The

SUPPLEMENT

to The

Modern Encyclopedia

of

Russian, Soviet

and Eurasian

History

CONTRIBUTORS

Rafis Abazov
Harriman Institute, Columbia University

John T. Alexander
University of Kansas

Audrey L. Alstadt
University of Massachusetts

Marina N. Baldano
Institute of Mongolian, Buddhist, and Tibetan Studies, Ulan Ude

Svetlana V. Baldano
Institute of Mongolian, Buddhist, and Tibetan Studies, Ulan Ude

Daniel Balmuth
Skidmore College

Brian J. Boeck
Loyola Marymount University

Elena N. Boeck
Yale University

Paul D. Buell
Western Washington University

Henry W. Castner
Queens University

Georgii N. Chagin
Perm State University

J. Eugene Clay
Arizona State University

Jonathan W. Daly
University of Illinois at Chicago

David W. Darrow
University of Dayton

Nadir Devlet
Yeditepe University, Istanbul

Ilia Dorontchenkov
Saint Petersburg Academy of Fine Arts

Andrew R. Durkin
Indiana University

Gregory J. Embree
Arlington, Virginia

Lee A. Farrow
Auburn University, Montgomery

Gero Fedtke
Humboldt-Universität zu Berlin

Darius Furmonavičius
University of Bradford

Abbott Gleason
Brown University

Darra Goldstein
Williams College

Michael D. Gordin
Princeton University

Edythe C. Haber
University of Massachusetts, Boston

Jennifer Hedda
Simpson College

Anders H. Henriksson
Shepherd College

J. Michael Hittle
Lawrence University

Michael A. Hudson
University of California, Santa Cruz

Pamela J. Kachurin
Indiana University

Scott M. Kenworthy
Miami University, Ohio

Evgenii I. Kirsanov
Novocherkassk

Alexei B. Kojevnikov
University of Georgia

Nikolay Komedchikov
Institute of Geography, Russian Academy of Sciences

Mark Konecny
University of Southern California

Roman K. Kovalev
The College of New Jersey

Randall D. Law
Northwestern College, Iowa

Edward J. Lazzerini
University of New Orleans

(continued on page vi)

The
SUPPLEMENT
to
The Modern Encyclopedia
of
Russian, Soviet and Eurasian
History

>>>->>>->>:->>>->>>->>>->>>->>>->>X<<-<<<-<<<-<<<-<<<-<<<

Edited by
Bruce F. Adams

>>>->>>->>>->>>->>>->>X<<-<<<-<<<-<<<-<<<-<<<-<<<-<<<

Vol. 5

Academic International Press

2004

THE SUPPLEMENT TO THE MODERN ENCYCLOPEDIA OF RUSSIAN, SOVIET AND EURASIAN HISTORY
Volume 5

ISBN: 0-87569-142-0

Composition by Ethel Chamberlain

Printed in the United States of America

By direct subscription with the publisher

www.ai-press.com

ACADEMIC INTERNATIONAL PRESS
POB 1111 • Gulf Breeze FL 32562 • USA

Preparation of this volume

was facilitated greatly by the

support of the

University of Louisville

CONTRIBUTORS (continued)

Scott C. Levi
University of Louisville

David MacFadyen
University of California, Los Angeles

David MacKenzie
University of North Carolina, Greensboro

George P. Majeska
University of Maryland

Steven G. Marks
Clemson University

John M.P. McErlean
York University

Yana Meerzon
University of Toronto

Konstantin B. Mitupov
Buriat State University, Ulan Ude

Eugenia K. Mitupova
Moscow State University

Robert W. Montgomery
Baldwin-Wallace College

Victor L. Mote
University of Houston

Pieter J. Mulder
Haarlem, Netherlands

Gregory Myers
University of British Columbia

Marshall T. Poe
Washington, D.C.

Jeff F. Sahadeo
University of Tennessee at Knoxville

Norman E. Saul
University of Kansas

Tim J. Scholl
Oberlin College

Donald A. Thumim
University of Phoenix, Colorado Campus

Manon van de Water
University of Wisconsin, Madison

Wim P. van Meurs
University of Munich

Irena Vladimirsky
Tel-Aviv University

Brian Glyn Williams
University of Massachusetts, Dartmouth

Markus Wolf
Munich, Germany

Richard L. Wolfel
Southern Illinois University, Edwardsville

Bradley D. Woodworth
Indiana University

Dov Yaroshevski
Tel-Aviv University

Denise J. Youngblood
University of Vermont

B

BUGANOV, VIKTOR IVANOVICH (1928-1996). Russian historian, specialist in source study of the early modern period, author of over twenty books, dozens of articles, and the editor of many important source publications.

The son of peasants, Buganov was trained in the 1950s by Mikhail Nikolaevich Tikhomirov (1893-1965) and Sigurd Ottovich Shmidt (1922-), successive chairmen of the Russian Archaeographic Commission. Under their influence he gained a deep appreciation of detailed source study, to which he devoted most of his scholarly life and made his greatest historical contribution. His candidate dissertation, defended in 1955, was a comprehensive analysis of Muscovite Service Registers (razriadnye knigi) of the fifteenth, sixteenth, and seventeenth centuries. The Service Registers recorded the civil, military, and court activities of the Muscovite elite and together constitute one of the few primary sources of biographical information on early Russian notables. In his thesis and subsequent monograph Buganov explored the genesis of the Service Registers, explained their role in court life, and offered a catalog of surviving copies.

Buganov's work on the Service Registers represented a vast improvement in historical understanding of these vital sources. Prior to the appearance of his monograph in 1962 scholars had identified perhaps thirty copies of the Service Register, and the relation among them remained unclear. Buganov cataloged more than 260 copies and divided them into several distinct redactions. Moreover, Buganov published several redactions of the Service Registers, making them available to the wider scholarly community for the first time. In the 1960s Buganov worked in the Chronicle Section of the Institute of History of the USSR, the group responsible for the publication of old Russian chronicles. His doctoral dissertation, defended in 1968, concerned civil unrest in seventeenth-century Muscovy. He published a monograph based on his research the following year. His interest in social unrest continued in the 1970s when he studied peasant war in the seventeenth and eighteenth centuries. In the 1980s Buganov wrote a series of popular books on the leaders of various so-called peasant uprisings, including Bolotnikov, Bulavin, Razin, and Pugachev. Buganov was an active teacher who passed on his interest in source study to his students. Fifteen of them defended candidate dissertations and five of them doctoral dissertations. Buganov died 23 February 1996.

Bibliography: Viktor I. Buganov, *Razriadnye knigi poslednei chetverti XV-nachala XVII vv.* (M., 1962), *Moskovskie vosstaniia kontsa XVII v.* (M., 1969),

Krestianskie voiny v Rossii XVII-XVIII vv. (M., 1976). A complete list of Buganov's numerous publications to 1988 is available in "Spisok pechatnykh trudov V.I. Buganova," *Arkheograficheskii ezhegodnik za 1988 g.* (M., 1989), 278-287. More complete is *Viktor Ivanovich Buganov. Bibliograficheskii ukazatel'* (M., 1993).

Marshall T. Poe

BUKHARAN JEWS. Ethnic minority in Uzbekistan and Tadzhikistan, speakers of Judeo-Tadzhik, probably numbering around 40,000 people in the mid-1980s.

The most ancient references to a presence of Jews in the area broadly defined as Central Asia, north of contemporary Iran, Afghanistan, Turkmenistan, Uzbekistan, and Tadzhikistan, can be dated to the first century B.C. In the territory of Turkmenistan archaeologists have found ossuaries with Hebrew letter inscriptions traceable to the period between the fifth and seventh centuries A.D. From the eighth century on there is evidence of Persian-speaking Jews in the Central Asian area. Sources mention the presence of Jews, including traders, silk weavers, mining experts, and writers of religious books, during the periods of Arab and Mongol domination in Central Asia as well as in states which existed there during the fifteenth to seventeenth centuries.

Bukharan Emirate. In this traditional Muslim state (1753–1920), as everywhere in the Muslim world, the local Jews were considered a protected community with the legal status of second-class subjects. They were subject to restraints in dress, transportation, housing, and access to state service positions but enjoyed broad autonomy in governing their neighborhoods through elected notables, with rabbis and other officials responsible for religious services, education, and community needs.

The major centers of the Jewish concentration in the emirate were the capital cities Bukhara and Samarkand. The Jews were generally engaged in trade and crafts, and particularly in the dye industry. As in other Islamic countries some Jews converted, or were forcefully converted, to Islam, and there emerged a small community of crypto-Jews, called chala, formally attached to Islam but secretly practicing Judaism and standing aloof from both local Muslim and Jewish communities.

While Jews generally were barred from high positions in Bukhara, for some conversion opened the doors to the emirate's government. Such was the case of Aharon Kandin who became kushbegi (minister of finance) in the mid-nineteenth century. After the Russian conquest of Central Asia Kandin fled to Russian Turkestan, returned to Judaism, and later emigrated to Palestine.

A major cultural revolution among the Jews of the Bukharan emirate was brought about in the eighteenth century by a rabbinical messenger from Palestine, Moroccan-born Yosef Maman (1752–1838). Maman stayed with the Bukharan Jewish community for the rest of his life and introduced profound changes into religious services, study, and ritual.

From 1868, when the Bukharan emirate turned into a protectorate of the Russian Empire, the merchants of the emirate were entitled to settle everywhere in the Turkestan region or krai, the border province of the empire comprising conquered Central Asian territories, and to enjoy the same rights as Russian merchants. Similarly, Russian merchants in the emirate were entitled to the same rights as their local counterparts. This provision lured some 320 families of the most resourceful Bukharan Jews to leave for the Turkestan krai and to open businesses there in the dry goods and cotton trade. Construction of the Central Asian railway at the end of the nineteenth century, which crossed the territory of the Bukharan emirate, facilitated shipment of Russian goods into the protectorate and induced some Bukharan Jews to launch careers as local agents for Russian textile industrialists.

Changed social and economic conditions in Russian Central Asia allowed the Bukharan Jews to undertake one of the most pioneering enterprises in the history of this community, namely the establishment in the 1890s of a society for the construction of a Bukharan quarter in Jerusalem. This continuing enterprise made possible both pilgrimages to the Holy Land and the founding of modern religious schools in the Bukharan emirate, aided by teachers brought over from Palestine.

The gradual incorporation of Bukhara into the Russian Empire exposed Bukharan Jews to new political ideas. During the Russian revolution of 1905-1907 some Jews from Bukhara city applied for membership in the Society for Achievement of Civic Equality for the Jewish People in Russia. In the aftermath of the 1917 February Revolution in Russia hundreds of Bukharan Jews, following David Doros (meaning tall in the Tadzhik language) Yakubov, participated on 4 April 1917 in a unique anti-government demonstration of five thousand Bukharans which took place in Bukhara city and was organized by local modernists, jadids, demanding political reforms and civic equality. The emirate authorities realized that the Bukharan Jews had become an important political entity. In 1918, when the emir of Bukhara had to fight for his survival with the neighboring radical Bolshevik regime of the Turkestan Soviet Republic, he ordered the execution of the Bukharan Jewish opposition leadership, which at the time comprised three members of the Yunusov family. To emphasize his benevolent attitude toward loyal Jews he invited Jewish notables to his palace and decorated them with medals.

Upon proclamation of the Bukharan People's Soviet Republic in 1920, for the first time in the history of Bukhara the Bukharan Jews were considered an important factor in the country's modernizing efforts, and many of them became prominent in the republican government. The most outstanding Jewish personality, Ezra Khakhamov, served as the deputy head of the Bukharan secret police and later as director of the Government Information Office. In the Ministry of the Interior there was a Collegium for Jewish Affairs with Abo Khakhamov as its chairman. In the provinces Jewish committees were founded for the administration of communal affairs, and new Jewish schools for both girls and boys were established in Bukhara city.

Turkestan Region (Krai). After the Russian conquest the indigenous Jews, formerly second-class citizens of the Bukharan emirate and Kokand khanate, were promoted to the status of natives (tuzemtsy). This elevation contributed toward the inclusion of the Jewish population in the process of economic and social modernization of the region. Bukharan Jews were instrumental in the development of the cotton industry in Turkestan, and in the period between the 1890s and the 1910s there emerged a group of leading local Jewish capitalists, most notable among them the Vadiaevs, Davidovs, Poteliakhovs, and Simkhaevs. Many other Bukharan Jews were employed in middle and lower positions in the cotton industry and trade. This resulted in a great deal of animosity towards Bukharan Jews on the part of nationalist Russian officialdom and the press, as well as the jealousy of local indigenous rivals.

The Bukharan Jewish community in the Turkestan krai maintained a rather traditional communal life through its network of synagogues and religious schools, actively participated in the Jerusalem construction enterprise, and brought in teachers from Palestine for its schools on a regular basis. There were also attempts to create private modern educational facilities, so-called Jewish Native schools similar to the Russian Native schools for the Muslim population supported by the Russian colonial administration. In addition there was a commercial school in Kokand, supported in part by Bukharan Jewish magnates, and during World War I the first Hebrew high school was established in Samarkand.

The most disturbing political problem for the community during the period of tsarist rule was persecution of Bukharan expatriates by the authorities who viewed them as a dangerous element and strove to deport them back to the Bukharan emirate. Their process of naturalization was halted, and their fate was discussed by the imperial government in 1908 and 1910. The Bukharan Jewish community in Turkestan sent a special delegation headed by chief rabbi S. Tajer to St. Petersburg, mobilized the support of Russian industrialists for the right of Bukharan Jewish expatriates to remain in Turkestan, and finally succeeded in postponing deportation.

After the February Revolution of 1917 the Bukharan Jews in Turkestan were active in the public and municipal life of the region, and they were promised by the local Muslim modernist leaders to receive one place on the list of the regional Muslim delegation to the Russian Constituent Assembly which was dispersed by the Bolsheviks in 1918. At the end of 1917 the first Muslim government of the region, the Kokand autonomy, emerged, and the Bukharan Jewish industrialist Sion Vadiaev was included as the minister of finance. Within the Bukharan Jewish community there were people of the lower and middle strata who were inclined to support the Russian radical leadership in Turkestan, the Tashkent-based Council of People's Commissars. Particularly distinctive among the latter were former draftees sent during World War I in work units to European Russia for labor at industrial plants. They returned home extremely revolutionized and hostile toward the community notables.

Turkestan Republic. For seven years (1918-1924) this borderland Soviet republic struggled for survival against many internal and external foes, and the Bukharan Jewish community there was subject to many upheavals. The major source of its economic existence, the cotton and dry goods trade, collapsed due to the civil war in the countryside, state nationalization of the cotton industry, and lack of communications with the European part of Russia, especially in 1918-1919. Many Jews died in the famine. Wealthy merchants were deprived of their property, arrested, and some executed. Many fled abroad.

On the other hand the revolutionary regime did a great deal to alleviate the plight of the lower strata of the Bukharan Jewish community in the cities and to develop new sources of livelihood for them. Its most strenuous efforts were undertaken in the field of socialization of the community to the new revolutionary values and principles, as was done with other ethnic minorities in the republic. Towards this end a broad network of schools for Bukharan Jews was established, and the vernacular Judeo-Tadzhik was offered as a teaching language instead of the traditional Hebrew. For a while this turned into a bone of contention between young Bukharan Jewish cultural activists and their patrons, Ashkenazi (European) Jewish communists from the republican Ministry of Education.

Uzbek Soviet Republic. In 1924 the multinational Turkestan, Bukharan and Khorezm republics were replaced by new ethnic political bodies, the Turkmen and Uzbek Soviet republics. As a result the Bukharan Jewish community underwent two major socio-economic and demographic changes. During 1925-1934 part of this predominantly urban group moved to the countryside and lived and worked on Jewish collective farms. Later, between the 1930s and 1950s one fifth of this group, approximately five thousand persons, migrated toward neighboring Tadzhikistan, which until 1929 was part of the Uzbek Republic, and settled in its cities. These changes were caused by huge social dislocations in the republic during the late 1920s, particularly agrarian reform, imposed collectivization of the rural farms, and reconstruction of the urban economies which left no place for traditional forms of private urban trade and crafts. Many of those who could not accommodate themselves to the new conditions undertook the dangerous illegal journey across the southern USSR border with Afghanistan on their way to Palestine. This transformation was reflected in new patterns of settlement of Bukharan Jews in Uzbekistan towards 1934. About 40 percent concentrated in the capital cities, Samarkand and later Tashkent, about 20 percent in rural areas on collective farms (kolkhozes), and the rest dispersed among large and small cities. The Bukharan Jewish agricultural settlements were considered by the Uzbek republican leaders of the time an outstanding achievement of the early social reconstruction in Uzbekistan.

The process was arrested in the late 1930s and 1940s and discontinued in the 1950s.

Similar developments occurred in the fields of education and culture. The network of schools teaching in Judeo-Tadzhik, which at first used the Hebrew alphabet and later the Latin, was promoted by the state in the 1920s and early 1930s, complemented by extensive publication of textbooks, translations, and original writings of Bukharan Jewish authors and supported by the Bukharan Jewish theater and press. Toward the 1940s this cultural undertaking was destroyed by the authorities. Some hundreds of Bukharan Jews fell victim to political purges in Tashkent and Samarkand at the end of the 1930s.

During the 1940s-1980s the Bukharan Jews became urbanites again, most members of the community earning their livelihood in various service and trade niches. A growing number of the younger and better educated generation, well versed in Russian, entered professional careers, especially in medicine, education, universities, and research despite discriminatory measures by the authorities.

It was only in the perestroika period (1987-1991) that Bukharan Jewish activists in Uzbekistan commenced to restore community life by reestablishing its institutions such as cultural centers in Tashkent and Samarkand, reopening its theaters and reinstituting publishing activities, strengthening the traditions of the community, and supporting the synagogues and religious studies. These trends were opposed by another prevalent current. Like other Jews of the former Soviet Union, Bukharan Jews emigrated to Israel and the United States beginning as early as 1971, and this process was accelerated on 2 May 1990 when the Uzbeks of Andizhan assaulted families of minorities, among them thirteen Bukharan Jewish families, and looted their property.

Tadzhik Soviet Republic. The founding of the Tadzhik Soviet Socialist Republic in 1929, the most backward yet fast developing region of Soviet Central Asia, opened many positions in the economy, as well as in cultural and educational institutions, to enterprising persons. It presented an outlet for those Bukharan Jews in Soviet Uzbekistan who were dissatisfied with their political status and economic hardship and felt culturally and nationally deprived. The mother tongue of these migrants was Tadzhik, which was surely an advantage in entering the native society.

Settled in Tadzhikistan in the 1930s-1950s, mostly in the capital Stalinabad (Dushanbe) and Leninabad (Khodzhent, Khojand), Bukharan Jews found occupations in the growing service sector, such as photography shops, shoe repair, and tailoring. Some of them became prominent in Tadzhik culture and sciences. The most outstanding cinema director of Tadzhikistan in the 1940s-1960s was Boris (Bentsion) Kimiagarov (1920-1979), and Sarodzhan (Sara) Yusupova (1910-1960), a geologist, was chosen as a member of the Tadzhik Academy of Sciences and member of the Tadzhik Supreme Soviet. Approximately half of those popular in Tadzhik music and dance were Bukharan Jews. There emerged also a broad stratum of Bukharan Jewish professionals in middle and high positions in city government, educational institutions, hospitals and research.

Even so, for years the national life of the Bukharan Jews was suppressed. While many observed traditions in their everyday, private life and the existence of synagogues was permitted, the process of assimilation of the younger generation, particularly from the 1960s on, accelerated. At the onset of the perestroika period the first attempts at rekindling Bukharan Jewish communal life were made, and the Society of the Friends of Jewish Culture (Hoverim) emerged in 1989 in Dushanbe. The movement for Tadzhik independence, disturbances in Uzbekistan, and riots in Dushanbe in April 1991 caused panic among the Bukharan Jews of Tadzhikistan and contributed to massive emigration to Israel and the United States at the beginning of the 1990s.

There remains an unresolved statistical puzzle concerning the size of the Bukharan Jewish community in Soviet Tadzhikistan. Sources from the 1960s cite a figure of around five thousand. The last Soviet census in 1989 gives an estimate of 4,859 Jewish persons, but this is open to doubt since census criteria gave great weight to the mother tongue, and an unknown number of younger Bukharan Jews may have named Russian in that category. Bearing in mind a traditionally high birth rate in Bukharan Jewish families, the numbers cited by another source, 13,000 for 1990, seems reasonable.

Post-Soviet States. After 1991 the mass emigration of Bukharan Jews from independent Uzbekistan and Tadzhikistan to Israel and the United States became the central factor in the life of this ethnic community. Particularly large was the flight from Tadzhikistan before and during the 1992-1994 civil war. According to the Jewish Agency of Israel, 19,000 Jews from Uzbekistan and 10,500 from Tadzhikistan arrived in Israel between 1989 and 1998. What percentage of this population was Bukharan Jews is unknown, since the statistics for these arrivals are not recorded by subgroups. Therefore the category of Jews from Central Asia includes Bukharan, as well as Ashkenazi (European) and Mountain (Caucasian) Jews. The emigration actually led to the disappearance of many Bukharan Jewish communities in middle-sized and small cities. At the same time there was a rejuvenation of Jewish communal life in Uzbekistan, as evidenced by the activities of the (Bukharan Jewish) Samarkand Cultural Center, particularly educational activities supported by Israeli and American sponsors. The numbers of Bukharan Jews living in both countries in the mid-1990s have not been definitively determined.

Bibliography: V.I. Bushkov and D.V. Mikulskii, *"Tadzhikskaia revoliutsiia" i grazhdanskaia voina (1989–1994 gg.)* (M., 1995), gives emigration statistics. *Evrei v Srednei Azii. Proshloe i nastoiashchee* (SPb., 1995) presents ethnographic materials assembled by researchers of St. Petersburg Jewish University during the expedition to Central Asia in 1992. *Gody, Liudi, Fakty* (Samarkand, 1993) is a collection of articles on Bukharan Jewish history, tradition, and lifeways published previously in the Samarkand Bukharan Jewish newspaper

Shofar. Meyer R. Benyaminov, *Bukharan Jews* (New York, 1992) and *Grazhdanskie dvizheniia v Tadzhikistane* (M., 1990), 89-91 and 186-191, deal with Bukharan Jews and the Hoverim Society program. Michael Zand, "Bukharan Jews," *Encyclopedia Iranica,* Vol. 4, Fasc. 5 (1989), 530-545, contains the most complete bibliography on the history of the Bukharan Jews.

Dov Yaroshevski

BUKHARAN SCHOOL OF PAINTING. A style of Uzbek painting and calligraphy that flourished in Bukhara during the late sixteenth and seventeenth centuries, producing mostly miniatures for inclusion in manuscripts.

Until the consolidation of the Uzbek state and the establishment of Bukhara as its capital in the mid-sixteenth century the workshops of the city produced undistinguished miniatures to accompany manuscript texts. The styles and techniques were overwhelmingly legacies of the Timurid empire created by Tamerlane (Timur) in the early fourteenth century, and their quality is characterized by the French scholar Yves Porter as provincial at best. Under Uzbek political control through the Shaybanid and Janid dynasties, both production and quality rose and a school, or style, of Bukharan painting emerged during the later sixteenth century and flourished until the end of the seventeenth.

Perhaps most important about Bukharan painting of this period is its gradual severing of slavish imitation of the Timurid aesthetic. Much of this is explained by the migration of artists from many different parts of Central Eurasia to Bukhara, bringing with them variations in style, interest, and temperament.

One example of this evolution is the frequent use of architectural decor for the central focus of a painting. This takes the form of a seeming enclosure framed by two columns at the entrance, above which typically rests a frieze containing an epigraph. An inheritance from the Timurid period, this decor lost its epigraphical detail as the Bukharan school developed its own identity.

The habit of not signing paintings makes scholarly efforts to identify the painters of the Bukharan school extremely difficult, subject to error and controversy, and assuredly incomplete. A partial list of those generally accepted as painting in the Bukharan style of the period is provided.

Identified Painters of the Bukharan School

Name	Manuscripts with Paintings Identified
'Avaz Mohammad	Nezâmi's *Khamsa* (1668-1671)
Farhad	Sa'di's *Bustân* (1649); *Majâles al-'oshshâq* (c. 1645-1649)
Gol-Mohammad	Abu Tâher ibn Hasan ibn Musa al-Tarsusi's *Dâstân-e Qerân-e Habashi* (n.d.)
Mohammad Amin	Nezâmi's *Khamsa* (1668-1671); Khwâju Kermâni's *Divân* (n.d.)
Mohammad Darvish	Sa'di's *Bustân* (c. 1570), with illustrations added in 1616

Identified Painters of the Bukharan School (continued)

Name	Manuscripts with Paintings Identified
Mohammad Moqim	Ferdowsi's *Shâh-nâma* (1650-1660); Ferdowsi's *Shâh-nâma* (1664); Nezâmi's *Khamsa* (1668-1671); Abu Tâher ibn Hasan ibn Musa al-Tarsusi's *Dâstân-e Qerân-e Habashi* (n.d.)
Mohammad Nader Samarqandi	Untitled album (1616)
Mohammad Sharif	Sa'di's *Bustân* (c. 1570), with illustrations added in 1616
Molla Behzad	Nezâmi's *Khamsa* (1628); Nezâmi's *Khamsa* (1668-1671); Abu Tâher ibn Hasan ibn Musa al-Tarsusi's *Dâstân-e Qerân-e Habashi* (n.d.); Khwâju Kermâni's *Divân* (n.d.)
Morad-e Samarqandi	Ferdowsi's *Shâh-nâma* (1556-1557), illustrated at the end of the 16th and beginning of the 17th centuries; Sa'di's *Bustân* (c. 1570), with illustrations added in 1616; Yazdi's *Zafar-nâma* (1628), although some attribute illustrations to Mohammad Moqim.
Mohammad Salim	Ferdowsi's *Shâh-nâma* (1650-1660); Abu Tâher ibn Hasan ibn Musa al-Tarsusi's *Dâstân-e Qerân-e Habashi* (n.d.)

This table is derived from the work of Yves Porter, "Farhad le peintre. À propos des ateliers de peinture de Boukhara à l'époque de 'Abd al-'Aziz Khan (1645-1680)," *Cahiers d'Asie centrale*, 3-4 (1997), 267-278.

Bibliography: O.I. Galerkina, "Sredneaziatsko-indiiskie sviazi v miniatiure XVI-nachale XVII vv." in *Kul'tura i iskusstvo narodov Srednei Azii v drevnosti i srednevekov'e* (M., 1979), 105-191; O.F. Akimushkin and A.A. Ivanov, "Une école artistique méconnue. Boxârâ au XVIIe siècle. Notes sur les calligraphes et les peintres de la Bibliothèque des Ashtarxânides d'après Mohammad-Amin Boxâri" in *Art et société dans le monde iranien*, ed. by C. Adle (Paris, 1982), 127-139; B. Schmitz, "The Bukharan School of Miniature Painting," *Encyclopaedia Iranica*, Vol. 6, 527-600; Yves Porter, "Farhad le peintre. À propos des ateliers de peinture de Boukhara à l'époque de 'Abd al-'Aziz Khan (1645–1680)," *Cahiers d'Asie centrale*, Nos. 3-4 (1997), 267-278, and "Remarques sur la peinture de Boukhara au XVIe siècle," *Cahiers d'Asie centrale*, Nos. 5-6 (1998), 147-167.

Edward J. Lazzerini

BULGAKOV, MIKHAIL AFANASIEVICH (1891–1940). Prose writer and dramatist best known for witty and daring satire.

Bulgakov was born in Kiev, the eldest of seven children of Afanasy Ivanovich Bulgakov (1859–1907), a professor of church history at the Kiev Theological Academy, and Varvara Mikhailovna Bulgakova (1869–1922). His was a happy childhood in which the high moral principles instilled by his father coexisted with an atmosphere of high spirits and immersion in the arts, especially music and theater.

Bulgakov evinced a gift for literature while still an adolescent but chose the more practical field of medicine. In 1916, immediately after receiving his medical degree with distinction from Kiev University, he went to serve as a Red Cross volunteer in the World War. In September 1916 he was mobilized and assigned as the only doctor in a zemstvo hospital in the village of Nikolskoe, Smolensk province. He saw over 15,000 patients while in Nikolskoe and regularly confronted medical emergencies of the kind he later fictionalized in his story cycle, *Notes of a Young Doctor* (Zapiski yunogo vracha, 1925–1926). According to his first wife, Tatiana Nikolaevna Lappa (1892–1981), he also became a morphine addict and remained so until after his return to Kiev. In September 1917, having received an evaluation as "energetic and tireless worker in the zemstvo field," Bulgakov was transferred to the town of Viazma, where he specialized in venereology. He was there during the October revolution and in his correspondence complained of his isolation and desire to leave for Kiev or Moscow. In February 1918 he managed to get a medical discharge and returned to Kiev.

When Bulgakov arrived in Kiev, the Germans, in accordance with the Brest-Litovsk Treaty, occupied Ukraine and had established a government under the rule of the hetman Pavel Skoropadsky. The hetman's rather superficial Ukrainianism suited the Bulgakovs, who feared stronger nationalist sentiments. Therefore when the Germans withdrew from Kiev in December 1918, the Bulgakov brothers, Mikhail as a doctor, were among the troops who staged an unsuccessful defense of the hetmanate against the nationalist forces of Simon Petliura. Bulgakov's experiences during this period provide the core of his first novel, *The White Guard* (Belaia gvardiia, 1925) and his play, Days of the Turbins (Dni Turbinykh, 1926).

In his civil war writings Bulgakov expressed horror at the atrocities committed by Petliura's troops. He returned repeatedly to one incident in particular, which he witnessed after his mobilization by the Petliurites during their final days in Kiev in February 1919, a Cossack commander beating a Jew to death with a ramrod. During Petliura's withdrawal from Kiev Bulgakov managed to desert, but life became no easier under the occupying Bolsheviks. Because of his family's class affiliation the situation grew so risky that they hid in the forest during the summer of 1919. When after a brief occupation Denikin's White Army withdrew from Kiev in September 1919, Bulgakov left with them for the northern Caucasus city of Vladikavkaz.

Bulgakov's professional writing career began soon after his arrival in the Caucasus. His earliest work discovered so far, the story Prospects for the Future (Griadushchie perspektivy), expressed his fervent support of the Whites. "The heroes of the Volunteer Army are ripping the Russian land from Trotsky's hands inch by inch...everyone is passionately awaiting the liberation of the country." According to his fictionalized memoirs, Notes on the Cuff (Zapiski na manzhetakh, 1922–1923), Bulgakov would have fled the approaching Bolsheviks in February 1920 had he not come down with typhus. By the time he recovered in March the Bolsheviks already controlled Vladikavkaz and were in the process of setting up a local arts bureaucracy under the aegis of the Peoples's Commissariat of the Enlightenment. Bulgakov, in his struggle for survival, actively participated in the effort. Beginning in spring 1920 he worked as an administrator in the Subdepartment of the Arts (Podotdel iskusstv), gave talks before performances and concerts, published feuilletons and reviews in local newspapers, and wrote five plays, four of which were produced. He later destroyed all the plays, although a copy of one, Sons of the Mullah (Synovia mully, 1921), was discovered later. In Vladikavkaz Bulgakov also experienced his first conflicts with the critics, who especially reviled his play, The Turbin Brothers (Bratia Turbiny, 1920), for its allegedly anti-proletarian sentiments.

In May 1921 Bulgakov left Vladikavkaz, going first to Tiflis, then to Batumi. From there he seriously considered continuing his journey into emigration but chose instead to go to Moscow and test his literary powers in his own country. In late 1921 he arrived in the capital, penniless and homeless, his situation aggravated by galloping inflation and a severe housing shortage. He soon found shelter in the communal apartment of his brother-in-law at 10 Bolshaia Sadovaia Street, the prototype for 302B Sadovaia Street in *The Master and Margarita* (Master i Margarita, 1928-1940), and by spring 1922 was gaining a foothold in the Soviet periodical press. He became a regular contributor to the newspaper On the Eve (Nakanune), associated with the émigré Change of Landmarks (Smenovekhi) group, published in Berlin but distributed in emigration and in the Soviet Union. The satirical feuilletons and stories he published there between 1922 and 1924, with their vivid depictions of Moscow during the period of the New Economic Policy (NEP), brought him his first measure of recognition. They did not provide sufficient income, leading him to join the staff of The Whistle (Gudok), newspaper of the railroad workers' union.

The Whistle was breeding ground for some very gifted young writers, including Ilf and Petrov, Yury Olesha, and Valentin Kataev, yet Bulgakov regarded the feuilletons he wrote for the newspaper between 1922 to 1926 as mere hackwork. He reserved his serious writing for the nighttime, when he returned in imagination to the civil war and its immediate aftermath. The result was a number of short prose works written between 1922 and 1924. Some have an autobiographical core, depicting a doctor or writer caught up in the chaos and violence of the time, among them Notes on the Cuff, Unusual Adventures of a Doctor (Neobyknovennye prikliucheniia doktora, 1922), The Red Crown (Krasnaia korona, 1922), and On the Night of the Second (V noch na 3-e chislo, 1922). Other stories have no basis in the writer's life but like them center upon responses of lone individuals to the destruction of the old world: The Chinese Story (Kitaiskaia istoriia, 1923), The Raid (Nalet, 1923), and The Khan's Fire (Khansky ogon, 1924).

Both sides of Bulgakov's talent, the satirical and serious, reached a new plateau in 1925 with publication of his first separate book, *Diaboliad* (Diavoliada) and the serialization of his first novel, *The White Guard*, in the journal Russia (Rossiia). The book included the best and most ambitious of his satirical works thus far, most notably the two novellas Diaboliad (1924), a portrayal of devilish goings-on within the Soviet bureaucracy, and The Fatal Eggs (Rokovye yaitsa, 1925), which depicts the perils inherent in both scientific and governmental efforts to accelerate evolutionary processes. In *The White Guard* Bulgakov achieved a synthesis of his earlier fragmentary efforts to recreate his civil war experiences, placing his formerly solitary intellectual hero within a broad social, political, and metaphysical context.

From the very beginning Bulgakov's writings and their sharply satirical depictions of contemporary Soviet life and sympathetic portrayal of the old world encountered hostility from the critics. Beginning in 1925 his increasing prominence as well as the changing political climate led to ever greater problems with the authorities. *Diaboliad* was confiscated soon after publication although it was reissued the following year. The serialization of *The White Guard* ended abruptly when the authorities shut down the journal Russia. The next step was the first outright ban of a Bulgakov work, his third and most fully realized novella, *Heart of a Dog* (Sobache serdtse, 1925), a satire on scientific and socialist attempts to create a new, perfected human being. A few of Bulgakov's works came out in 1926 but in 1927 only one story, Morphine (Morfii), appeared.

At the very time Bulgakov's name was disappearing from print, he was achieving prominence as a dramatist, the result of the Moscow Art Theater's renowned 1926 production of Days of the Turbins. The play, a reworking of *The White Guard*, enjoyed enormous success with the public, but aroused almost unanimous outrage among critics. One reviewer coined the term Bulgakovism (Bulgakovshchina), the model for the Pilatism (Pilatchina) of his novel *The Master and Margarita*. The production nevertheless was permitted, due in part at least to the support of Stalin, who reportedly saw it fifteen times. After Days of the Turbins two of Bulgakov's plays had successful productions: Zoyka's Apartment (Zoikina kvartira, 1926), a satirical comedy on NEP decadence staged at the Vakhtangov Theater, and The Crimson Island (Bagrovyi ostrov, 1927), a parody of revolutionary drama produced in 1928 by Tairov's Kamerny Theater.

It was not long before Bulgakov's theatrical works suffered the same fate as his prose. In early 1929 Stalin expressed disapproval of his new civil war drama, Flight (Beg), then in rehearsal at the Moscow Art Theater, and soon after all of Bulgakov's plays closed. During the same year he and other insufficiently conformist writers became objects of virulent attacks by the Russian Association of Proletarian Writers (RAPP), then enjoying hegemony over literature. A final blow was the ban in 1930 of his play, Molière, or A Cabal of Hypocrites (Kabala sviatosh), the first of Bulgakov's works to treat his major theme of the 1930s, the conflict between the writer and the authoritarian state.

Bulgakov responded to this crisis with a characteristic mixture of fear and boldness. On one hand, he suffered attacks of extreme anxiety, during one of which in March 1930 he burned early drafts of *The Master and Margarita* and other works. On the other hand, between 1929 and 1931 he wrote a series of courageous letters to Stalin and others in the Soviet government. In the key letter of 28 March 1930 he declared himself a "mystical writer" and expressed his "profound scepticism toward the revolutionary process." He went on to ask permission to leave the Soviet Union or, if that proved impossible, to work in any capacity for the Moscow Art Theater. The response was swift and dramatic. On 18 April Stalin telephoned Bulgakov and granted his second wish.

Bulgakov worked from 1930 to 1936 for the Moscow Art Theater as literary adaptor and consultant, assistant director, and even actor. His adaptation of Gogol's *Dead Souls* (Mertvye dushi) premiered in 1932 and Days of the Turbins was revived the same year. Otherwise all his attempts to have his works published or produced during the 1930s met with frustration. The biography, *The Life of Monsieur de Molière* (Zhizn gospodina de Moliera, 1933), was rejected. None of his new plays—Adam and Eve (Adam i Eva, 1931), Half-Witted Jourdain (Poloumnyi Zhurden, 1932), Bliss (Blazhenstvo, 1934), Ivan Vasilievich (1935), Alexander Pushkin, later entitled Last Days (Poslednie dni, 1935), Don Quixote (1938), Batumi (1939)—nor the repeatedly revised Flight were produced, although several went into rehearsal. One partial exception was Moliere. After years of conflict-ridden rehearsals, it opened at the Moscow Art Theater in 1936 but closed in a few days after a vituperative attack in Pravda. Because of what he perceived as capitulation by the theater, Bulgakov resigned from its staff and joined the Bolshoi Opera as librettist, where his work fared no better.

During the time that Bulgakov was struggling in vain to see his works before the public, certain of his writings he did not even attempt to disseminate beyond a small circle of friends. One is the novel *Notes of a Dead Man. A Theatrical Novel* (Zapiski pokoinika. Teatralnyi roman), a biting satire on the Moscow Art Theater based upon the writer's experiences during the staging of Days of the Turbins. This was later translated into English as *Black Snow*. Bulgakov worked on the manuscript in 1936-1937, then left it unfinished in order to devote more time to his masterpiece, *The Master and Margarita*. After burning the earliest drafts of his novel about the devil in 1930 Bulgakov returned to it in 1931 and continued to revise and expand it for the rest of his life. The first version, begun in 1928, centered upon devilish doings in Soviet Moscow and was closely akin to his earlier satire. Only in 1931 did he introduce the characters of the persecuted writer and his true love, inspired by his third wife, Elena Sergeevna Shilovskaia (1893-1970). Here he achieved a synthesis of the satirical and the lyrical-autobiographical in his earlier writing. Later versions modified and expanded the significance of the Biblical subplot and the diabolical line, deepening the interconnections of the various plot levels.

Bulgakov suffered from repeated bouts of fear and depression throughout the 1930s yet stubbornly resisted the almost unbearable pressure to write paeans to the new Soviet reality. Only in 1939 did he relent and write a play about the young Stalin, Batumi, but the project came to an abrupt end when Stalin criticized it. Soon after, in August 1939, Bulgakov fell ill with nephrosclerosis, the disease that killed his father at a similar age. He continued revisions of *The Master and Margarita* during his final illness, dictating changes to his wife even after losing his sight. Revisions were not complete when he died on 10 March 1940.

At the time of his death Bulgakov was virtually a forgotten writer, known primarily as author of Days of the Turbins. He remained so until the 1960s when his works began again to appear in the Soviet Union. His broad renown came in 1966-1967 upon the first publication of *The Master and Margarita* in the journal Moscow (Moskva). The writer's reputation has continued to grow and many now regard *The Master and Margarita* as the greatest novel of the Soviet period.

Bibliography: The best Russian edition of Bulgakov's writings is *Sobranie sochinenii v piati tomakh* (M., 1989-1990). For his works in English see *The Master and Margarita*, trans. by Diana Burgin and Katherine Tiernan O'Connor (Ann Arbor, Mich., 1995), the most authoritative English translation, *Black Snow. A Theatrical Novel*, trans. by Michael Glenny (New York, 1967), *A Country Doctor's Notebook*, trans. by Michael Glenny (Glasgow, 1975), *Diaboliad and Other Stories*, trans. by Carl R. Proffer (Bloomington, Ind., 1972), *The Early Plays*, trans. by Ellendea Proffer and Carl R. Proffer (Bloomington, Ind., 1972), *Heart of a Dog*, trans. by Mirra Ginsburg (New York, 1968), *The Life of Monsieur de Molière*, trans. by Mirra Ginsburg (New York, 1970), *Six Plays*, trans. by Michael Glenny (London, 1991), and *The White Guard*, trans. by Michael Glenny (New York, 1971). The principal archival collection is Manuscript Division (Otdel rukopisei), Russian State Library, Moscow, fond 562. For memoirs, diaries, letters, see L.E. Belozerskaia-Bulgakova, *O, med vospominanii* (Ann Arbor, Mich., 1979), the memoirs of Bulgakov's second wife, Elena Bulgakova, *Dnevnik Eleny Bulgakovoi* (M., 1990), the diary of his third wife, Mikhail Bulgakov, *Dnevnik. Pis'ma. 1914-1940*, comp. by V.I. Losev (M., 1997), J.A.E. Curtis, comp. and trans., *Manuscripts Don't Burn. A Life in Letters and Diaries* (London, 1991). For critical studies, see Andrew Barratt, *Between Two Worlds. A Critical Introduction to The Master and Margarita* (Oxford, 1987); David Bethea, "*The Master and Margarita*. History as Hippodrome," in Bethea, *The Shape of Apocalypse in Modern Russian Fiction* (Princeton, N.J., 1989), 186-229; Marietta Chudakova, "*The Master and Margarita*. The Development of a Novel," trans. by Phyllis Powell, *Russian Literature Triquarterly*, Vol. 15 (1978), 177-209; Marietta Chudakova, *Zhizneopisanie Mikhaila Bulgakova* (M., 1988); J.A.E. Curtis, *Bulgakov's Last Decade. The Writer as Hero* (Cambridge, 1987); Henry

Elbaum, "The Evolution of *The Master and Margarita.* Text, Context, Intertext," *Canadian Slavonic Papers*, Nos. 1-2 (1995), 59-87; Boris M. Gasparov, "Iz nabliudenii nad motivnoi strukturoi romana M.A. Bulgakova *Master i Margarita*," *Slavica Hierosolymitana*, No. 3 (1978), 198-251; Edythe C. Haber, "The Mythic Structure of Bulgakov's *The Master and Margarita*," *Russian Review*, No. 4 (1975), 382-409, and *Mikhail Bulgakov. The Early Years* (Cambridge, Mass., 1998); Lidia Yanovskaia, *Tvorcheskii put' Mikhaila Bulgakova* (M., 1983); Lesley Milne, *Mikhail Bulgakov. A Critical Biography* (Cambridge, 1990); Lesley Milne, ed., *Bulgakov. The Novelist-Playwright* (Luxembourg, 1995); Ellendea Proffer, *Bulgakov. Life and Works* (Ann Arbor, Mich., 1984); Anatoly Smelyansky, *Is Comrade Bulgakov Dead? Mikhail Bulgakov at the Moscow Art Theatre*, trans. by Arch Tait (London, 1993); and Laura D. Weeks, ed., *The Master and Margarita. A Critical Companion* (Evanston, Ill., 1996).

Edythe C. Haber

BULGARI, ABDURRAHIM IBN USMAN AL- (1754-1835 or 1836). Known also as al-Utyz-Imäni. Scholar, poet, and sheikh in the Naqshbandiye Sufi brotherhood.

Al-Bulgari was born in 1754 in the village of Utyz-Imäni in present-day Tatarstan. Orphaned in his youth, he attended lower (maktab) and higher (madrasa) Islamic schools, the latter at the second mosque in the village of Kargaly. His attraction to the Naqshbandiye brotherhood was likely fostered by at least one of his teachers at the madrasa, Valida ibn Mukhammad al-Amina al-Kargali, himself a Naqshbandiye sheikh.

According to some sources, in 1785 al-Bulgari was forced to leave the Russian Empire with his entire household for engaging in anti-state religious propaganda. The details of his troubles with Russian authorities are unknown but likely stem from his criticisms of Christianity and Russian authority over Muslims. He settled in Bukhara where he combined additional study with service as a mulla at the Magak mosque. During the remaining years of the eighteenth century he traveled to various Central Asian and Afghan intellectual centers, including Samarkand, Herat, Balkh, and Kabul, before returning to the Volga-Ural region to devote the rest of his life to teaching and scholarship. Sources differ as to the date of his death.

Al-Bulgari was a prolific writer in both Arabic and Persian. His subjects ranged over Islamic theology, ethics, law, and mysticism. Except for some Turkic-language poetry in the masnavi genre, much of it polemical, his scholarship remained unpublished. His commitment to Sufism, its ethics and asceticism, flows consistently throughout all of his writings, although even on this theme he could be critical of the superficiality of some adherents.

In the history of Central Eurasian Islamic thought during the eighteenth and early nineteenth centuries al-Bulgari represents a major voice for a particular type of reformist inclination rooted deeply in the Islamic experience. Responding to what he perceived as a crisis in the practice of Islam that inevitably led to a weakening of the community of Muslims, he challenged his religious brethren to forsake the innovations (sing. bid'a) and errors that had crept into Islamic practice and now were considered genuine. Liberal interpretations of Islamic law, moral laxity, ethical ambiguity, fraternization with Christians, consumption of alcohol, and other forms of questionable behavior informed al-Bulgari's profound dissatisfaction with current realities. The cure, he pronounced repeatedly, was a return to the pure, unadulterated sources of the faith as established during its earliest history. Trust in recognized authority (taklid) to show the proper way and insistence upon strict adherence to moral teachings further shaped al-Bulgari's world view.

The content and direction of al-Bulgari's thought, with its emphasis on the struggle for continual personal improvement (jihad), led him into open argument with Islamic scholars past and contemporary. A militancy pervades his writings, and some would take words like his as a call to restore the purity and power of Islam in human affairs through force of arms. The nineteenth and early twentieth centuries in Central Eurasia witnessed a series of Islamic uprisings in the Caucasus, in the Volga-Ural region, and in Andizhan under the banner of communal jihad, a debatable but not surprising extension of the term's fundamental meaning. As a mode of reform in the face of growing disruption of traditional ways of life among Muslims, al-Bulgari's analysis and prescriptions competed with the more secularist trends epitomized by the jadidist mode of reform.

Bibliography: Shihabeddin al-Mardzhani, *Mustafad al-ahbar fi ahval Kazan wa Bulgar*, Vol. 2 (Kazan, 1303 [1885-1886]), 239-241; Rizaeddin ibn Fahreddin, *Asar*, Vol. 1, Fasc. 6 (Orenburg, 1904), 300-316; U. Beliaeva, "Gabderakhim Utyz Imiani tormysh yoly kham izhaty," in *Drevniaia tatarskaia literatura* (Kazan, 1964), 532-577; Michael Kemper, *Sufis und Gelehrte in Tatarien und Baschkirien, 1789-1889. Der Islamische Diskurs unter russischer Herrschaft* (Berlin, 1998); "al-Bulgari (al-Utyz-Imiani)," *Islam na territorii byvshei Rossiiskoi imperii. Entsiklopedicheskii slovar'*, Vol. 2 (M., 1999), 18-19; Aidar Iuzeev, *Tatarskaia filosofskaia mysl' kontsa XVIII-XIX vekov*, 2 vols. (Kazan, 1998).

Edward J. Lazzerini

BULGARIN, FADDEI VENEDIKTOVICH (1789-1859). Polish-Russian journalist and author. Publisher of the Northern Bee (Severnaia pchela, 1825-1859) and author of *Ivan Vyzhigin* (1829). See Bulgarin, Faddei Venediktovich, MERSH, Vol. 6.

The scion of a Polish szlachta family, Bulgarin was born in the village of Pieryszewo near Grodno on June 24, 1789. His father Benedykt was exiled to Siberia for his role in the uprising of April 1794 that led to the Third Partition of Poland. Young Bulgarin moved to St. Petersburg in 1798 and enrolled in the Imperial Cadet Corps. After obtaining his military commission Bulgarin served in the Russian army, distinguishing himself for valor at the Battle of Friedland in 1807. He later participated in the war against Sweden (1809) as a result of which Russia obtained the Duchy of Finland. Bulgarin was discharged for bad behavior in 1811 and later that year joined many of his countrymen as part of Napoleon's Grande Armée. After serving with the Polish units in the French army, Bulgarin was captured by the Allies in 1813 and was freed the following year as part of a prisoner exchange. He spent the next several years wandering Europe and finally settled in St. Petersburg in 1819. In 1825 he married Elena fon Ide (1809-1889), a distant relative of Alexander Bestuzhev-Marlinsky (1797-1837), and was the father of five children. A close friend of Alexander Griboedov (1795-1829), Bulgarin preserved the complete manuscript of his *Woe from Wit* (Gore ot uma, 1825) and served as the executor of Griboedov's financial affairs in St. Petersburg when the playwright was sent to Persia in 1829.

Bulgarin's aim as a writer was, as he put it, to make himself useful to the imperial government, which he saw as his duty both as a Pole and as a subject of the Russian Empire. In the early 1820s he began to publish literary, historical, and journalistic works and introduced the feuilleton into Russian journalism. Beginning with his Northern Archive (Severnyi arkhiv, 1822-1829) and continuing with journals such as the Children's Interlocutor (Detskii sobesednik, 1826-1829) and Russian Thalia (Ruskaia Taliia, 1824), and especially his newspaper Northern Bee (Severnaia pchela), Bulgarin embarked on a literary and journalistic career that spanned over thirty years. Northern Bee was the first privately owned newspaper in Russia and at its height in the 1830s boasted a circulation of thirty thousand copies, no mean feat in a country in which the reading public was very small.

In addition to The Northern Bee Bulgarin's best-known works were his novels. The first of these, Ivan Vyzhigin (1829), was an immediate best-seller and was the first Russian novel to be translated into foreign languages. His other major novels were *The False Dmitry* (Dmitrii Samozvanets, 1830), *Petr Ivanovich Vyzhigin* (1831), *Mazepa* (1833), and *The Memoirs of Titular Councillor Chukhin* (Pamiatnye zapiski Tituliarnorgo Sovetnika Chukhina, 1836). Bulgarin also wrote six volumes of memoirs (Vospominaniia, 1846-1849) and numerous shorter works of history.

The image of Bulgarin that has persisted through the years is that of a man who was a hack and a police spy who did his best to besmirch the good name of Russia's greatest poet, Alexander Pushkin (1799-1837), and who regularly denounced his rivals to the Third Section of His Imperial Majesty's Own Chancellery. As with all such images this one is a mixture of fact and fiction. His numerous literary conflicts with Pushkin are well known. More important are the other aspects of his activities and what they reveal about Russia in his time. For a period of five years (1826-1831) Bulgarin was in frequent communication with the Third Section, although it is often difficult to tell which contributions are his and which are those of other individuals who were similarly inclined. Bulgarin's notes are marvelous studies of the social and intellectual life of St. Petersburg in the late 1820s and are valuable for this reason. While it is true that Bulgarin complained about the mistreatment he received at the hands of some of his rivals, he did so only after suffering in silence for lengthy periods of time, and there is no concrete evidence that his complaints resulted in the suppression of others' works. It appears that the censors treated Bulgarin no differently from any other writer or publisher under Nicholas I.

Bulgarin's greatest legacy lies in his contributions to Russian literary and social history. The popularity of his novels and their translation into multiple European languages made Europeans aware for the first time that Russia had literature resembling that with which they were familiar. For many Europeans Bulgarin and Pushkin were Russian literature, at least until the major Russian novelists of the nineteenth century appeared on the world literary scene beginning in the 1850s. The chief reason for this is that Bulgarin promoted a constellation of values in his works that are now considerd to be middle-class: disinterested public service and commercial activity, anti-aristocratic sentiment, and a reformist attitude. The very popularity of Bulgarin's works in Russia itself suggests that many, if not most, of his readers shared these values as well. As the critic Vissarion Belinsky (1811-1848) admitted in his review of Bulgarin's *Memoirs*, people such as Belinsky himself would not have had an audience without Bulgarin's efforts. An analysis of the subscription lists for Bulgarin's major works reveals a population of readers who were primarily officers or civil servants, with individuals thrown in from other occupations and strata of society. The important thing to note here is that Bulgarin's readers identified themselves more by what they did than by their social origins. In essence Bulgarin's readership formed a group which he himself called the middle constituency (srednee sostoianie) and which has very strong parallels to the middle classes or bourgeoisie familiar in Europe at the time.

After a long career in journalism Bulgarin suffered a stroke in 1857 that left him paralyzed. He died at Karlovo, his estate outside the city of Dorpat (now Tartu in Estonia), on 20 August 1859.

Bibliography: Faddei Venediktovich Bulgarin, "Plausible Fantasies or a Journey in the 29th Century" in Leland Fetzer, ed., *Pre-Revolutionary Russian Science Fiction. An Anthology. Seven Utopias and a Dream* (Ann Arbor, Mich., 1982), *Sochineniia* (M., 1990), *Vospominaniia* (M., 2001); Thaddeus Bulgarin, *Ivan Vejeeghen, or Life in Russia* (London, 1831); Abram Il'ich Reitblat, ed., *Vidok Figliarin. Pis'ma i agenturnye zapiski F.V. Bulgarina v III otdelenie* (M., 1998); Donald Andrew Thumim, "In the Spirit of the Government. Faddei Bulgarin and the Formation of the 'Middle Class' in Russia, 1789-1859" (Ph.D. diss., Harvard University, 1995).

Donald A. Thumim

BULLITT, WILLIAM C. (1891-1967). Diplomat, writer. First US ambassador to the Soviet Union (1933-1936).

Born in Philadelphia of mixed Polish-Jewish and mainline Protestant parentage, William Bullitt graduated from Yale University, Phi Beta Kappa, class of 1912, and after a brief stint at Harvard Law School took odd jobs as a journalist while dabbling with poetry and beginning a novel he published many years later. After the death of his father and with a modest inheritance Bullitt traveled through Europe with his mother and was in Moscow in 1914 when the war was about to begin, escaping on the last train to Berlin. His journalistic career began in earnest in 1915 when he earned praise for covering the Henry Ford peace ship. Another assignment to Europe, mainly in Germany for the Philadelphia Public Ledger in 1916, brought more attention and an assignment as the Ledger's Washington correspondent. This coincided with his marriage to Ernesta Drinker, a fellow Philadelphia socialite and sister to the writer Catherine Drinker Bowen, that ended in divorce five years later.

He soon attracted the attention of Colonel Edward House, President Woodrow Wilson's consultant and confidante on a variety of domestic and foreign affairs and a fellow Yale graduate. As House's protege and informant, Bullitt served briefly on the Committee for Public Information and in the West European Division of the Department of State in 1917-1918, where he differed from most of his colleagues in taking a positive view of the Bolshevik Revolution. He was essentially House's spy in the department, and a memorandum that he wrote on 3 January 1918, perhaps prompted by House, that emphasized the Russian issue in a postwar settlement may have influenced the president's final draft of the Fourteen Points. Bullitt advised House that "Trotsky is the sort of man we need in power in Russia" (Saul, 216-217). Subsequently Bullitt protested against the trend toward allied military intervention in Russia.

Due to House's patronage Bullitt was one of several secretaries to the American mission at the Paris peace conference in 1919, meeting and impressing the president on the voyage to Europe. In Paris he protested the injustice of excluding Russia, a major participant in the war, from the negotiations. But the project of including the Bolsheviks in a separate Russian conference at Prinkipo, remotely located near the Turkish capital of Constantinople, failed. A hurriedly improvised effort, backed especially by British leader David Lloyd George, to find some accommodation with the new government of Russia and bring about a cease-fire in the escalating civil war in Russia resulted in Bullitt's leading a mission to Moscow in March 1919. House's choice of the inexperienced and relatively unknown Bullitt was meant to alleviate French opposition, but it naturally confused the Bolshevik leaders, especially with the enigmatic veteran socialist Lincoln Steffens accompanying Bullitt. Nevertheless, the American contingent met with Foreign Affairs Commissar Georgy Chicherin and with Lenin and received assurances of a willingness to negotiate concessions that would relinquish Bolshevik control of Finland, Ukraine, the Caucasus, and Siberia. Though this first allied mission to Moscow came to nothing due to French opposition and Wilson's preoccupation with other peace objectives, Bullitt achieved a degree of fame as a hero for those who favored accommodation instead of hostility toward the Bolshevik regime.

In the 1920s Bullitt spent most of his time in Europe as an Eastern-establishment and globe-trotting playboy. He frequented the salons of Paris while married to John Reed's widow Louise Bryant, pen name of Anna Louise Mohan, from 1923 to 1929 and consorted with a variety of notable people of the times, including Sigmund Freud, Yale classmate Cole Porter, F. Scott Fitzgerald, and Ernest Hemingway. Bullitt finally returned to the American political limelight with the help of House and New York attorney Louis Wehle with a second trip to Russia in 1932, during which he laid a much publicized wreath at the grave of Reed. Upon his return he was introduced to and impressed Franklin D. Roosevelt, who was just beginning his campaign for the presidency. As an internationalist and an advocate of Soviet recognition, he went to Europe as an agent of the president-elect in early 1933. In London he met with Soviet Commissar of Foreign Affairs Maxim Litvinov and returned with clear evidence, as if any were needed, of Soviet willingness to negotiate differences toward diplomatic recognition, owing especially to Moscow's alarm about Japanese aggression in Manchuria.

The result was an official invitation, after Roosevelt's election, to Soviet president Mikhail Kalinin for Litvinov to visit the United States in November 1933. The subsequent negotiations in Washington were conducted mainly by Bullitt, assisted by Soviet expert George F. Kennan, and concentrated on Soviet recognition of the foreign debt to the United States acquired by the Provisional Government, redemption for confiscated property, and non-interference by the Comintern in America on one side, and long-term American credits to Russia on the other. After much tedious discussion the two parties agreed to formal diplomatic recognition on 19 November with promises to resolve outstanding issues later. As a reward for his service and dedication to this cause Bullitt was named the first American ambassador to the USSR. He hurriedly journeyed to Russia with Kennan in December for the formal exchange of letters and returned early the next year with his daughter Anne, by Louise Bryant, to begin his tenure as ambassador. His first meetings with Joseph Stalin signaled mutual mistrust at first sight. The Soviet failure to live up to the Litvinov agreements and additional aggravations concerning currency exchanges and accommodations for embassy personnel led Bullitt to become increasingly disappointed and embittered. He quickly shifted from the pro-Soviet stance he had held since 1917 to strong hostility to the Stalinist regime.

Bullitt's third mission to Moscow was no more successful than the first, since making arrangements for Soviet payment of debts owed from before the Bolshevik Revolution remained elusive and the hoped for boost in trade and business between the two countries was disappointing. Nevertheless, with the able assistance of Kennan, Charles "Chip" Bohlen, Charles "Charley" Thayer, Leroy "Loy" Henderson, and others, the Bullitt embassy established a firm foundation for expertise and competence about Soviet Russia that survived the Moscow turmoil of ideological discord, purges, and the Nazi-Soviet Pact to lay the foundation for lend-lease and the grand alliance in 1941. Though disenchanted with his Russian mission, Bullitt continued in the diplomatic service as ambassador to France from 1936 to 1940, staying through the fall of Paris, and then as a roving ambassador for the president until their disagreement in 1942. He then served as an advisor to the French army until crippled by an auto accident in 1945. In the postwar years Bullitt remained a staunch critic of the Soviet Union and an architect of the Cold War until his death in 1967.

Bibliography: An excellent biography of Bullitt by Will Brownell and Richard N. Billings is *So Close to Greatness. A Biography of William C. Bullitt* (New York, 1987), while Orville H. Bullitt, ed., *For the President, Personal and Secret. Correspondence Between Franklin D. Roosevelt and William C. Bullitt* (New York, 1972) includes biographical information in the introductions by George F. Kennan and Bullitt's brother Orville and documentation on the recognition negotiations. Bullitt himself authored *The Bullitt Mission to Russia* (New York, 1919) and *The Great Globe Itself* (New York, 1946). The memoirs of Bohlen, *Witness to History, 1929-1969* (New York, 1973) and Kennan, *Memoirs, 1925-1950* (Boston, Mass., 1967) are very revealing. See also Kennan's *Russia and the West Under Lenin and Stalin* (Boston, Mass., 1961), Michael Cassella-Blackburn, *The Donkey, the Carrot, and the Club. William C. Bullitt and Soviet-American Relations, 1917-1948* (Westport, Conn, 2004), and Norman E. Saul, *War and Revolution. The United States and Russia, 1914-1921* (Lawrence, Kan., 2001).

Norman E. Saul

BUNIATZADE, DADASH KHOJA OGLU (1888-1938). Major party and government figure in Azerbaijan.

Buniatzade became a member of Hummet, a social democratic party for Muslim workers, in 1908. He worked in the Baku press writing party propaganda and translating Russian materials into the Turkic language of Azerbaijan. In May and June 1918 he participated in the short-lived communist government in Baku, the so-called Baku Commune. Although he was not a commissar, the only Azerbaijani commissar being Nariman Narimanov, he was a member of the executive committee of the governing soviet. After the fall of the commune to a combined nationalist and Ottoman force in August 1918 Buniatzade went with other Azerbaijani socialists to Astrakhan where he headed the party section for Muslim affairs for Transcaucasia. He concomitantly edited the Turkic-language newspaper Tartysh (Battle).

In August 1919, at the time the British occupation forces under General W.M. Thomson left Baku, Buniatzade was sent to work with Anastas Mikoian who oversaw the semi-legal Baku Committee of the Russian Communist Party (Bolshevik). Buniatzade was surely a link to Hummet, which reconciled pro-Bolshevik and pro-Menshevik members from an earlier split the previous December.

Under the laws of the Azerbaijan Democratic Republic (1918-1920) many different political organizations were allowed. The Bolshevik-led Baku Committee incorporated Hummet and planned the overthrow of the republic's coalition government. Aided by an ultimatum from the Red Army, the party overthrew the republican government on the night of 27-28 April 1920. A revolutionary-military committee (Voenrevkom) was created with Narimanov at the head and Buniatzade as commissar of Enlightenment and Worker-Peasant Inspectorate.

As commissar of enlightenment Buniatzade oversaw the press, propaganda, adult literacy campaigns, and school reform. Like the head of state Narimanov, Buniatzade believed that the sovietization of Azerbaijan was part of a world-wide anti-colonial struggle liberating Azerbaijan from Russia, rather than an imitation of the Russian proletarian revolution. In an interview in the Azerbaijani-language newspaper Kommunist in October 1920 Buniatzade said that education had to show the workers and peasants of Azerbaijan that "the new government is their own." Buniatzade was replaced as commissar in the summer of 1922, seemingly as part of a consolidation of control over culture by then secretary of the Azerbaijan Communist Party, Sergei Kirov, a protégé of Stalin.

Buniatzade went on to occupy a series of important posts as commissar of food and of lands, as head of the republic's state planning agency (Gosplan), and by the late 1920s as vice-chairman of the Council of Commissars (Sovnarkom), the governing body of Soviet Azerbaijan. In March 1930 he was elected chairman of Sovnarkom, a post he held into 1932. He then became commissar of lands of the Transcaucasian Federation (ZSFSR), which united Azerbaijan, Armenia, and Georgia in a single economic and political unit, as well as a member of its central executive committee (CEC). He was elected also to the presidium of the Azerbaijan CEC and the CEC of the USSR.

In June 1937 he was not among those reappointed to the Central Committee of the Azerbaijan Communist Party. Other prominent party members were also excluded. The reason became plain in October. He was made a co-defendant in the trial of the major Azerbaijani old Bolsheviks. The group was accused of fostering counterrevolution in Azerbaijan, including supporting an uprising that occurred recently in the city of Shemakhi just to the west of Baku. All were convicted and the most prominent members, including Buniatzade, were sentenced to be shot. The sentences were carried out in 1938.

Bibliography: There is little written on Buniatzade. He did not appear in the first edition of the *Bol'shaia Sovetskaia Entsiklopedia* perhaps because when the "Bu" volume appeared in 1927 he was not deemed sufficiently important for an entry. By the time the second edition appeared, he had been purged. The longest biographical information on him is given in *Aktivnye bortsy za Sovetskuiu vlast' v Azerbaidzhane* (Baku, 1957), 45-47.

Audrey L. Alstadt

BURGOMASTER REFORM. See Burmistr Reform of 1699.

BURIAT LAMAISM. The Buddhism that took root in Buriatia is Tibetan, Mahayana Buddhism, or lamaism.

Buriat lamaism is related to the school of Gelugpa, which was founded by the Tibetan philosopher Tsonkapa (1357-1419). Buddhism linked Buriatia to the cultural traditions of the East as found in India and Tibet, Mongolia and China. It began to penetrate the territory of Buriatia and Mongolia during the period of the Turkic khanates, at which time and until the seventeenth century the traditional belief of the Buriats and Evenks was shamanism.

Buddhism became a more powerful stimulus of the social and cultural development of the Buriat people than was shamanism. Important aspects of the history of Buddhism in Buriatia include the spread of the Mongolian and Tibetan written languages, the growth of literacy among a certain part of the population, and the adoption of Indo-Tibetan and Chinese astronomy. It was from the latter that a sixty-year animal cycle for counting the years was introduced and practical annual calendars were developed.

By 1741 there were eleven lamaistic temples and 150 lamas in the Trans-Baikal region. By an order of Empress Elizabeth an official roster of 150 lamas was drawn up for the first time. In exchange for being freed from the tax in kind (yasak) and other taxes, they were required to swear an oath of allegiance and to preach Buddhism to the nomadic tribes.

Monasteries (datsans) were founded in practically all significant population centers of Buriatia in the first half of the nineteenth century. In 1822 there were 2,502 lamas. By 1831 they numbered 4,637. Many datsans had their own novices, but purely theological schools appeared in Buriat datsans only in the nineteenth century. The most popular of them were the Tsanit schools in the Tsugol, Gusinoozersk, Aga, and Ana datsans, all of which taught Buddhist philosophy.

The development of a network of datsans, the growing complexity of temple services, and the penetration of lamaistic religious practices into the everyday life of the Buriat people created the need to provide the clergy and believers with theological literature and cultic objects, such as sculpted and painted images of the gods and goddesses of the lamaistic pantheon as well as other items for temples and domestic shrines. This spurred the development of publishing, icon painting, religious architecture, specialized metal- and woodworking, and sewing, appliqué, and other needlework in the datsans and villages of Buriatia.

Buddhist datsans and lamas also spread Tibetan medicine throughout Buriatia. Schools to train lama-healers were opened in the Aga, Atsagat, Gusinoozero, and other datsans during the nineteenth century. Tibetan medicine had names for more than 1,300 pharmaceutical preparations. In Mongolia and Buriatia Tibetan healers developed a distinct pharmacopeia based on local conditions and using the experience of popular medicine. Tibetan medicine also employed blood-letting, acupuncture, and cauterization.

In response to the policies of forceful assimilation, russification, and Christianization, a movement of renewal appeared among the national-democratic intelligentsia and liberal Buddhist clergy at the end of the nineteenth and beginning of the twentieth centuries. Many western students of Buddhism think that the Buriat renewal movement was inspired by the Bolsheviks and given birth by the Soviet authorities. The idea of Buriat renewal actually derived from modernistic interpretations of Buddhism, which began to intrigue European thinkers at the turn of the twentieth century. Proponents of Buriat renewal attempted to preach several ideas among Buriat believers. Buddhism is not a religion nor an ethical-philosophical teaching; Buddha was not a god, but a brilliant person, a scholar and thinker; Buddhism does not contradict science, materialism, communism or Marxism; Buddhism is a system of empirical ethics and rational thought, not a ritualistic worship of gods; there is nothing pessimistic about Buddhism, which is an optimistic teaching interested in improving real life here on Earth. The great majority of the clergy and believers did not accept modernization of the religion. In practical fact the renewal movement led to the recognition of Soviet authority by the church and to an attempt to reform the daily lives of the Buddhist clergy.

The legal condition of lamaism in the Soviet state was set out in an order of the Central Executive Committee of the Council of People's Commissars of the Buriat-Mongol Autonomous Soviet Socialist Republic of 17 December 1925, which adopted the Soviet decree on separation of church from the state and schools from the church. Monasteries and monastery property were nationalized. Until the end of the 1920s the struggle against lamaism took place primarily in the ideological sphere. Later the renewal movement and the lamaistic clergy were more forcefully repressed. Worship practically ceased. By the end of the 1930s most lamas had been arrested, and not a single Buddhist monastery was in operation. All were destroyed and their property taken. Many spiritual and material valuables were lost forever.

From 1937 to 1945 there were no officially operating religious centers of lamaism in Buriatia. The religious movement went underground, and by 1944-1945 many itinerant lamas were active in Buriatia. A meeting of Buddhist activists took place in Ulan-Ude in 1946. That same year the Central Spiritual Administration of Buddhists was established and L.N. Darmaev was elected its chairman at its first congress. Darmaev resided at Khamba Temple (Sume), which is now Ivolga datsan. The Buddhist church continued to operate within the framework of the decree and charter of 1946 into the 1990s. Only two Buddhist monasteries functioned in the Trans-Baikal region until 1990, the Ivolga datsan in Buriatia and the Aga datsan in the Chita region. Ivolga datsan was the residence of the Pandita-Khambo lama, the chairman of the Central Spiritual Administration of Buddhists of the Soviet Union.

At the current time there are several dozen datsans active in the territory of ethnic Buriatia under the leadership of the traditional Buddhist clergy (sangkhi), whose chairman is Khambo-lama D. Aiusheev. Besides the daily prayers and minor assemblies (khuraly), six large traditional worship services, associated with the cult of Buddha Shakyamuni, Maitreya, and Tsonkapa, take place annually in all datsans.

Bibliography: John Snelling, *Buddhism in Russia. The Story of Agvan Dorzhiev, Lhasa's Emissary to the Tsar* (Shaftesbury, 1993); Nicholas Poppe, "The Buddhists" in *Genocide in the USSR. Studies in Group Destruction*, ed. by Nikolai D. Deker and Andrei Lebed (New York, 1958), 181-192; B. Bashkevich, *Lamaisty Vostochnoi Sibiri* (SPb., 1998); K.M. Gerasimova, *Obnovlencheskoe dvizhenie buriatskogo lamaistskogo dukhvenstva, 1917-1930 gg.* (Ulan-Ude, 1964); B.D. Dandaron, *O religioznykh obriadakh lamaisma. O nekotorykh religioznykh kul'takh i ikh sushchnosti* (Ulan-Ude, 1961); N.L. Zhukovskaia, *Vliianie mongolo-buriatskogo shamanstva i doshamanskikh verovanii na lamiasm* (M., 1968); *Lamaizm v Buriatii XVIII-nachale XX vv.* (Novosibirsk, 1983); V.Ts. Mandakova, *Buddiiskaia misteriia Tsam v Buriatii* (Ulan-Ude, 1997); *Polozhenie o lamaistskom dukhvenstve v Vostochnoi Sibiri* (SPb., 1998).

Eugenia K. Mitupova

BURIAT LANGUAGE. Buriat belongs to the Mongolian family of languages.

Buriat became a separate language after Mongol-speaking tribes settled in the cis- and trans-Baikal regions during the seventh and eighth centuries and slowly evolved a distinct Buriat ethnos. After the adoption of Buddhism, Old Mongolian, then the only written language among the Mongol-speaking tribes of Central Asia, spread widely among the Buriats. The formation of Buriat as a distinct and unified language took place in the presence of various Buriat dialects, whose existence can be explained in part by the dispersed settlement of the Buriat population. Buriat still has many dialects which are, as a rule, based upon the tribal organization of the Buriat people, but that is not absolutely true. For hundreds of years the development of dialects and their interactions in various regions were influenced substantially by tribal relationships. For example, the Bulagat tribes, who migrated to the northern regions of the Selenga River, adopted the Khori dialect almost completely. Frontal study of Buriat dialects and analysis of studies of their classification and systematization by leading linguists of Mongolian languages show that contemporary Buriat is divided into four dialectical groups.

Khori Dialect. This is the largest dialectical division of the Buriat language. It includes Khori subdialect, which is spoken throughout the three large administrative regions of the Buriat republic, Eravna, Khori, and Kizhinga. Tugnui subdialect and Aga subdialect, which is spoken throughout the Chita region except where the Onon Khamnigans have their own subdialect, are related to Khori. The subdialects of the Ivolga and northern Selenga Buriats, who are genealogically related primarily to the Bulagat and to a lesser degree to the Ekherit tribes, are also related to Khori.

Ekhirit-Bulagat Dialect. This includes the Ekhirit-Bulagat, Bokhan, and Olkhon subdialects, as well as the subdialects of the Barguzin and Baikalo-Kudara Buriats. The Ekhirit-Bulagat dialect is the largest dialectical group in the Buriat-speaking territory of Irkutsk region. It includes the relatively independent Ida and Osa subdialects as well as those of the Saigut and Chinese Buriats, who have not lost their ties to the Ida and Bulusa Buriats.

Alaro-Tunka Dialect. This comprises the Alar subdialect, the Tunka-Oka and Zakamen subdialects as well as the subdialect of the Unga Buriats.

Tsongolo-Sartul Dialect. This comprises two subdialects, the Tsongol and Sartul. Speakers of this dialect are comparatively recent migrants from Mongolia (early eighteenth century) who have not lost yet features of the Mongol tongue, which has remained in one way or another in direct contact with adjacent Buriat subdialects for the last three centuries.

The Khori dialect forms the basis of contemporary literary Buriat. How one writes the language is closely related to the cultural-religious and sometimes to the political orientation of the speaker, and it has been debated for decades. The issue of the written language is a complex and sensitive one. Early in the twentieth century two major schools of thought about graphic reform, identified with A. Dorzhiev and B. Baradin, struggled for supremacy. An important factor in this debate in the 1920s and 1930s was a change in cultural orientation to europeanization, which tilted the debate in favor of B. Baradin's arguments for adopting the Latin alphabet. In 1931 it was officially decided to write Buriat in Latin characters. Although this period is characterized by many researchers as a time in which Buriat artistic literature flourished, the level of education rose, and the Latin alphabet grew in popularity, it became clear by 1934 that the new alphabet was not taking deep root. The failure seems to have been caused by basing the new Buriat language on the Khalkha-Mongol language, and moreover on the Selenga dialect, rather than on the living, conversational language of the people. In 1939 it was decided that Buriat would be written instead in the Cyrillic alphabet.

These two abrupt changes within a single decade, first to the Latin and then to the Cyrillic alphabet, destroyed cultural and linguistic traditions. For a time it halted development of the Buriat language. Requiring people to learn two new systems of writing sped the adoption of the Russian language by non-Russian speakers in the nationalities regions and consequently the development of national and Russian bilingualism. The fact that literacy campaigns were undertaken using the Cyrillic alphabet and that international culture largely was absorbed through the Russian language reinforced bilingualism.

At the present time the Buriat language possesses both a conversational and a relatively well developed literary language. Literary Buriat is based on the dialect of the Khori Buriats, Old Mongolian, and Buriat folklore, as well as a number of dialects and subdialects, which function mostly in the day-to-day sphere. Conversational Buriat contains elements of the Buriat literary language and dialects as well as of the Russian language. The level of standardization of literary Buriat is rather high. The last code of orthographic rules was confirmed in 1961, and in 1962 an academic grammar of Buriat was published. There are multi-language and orthographic dictionaries for Buriat, and a variety of school text books and grammars are available. Within literary Buriat there is a great deal of stylistic diversity. High-literary, popular-journalistic, pedagogical, and literary-conversational styles exist. Lexical-pronunciation standards are well established. Official business and scholarly styles are not fully developed yet.

The majority of Buriat speakers live in the Russian Federation. According to the 1989 census there were 421,380 Buriats in the USSR, including 417,425 in the Russian Federation. Most of them live in one of three subdivisions of Eastern Siberia: the Buriat republic, and the Aga and Ust-Orda Buriat autonomous territories. The Buriats in these regions, who account for one-quarter of their total populations, number 341,185. Outside the Russian Federation about 60,000 Buriats live compactly in Mongolia and about 6,000 in China.

The Buriats, their culture, and their language have always been in active contact with neighboring peoples. From them they assimilated aspects of Buddhist and Christian cultures and traditions. The presence of two different cultures and languages on their borders, Mongolian and Russian, deposited in the Buriat language a significant number of elements, sometimes relics, of both languages. Mongolisms are more common in medicine, culture, and religion. Russian terms are common in administrative and scientific terminology, trade, and objects of everyday use. The core of the Buriat language remains native elements as is clearly seen in Buriat literature.

Bibliography: Nicholas Poppe, *Buriat Grammar* (Bloomington, Ind., 1960); James Bosson, *Buriat Reader* (Bloomington, Ind., 1962); D.A. Abasheev, "K voprosu realizatsii buria-mongol'skogo iazyka," *Buriatovedcheskii sbornik*, Nos. 3-4 (1927); B.B. Batoev, *Buriatskii iazyk. Grafika, orfografiia i punktuatsiia* (Ulan-Ude, 1993); Ts.B. Budaev, *Buriatskie dialekty. Opyt diakhronnogo issledovaniia* (Novosibirsk, 1992); *Buriatskii iazyk. Sovremennoe sostoianie, sotsiolingvisticheskii aspekt* (Ulan-Ude, 1999); D.D. Dorzhiev, *Rannie pamiatniki buriatskoi pis'mennosti* (Ulan-Ude, 1969); G.A. Dyrkheeva, *Buriatskii iazyk v usloviiakh dvuiazychiia. Problemy funktsioniriovaniia i perspektivy razvitiia* (Ulan-Ude, 2002); N.N. Poppe, *K voprosu o sozdanii novogo mongol'skogo alfavita* (Baku, 1929).

Konstantin B. Mitupov

BURIAT LITERATURE. Mongolic literature could be said to begin with the appearance of the *Secret History of the Mongols*, written in 1240. Presented in the style of a historical chronicle, the *History* was compiled from epic tales and genealogies and incorporates legends, poems, blessings and admonitions, songs, and sayings. Little changed in Buriat folklore and literature until Buriat lands were absorbed into the Russian Empire late in the seventeenth century. Then along with traditional heroes such as Babzha-Baras bator, Shilde-Zangi, and Shono-bator, new heroes such as Tsar Peter I, began to make their appearance.

The great heroic epic of Buriatia, which runs to tens of thousands of poetic lines, is called *Geser*. Mikhail Khangalov, Tsyben Zhamtsarano, and Sergei Baldaev were among its more important compilers. The enormous work of studying and collating its myriad variations and creating a composite text that retained the topical and linguistic wealth of the many versions was accomplished by Namzhil Baldano. The composite text he produced provided the basis for *Geser*'s translation into Russian, first by the famous translator Semen Lipkin in 1970 and later by the poet Vladimir Soloukhin in 1982.

Dramaturgy became a popular literary genre at the beginning of the twentieth century. Plays by D. Abasheev (Death, Ukhel, 1908), I.G. Saltykov (Two Worlds, Khoer mozho, 1911), Ch.-L. Bazaron (The Gambler, Khaartashan, 1912, and Bread, Tariaan, 1921), S.P. Baldaev (Tsiren the shepherd, Tsirenmalchin, 1909), and D.-R. Namzhilon (Renewal, Khuushan khubilba, khuuli shenerbe, 1918), among others, reflect the life of Buriat society during this important period when the ideas of the Enlightenment, nationalism, and democracy were spreading more widely among the Buriat intelligensia.

Between 1917 and 1937 Buriat writers began to work in new genres. The popular oral tradition of folk tales gave rise to short stories. And folkloristic poetry, which grew out of older epic works and folksongs, gradually developed into recognizably modern poetry. Earlier one-act farces and melodramatic plays by village playwrights became more complex and developed into contemporary professional drama.

Numerous works written in the 1920s became classics. Among them were the historical dramas of Bazar Baradin, such as Mrs. Choizhid (Choizhid khatan, 1924) and The Great Sister-Shaman (Ekhe udagan Abzhaa, 1925), Khotsa Namsaraev's poem The Word of Old Gelen (Ubgen Gelene Uge, 1929), a series of stories from the cycle The Way It Was, the lyrical poetry of Munko Saridak, and Bavasan Abiduev's poem The Airplane (Agaaryn ongoso, 1928).

The most significant literary accomplishments of the 1930s were prose works. Essays, feuilletons, and sketches that appeared regularly in the periodical press played an important role in their development. Ts. Don (Tsyrenzhap Dondubon) wrote the first Buriat novellas, *Lunar Eclipse* and *Poison,* in 1932 and 1935 respectively. They examined the complex and rather painful changes in the mentality of Buriat peasants as they came under the influences of modernization and Soviet ideology.

Important new plays also were written in this period. The Buriat National Theater in Verkhneudinsk, now Ulan-Ude, opened with a performance of Namzhil Baldano's play Breakthrough in 1932. Apollon Shadaev's comedy Mergen and Namzhil Baldano's historical drama One of the Many also were performed there. Gombo Tsydynzhapov and Apollon Shadaev composed the first Buriat musical drama, Bair, and composer Markian Frolov wrote the first opera,

Enkhe-Bulat bator (1940) with a libretto by Namzhil Baldano. The plays of Tsyren Shagzhin and Dashi-Rabdan Batozhabai were successful and popular in the 1950-1960s.

Buriat poetry underwent significant changes in the 1940-1950s. Graphically poetry grew more dynamic and symmetrical and adopted stanzaic structure. Khotsa Namsaraev, Solbone Tuia, Damba Dashinimaev, Bato Bazaron, Babasan Abiduev, Zhamian Baldanzhabon, Tsokto Nomtoev, Danri Khiltukhin, Shirab Nimbuev, and Tseden Galsanov were among the most outstanding poets.

The publication of the first novels in Buriat literature, *The Steppe Awoke* (Step prosnulas, 1949) by Zhamso Tumunov and *At Dawn* (Na utrennei zare, 1950) by Khotsa Namsaraev, was a major literary event. Chimit Tsydendambaev wrote a trilogy about the leading Buriat scholar, Dorzhi Banzarov, which was published in 1953 and 1959. Baradii Mungonov's novel about the contemporary Buriat village, *Our Turbulent Khilok* (Khilok nash burlivy), was published in 1959. Other notable novels from the 1950s and 1960s include the trilogy *Stolen Happiness* (Pokhishchennoe schastie, 1959) by Dashirabdan Batozhabai, *The Steamboat Whistles* (Gudit parovoz, 1960) by Zhamian Baldazhabon, *The Last Retreat* (Poslednee otstuplenie, 1961) and *Break-Grass* (Razryv-trava, 1969) by Isai Kalashinkov, *Singing Arrows* (Poiushchie strely, 1962) by Afrikan Balburov, and *Night Dies at Dawn* (Noch umiraet s rassvetom, 1963) by Mikhail Stepanov.

In the following years excellent short stories were published by such writers as Vladimir Kornakov, Dashi Erdyneev, Olga Serova, Kim Balkov, Sergei Tsyrendorzhiev, Bair Yabzhanov, Konstantin Karnyshev, Sergei Bukhaev, and others. Vladimir Mitypov, who wrote the novellas *Degrees of Perfection* (Stupeni sovershenstva, 1965), *The Green Madness of the Earth* (Zelenoe bezumie zemli, 1966), *Arrival of the Big Apes* (Prikhod bolshikh obezian, 1968), and *Valley of the Immortals* (Dolina bessmertnikov, 1975), was the best known writer of science fiction. Mikhail Zhigzhitov's novellas *Steppe Landslide* (Stepnoi obval, 1975), *Beyond Seven-Wolf Gorge* (Za ushcheliem semi volkov, 1978) were concerned with ecology, as were Konstantin Karnyshev's *From the Holy to the Hapless* (Ot sviatogo do goremyka, 1971), Daba-Damby Dugarov's *Black Sable* (Cherny Sobol, 1969), and Kim Balkov's *Bridge* (Most, 1982). *Cruel Century* (Zhestoki vek, 1974) by Isai Kalashinkov, *Army in Boots* (Untovoe voisko, 1976) by Viktor Sergeev, *Year of the Fiery Serpent* (God ognennoi zmei, 1972) by Tsydenzhap Zhimbiev, and *On the Turgen River* (Na Turgenreke, 1979) by Mikhail Stepanov were all historical novels.

In the 1960s to the 1980s some of the better Buriat poets have included Tsyren-Dulma Dondokova, Damba Zhalsaraev, Chimit-Rygzen Namzhilov, Tsydenzhap Zhimbiev, Nikolai Damdinov, Tsyren Galanov, Vladimir Petonov, Dondok Ulzytuev, Tsyren-Dulma Dondogoi, Vladimir Lipatov, Mels Sambuev, Georgy Dashabylov, Andrei Rumiantsev and, Namzhil Nimbuev. Among their most notable works are Dondok Ulzytuev's White Month (Belyi mesiats, 1968) and Song of the Universe (Pesn vselennoi, 1969), Nikolai Damdinov's My Father's Name (Imia otsa, 1960), Chimit-Rygzen Namzhilov's A Mother's Heart (Serdtse materi, 1968), Tsyren-Bazar Badmaev's Battle for the Sun (Borba za solntse, 1967) and Tsyren-Dulma Dondokova's The Girl from Baikal (Devushka s Baikala, 1963).

Among the more talented children's writers are Danri Khiltukhin, Tsokto Nomtoev, Shirab Nimbuev, Tsyren Badmaev, Gunga Chimitov. The creative works of Lobson Tapkhaev, Galina Radnaeva, and the Russian-language poet Bair Dugarov are of great interest. Their poems preserve and develop the best traditions of citizenship and philosophical outlooks, and present a synthesis of lyrical and epic forms along with an unceasing search for new ideas and forms of expression.

Ardan Angarkhaev, Bair Erdyneev, Dorzhi Erdyneev, Rinchin Badmaev and Shirab-Nimbu Tsydenzhapov have continued to write high-quality dramas for the theater. Bair Erdyneev and Rinchin Badmaev's play Damdin Lama (1991), Mikhail Batoin's That Many-Faced World (Etot raznoliky mir, 1992), and Bulat Gavrilov's Where are You, Shambala's Country? (Gde ty, strana Shambala? 1992) are among the best plays of the last several decades.

Works by Buriat writers now are published in many languages in Russia and abroad.

Bibliography: Jeremiah Curtin, *A Journey in Southern Siberia. The Mongols, their Religion, and their Myths* (Boston, Mass., 1909); G. Bashkuev, *The Buryats. Traditions and Culture* (Ulan Ude, 1995); E.E. Baldanmaksarova, *Buriatskaia poeziia. Traditsii i novatorstvo, 1920-80-e gg.* (Ulan-Ude, 1999); S.Zh. Baldanov, "Buriatskaia literatura segodnia. Sostoianie, problemy, perspektivy," *Vershiny* (2000), Vol. 1; *Biobibliograficheskii slovar' repressirovannykh pisatelei Buriatii* (Ulan-Ude, 1995); *Istoriia buriatskoi sovetskoi literatury*, 3 vols. (Ulan-Ude, 1967, 1995, 1997); I.A. Kim, *Buriatskaia sovetskaia poeziia dvatsatykh godov* (Ulan-Ude, 1968); V.Ts. Naidakov, *Buriatskoe dramaticheskoe iskusstvo* (Ulan-Ude, 1962), *Sovremennye pisateli Buriatii* (Ulan-Ude, 1969), *Traditsii i novatorstvo v buriatskoi sovetskoi literature* (Ulan-Ude, 1976), *Stanovlenie i razvitie buriatskoi literatury, 1917-1995* (Ulan-Ude, 1996); S.M. Tulokhonov, *Istoriia literatury Buriatii* (Ulan-Ude, 2000); M. Tsyrenova and L. Dampilova, *Osnovnye tendentsii v razvitii sovremennoi buriatskoi poezii* (Ulan-Ude, 2000).

Svetlana V. Baldano

BURIAT REPUBLIC (1923-).The Republic of Buriatia is now part of the Russian Federation. It was established on 30 May 1923 as the Buriat-Mongol Autonomous Soviet Socialist Republic (ASSR). The capital of the republic, which was founded in 1666 and received the status of a city in 1783, now is called Ulan-Ude. Until 1934 it was named Verkhneudinsk. Buriatia's southern border coincides with Russia's border with Mongolia. On its other borders it touches the Republic of Tuva and the Irkutsk and Chita regions of Russia.

Government Structure. From 1923 to 1991 Buriatia was an ASSR within the Soviet Union. According to the federation agreement of the constitution of the Russian Federation adopted in 1993, the Republic of Buriatia is now a constituent part of the Russian Federation. State power in the republic is held by the president, the People's Assembly (Khural), the government, and the courts. According to the constitution the president is the head of the republic, its chief executive authority, and chairman of the government. Leonid Vasilievich Potapov was elected to his third term as president on 23 June 2002. The parliament of the republic, the People's Assembly, is a representative and legislative organ. Within its competence lie amendments to the constitution; development and passage of laws; approval of national programs of economic and social development; consideration, approval, and oversight of the state budget; decisions concerning changes to the republic's borders; determination of the administrative-territorial organization of the republic; receipt of the president's annual message about the internal and external policies of the republic; receipt of reports from the constitutional court, etc.

Executive power in the Republic of Buriatia is exercised by the government. It develops and presents the republic's budget to the People's Assembly and assures that it is carried out; presents a report on the fulfillment of the budget; oversees the implementation of financial, credit and monetary policies, as well as policies in the areas of culture, science, education, public health, social security, and ecology; administers the republic's property; oversees measures for the observation of legality, including civil liberties, the preservation of property and social order, and the struggle against crime; and carries out other charges laid upon it by the constitution, republican laws, and directives of the president.

Judicial authority is held by constitutional, civil, administrative, and criminal courts. In accordance with the constitution a Constitutional Court, Supreme Court, and Higher Court of Arbitration have been established and are in operation. The republic's procuracy is part of the unified system of the procuracy of the Russian Federation. Local self-administration is recognized and guaranteed in the republic. It has been established in all regions and cities subordinate to the republic.

Political parties and non-governmental organizations play an important role in the political life of the republic. Nineteen parties and twenty-two other political organizations are registered. Most of them are regional branches of parties and movements active throughout Russia.

The Republic of Buriatia has its own state symbols, including an emblem, flag, and hymn, which express its statehood, independence, and the traditions of its multiethnic population. The relationships among the executive institutions of the Republic of Buriatia and the Russian Federation are constitutionally established.

Nature. Buriatia is located at the junction of Central and Northern Asia in an area influenced by both the Pacific and Atlantic oceans. It occupies an area of

135,053 square miles (351,700 sq. km) or two percent of the total area of Russia. The territory of the republic stretches from the west to the east between 98°40' and 116°55' longitude and from north to south between 57°15' and 49°55' latitude.

Buriatia is primarily a mountainous country. It possesses a few level valleys, which are all located at elevations between 1,640 and 2,396 feet (500-700 m). The lowest point in Buriatia, the shore of Lake Baikal, is 1,492 feet (455 m) above sea level. The territory has a complex geological structure. The process of mountain formation, which began in the Upper Proterozoic age, continued into the middle of the Cambrian period, 700-500 million years ago. Folded mountain structures are composed primarily of archaezoic and proterozoic rocks. Frequent volcanic eruptions occurred in the Paleozoic era in the Vitim Plateau, Eastern Saian, and Khamar-Daban areas. Broad depressions of the trans-Baikal type, such as at Selenga mid-mountain, formed at the beginning of the Mesozoic era. In the Paleogene period of the Cenozoic era insignificant tectonic movements took place, and more recently in the Neogene-quarternary era the topography seen today with depressions of the Baikal type, like Baikal, Tunka, and Barguzin, took shape.

The republic possesses abundant mineral resources. More than 500 deposits of useful minerals have been discovered on its territory, more than 300 of which are registered by the government. They include deposits of gold, uranium, polymetallic complexes, quartz, zinc, nickel, beryllium, asbestos, and others. There are unique deposits of green and pale nephrite. There are also large deposits of coal, fluorspar, limestone, dolomite, fireclay, and various materials useful for construction such as pearlite, zeolite, brick and ceramic clays, sand and gravel, and other stone. The total value of the proven resources of the larger deposits is more than US $130 billion.

One of Buriatia's most important resources is its forests. The total area of forest land is 67.2 million acres (27.2 mn ha), of which 50.1 million acres (20.3 mn ha) are covered with forests. The total supply of timber is estimated at 65,286,500 cubic feet (1,850,000 cu m). Sixty-five percent of the trees are deciduous varieties, 21 percent pine, 10 percent Siberian cedar, the rest spruce and fir.

Buriatia's economy is heavily influenced by the unique ecosystem of Lake Baikal. The lake's water is exceptionally clean and comprises one-fifth of the world's supply of fresh water. There are also more than 360 mineral and thermal springs in the republic. In one way or another more than 90 percent of the territory is connected with the Baikal ecosystem.

Buriatia's climate is harshly continental. The republic's location in the center of the Asian continent, its great distance from the oceans, and its mountainous terrain are the primary factors in its climatic processes. Winter is long, cold, windless, and not very snowy. Summer is short and warm. The mean temperature in January is approximately -24°C (-11°F), in July 18°C (64°F).

Rainfall in many agricultural regions, including the valleys of the Selenga, Uda, Barguzin, and other rivers, averages ten to twelve inches (250-300 mm). In mountainous regions twelve to twenty inches (300-500 mm) or more fall annually.

The formation of topsoil in Buriatia is influenced by the land's latitude and high altitude, and by the exposure and steepness of its mountain slopes. The width and orientation of mountain valleys and depressions, and the nature of the rock from which the soil is formed also play a large role. Vegetation varies widely from semi-arid to mountain-tundra species. Sheep's fescue, hairgrass, stemless cinquefoil, cold wormwood, and virgin grass dominate in the steppe. Saline soils are spottily covered by alkaline meadows with chee grass and hemp nettle. The forest-steppe areas are covered with birch, mixed birch and pine, and larch forests. In the taiga zone larch dominates. The fauna of Buriatia ranges through animals of the arid steppes, the Siberian taiga, the high mountains, and the northern tundra. Of 2,630 species of flora and fauna more than 60 percent are found only in Buriatia. In the mountain-taiga and forest regions there are sable, squirrel, weasel, hare, wolverine, lynx, and bear. Among hoofed animals are elk, boar, mountain goat, and roe, musk, Manchurian, and northern deer. Fox, wolf, ermine, steppe polecat, long-haired ground squirrel, and roe deer are more common in the forest-steppe and steppe zones. Central Asian fauna, such as the Tarbagan marmot, striped and hairy-footed hamsters, Mongolian jerboa, Daur hedgehog, Pallas' cat, Tolai hare, and others mingle with typical Siberian species in the southern regions. Muskrats are widespread in the lakes of Buriatia.

In the territory of Buriatia 6,150,000 acres (2,490,000 ha) of natural landscape have been protected. In addition to three wildlife sanctuaries (zapovednik), two national parks, and sixteen reserves (zakaznik), 266 natural monuments, and more that 3,000 historical and cultural monuments have been established. The Barguzin sanctuary plays an important role in the preservation and breeding of the Barguzin sable.

There are many rivers, lakes, and mineral springs in Buriatia. All the rivers are part of the Arctic Ocean basin. The largest of them are the Selenga and Vitim. There are seventeen lakes in the republic with a surface area of more than 3.8 square miles (10 sq. km). The largest by far is Baikal 12,109 square miles (31,500 sq. km). The most famous of the more than 360 mineral springs in Buriatia are the Arshan, Gremiachinsk, Nilova Pustyn, Baunt, Kuchiger, Alla, Garga, and Khongor Uula.

Population. Buriatia is very thinly populated with about 1.15 people per square mile (3 per sq. km). On 1 January 2000 some 1,050,900 people lived in the republic. In the last decade the population declined as a consequence of a higher mortality rate and a lower birth rate.

The ethnic composition of Buriatia is 70 percent Russian, 24 percent Buriat, .1 percent Evenk, and 5.9 percent others. Until 1923 only 6 percent of the population was urban. By 2000 approximately 60 percent was. There are six cities in Buriatia: Ulan-Ude, Gusinoozersk, Severobaikalsk, Zakamensk, Kiakhta, and Babushkin.

Economy. Buriatia's economy relies on both agriculture and industry. Animal husbandry accounts for 70 percent of Buriatia's agriculture. The most important animals are fine fleeced and semi-fine fleeced sheep, meat and dairy cattle, pigs, and fowl. Spring wheat is the most important grain crop. Oats, barley, potatoes, feed crops, and other vegetables are also important. Among industries, machine tools, metal working, wood processing, building materials, foods, textiles, and mining of coal, rare metals, and gold are all significant. Buriatia is rich in fur-bearing and hoofed game animals, allowing for the development of hunting and trapping as part of the economy.

The Eastern Siberian and the Baikal-Amur Mainline railroads play leading roles in transport in Buriatia. Within the republic, which has over 3,720 miles (6,000 km) of roads, auto transport is important. Air transport connects Buriatia with various regions of Russia and neighboring countries and also with the northern regions of the republic. Boats ply Lake Baikal and the Selenga River. The Vitim River is navigable in high-water seasons from Romanovka to Ust-Muia.

Education. When the Buriat-Mongol ASSR was founded in 1923, a People's Commissariat of Education was established. In the 1923-1924 academic year 485 primary and twelve secondary schools were in operation. The introduction of universal primary education brought 94.2 percent of all children ages eight to eleven into schools by the end of the first Five Year Plan in 1932. At that time schools were separated into elementary, seven-year, and high schools. In the 1970s universal high-school education began. In 2004 Buriatia has a network of more than 1,000 general education institutions, including 618 schools attended by approximately 200,000 children, 112 institutions of post-primary study, and others. In accordance with existing laws they provide a cost-free education for all students. There are more than twenty higher-level institutions, such as lycées, gymnasiums, and colleges, and more than 100 educational institutions of innovative types, including schools organized on non-denominational, ethnic lines for Buriat, Russian, Evenk, and trans-Baikal Cossack students.

The republic maintains a system of vocational and professional educational institutions. Buriatia's first vocational schools were opened in the 1920s and 1930s. All professional-vocational schools were made eight-year schools in 1957-1958. In 1963 separate urban and rural professional-vocational schools were established. In 2004 forty-three vocational and professional institutions function in Buriatia, including twelve professional lycées, twenty-four schools, one special school, and six schools of the Ministry of Internal Affairs. Approximately 20,000 students attend these schools, working under 495 teachers and 700 industrial training specialists to prepare themselves for careers in eighty-three professions.

In the 1930s and 1940s a number of mid-level special educational institutions were established to prepare qualified workers for heavy industry and agriculture. During the transition of the economy to a market economy in the 1990s this system of mid-level professional education was reformed. In the early 2000s eighteen mid-level special educational institutions, eight of which have the status of colleges, are active in the republic, preparing workers in sixty-nine specializations.

Higher education is carried out in four state institutions of higher learning: Buriat State University, Eastern Siberian State Technological University, Buriat State Agricultural University, and Eastern Siberian State Academy of Culture and Arts. To date they have graduated more than 80,000 students. More than 12,500 students currently attend these institutions, and another 8,000 plus study by correspondence. The annual entry of students for the first year of study exceeds 2,300. The staff numbers more than 1,900 professors and teachers. The preparation of specialists in institutions of higher education takes place in 6 broad fields and 106 specializations. Institutions of higher education of Buriatia have opened branches in Mongolia, the Republic of Sakha (Yakutia), Tuva, and the Irkutsk and Chita regions.

Post-graduate degrees are available in seventy-five scholarly and pedagogical specialties. Three dissertation councils for doctorates and twelve councils for the defense of candidate degrees are in operation.

Public Health. The Peoples Commissariat of Public Health was established in 1923. It oversaw the operation of sanitary-hygiene centers, bacteriological laboratories, and rabies and malaria stations. These were transformed later into sanitary-epidemiological stations. Doctors carried out extensive campaigns against infectious diseases and their underlying causes, including an effort to educate the population about sanitation and hygiene. The commissariat paid special attention to maternal and pediatric care and to the development of a network of pharmacies. The Ulan-Ude Medical Technicum was opened in 1930.

In 2004 150 hospitals with almost 12,000 beds, 235 outpatient clinics and polyclinics, 350 medical-assistants and midwives centers, and eleven dispensaries operate under the Ministry of Public Health and other ministries. For each 10,000 people there are approximately 40 doctors, 103 medical specialists, and 112 hospital beds. About eighty physicians with doctoral and candidate degrees in medical, biological, and pharmaceutical sciences work in the public health system. Medical students are trained by the medical faculty of Buriat State University.

In recent years new wings have been added to Buriatia's veterans' hospital, children's hospital, perinatal center, and to the central national hospital. New technology and techniques have been introduced, including organ transplants, electrocardio stimulation, angiocardiograms, endovascular and endoscopic surgery, ultrasound diagnostics, and hemodialysis. Efforts are being made to combine the achievements of modern medical science with the rational experience of Tibetan medicine. The Center for Eastern Medicine, the only such inter-regional center in Siberia, has worked since 1989 to provide mobile medical and therapeutic services.

Science and Scholarship. The foundation for science and scholarship in Buriatia was laid three centuries ago by pioneers, travelers, scholar-explorers, and members of the Russian Academy of Sciences who began the study of the nature and history of the trans-Baikal region. Buddhist monasteries, where Eastern medicine, astrology, philosophy, and other sciences were studied, served as breeding grounds of scientific activity. The contemporary structure of science in the republic took form in the Soviet period, beginning with the establishment of the Buriat Scientific Committee, and has grown into a wide network of scientific institutions, the most important of which now is the Buriat Scientific Center of the Siberian Branch of the Russian Academy of Sciences. The Buriat Scientific Center unites the republic's scientific-research institutes such as the Institute of Mongolian, Buddhist, and Tibetan Studies, the Institute of General and Experimental Biology, the Baikal Joint Institute for the Exploitation of Nature, the Geological Institute, and the Department of Physics. Education in scientific fields is provided by the scientific-research departments of the republic's four institutions of higher learning. Republican branches of Russian organizations are active in Buriatia. They include the Eastern Siberian Scientific-Research and Planning and Design Institute of the Fishing Industry of the Ministry of Fishing Industry of the Russian Federation, the Barguzin Sanctuary of the Main Administration of Hunting, the Trans-Baikal Scientific-Research Laboratory of Forensic Expertise within the Ministry of Justice, the Buriat Institute for Improvement of Preparation of Educators, the Buriat Scientific-Research Institute of Agriculture, and other institutes. The Buriat Center of Geological Work, the Trans-Baikal Territorial Administration for Hydrology and Meteorology, the Buriat Experimental Land Reclamation Station, the Buriat Center for Standardization, Metrology, and Certification, and the Center for Hydrology, Meteorology and Environmental Monitoring provide various scientific services. The academic and branch institutes, laboratories and centers of the Buriat Republic carry out scientific research in all basic areas of modern science.

Bibliography: Cathryn Brennan, *Cultural Upheaval in Revolutionary Russia. The Buriats and the Far Eastern Republic, 1920-1922* (Richmond, 2002); James Forsyth, *A History of the Peoples of Siberia. Russia's North Asian Colony, 1581-1990* (Cambridge, 1992); Natal'ia L. Zhukovskaia, *Istoriko-kul'turnyi atlas Buriatii* (M., 2001); *Atlas Baikala* (M., 1993); M.L. Alekseev, *Kapital'noe stroitel'stvo Buriatskoi ASSR* (Ulan-Ude, 1981); B.V. Bazarov, *Obshchestvenno-politicheskaia zhizn' 1920-1950-kh gg. i razvitie literatury i iskusstva Buriatii* (Ulan-Ude, 1995); M.N. Baldano, *Industrial'noe razvitie Buriatii, 1923-1991 gg. Dostizheniia, izderzhki, uroki* (Ulan-Ude, 2001); A.A.

Bartanova, *Obrazovanie Buriat-Mongol'skoi ASSR* (Ulan-Ude, 1964); *Istoriia, kul'tura, ekonomika Buriatii. Iubileinyi statisticheskii sbornik* (Ulan-Ude, 1995); D.D. Mangataeva, *Naselenie Buriatii. Formirovanie i razvitie* (Ulan-Ude, 1995); K.B. Mitupov, *Stanovlenie sotsialisticheskoi sotsial'noi struktury Buriatii, 1938-1960 gg.* (Novosibirsk, 1986); *Rastitel'nost' Sibiri. Predbaikal'e i Zabaikal'e* (Novosibirsk, 1985); *Respublika Buriatiia. Kratkii entsiklopedicheskii spravochnik* (Ulan-Ude, 1998); *Respublika Buriatiia v tsifrakh. Statisticheskii sbornik* (Ulan-Ude, 1997); *Sotsial'noe razvitie Buriatskoi ASSR* (Ulan-Ude, 1989).

Konstantin B. Mitupov

BURIATIA IN THE RUSSIAN EMPIRE (c. 1680-1917). Russian troops reached Lake Baikal early in the seventeenth century and fought to conquer lands that were reputed to be rich in silver and fur and whose native population could be made to supply significant tribute payments. As they progressed to the east, Cossack units constructed forts (ostrogi) which became starting points for the further penetration of tsarist troops into the trans-Baikal region. Some Buriat tribes and clans resisted Russian troops with arms, others submitted to the Russians under armed pressure and agreed to pay tribute in furs (yasak). Most of western Buriatia was absorbed into the Russian state by the end of the seventeenth century.

The conquest of Buriatia opened the way to China. By the late 1680s Russian troops reached the uncertain borders with China. After long negotiations among representatives of the two governments, on 25 August 1689 Russia and China signed the Treaty of Nerchinsk, which determined Russia's eastern boundary with China. Although the question of the region's southern border remained open until 1727, the treaty strengthened Russia's hold on the trans-Baikal region. The Bura Treaty, which set the southern boundary with China, was completed on 20 August 1727. The two nations signed the Kiakhta Treaty on international trade in 1728. These agreements officially completed the establishment of Russia's boundaries with China, part of which were at the same time the southern and eastern borders of Buriatia, and Buriatia became part of the Russian state.

Russian Administration of Buriatia. Buriat society was governed by patriarchal and feudal relationships in the seventeenth century. Territorially and administratively Buriats were organized into clans. Traditional law, marriage, family relationships, and land use were governed within clans, which sometimes extended mutual help to one another. In some instances the Russians extended and strengthened existing institutions of Buriat local self-administration. Beginning in the 1740s steppe bureaus (kontory) were established in Buriat departments (vedomstsva), consisting of the chief (shulenga or taisha) and six deputies. Official congresses (suglan) were organized within the bureaus for apportioning various taxes and assessments and for deciding other important matters. Taishas, their deputies, and clan leaders (zaisany, shulengi, zasuly, all plural) participated in the suglan. So-called peace huts existed in clan gatherings. Taishas, zaisans, and shulengas were chosen from the wealthiest families, those who owned the largest herds. They comprised a steppe aristocracy (saity).

After the conclusion of the Bura Treaty in 1727 the Russian government made efforts to secure the border with China and Mongolia. They recruited Buriats, among others, and sent units of Russian soldiers, Cossacks, and Buriat and Evenk retinues (druzhiny) to guard the borders. Wherever the Russians built forts, towns, and villages, they also built chapels and prayer houses, and later, stone churches. By the end of the nineteenth century there were 278 Orthodox churches, four monasteries, and 302 chapels in the trans-Baikal region. The tsarist autocracy and the Orthodox Church attempted to russify and to christianize the native peoples of the region. In the first half of the seventeenth century Orthodox priests conducted forceful baptisms of Buriat and Evenk prisoners of war.

The Baikal and trans-Baikal regions were made part of Irkutsk province. In 1803 the Siberian governor generalship was established with its capital in Irkutsk. The Russian population was administered through territorial units called districts (uezdy). The Buriat population was further divided into departments (vedomstva), which were assigned to four districts: Irkutsk, Nizhneudinsk, Verkhneudinsk, and Nerchinsk. In the first half of the nineteenth century the Buriat departments west of Lake Baikal were Alar, Balagansk, Ida, Kuda, Verkholensk, Olkhon, and Tunka. In the trans-Baikal region they included Barguzin, Kudara, Khorinsk, Selenga, and Zakamensk. The reform of Siberian governance introduced by Governor General M.M. Speransky in 1822 included a Charter on the Administration of Non-Russians and new Institutions for the Administration of the Siberian Provinces. The charter established new offices of ethnic self-government called steppe councils (dumy), which possessed considerable rights and powers in their departments. The Alar, Balagansk, Ida-Kuda, Verkholensk, Olkhon, and Tunka councils were established in the Irkutsk region. Among the trans-Baikal Buriats the Kudara, Barguzin, Selenga, and Uda councils were created. Another significant administrative reform occurred between 1886 and 1890 when the Buriats' steppe councils of Irkutsk province were abolished and weaker boards (upravy) were established in their place.

Buddhism began to spread widely in Buriatia near the end of the sixteenth century. By the time that Russia's southern border with China was established, Buddhism was firmly rooted. In 1741 Empress Elizabeth decreed that 150 full (komplektnye) lamas were to staff the Buddhist monasteries (datsans). They were sworn to loyalty to Russia, freed from the fur tribute and other taxes, and received permission to proselytize among the nomads. By order of the tsarist government the monasteries of the trans-Baikal region were joined into a unified system, and the church organization of Buriat lamaism was formed. The tsarist government recognized lamaism as a state religion.

In the trans-Baikal region the tsarist government made repeated efforts to strengthen its domination of the Buriats. During the nineteenth century it abolished the steppe councils and non-Russian boards along with the positions of taishas and zaisans and in their place established rural districts (volosty) and district administrations (upravleniia). Fifteen districts were established in the territory of the trans-Baikal Buriats. Local authority in Buriat settlements (ulusy) was transferred to leaders appointed from among Russian peasants. District administrations were introduced among the Buriats of Irkutsk province in 1912 when the non-Russian boards were abolished there also.

Settlement and Economic Assimilation of Buriatia. The settlement and economic assimilation of Buriatia began almost simultaneously with its conquest and annexation. Cossacks, musketeers, and other servicemen first constructed a network of winter quarters and forts. Non-military settlers then built homes around the forts, which became economic centers for the surrounding regions. Russian migrants settled in the areas most favorable for agriculture, primarily in the valleys of the major rivers. The area west of Lake Baikal was settled more quickly than the trans-Baikal region. The Buriat population also grew in the seventeenth century. Buriats who had migrated into Mongolia returned. The establishment and defense of Russia's borders reduced raids by Mongolian, Manchurian, and Oirat bandits, providing a relatively peaceful and secure life for the Buriats. In the middle of the eighteenth century Old Believers from Poland and the western provinces of Russia, who were accused of being schismatics, were resettled beyond Lake Baikal. A large group of Jewish colonists, who also played a part in the economic assimilation of the area, were settled in Barguzin region. Buriatia was also a region of exile and of punishment at hard labor (katorga). Decembrists, participants in peasant uprisings and the workers' movement, Polish rebels, revolutionary democrats, populists, and social democrats were sent to Buriatia.

Toward the end of the eighteenth century a number of positive changes occurred in the Buriat economy. An increasing number of Buriats settled out of the nomadic way of life and took up agriculture and haying along with cattle breeding. Connections to the Russian market grew stronger, especially as Buriats adopted some of the economic skills of Russian peasants and craftsmen. They also began to use firearms for hunting. In the nineteenth century, especially after 1850, the Russian and Buriat peasant economies grew even more rapidly. Cattle breeding remained the most important part of the rural economy of the Buriats, Russian peasants, and the trans-Baikal Evenks. Late in the nineteenth century the herders of the trans-Baikal region had more cattle and horses, their most important animals, per capita than did residents of any other province and region of Asian Russia. In number of sheep and goats they occupied seventh place. Measured by the total number of horses and cattle the Buriats of the trans-Baikal region stood in first place in Russia, by the number of sheep, fourth place.

As a money economy and capitalistic relations grew in Buriatia so too did social differentiation among the Buriats and Russians. Yet traditional relations were dominant in Russian villages and Buriat ulus for a long time. Despite the penetration of capitalistic relations, feudal-patriarchal relations remained primary. There were no serf estates in the region, although the Russian state and the tsarist family were landowners, and Buriats and other native people continued to pay fur tribute. The abolition of serfdom in 1861 along with later reforms and the continuing development of a money economy created more favorable conditions for the development of the Siberian economy.

Before the Russian conquest of Buriatia there was no industry to mention. Although the Buriats conducted some iron, salt, and silver mining and Buriat smiths had domestic foundries, the annexation of Buriatia opened the way for further development. Silver, copper, and iron smelting works, silver, gold and copper mines, saltworks, soapworks, distilleries, and textile and leather manufactories were soon active. Most enterprises were privately owned and employed hired labor, and many relied on primitive technology and were little more than crafts shops. After Buriatia was annexed to Russia, it became increasingly integrated with the wider Russian market.

In the early period barter trade dominated, but monetary exchanges grew over time. Russian trade with China through Kiakhta increased after 1727. The Kiakhta trade spurred the growth of several Baikal area industries, in particular leather production, which helped the Buriats' rural economy. Selenginsk and Nerchinsk were important centers for trade with Mongolia and China. Markets in the towns and districts of the region increased in size and importance. Along with trade and markets came an increase of urban population, which grew more than 250 percent from 1863 to 1897 in the trans-Baikal region.

After the union of Buriatia with Russia, through christianization and russification campaigns, the tsarist government attempted with some success to transplant its political culture to the Buriats and Evenks. They established schools in the towns and forts. Russian culture, literature, and art took root in villages with Russian population. As Buddhism spread through the trans-Baikal region, religious schools opened in monasteries. Printers and publishers set up shop in the region. It was then that Russian literacy penetrated to the Buriats, where the cultures of East and West met and interacted. The authorities established three types of schools: gymnasiums, district, and parish schools. Agvan Dorzhiev, a prominent Buriat Buddhist activist and diplomat who worked in St. Petersburg, reformed written Mongolian and published the classics of Mongolian literature at the beginning of the twentieth century.

The Moscow trace was cleared at the end of the eighteenth century. For a long while it provided the only access to Siberia and Buriatia from European Russia. The Trans-Siberian Railroad, built in the first years of the twentieth century, played a huge role in the social, economic, and cultural development of the region. It immediately spurred the growth of the coal industry and encouraged the growth of trade.

With growth of industry came intensification of working class movement. Workers' groups grew increasingly well organized and began to make economic and political demands. At the same time the introduction of district (volost) institutions and the transfer of local authority into the hands of Russian peasant leaders sharply increased colonial subjugation of the Buriat population. Peasant and Buriat national movements began to stir. The Russo-Japanese War hastened the growth of social and political movements, and they exploded during the revolution of 1905-1907. At the beginning of 1906 revolutionary unrest in the trans-Baikal region was put down by punitive expeditions led by generals Rennenkampf and Meller-Zakomelsky. Leaders of the Verkhneudinsk Social Democrats and strike committee, A.A. Goldsobel, I.G. Shults, M.D. Medvednikov, A.A. Gordeev, and N.A. Miliutinsky, were hanged. After the revolution was crushed, the tsarist administration strengthened police oversight in Buriatia's factories and transport and in Buriat uluses. Land surveying was conducted throughout Buriatia in the following years for Moscow's peasant resettlement policy, part of the Stolypin land reforms.

Strikes, agrarian disturbances, and the Buriat national movement resumed in 1912-1913. In the spring of 1914 a number of armed demonstrations by Buriats took place. Despite such turbulence the economic growth of the region continued, reaching record highs in 1913 and continuing well into the period of the First World War. The conditions of wartime had an effect on the population nonetheless. Dissatisfaction with the war and with the tsarist government as a whole grew. Democratic, agrarian, workers', and national movements all increased in strength during the World War. Political exiles such as M.V. Frunze, V.M. Serov, N.C. Kabashev, E.A. Petrov, V.A. Chashchin, and A.M. Buiko, played important roles in the growth of revolutionary thought and organization. The directive of 1916 to draft non-Russians, which began the call-up of Buriats for labor in areas behind the war's front lines, played a large role in the growth of the national movement. Approximately 20,000 Buriats were mobilized for labor near the front, particularly in Belorussia and Arkhangelsk provinces, and in enterprises in Eastern Siberia.

The victory of the February Revolution, which toppled the tsarist autocracy, encouraged many movements to action in Buriatia. Illegal political party organizations began to emerge from underground. New Socialist Revolutionary (SR), Populist-Socialist, Laborite (Trudovik), and Kadet party organizations were established as was an Executive Committee of Social Organizations in Verkhneudinsk. E.A. Petrov, a former Bolshevik delegate to the Second State Duma, was elected its chairman. At the same time the Verkhneudinsk Council (Soviet) of Workers' and Soldiers' Deputies was formed by representatives of the democratic and SR organizations. V.M. Serov, another former Bolshevik delegate to the Second State Duma, was elected its chairman. Chita's mayor, N.N. Savich, represented the executive authority of the Provisional Government in the trans-Baikal region. The mayors of Verkhneudinsk and Troitskosavsk fulfilled the same function in their districts. In Selenga and Barguzin districts city elders took that responsibility. The dual power that held sway across the country as a whole took shape in Buriatia as well. The Verkhneudinsk Executive Committee of Social Organizations and the Council of Workers' and Soldiers' Deputies worked in close harmony at first to support the policies of the Provisional Government, but they had little power outside the Russian population of the western trans-Baikal region.

The democratic transformations begun in Buriatia gave new strength to the national liberation movement. Buriatia's workers supported the revolution, spoke out for the establishment of autonomous and democratic institution of self-government, for the abolition of old district institutions, and for creation of new, provisional administrative offices. The first congress to represent Buriats of both the trans-Baikal region and of Irkutsk province took place in Chita on 23-25 April 1917. It declared itself to be the supreme governing body for the Buriat population and established the Central Buriat National Committee (Burnatskom) to function between its congresses. Prominent Buriat social activists such as B. Baradin, N. Bogdanov, Ts. Zhamtsarano, and E.-D. Rinchino became leaders of Burnatskom. Buriat peasant demonstrations also increased. A congress of eleven clans of the Khori Buriats, representing a significant part of the trans-Baikal Buriats, took place in March 1917. It condemned the agrarian policies of tsarism and called for a thorough restudy of the land question and for the abolition of the institutions of land captains. The peasant movement was closely tied to the Buriat national movement. During the summer of 1917 popular dissatisfaction with the policies of the Provisional Government intensified.

Bibliography: James Forsyth, A History of the Peoples of Siberia. Russia's North Asian Colony, 1581-1990 (Cambridge, 1992); Natal'ia L. Zhukovskaia, *Istoriko-kul'turnyi atlas Buriatii* (M., 2001); T. Mikhailov, K. Kim, and G. Sanzhiev, eds., *Aktualnye problemy istorii Buriatii* (Ulan-Ude, 1987), *Aktualnye problemy istorii intelligentsii Buriatii* (Ulan-Ude, 1999); I.A. Asalkhanov, *Sotsial'no-ekonomicheskoe razvitie Iugo-Vostochnoi Sibiri vo II polovine XIX v.* (Ulan-Ude, 1963); I.B. Batueva, *Buriaty na rubezhe XIX-XX vv.* (Ulan-Ude, 1992), *Istoriia razvitiia khoziaistva zabaikal'skikh buriat v XIX v.* (Ulan-Ude, 1999); F.F. Bolonev, *Staroobriadtsy Zabaikal'ia v XVIII-XIX vv.* (Novovsibirsk, 1994); *Buriatiia XVII-nach. XX v. Ekonomika i sotial'no-kul'turnye protsessy* (Novovsibirsk, 1989); *Voprosy istoriografii istorii Buriatii XIX-nachala XX v.* (Ulan-Ude, 1994); G.P. Galdanova, *Zakamenskie buriaty. Istoriko-etnograficheskie ocherki II pol. XIX - I pol. XX v.* (Novosibirsk, 1992); D.Sh. Gomboev, *Zemel'nye otnosheniia v Buriatii* (Ulan-Ude, 1988); T.V. Polikova, *Kul'tura gorodov Pribaikal'ia II pol. XIX v - 1917 g.* (Ulan-Ude, 1999); G.L Sanzhiev and E.G. Sanzhiev, *Buriatiia. Istoriia, 17-19 vv.* (Ulan-Ude, 1999); V.S. Khankharaev, *Buriaty v 17-18 vv. Demograficheskaia istoriia i etnicheskie protsessy* (Ulan Ude, 2000).

Marina N. Baldano

BURIATIA, PRE-RUSSIAN. The earliest archaeological evidence for the appearance of humans on the territory of Buriatia dates to the Upper Paleolithic Age between 25,000 and 40,000 years ago. Archaeological finds at Varvarina Mountain and Kamenka in Zaigraevsky, Malyi Kunalei in Bichursky, Podzvonkaia in Kiakhta, and Sanny Cape in Khorinski region date from that time. The Paleolithic population lived by hunting and gathering as did their descendants well into the Neolithic Age. Five to six thousand years ago people still lived primarily by hunting, gathering, and fishing. Evidence for the first attempts to cultivate grains appears late in the Neolithic period. It was then also that people were buried for the first time with possessions, apparently signifying appearance of the concept of life after death.

The ancient population of the Baikal area first became acquainted with metal working near the beginning of the second millennium B.C. Articles made of pure copper were found at camps and settlements from that era. Herding economies began to develop in the Bronze Age. The distinctive archaeological culture that took shape in the Central Asian steppe at that time is usually called the Karasuk historical-cultural community. It extended over a vast territory in southern Siberia, Saiano-Altai, Mongolia, and the trans-Baikal region. A new type of archaeological monument also appeared in the steppe and forest-steppe zones east of Lake Baikal in the late Bronze Age and the Early Iron Age, graves marked by stones. The varying dimensions of the graves testify to the beginning of social and economic differentiation in society. The population was organized by clans and tribes. Tribal alliances were sometimes formed for the purpose of making war.

In the last third of the first millennium B.C. alliances of nomadic tribes, known to history as the Huns or the Siuns, appeared in Central Asia. Archaeological remains of their society are found in the southern area of contemporary Buriatia in the river valleys of the Selenga and its tributaries, the Dzhida, Chikoi, Khilok, and the Temnik. Chinese historiography links the rise of the Huns with the names shaniui Touman and, especially, his son Mode.

To administer their lands the Huns divided the state into separate regions and territories and developed a group of servitors to carry out government functions. Their powerful military organization allowed the Huns to alter their economy significantly by adding the flow of goods from outside to already existing internal practices. The primary sources of additional material resources were tribute collected from conquered peoples and war booty taken in raids and invasions. The Huns acquired the greater part of their booty on raids into the Han Chinese empire. The Huns also created settlements to supply the population with a variety of products. Scholars note that Hun society was highly organized in comparison with other nomadic societies.

The Northern Hun confederation was broken up by Han troops in A.D. 93. After the fall of the Huns the nomadic tribes of the trans-Baikal region battled for control of the steppe. Power soon passed to the Sianbi. The Sianbi descended from the Dunkhus, who were at one time defeated by shaniui Mode. Their rise to power is associated with Tianshikhuai, who established a large, powerful army and carried out a series of reforms. In a series of military campaigns he defeated the Dinlins and Usuns and gradually came to rule all the former lands of the Huns. For administrative purposes he divided his lands into right, center, and left wings, establishing a relatively streamlined system. After the death of Tianshikhuai the Sianbi state broke into several parts which were controlled by the stronger of the remaining nomadic alliances.

The next powerful nomadic alliance to control this region was the Zhuzhan khanate which lasted from 402 until 555. Its founder, Shelun, carried out a series of successful campaigns and gathered a territory that was enormous for that time. The Zhuzhans were typical nomads. They practiced herding, lived in felt tents, and were constantly on the move yet possessed fortified towns. Some Zhuzhans were literate, and they were acquainted with Buddhism. After more than 150 years uprisings of the Turks who lived in the Altai region as slaves of the Zhuzhans destroyed the Zhuzhan empire. During the time between the rise of the Turks and the beginning of the seventeenth century the Baikal region became an inseparable part of the Mongolian ethnic world. All preconditions for the development of the Buriat people were in place.

After the collapse of the Zhuzhan khanate and the rise of the Turks-tiukiu in Central Asia, a Mongolian tribe called the Chino occupied the territory immediately east of Lake Baikal. Toward the middle of the ninth century the Chino, who reverenced the wolf as a totem, settled in the so-called Three Rivers area of the Onon, Kerulen, and Tola rivers, and there the Mongolian nationality began to coalesce. Mongolian-speaking people settled throughout the region to the east of Lake Baikal in this era.

Large confederations of Turkic tribes dominated the steppe from the sixth to the tenth century. Their influence spread across an enormous area from western China to the Volga. In 604 as a result of civil strife a larger state broke up into eastern and western khanates. During the next several centuries Turkic tribes came into closer contact with non-Turkic residents of the region, both nomadic and settled, and began to coalesce into the nationalities and the Turkic ethnos that familiar today throughout Central Asia and neighboring parts of southern Siberia.

At the end of the twelfth and early thirteenth centuries Mongol tribes were consolidated into a powerful state in the trans-Baikal region, led by Temudzhin, later given the title Chingis (Genghis) Khan. The period of the great empire established by Chingis (Genghis) Khan brought the Baikal region into even closer contact with Mongolia. The Bargudzhin-Tokum tribes joined the increasingly centralizing Mongol realm voluntarily in 1201. Because of their close partnership newcomers from the Bargudzhin-Tokum tribes actively participated in the military and political life of the Mongol state and made significant contributions to its establishment and growth. The Mongols conquered the Saiano-Altai tribes in 1207.

When the Great Empire collapsed in the fourteenth century, the country disintegrated into many smaller parts, and ties between the Baikal region and Mongolia proper weakened. Later in the fourteenth century the Mongols seized the northern part of the trans-Baikal region again. This consolidation process led to an alliance of tribes, such as often precedes the formation of a nationality. Considerations of defense and the raids of the Kyshtyms dictated the need for alliance. The tribal alliance of the lands near Lake Baikal, which came to be called Buriat, dates to the sixteenth century. Until the arrival of the Russians this tribal alliance was a significant force in southern Siberia. The Baikal tribes took tribute from their closest neighbors, the Kyshtyms, who lived at Biriusa, Uda, Chuna, Vikhorevaia, and elsewhere, and from more distant tribes. The Russian conquest of the Baikal region began in the 1630s.

Bibliography: James Forsyth, *A History of the Peoples of Siberia. Russia's North Asian Colony, 1581-1990* (Cambridge, 1992); Natal'ia L. Zhukovskaia, *Istoriko-kul'turnyi atlas Buriatii* (M., 2001); I.B. Batueva, *Ocherki istorii selenginskikh buriat* (Ulan-Ude, 1993); *Buriatskie letopisi* (Ulan-Ude, 1995); B.B. Dashibalov, *Baikal'skaia Sibir' v srednie veka* (Ulan-Ude, 1997); B.Sh. Dorzhiev, *Buriatiia v srednevekovuiu epokhu* (Ulan-Ude, 1998); N.P. Egunov, *Buriatiia do prisoedineniia k Rossii. Ocherk o sotial'no-ekonomicheskom i politicheskom razvitii buriatskikh plemen v XIII-XVII vv.* (Ulan-Ude, 1984); Ts.A. Zhimbiev, *Rodoslovnaia khorinskikh buriat* (Ulan-Ude, 2001); B.P. Zoriktuev, *Pribaikal'e v seredine VI-nachale XVII vv.* (Ulan-Ude, 1997); P.B. Konovalov, *Khunnu v Zabaikal'e* (Ulan-Ude, 1976); *Kul'tura i pamiatniki bronzovogo i rannego zheleznogo vekov Zabaikal'ia i Mongolii* (Ulan-Ude, 1995); A.D. Tsybiktarov, *Buriatiia v drevnosti* (Ulan-Ude, 1999).

Marina N. Baldano

BURIATS. Also spelled Buryats. Self-appellation Buriaad. Indigenous people of Siberia.

The Buriats are an Asiatic nationality inhabiting the area surrounding the southern half of Lake Baikal in southeast Siberia. According to the 1989 census the Buriats numbered 421,380 people. Approximately 249,500 of them inhabited the Russian Federation's Buriat Republic, comprising only about 25 percent of the population. An additional 66,600 Buriats lived in Chita region, including 42,400 in the Aga Buriat National Territory, and 81,000 in Irkutsk region, including 49,300 in the Ust-Orda Buriat National Territory. Outside Russia there are 35,600 Buriats in Mongolia and between 6,000 and 7,000 in China. Traditionally a rural people, the Buriats grew progressively urbanized. The proportion of city- and town-dwelling Buriats is about equal that found residing in the countryside of their titular republic. The Buriat language belongs to the Mongolian branch of the Altaic family and is composed of numerous dialects of varying mutual intelligibility. The modern Buriat literary language is based on the Khori dialect and is written in a modified Cyrillic alphabet. According to the 1989 census 86 percent of Buriats spoke their mother tongue, although the real percentage was probably closer to 70 percent.

At the time of their initial contact with Russian adventurers and Cossacks in the early seventeenth century the Buriats numbered around 30,000 and their primary economic activity was animal husbandry. Buriats east of Baikal lived as nomads in felt yurts and herded cattle, horses, sheep, and goats over the steppes. Buriats south and southwest of Lake Baikal also raised yaks and camels. Most of the Buriat lands west of Lake Baikal are mountainous and heavily forested, so animal husbandry there was usually more sedentary and the Buriats as a rule dwelled in four- to eight-sided wooden cabins. Some western Buriats also raised hay for their livestock and millet, barley, buckwheat, and oats for their own use. Pre-conquest Buriats also fished, by netting, hooking, and trapping, and hunted bear, fox, lynx, wolverine, deer, geese, ducks, beaver, squirrels, wolves, and wild goats as some of their main prey. Besides the primary hunting implement, the bow and arrow, Buriats used edged weapons. Buriat blacksmiths shaped iron ore into weapons for hunting and war and fashioned plow tips, horseshoes, and various household items. Jewelry and ornaments were made from gold and more commonly from silver purchased from Chinese traders. Buriat silversmiths are still celebrated for the delicacy and intricate detail of their creations.

Traditional Buriat society rested on a complex system of clan and tribal divisions. Tribal and clan loyalties still exert a strong, though often clandestine, influence on everyday life. The Buriat tribes, of which the largest are the Khori, Bulagat, Ekhirit, and Khongodor, are subdivided into dozens of smaller clans. The tribal and clan nobility (noyon) gained their wealth from ownership of large herds, collection of tribute from non-Buriat neighboring peoples and lesser Buriats, and trade with China and Mongolia. Commoners (ulad zon), who maintained smaller herds, made up the majority of Buriats. Slaves (barlag) were usually non-Buriat prisoners of war. Destitute Buriats sometimes indentured themselves to their noble creditors although, unlike slaves, they could not be sold. Common ownership of clan grazing lands, as well as an ethic of noblesse oblige among wealthy Buriats, most likely ameliorated the negative effects of Buriat social differences.

The Buriat nobles served as vassals of the Oirat and Khalkha Mongol khans and delivered yearly shipments of furs to them, but these Mongol rulers exercised no control over Buriat territory. The Buriats and their Mongol overlords frequently engaged in battles as a result of the former's refusal to deliver tribute and the latter's plundering of Buriat settlements. The Russian conquest exacerbated these conflicts by introducing Russian-Mongolian competition for Buriat tribute. The Buriats also traded with the Mongols, exchanging furs for silver, cloth, various Chinese manufactured goods, mirrors, and most likely tea and tobacco.

All pre-conquest Buriats were shamanists, and many Buriats, especially west of Baikal, still practice shamanism. The shaman (böö), whose profession usually was inherited, led religious ceremonies, including the ritual sacrifice of horses to the sky god Tengri and rites of birth, healing, marriage, and burial. Buriat shamanists use representations of shamanist deities (ongons) to ward off ill fortune and raise stone cairns (oböös) to mark sacred places. Buriat shamanism contains some elements of fire worship, for example, offerings of meat, milk, fat, liquor, and butter.

The Buriats initially attracted the notice of the Russians in late 1608, when Russian military servitors (sluzhilye liudi) first obtained reports from native hunters in the Kan and Kazir river valleys of a wealthy and prolific Bratsky people far to the east. The first contact between Russians and Buriats occurred in 1628 near the confluence of the Oka and Angara rivers, where Russian troops led by Yakov Khripunov attacked and defeated a small group of Buriats, taking several hostages and a few furs. The Russian conquest of Buriatia continued over the course of the seventeenth century. Some Buriats launched massive uprisings in an attempt to cast off the Muscovite yoke, others fled south to Mongolia proper. Two treaties with the Qing Empire, the Treaty of Nerchinsk (1689) and the Treaty of Kiakhta (1727), affirmed Russia's hold over Buriat lands and brought under tsarist control all Buriats who had not fled south.

Even as Russia was consolidating its hold on the Buriats, the Tibetan variety of Mahayana Buddhism was penetrating Buriat lands. Lamaist Buddhism entered Buriatia via Mongolia by the second half of the seventeenth century and subsequently attracted adherents east of Baikal. Tolerance of the incorporation of many shamanist rituals and concepts aided Buddhism in its success. The Buriats' adoption of Buddhism was an event of more than merely religious significance. Many monasteries (datsans) operated schools that taught literacy in Tibetan and classical, or written, Mongolian, the literary language of Buddhist Buriats, and provided instruction in theology, philosophy, medicine, and other disciplines. In that way the datsans served important cultural and educational functions in addition to spiritual ones.

Empress Elizabeth Petrovna granted official recognition to Buriat Buddhism in 1741. She and her successors made only half-hearted attempts to limit the number of Buriat datsans and lamas (monks) because they viewed the independent Buriat Buddhist infrastructure as a means of preventing native believers from falling under Qing influence. Tibet and Mongolia, the other two centers of Lamaist Buddhism, were under Chinese rule. Orthodox missionaries' attempts to convert the Buriats during this period were infrequent and usually unsuccessful.

The tsarist administration's contacts with the Buriat population before the early nineteenth century were sporadic and ad hoc, being limited largely to the collection of the tribute in kind (yasak) and other obligations. At the same time, corruption and exploitation among Russian and clan and tribal officials were rampant. Governor General Mikhail Speransky's reform of the Siberian administrative system in 1822 created a system of native self-government based on traditional clan and tribal officials overseen by steppe councils (stepnye dumy) and clan directorates (rodovye upravlenia). Courts attached to these bodies held jurisdiction over most cases, other than those involving Russians or such serious crimes as murder, robbery, rape, and counterfeiting. The Speransky reforms did not eliminate venality or abuses of power, but they did provide the Buriats with an administrative structure that used traditional forms of authority and operated in the native tongue. Moreover, the need for literate Buriats to staff the native administrative offices provided impetus for development of a modest system of Russian education for Buriat youth.

Russification policies were extended to the Buriats along with the empire's other non-Russian peoples in the latter half of the nineteenth century. Buddhism and shamanism came under increasing official pressure from the mid-nineteenth century on. The number of Buriat lamas was arbitrarily limited to 285 in 1853 and the construction of new datsans was forbidden. Although these restrictions sometimes were evaded, they hampered the spread of Buddhism and classical Mongolian west of Baikal, where Buddhism thus far had made few inroads. The western Buriats were thereby deprived almost to a man of literacy in their people's written language. Compulsory conversion of Buriats was another means of russification. Between the 1860s and 1890s Orthodox missionaries forcibly baptized tens of thousands of Buriats and enrolled Buriat children in missionary-run boarding schools. When official restrictions on religion were relaxed after 1905, most converts renounced Orthodoxy. At the same time the regime strongly discouraged the use of Buriat and classical Mongolian in native schools. Moreover, the native administrative offices created by Speransky were abolished and replaced with Russian ones at the turn of the century. Simultaneously, native lands in excess of 43.5 acres (17.6 hectares, 15 desiatinas) were confiscated and given to Russian settlers. These moves resulted in fierce resistance and protests by the Buriats and played no small part in encouraging the development of Buriat nationalism.

Despite these attacks on Buriat cultural identity a small but vigorous Buriat intelligentsia developed over the course of the nineteenth and early twentieth centuries. Dorzhi Banzarov (1822-1855), a graduate of Kazan University, authored *The Black Faith, or Shamanism among the Mongols*, the first scholarly investigation of Buriat shamanism. Tsyben Zhamtsarano (1880-1938) collected and recorded Buriat and Mongol folklore and published research on Mongol historical chronicles. Matvei Khangalov (1858-1918) investigated the material culture, customary law, economic activities, and cultural traditions of his people. Gombozhab Tsybikov (1873-1930) authored important works on Tibetan ethnography and Mongolian philology. Bazar Baradin (1878-1937) taught Mongolian at St. Petersburg University and investigated Tibetan religious practices before 1917. During the 1920s he headed the Buriat Commissariat of Education and lobbied, ultimately successfully, for the adoption of the Latin alphabet by the Buriats. The Buddhist leader Agvan Dorzhiev (1853-1937) served as the tutor of the Thirteenth Dalai Lama, acted as a liaison between the Russian and Tibetan courts at the turn of the century, traveled widely throughout Europe and Asia, took part in developing a new Buriat writing system based on the vertical Mongolian script, and constructed a Buddhist temple in St. Petersburg between 1909 and 1915.

The fall of the autocracy in February 1917 unleashed a storm of Buriat political activity. Intellectuals created a Buriat National Committee, usually known by its Russian acronym Burnatskom, to coordinate nationalist activities and draft plans for political autonomy. Native teachers devised programs for native language education, and rural Buriats formed militias to combat land seizures by Russian settlers. Most Buriats supported the Socialist Revolutionaries, whose emphasis on rural needs and political decentralization was compatible with the Buriats' own desire for autonomy. Only a dozen or so Buriats joined the Bolsheviks before

October 1917. Bolshevik centralism and opposition to nationalist movements antagonized most Buriats.

The Buriat lands were an area of intense military activity during the Civil War. The depredations of White and Red troops, as well as Japanese interventionists, led to famine in the Selenga River Valley and several other hard-hit areas and forced thousands of Buriats to flee across the border to Mongolia. A handful of Buriats attempted in February 1919 to unite the Mongol peoples into a Greater Mongolian state sponsored by Japan to include Outer and Inner Mongolia and Buriatia, along with Tuva and at least part of Manchuria. The planned state never took shape, but the specter of Pan-Mongolism and Buriat-Japanese intrigue reemerged during the Great Purges, when thousands of Buriats were imprisoned and executed on precisely these charges.

The end of the Civil War brought a cultural renaissance to the Buriat lands. A Buriat-Mongolian ASSR encompassing almost all areas of Buriat settlement was created in 1923, giving the Buriats an officially recognized homeland for the first time. Significant gains were made in native-language literacy, education, and publishing. Bolshevik policies designed to gain non-Russian support encouraged the hiring and promotion of indigenous peoples and the use of local languages in governmental and economic institutions. By 1928 the Buriat-Mongolian ASSR's economic activity had returned to pre-World War I levels. The new regime's initially liberal approach to Buddhism led to an expansion of Buddhist institutions, even in the traditionally shamanist region west of Baikal. In some areas of Buriatia more Buriat children were enrolled in datsan schools than in secular ones. A Buddhist reform movement, led by Agvan Dorzhiev, reduced corruption and vice in the datsans and achieved a modus vivendi with the new regime's rulers by arguing the compatibility of Buddhism and communism.

The social, cultural, and economic policies of the Stalinist period nullified these advances. The Mongolian alphabet was abolished and replaced first by the Latin alphabet and then by Cyrillic. This effectively detached the Buriats from the centuries-old Mongolian literary tradition. At the same time the official preference for Russian loan words led to marked russification of the Buriat written language's vocabulary. Datsans were shut down and destroyed, and lamas and shamans arrested and executed. The collectivization of animal husbandry and agriculture and the forcible settling of nomads in state farms resulted in the mass slaughter of livestock and a series of rural uprisings in southern and western Buriatia, all of which were violently suppressed.

The drive for rapid industrialization led to the influx of thousands of non-natives into Buriatia, which limited the use of the Buriat language in public life. Attempts to maintain the Buriat language in the workplace were abandoned by the mid-1930s. Transfers of Buriat lands to Irkutsk and Chita regions in 1937 significantly reduced the territory of the Buriat-Mongolian ASSR. The Great Purges destroyed many of the Buriat intelligentsia, who were arrested and executed on charges of Pan-Mongolism, Buriat nationalism, and espionage in the service of Japan. The small number of educated Buriats exacerbated the cultural effects of these losses. Non-Buriat, primarily Russian, immigration increased because of the eastward evacuation of industry during World War II. Although Stalin's wartime liberalization of religious policy resulted in minor concessions to the Buriats—two datsans were reopened at Aga and Ivolga—the onslaught on Buriat cultural identity in general resumed in 1948. In that year Communist Party officials denounced the Buriat national epic *Geser* as feudalistic and nationalistic, and its study and publication were forbidden until 1953.

The thaw during the Khrushchev era saw relaxation of the most violent attacks on Buriat culture. Several purged intellectuals, for example, the communist leader Mikhei Erbanov and the poet Solbone Tuiaa, were rehabilitated, and expression of interest and cautious pride in native culture no longer ensured persecution. Moreover, a general rise in Soviet living standards in the post-Stalin period permitted a notable increase in the Buriat population, which grew by 67 percent between 1959 and 1989 alone. Rising educational levels brought an increase in the number of Buriats employed in executive positions, particularly in government and scientific life.

Nevertheless the basic contours of official policy toward the Buriats and other national minorities continued to be the promotion of a quasi-Russian Soviet culture at the expense of indigenous identities. Nor did official discouragement of pan-Mongolism abate. The Buriat-Mongolian ASSR was renamed the Buriat ASSR in order to downplay the Buriats' ethnic ties with the rest of the Mongol world. The theory of the rapprochement (sblizhenie) and eventual merger (sliianie) of nations, promoted by communist ideologists from the 1960s on, heralded a further devaluation of Buriat identity. During the 1970s Russian was made the language of instruction in practically all Buriat schools. Attacks on Buddhism resumed at the same time. The Buddhologist and Tibetan scholar Bidia Dandaron was arrested in 1972 along with dozens of his students, relatives, and colleagues. Dandaron later died in prison.

The Gorbachev era ended the official russification that endured over most of the Soviet period. The Buriats' pre-revolutionary cultural heritage and their historical connections with other Mongols ceased to be taboo subjects. For example, the lunar new year, Sagaan hara, or Sagaalgan, began to be celebrated openly for the first time in decades, and *The Secret History of the Mongols*, an account of Chingis (Genghis) Khan's rise to power, appeared in a new bilingual Buriat-Russian edition in 1989. Native politicians managed to have their autonomous republic upgraded to union-republic status. Gorbachev's relaxation of religious policy permitted a revival of Buriat Buddhism. Several new datsans were founded, and the Dalai Lama visited Buriatia in 1991 and 1992 amid much fanfare. The Buriat language has occupied a prominent place in this cultural revival. Significant efforts have been made to expand its place in education, publishing, radio, and television, and a language law of 1991 declared the official equality of Buriat and Russian in the political, educational, administrative, and other public institutions of the Buriat republic. Classical Mongolian also returned to the curriculum in at least some schools. A series of festivals, lectures, and publications commemorated the *Geser* epic in 1995, and young Buriats again are being trained as bards (üligershen).

The end of the Communist Party's monopoly on political activity allowed the formation of new political, social, and cultural organizations and institutions to promote Buriat interests. Negedel (Unity), the All-Buriat Association of the Development of Culture, and the Rebirth Humanitarian Center were created to facilitate the revival of Buriat traditions, language, arts, and handicrafts, and other aspects of native culture. Local environmental groups, such as the Baikal Fund, Akhalar, and Ekomir, attempt to ameliorate the damage wrought by Soviet industrial and extractive practices and to prevent further damage to the local ecology. Buriat nationalist groups, such as the Buriat-Mongolian People's Party, advocate greater political and cultural autonomy for the Buriats. Purely political forms of nationalism are relatively weak. Calls for independence or secession from the Russian Federation are practically nonexistent. An attempt to restore the word Mongol to the republic's title at the end of the 1980s failed, due at least in part to lack of public support. A campaign to restore Buriatia's pre-1937 borders likewise bore no fruit. Given the Buriats' minority status within their own republic and the tremendous economic difficulties in post-communist Buriatia occasioned by Russia's economic crisis, it is not surprising that the Buriat national movement has chosen to focus on issues of cultural, rather than political, autonomy.

Bibliography: Marjorie Mandelstam Balzer, "From Ethnicity to Nationalism. Turmoil in the Russian Mini-Empire" in *The Social Legacy of Communism,* ed. by James R. Millar and Sharon L. Wolchik (Cambridge, Mass., 1994); Sh.B. Chimitdorzhiev, *Buriaadai tüükhe beshegüüd* (Buriat Historical Writings) (Ulan-Ude, 1992); James Forsyth, *A History of the Peoples of Siberia. Russia's North Asian Colony, 1581-1990* (Cambridge, 1992); Carolyn Humphrey, "Buryatiya and the Buryats" in *The Nationalities Question in the Post-Soviet States,* ed. by Graham Smith (New York, 1996), *Karl Marx Collective. Economy, Society and Religion in a Siberian Collective Farm* (Cambridge, 1983); Helen Sharon Hundley, "Speransky and the Buriats. Administrative Reform in Nineteenth-Century Russia" (Ph.D. dissertation, University of Illinois, 1984); T.M. Mikhailov, N.V. Kim, and B.V. Bazarov, eds., *Istoriia Buriatii v voprosakh i otvetakh,* 3 vols. (Ulan-Ude, 1990-1992); P.T. Khaptaev, et al. eds., *Istoriia Buriat-Mongol'skoi ASSR* and *Istoriia Buriatskoi ASSR* (Ulan-Ude, 1951-1954, 1957); A.A. Badiev, et al. eds., *Kul'turnoe stroitel'stvo v Buriatskoi ASSR (1917-1981). Dokumenty i materialy* (Ulan-Ude, 1983); T.M. Mikhailov, "Buriaty" in *Narody Rossii. Entsiklopediia,* ed. by V.A. Tishkov (M., 1994); Robert Montgomery, "Buriat Language Policy, 19th c.-1928. A Case Study in Soviet Nationality Practice" (Ph.D dissertation, Indiana University, 1994); N.V. Kim, et al. eds., *Natsional'no-osvoboditel'noe dvizhenie buriatskogo naroda* (Ulan-Ude, 1989); B.V. Bazarov, et al. eds., *Neizvestnye stranitsy istorii Buriatii (iz arkhivov KGB),* 2 vols. (Ulan-Ude, 1991-1992); E.M. Zalkind, et al. eds., *Ocherk istorii kul'tury Buriatii,* 2 vols. (Ulan-Ude, 1972); Nicholas Poppe, "The Buddhists" in *Genocide in the USSR. Studies in Group Destruction,* ed. by Nikolai D. Deker and Andrei Lebed (New York, 1958), 181-192, *Buriat Grammar* (Bloomington, Ind., 1960); Robert Rupen, *Mongols of the Twentieth Century,* 2 vols. (Bloomington, Ind., 1964); John Snelling, *Buddhism in Russia. The Story of Agvan Dorzhiev, Lhasa's Emissary to the Tsar* (Shaftesbury, 1993); K.V. Vyatkina, "The Buriats" in *The Peoples of Siberia*, ed. by M.G. Levin and L.P. Potapov, trans. by Stephen Dunn (Chicago, Ill., 1964); Natalia Zhukovskaya, "The Buriats" in *Encyclopedia of World Cultures,* Vol. 6, *Russia and Eurasia/China*, ed. by Paul Friedrich and Norma Diamond (Boston, Mass., 1994).

Robert W. Montgomery

BURLIUK, DAVID DAVIDOVICH (1882-1967). Artist, poet, and major figure of Russian futurism.

David Burliuk was born in the Kharkov region to a successful merchant and landowner. He was the brother of Nikolai Davidovich (1890-1920), Liudmila Davidovna (active 1907-1908), and Vladimir Davidovich (1886-1917) Burliuk. David Burliuk studied at the Kazan School of Art and the Odessa Art School between 1898 and 1900. He also attended the Munich Academy in 1902-1903 and the Atelier Cormon in Paris in 1904.

David Burliuk is known for his artistic and literary innovations as well as his organizational activities. In the winter of 1907 David Burliuk and his three siblings exhibited in Moscow and St. Petersburg with the World of Art (Mir iskusstva) and Union of Youth (Soiuz molodezhi) groups. Between 1907 and 1910 Burliuk organized and participated in the Wreath and Stephanos exhibitions and continued to exhibit regularly with the Union of Youth. Natalia Sergeevna Goncharova (1881-1962), Mikhail Fedorovich Larionov (1881-1864), and Aleksandra Aleksandrovna Ekster (1884-1949), among the future leaders of the avant-garde, also participated in these early exhibitions.

In the winter of 1909 David and Vladimir Burliuk formed a Modern Russian poets circle which included Vasily Vasilievich Kamensky (1864-1961), Mikhail Vasilievich Matiushin (1861-1934), and Velimir Vladimirovich Khlebnikov (1885-1922). This group collaborated on avant-garde poetry and art books such as the infamous *A Trap for Judges* (Sadok sudeii, 1913) which included poems by Kamensky, Khlebnikov, and Elena Genrikhovna Guro (1877-1913).

While visiting Chernianka, the Burliuk's family estate in Crimea, in December 1911 the Burliuk brothers and poet Benedikt Konstantinovich Livshits (1886-1939) founded the group Hylaea. Their choice of the ancient Greek name for the region around Chernianka invoked southern Russia's Greek heritage and distinguished their artistic circle from western modernist counterparts, specifically Italian futurism. The principles of Hylaea were the cultivation of primitivism, and linguistic and pictorial innovation. Their activity was also informed by a nationalist impulse to re-enliven Russian art via native Russian sources rather than by importation of Western artistic styles. Both David and Vladimir Burliuk had a long-standing interest in archaeology, especially of the region of Southern Russia. Between 1907 and 1912 they participated in archaeological digs, excavating over fifty ancient Greek tombs in Crimea. To further distinguish their own futurist group from the Italian Futurists, they initially called themselves Men of the Future (budetliane), a word invented by

Khlebnikov from the future tense of the verb to be. David Burliuk's poetry, as well as Khlebnikov's, between 1910 and 1914 combined archaic sounds, invented words, and phrases used out of context. Value was placed on the sound of the utterance itself and new potential interpretations, rather than the standard meanings.

In 1911 David Burliuk re-entered art school in Odessa, wanting to obtain a diploma. While he was in Moscow for a state examination, Burliuk met the young poet and painter Vladimir Vladimirovich Maiakovsky (1893-1930). Burliuk is often credited with discovering Maiakovsky because he encouraged him to write poetry rather than become a painter.

At Chernianka in the summer of 1911 Larionov, Goncharova, and David and Vladimir Burliuk organized the Jack of Diamonds (Bubovny valet) exhibition, which took place during the winter of 1911. This exhibition united the leaders of Russian modernism, including artists Kazimir Severinovich Malevich (1878-1935), Vladimir Evgrafovich Tatlin (1885-1953), Vasily Vasilievich Kandinsky (1866-1944), Aleksandra Ekster, Goncharova, Larionov, and Petr Petrovich Konchalovsky (1876-1956), and propelled them to investigate more radical avant-garde pictorial innovations. David Burliuk's paintings from this period assimilate cubist pictorial language into abstracted landscapes which are seen from multiple points of view. He believed cubism was the most appropriate way of painting in the contemporary era. David Burliuk promoted cubism through lectures accompanied by slides and publication of his essay Cubism (Kubizm) in 1912. David Burliuk also participated in the second Jack of Diamonds exhibition in 1912, which included paintings by Henri Matisse (1869-1954), Pablo Picasso (1881-1973), and Robert Delaunay (1885-1941). In 1912 Burliuk travelled to Munich to participate in the Blue Rider exhibition and published one of his essays in *The Blue Rider Almanac*.

David Burliuk's provocative public appearances, in which he paraded the streets or gave lectures with his face painted, antagonized the public and provoked conservative art critics. One critic invented the verb to burliuk (burliukat) meaning to fool around. The publication of *A Slap in the Face of Public Taste* (Poshchechina obshchestvennomu vkusu, 1912), a collection of drawings and poems by David and Vladimir Burliuk and Kandinsky, solidified Russian futurists' reputation as provocateurs. Its deliberately outrageous title and contents earned David Burliuk the title father of Russian futurism. Other important futurist publications to which David Burliuk contributed are *Croaked Moon* (Dokhlaia luna, 1913), *Milk of Mares* (Moloko kobylits, 1914), and Futurists. The First Journal of the Russian Futurists (Futuristy. Pervy zhurnal russkhikh futuristov, 1914). David Burliuk appeared in the film, Drama in Cabaret No. 13, which recorded on film the daily lives of the futurists as they paraded the streets and visited cafes.

David, his brother Vladimir, Kamensky, and Maiakovsky embarked on a futurist tour of southern Russia between December 1913 and March 1914, coinciding with Italian futurist Fillipo Marinetti's visit to St. Petersburg and Moscow. They visited seventeen towns across Russia giving speeches and generally inciting the public.

David Burliuk lived in the Urals between 1915 and 1917, and many consider his publications from that period as dilutions of the original spirit of Hylaea. The one exception is Took. Drum of the Futurists (Vzial. Baraban futuristov, 1915), a polemical journal which included poetry by Maiakovsky and drawings by David Burliuk.

Although David Burliuk signed the Decree for the Democratization of Art in 1917, he was not associated with futurist activity after the Bolshevik Revolution. David Burliuk lived in Vladivostok between 1918 and 1920, collaborating on the art journal Creation (Tvorchestvo) and occasionally exhibiting and lecturing. Following a two-year stay in Japan, during which he was well received and sold many paintings, Burliuk and his wife and children moved to New York City in 1922.

Unable to support his family with sales of his paintings, Burliuk took a proofreading job at a Russian-language newspaper, where he ultimately became the arts editor. Christian Brinton took an interest in his work and arranged for Burliuk's participation in a Modern Russian art exhibition at the Brooklyn Museum of Art. Burliuk had his first one-man show in the United States in 1924 at Societé Anonyme and exhibited with them regularly through the 1920s and 1930s. He had a one-man show at the Phillips Collection in Washington, D.C., in 1939 where critics praised him for his strong peasant quality and the fantasy and folklore of this works. Although critically well received, Burliuk remained relatively obscure in the United States. David Burliuk edited the periodical Color and Rhyme from 1930 until 1966, and continued to contribute to exhibitions of contemporary Russian art until his death. Burliuk died in 1967 in Long Island, New York.

Bibliography: David Davidovich Burliuk, *Vospominaniia* (New York, 1932), *Fifty-five Years of Painting* (New York, 1962); Susan Compton, *The World Backwards. Russian Futurist Books, 1912-1916* (London, 1978); Catherine Dreier, *Burliuk* (New York, 1944); Camilla Gray, *The Russian Experiment in Art. 1863-1922,* revised and enlarged by Marian Burleigh-Motley (New York, 1986), 110-118; Benedikt Livshits, *The One and a Half-eyed Archer,* trans. by John Bowlt (Newtonville, Mass., 1977); Vladimir Markov, *Russian Futurism. A History* (Berkeley, Cal., 1968); *L'avant-garde russe, 1905-1924* (Nantes, 1993).

Pamela J. Kachurin

BURLIUK, VLADIMIR DAVIDOVICH (1886-1917). Painter and graphic artist. Important figure in Russian futurism.

Vladimir Burliuk was born in the Kharkov region to a successful merchant and landowner. Brother of David Davidovich (1882-1967), Nikolai Davidovich (1890-1920), and Liudmila Davidovna (active 1907-1908) Burliuk. Vladimir Burliuk studied at the art school in Odessa between 1898 and 1900, in Munich at the Azbé studio in 1903, and then in 1904 at the Atelier Cormon in Paris with his brother David.

Vladimir Davidovich's artistic career was associated with the avant-garde exhibitions such as the Jack of Diamonds (Bubovny valet) and Union of Youth (Soiuz molodezhi) with which he exhibited between 1910 and 1914. Propelled by his interest in native Russian pictorial sources and archaeology, Vladimir Burliuk cultivated a primitivist cubist style which became the hallmark of neo-primitivism, characteristic of the Jack of Diamonds artists and later the Donkey's Tail.

Vladimir Burliuk illustrated many of the futurist books to which his brother David and poets Vladimir Vladimirovich Maiakovsky (1893-1930), Vasily Vasilievich Kamensky (1864-1961), and Velimir Vladimirovich Khlebnikov (1885-1922) contributed poetry. He provided portraits of the contributors to the futurist book *A Trap for Judges* (Sadok sudeii) published in 1913. Among his best-known illustrations are those for the futurist collections, *Croaked Moon* (Dokhlaia luna, 1913), *Milk of Mares* (Moloko kobylits, 1914), and *The Bung* (Zatychka, 1913). The drawings for *The Bung* are notable for the fact that they were hand-colored lithographs emphasizing the individual validity of line and color, corresponding to similar efforts in poetry. Vladimir Burliuk also contributed the majority of illustrations to Maiakovsky's first play Vladimir Maiakovsky. A Tragedy (1914). These drawings reflect an interest in geometric abstraction, which was to find its ultimate expression in suprematism. Vladimir Burliuk was a member of the German art groups The Blue Rider and New Artists Union, and exhibited in Berlin in 1913 and in Paris in 1914. He was killed during active service in the Balkans in 1917.

Bibliography: David Davidovich Burliuk, *Vospominaniia* (New York, 1932); Susan Compton, *The World Backwards. Russian Futurist Books, 1912-1916* (London, 1978); Camilla Gray, *The Russian Experiment in Art, 1863-1922*, revised and enlarged by Marian Burleigh Motley (New York, 1986), 110-118; Benedikt Livshits, *The One and a Half-eyed Archer*, trans. by John Bowlt (Newtonville, Mass., 1977); Vladimir Markov, *Russian Futurism. A History* (Berkeley, Cal., 1968); *L'avant-garde russe, 1905-1924* (Nantes, 1993).

Pamela J. Kachurin

BURMISTERSKAIA PALATA. Established in 1699, this institution managed the tax, crown service, and judicial affairs of the Muscovite commercial population. Officially renamed the ratusha in November 1699.

The Burmisterskaia palata (hereafter ratusha, from the German, Rathaus) anchored the burmistr reform of 1699. Locally, the ratusha served as the town hall for the merchants, traders, and artisans from the thirty-eight units, two merchant corporations and thirty-six territorial corporations, that composed the Moscow city quarters (posady). Nationally, the ratusha became the central treasury of the state which gathered taxes collected by burmistry (pl.) in town halls throughout the country and then disbursed the proceeds to various government entities, mainly for military purposes. It also supervised the tax-collecting, city service, and judicial activities of all town halls, and it had responsibility for protecting Russia's taxpaying townsmen from unfair competition from foreign merchants and non-taxed domestic competitors through the enforcement of existing trade charters.

After a period of initial confusion over the meaning of the decree calling the ratusha into existence, the institution began operations on 1 September 1699. By that time thirty-three burmistry had been elected, four by the senior merchants (gosti), four by the guild of senior merchants (gostiniia sotnia), and twenty-five by various territorial corporations of the capital. Ultimately the ratusha consisted of twelve burmistry, who selected one of their number as president for a monthly term.

Tsar Peter himself identified a site for the ratusha, a building adjacent to the church of St. John the Baptist near the Borovitsky gate of the Kremlin. The tsar also ordered that the ratusha be provided a seal, depicting a commercial balance. The government assigned twelve clerks (podiachie) to the ratusha to manage accounts and correspondence and one hundred soldiers to assist in tax collection. The ratusha received the right to issue directives to chanceries (prikazy) and other central governmental institutions and to report directly to the sovereign. The ratusha thus became the equivalent of a chancery.

Its broad revenue sources from direct and indirect taxes quickly enabled the ratusha to supplant the Great Treasury (Bolshaia kazna) as the main financial institution of the state. The full value of the taxes assessed under its authority could have covered 90 percent of the state's military expenditures. The actual record of the ratusha was mixed. In 1701 it collected 1,302,016 rubles, nearly half of the government's income for the year and twice the amount gathered in 1680 from the same set of taxes. Revenues declined in the next three years and never again met government targets. The ratusha also had difficulty with disbursements. Much of its revenue went to non-budgeted purposes in response to directives from other chanceries. To straighten matters out, in 1705 Peter appointed Aleksei Aleksandrovich Kurbatov (d. 1721) as chief inspector of the ratusha. Kurbatov increased revenues in subsequent years, but they still fell short of budgeted goals. In reaction the government began to transfer groups of cities from the jurisdiction of the ratusha to that of governors (nachalniki). Kurbatov fought in vain against this practice which undermined the principle of centralization on which the burmistr reform was based and which depleted ratusha revenues. When decentralization triumphed in the provincial reform of 1708-1711, the ratusha lost its state-wide fiscal role. With a few exceptions it acted solely as the town hall for the Moscow commercial population until the initiation of Peter's magistracy reform. Even then the term ratusha survived. Article XXII of the Main Magistracy Regulation of 16 January 1721 called for two-story town halls (ratushy) in large and middle-sized cities to support the activities of local magistracies.

The overarching objective of the ratusha, as that of the burmistr reform writ large, was to increase government revenues. To accomplish that goal the government created an administrative structure that directly linked those responsible for revenue-gathering in the localities, burmistry, with a central office for collection and disbursement of these revenues. Financial activities that once were dispersed across thirteen chanceries came under the sole jurisdiction of the ratusha. The ratusha itself relied for its effectiveness on the fiscal knowledge, economic power, and deep pockets of Moscow's senior merchants who served as burmistry. The ratusha performed its role as central treasury with some success, though it failed to keep up with spiraling military expenditures. The decline of the ratusha thus can be attributed mainly to its failure to meet its budgeted revenues, and also to its inexperience in bureaucratic infighting, especially with newly established military chanceries, and to Peter's mid-reign turn toward administrative decentralization.

But the pendulum soon swung back toward centralization. The St. Petersburg main magistracy had many similarities with the ratusha. Both institutions played a crucial role in gathering revenues from and managing the state responsibilities of the Russian urban taxpaying population.

Bibliography: For the early history of the ratusha see M.M. Bogoslovskii, *Petr I. Materialy dlia biografii,* Vol. 3 (M., 1946), and N.P. Eroshkin, *Istoriia gosudarstvennykh uchrezhdenii dorevoliutsionnoi Rossii* (M., 1983). A thorough study of the ratusha based on legal sources is found in I.I. Ditiatin, *Ustroistvo i upravlenie gorodov Rossii,* Vol. 1 (SPb., 1875), and A.A. Kizevetter, *Mestnoe samoupravlenie v Rossii IX-XIX st. Istoricheskii ocherk* (Pg., 1917). P.N. Miliukov, *Gosudarstvennoe khoziaistvo Rossii v pervoi chetverti XVIII stoletiia i reforma Petra Velikogo* (SPb., 1905), emphasizes the fiscal nature of the ratusha. In English, see J. Michael Hittle, *The Service City. State and Townsmen in Russia, 1600-1800* (Cambridge, Mass., 1979), and Claes Peterson, *Peter the Great's Administrative and Judicial Reforms* (Stockholm, 1979).

J. Michael Hittle

BURMISTR REFORM OF 1699. A fiscal, social, and urban reform of Peter I.

Ever-growing military expenditures compelled the government of Peter I to increase state revenues dramatically. Up to 1699 local elected officials, such as town elders, customs and liquor tax heads, and their assistants, gathered the two principal sources of state revenue, direct taxes, especially the streletsky (musketeer), and indirect taxes, customs and liquor, and forwarded them to the various chanceries (prikazy) to which the localities were subordinated. The work of these local officials, as well as their own economic activities, suffered from red tape and corruption at the hands of their supervisors, military commanders (voevody) and chancery officials. As a consequence government revenues fell short of budgeted targets.

On 30 January 1699 two imprecisely worded decrees of the sovereign sought to enhance state revenues by creating new local and central government institutions, wholly independent of military commanders and chancery officials, whose main purpose was to collect and disburse these crucial revenues. One decree called for establishment of town halls (zemskie izby) staffed with elected officials, soon to be called burmistry (pl.), a term Peter imported from Holland. The law made the burmistry responsible for administration of state taxes as well as for supervising city service obligations and for rendering justice among the merchants, traders, and artisans who were known collectively as townsmen (posadskie liudi). Although the reform focused on a single social estate, its embrace was in fact much broader. The law permitted not only townsmen but also traders from state and crown communities (volosti) as well as taxable peasants to participate in the election of burmistry. This broad franchise reflected the government's concern that all payers of the chiefly state taxes be removed from the jurisdiction of military commanders. All eligible voters, urban and rural, voted in the first elections.

Initially the reform was voluntary. The law permitted the townsmen in each city to decide whether they wished to elect burmistry, and if so, how many. Those cities which adopted the reform were to pay taxes at twice the previous rate. The government apparently assumed that the townsmen would consider freedom from the depredations of military commanders worth the burden of double taxation. The responses of the cities did not support that assumption. Of seventy cities for which data exist, eleven accepted the government proposal fully, thirty-three refused it, and twenty-six elected burmistry but were silent about the double tax. On 20 October 1699 the government made the reform mandatory but dropped the double tax.

The second decree of 30 January 1699 called for the creation of a Burmistr Chamber (Burmisterskaia Palata) whose officials were to be elected by the entire commercial population of Moscow. The Burmistr Chamber, soon renamed the ratusha, had two functions. First, it served as the city hall for Moscow's merchants, traders, and artisans, and second, it acted as the central office of the burmistr institution throughout the state. In this latter capacity the ratusha was to receive once each year the taxes gathered by the various town halls.

What little is known about the actual operations of town halls reflects a mixture of difficulties and accomplishments. Some town halls encountered resistance from military commanders who refused to surrender to burmistry necessary tax records. In Kaluga conflicting factions of wealthy and poor taxpayers struggled for years over control of the city hall. At one point two city halls were operating simultaneously. And the burmistry were themselves not beyond the kinds of corruption, both bribery and outright theft of government funds, about which they had so long complained when military commanders and chancery officials supervised tax affairs. Still, the revenues gathered by the town halls and directed to Moscow were substantial, well in excess of what was taken in before the reform.

Although the ratusha began to lose some of its authority incrementally after 1705, the basic structure of the burmistr reform remained largely intact until the provincial reform of 1708-1711. This reform cost the ratusha its role as chief treasury of the state and reduced it to managing the Moscow mercantile population. Local burmistry continued their tax-collecting activities but handed over the revenues to governors or military commanders at the provincial level, rather than to central government officials. The overall direction of the activities of town halls shifted over time first to governors, then to the Senate, and finally to the Commerce College. The last vestiges of the burmistr reform passed from the scene with the appearance of the magistracy reform, first defined by legislation in 1718 and finally implemented starting in 1721.

Three lines of institutional development converge in the burmistr reform, the administration of taxes, the organization of the urban taxpaying estate, and urban policy. The language of the decrees of January 1699 underscores Peter's overarching aim, to increase tax revenues. This was nothing new, for the government took steps in 1679-1681 to consolidate taxes and to concentrate their collection. It also tried, although with limited success, to check the rapacious behavior of the military commanders. In 1674 the government stripped them of the right of subsistence by local residents, and in 1698 it ordered them to stay out of fiscal matters in the localities. Given these precedents, the burmistr reform can be seen as the culmination of an existing process of centralizing the administration of the chief state taxes and of protecting them from predation by representatives of the central government in the localities.

The burmistr reform, given its focus on the taxpaying townsmen, can be regarded also as an effort to give greater coherence and strength to a beleaguered social estate whose economic and fiscal potential the government increasingly prized. Precedents for such concerns go back to the protections granted the townsmen in the Law Code of 1649 and the trade charters of 1653 and 1667. The burmistr reform, in particular the ratusha, was in many ways the fulfillment of a recommendation of Afanasy Lavrentevich Ordin-Nashchokin (1605-1680), contained in Article 88 of the New Trade Statute of 1667, that the government establish "a chancery of mercantile people." But in practice the overriding emphasis on fiscal obligations negated the reform's potential for favoring the urban taxpaying estate.

Finally, the burmistr reform reflects Peter's early views on the role of cities. Impressed by the European cities he visited, Peter sought to upgrade Russia's cities by importing urban administrative institutions, especially from Holland and from cities operating under Magdeburg Law. The importation was selective. The burmistr reform embraced only one portion of the urban population, the taxpaying townsmen, and it lacked the principal of urban autonomy that lay at the heart of the model institutions. The burmistr reform essentially placed traditional service by the townsmen into a new centralized structure, garnished with foreign nomenclature. When it failed to come up with the needed revenues, the burmistr institution was sacrificed in the name of decentralization. Yet its structure and functions clearly presaged the magistracy reform, Peter's bolder and more mature attempt to create cities commensurate with the demands of a mercantilist state.

Bibliography: For the early history of the reform see M.M. Bogoslovskii, *Petr I. Materialy dlia biografii*, Vol. 3 (M., 1946). An urban-oriented, institutional study of the reform based on legal sources is found in I.I. Ditiatin, *Ustroistvo i upravlenie gorodov Rossii*, Vol. 1 (SPb., 1875), and A.A. Kizevetter, *Mestnoe samoupravlenie v Rossii IX-XIX st. Istoricheskii ocherk* (Pg., 1917). P.N. Miliukov, *Gosudarstvennoe khoziastvo Rossii v pervoi chetverti XVIII stoletiia i reforma Petra Velikogo* (SPb., 1905), emphasizes the fiscal nature of the reform. See also A.V. Murav'ev, "Iz materialov po istorii klassovoi bor'by v russkom gorode nachala XVIII veka" in *Arkheograficheskii ezhegodnik za 1959 god* (M., 1960). In English see J. Michael Hittle, *The Service City. State and Townsmen in Russia, 1600-1800* (Cambridge, Mass., 1979), and Claes Peterson, *Peter the Great's Administrative and Judicial Reforms* (Stockholm, 1979).

J. Michael Hittle

BURNASHEV, KHANIF KHISANOVICH (1900-1938). Central Asian Communist Party activist.

Burnashev was born into a Tatar family in the village of Shagand near Namangan in the Fergana Valley. He learned Russian early, probably in a Russian native school. Later he attended high school (gymnasium) in Tashkent, then he left after the 1917 revolutions without graduating to engage in politics. He worked in the Turkestan Commissariat of Nationalities' newspaper, Communist (Ishtirokiyun). On 1 December 1919 he joined the Communist Party of Turkestan (CPT).

Burnashev advanced quickly as secretary of the party committees of the city of Tashkent and then Syr-Daria region, achieving the status of candidate member of the CPT's Central Committee. In September 1921 he became secretary of the party committee of Fergana region. This was one of the key positions in Turkestan at the time, since Fergana was a hot spot, under heavy attack by Basmachi armed resistance to Soviet power. In 1923 Burnashev became one of the most active members of the so-called Young Communists, led by Usmankhan Ishan-Khojaev (1899–1938). The Young Communists declared themselves to be Turkestan's truest Marxists and sought to replace the current Muslim leadership, which they accused of maintaining a patriarchal system of sovieticized medieval despotism. The Young Communists called for an assault on Central Asia's backward way of life.

As a result of a crackdown on the Young Communists, initiated by the CPT secretary Abdulla Rahimbaev (1896–1938), Burnashev lost his positions and had to leave Turkestan. He went to Moscow, where Lazar Moiseevich Kaganovich (1893–1991) helped him enroll in the Institute of Red Professors, where he became a specialist in economics. While he was in Moscow Burnashev appealed successfully to Stalin in 1924 for support for the Young Communists.

After the national delimitation of Central Asia the Young Communists, now under the leadership of Akmal Ikramov (1898–1938), came to power in Uzbekistan. Burnashev became one the most important Uzbek leaders as head of the agitation and propaganda department of the Central Committee of the Communist Party of Uzbekistan (CPUz), editor of the party's newspaper Red Uzbekistan (Qizil Ozbekiston), head of Uzbekistan's State Planning Commission (Gosplan), and people's commissar for agriculture. Burnashev was responsible for Uzbekistan's first Five Year Plan.

In March 1929 the Ikramov group was severely defeated at the Fourth Congress of the CPUz by younger party activists, who accused them of having bourgeois origins. Burnashev lost all his posts. From 1930 onward he worked again in Moscow as head of the planning department in the USSR's People's Commissariat of Agriculture. Arrested on 25 March 1937, he was sentenced to death on 2 November 1937 and shot on 22 March 1938. He was posthumously rehabilitated on 18 August 1956.

Bibliography: The only biographical sketches are "Burnashev, Khanif Khisanovich," in *Revoliutsiei prizvannye* (Tashkent, 1987), 290-292, and "Burnashev, Xanif Xisanovich," in *O'zbek Sovet Entsiklopediyasi*, 14 vols. (Tashkent,

1971-1980), Vol. 2, 480. They are both formulaic biographies. Given the scarcity of information on historical figures in scholarly literature in Soviet Central Asia, additional material is found so far only in archives.

Gero Fedtke

BURNT BY THE SUN (1994). Motion picture personalizing tragedies of Soviet life in the 1930s. Directed by Nikita Mikhalkov. Produced by the TriTe Studio, Moscow.

The most important Russian film of the 1990s, Nikita Mikhalkov's Burnt by the Sun personalizes the tragedies of Soviet life in the 1930s by examining the corrosive impact of Stalinism on one family. The film's moral, ideological, and cultural conflicts are played out through its antagonists, Sergei Kotov (Nikita Mikhalkov) and Dmitry (Oleg Menshikov). At first the two men appear to be opposites in every way. The bluff Colonel Kotov is a simple man, a Bolshevik and Civil War hero. The enigmatic Dmitry is a well-educated pianist who fought for the Whites during the Civil War and has spent most of the intervening years in exile in France.

As the tragedy unfolds on a single summer day in 1936, the differences between Kotov and Dmitry become painfully obscured. Both love the same woman, the beautiful Mariusia (Ingeborga Dapkunaite), who is now Kotov's wife, but was Dmitry's lover. Both bask in the affections of Mariusia's eccentric family, who have embraced Kotov just as they once embraced Dmitry. What propels the story is the jarring fact that both men serve the same cause. Dmitry is not only a charming pianist and storyteller, a relic from the past. He is an NKVD agent, who has come to this nest of gentry for one reason, to arrest Kotov as an enemy of the people.

The personal was political in Stalinist culture, and Mikhalkov brilliantly illustrates this idea though a complex web of relationships. Kotov is amazingly naive for a man with his past and his current position of power. The colonel has married into a nest of gentry, a family of artists remarkably like Mikhalkov's own privileged clan. Through Kotov's influence his in-laws have managed to retain their picturesque summer home by turning into a rest home for artists and musicians. There the old folks, garbed in white linen, sigh for the aroma of the old days, speak French, and joke about Soviet holidays.

Truly proletarian touches are few. Kotov is proud that he doesn't speak French, yet. He informs Uncle Vsevolod that "things aren't so bad these days," which is a stunningly half-hearted affirmation of the Soviet system for a high-ranking army officer. Kotov insists that the family play soccer instead of the bourgeois game of croquet. Yet despite the evident luxury of his life, so different from the rest of Soviet society, Kotov fails to see his own hypocrisy in attacking Dmitry. Kotov argues to his wife that her former lover is a cynical opportunist, who left her because he was afraid. Kotov sneers at Dmitry, "Who forced you, my angel? We bought you. Like a whore."

Even as he is driven from paradise, Kotov's self-confidence is unshaken. He knows Stalin's personal telephone number, so "who will dare touch me?" He soon learns. Trussed like an animal, his face beaten to a pulp, whimpering like a baby,

Kotov sits propped between Dmitry and an NKVD enforcer, both of whom avert their eyes. It is the devil's bargain: a life for a life, Kotov's life in exchange for the life in the sun that Dmitry lost.

But the exchange is not equal. As Dmitry knows better than anyone, Kotov's destruction means the inevitable destruction of Mariusia and their little daughter Nadia as well. Even in Dmitry's eyes, his revenge is not justice, and he exacts his own justice by committing suicide.

The ending titles inform the viewer of Kotov's execution, of Marusia's arrest and death in the camps, of Nadia's arrest and eventual rehabilitation, and Mikhalkov dedicates the movie to "all who were burnt by the sun of the revolution." Though many Western critics appeared not to understand this, the dedication was as much for the tragically corrupted Dmitry as for the Kotovs.

The reaction among North American movie critics was unusually uniform for a Russian film. Despite the predictable complaints about the Russian penchant for digressions, heavy-handed symbolism, slow pacing, and eccentric flourishes, no one could deny the film's beauty and enormous emotional impact. On the other hand, Russian critics and Western scholars were shocked by the way Burnt by the Sun misrepresented Soviet life on the eve of the Terror as a Chekhovian fantasy world. Russian critics and viewers found the moral ambiguity of the movie troubling. Weren't Kotov and Dmitry portrayed too sympathetically, given that one was a Bolshevik and the other a traitor to his class?

Burnt by the Sun represents Mikhalkov's most complex artistic achievement to date as well as his greatest box office success. Mikhalkov's pictures won many international prizes, but the Oscar remained his elusive dream. Even though Burnt by the Sun already won the Jury Prize at the Cannes Film Festival in 1994, Mikhalkov made it clear that receiving the Oscar for Best Foreign Film in 1995 was the highlight of his career. Award in hand, Mikhalkov signed a North American distribution deal with Sony Pictures, and Burnt by the Sun earned more than $2 million in the US. Mikhalkov was so proud of his Oscar that he complained loudly to the Russian press when President Boris Yeltsin did not personally greet him at the airport on his triumphant return from Los Angeles.

Bibliography: Kinograf, No. 4 (1997), 148-65. In English see Louis Menashe, "Burnt by the Sun," *Cineaste,* Vol. 21, No. 4 (1995), 43-44, Nikita Mikhalkov, "Blind Faith," *Sight and Sound* (January 1996), Ludmila Bulavka, "Nikita Mikhalkov and *Burnt by the Sun.* A Monarchist Film-Maker Confronts Humane Socialism," *New Left Review* (January/February 1997), 139-48, Tatiana Moskvina, "La Grande Illusion" in *Russia on Reels. The Russian Ideal in Post-Soviet Cinema,* ed. by Birgit Beumers (London, 1999), Chap. 9; and Birgit Beumers, *Burnt by the Sun* (London, 2000).

Denise J. Youngblood

BURTSEV, VLADIMIR LVOVICH (1862-1942). Publicist, publisher, historian of the Russian revolutionary movements, revolutionary Sherlock Holmes.

Born in Fort Aleksandrovsky east of the Caspian Sea in 1862, the son of a minor officer in the Orenburg Cossack Host, Burtsev graduated from gymnasium in Kazan in 1882. He studied mathematics and law at the universities of St. Petersburg and Kazan but was arrested for political activity before taking his degree and was exiled in 1886 to Irkutsk province. He fled abroad, where he spent most of the rest of his life, settling briefly in Switzerland and France, then in England. There he published *For a Hundred Years, 1800-1896* (Za sto let, 1800-1896, 1897), a chronicle of the Russian revolutionary movements, and three issues of a journal, Populist (Narodovolets, 1897), in which he advocated political terrorism. In early 1898 he was sentenced by an English court to eighteen months of hard labor for incitement to political murder. From 1900 to 1904 he published six issues of The Past (Byloe), an important pre-revolutionary journal, which published memoirs and documents devoted to the history of the Russian revolutionary movements. In 1903 he was expelled from both England and Switzerland and settled in France.

Burtsev was a deeply religious boy who had dreamed of taking monastic vows. In the late 1870s he abandoned religion but soon became enthralled with the People's Will and developed an ardent faith in the revolutionary movement. In the early 1900s he drew close to the Socialist Revolutionaries yet never formally joined a political party. He advocated political terror but only, he claimed, as a means to achieve social and political reforms in Russia.

The general amnesty for political dissidents, which Nicholas II proclaimed in October 1905, permitted Burtsev to return to St. Petersburg. In January he launched a second series of Byloe, which appeared monthly until closed by the government in October 1907. He then returned to Paris where he published two newspapers, Common Cause (Obshchee delo, 1909-1910) and The Future (Budushchee, 1911-1914).

While in Russia, Burtsev began making contacts with former police officials, seeking to coax from them revelations about security police operations. In spring 1906 M.E. Bakai, a disgruntled security policeman, placed his broad expertise and a list of fifty to seventy-five informants at Burtsev's disposal and emigrated to Paris in 1908 to join him. Thus began the endeavor for which Burtsev is best known, the unmasking of police informants. Working systematically to discover their identities, roles, and names, he felt engaged in a sacred campaign against provocation, the term widely used by the educated elite to mean police deployment of secret informants. Burtsev's main target beginning in 1906 and his greatest triumph was to expose E.F. Azef, a highly paid informant who helped found the Socialist Revolutionary Party. As the leader of its combat organization, Azef organized the assassination of V.K. Plehve (1904) and Grand Duke Sergei Aleksandrovich (1905) before coming under more active police control and helping the government to foil numerous further terrorist plots.

Burtsev began to make informal accusations against Azef in spring 1907. A year later he unmasked M.A. Kensitsky and N.P. Starodvorsky. The Socialist Revolutionary leadership remained skeptical especially when Burtsev refused to divulge the sources of his suspicions. The Russian government pressured France to expel

Burtsev and Bakai but to no avail. Public opinion now supported their crusade against the Russian police apparatus.

To convince Azef's party comrades of his treason toward them, Burtsev needed convincing proof. After all, most Socialist Revolutionaries adulated Azef, despite his somewhat repulsive appearance and manner, as a brilliant terrorist mastermind. A.A. Lopukhin, Police Department director from 1902 to 1905, provided the expert testimony that sealed the double-agent's fate. Lopukhin resented his dismissal following the assassination of Grand Duke Sergei and, supposedly shocked to learn from Burtsev during a trip to Germany about Azef's role in that event, confirmed that he was indeed a police agent. More important was Lopukhin's reiteration of everything he knew about Azef to Socialist Revolutionary Party leaders in St. Petersburg and London in November and December 1908. They denounced Azef in January 1909, causing a major scandal in Russia and abroad.

During the next several months with the assistance of Bakai and L.P. Menshchikov, another turncoat police official, Burtsev unmasked several other police informants, including M.Ya. Tsikhotskaia, M.I. Deev, Z.F. Gerngross-Zhuchenko, and A.E. Serebriakova. He also denounced an erstwhile informant, then in charge of the Russian government's security police outpost in Paris, A.M. Garting, who was forced to flee the country. Burtsev also wrote numerous letters, copies of which he often published, to senior officials in Russia, members of the Duma, public figures, and even to Nicholas himself, decrying the use of police informants.

Many of the Russian revolutionary activists did not applaud Burtsev's anti-informant crusade. Aside from the fact that some of his targets faced violent interrogation at the hands of their comrades, three revolutionary activists, E.M. Lapina, Ya.F. Berdo, and V.M. Kamorsky, killed themselves when they fell under false suspicions of serving the police. The larger problem for Russia's revolutionaries was that Burtsev seemed to carry out his crusade as a man possessed, without regard to whether he was advancing the revolutionary cause or not. V.N. Figner complained that he sowed suspicion and loathing among revolutionary activists. Burtsev's campaign demoralized the Socialist Revolutionary Party and called into question its very purpose, especially its commitment to centralized political terrorism.

When the world war broke out, Burtsev abandoned his antigovernment struggle and returned to Russia. Arrested upon entering the country in August, he was exiled to Siberia, then amnestied in late 1915. He settled in Petrograd under close police surveillance. After the February Revolution he interrogated former police officials and resumed publication of Byloe and Obshchee delo. In summer 1917 he agitated against the Bolsheviks and advocated the replacement of A.F. Kerensky by L.G. Kornilov. When the Bolsheviks came to power, they immediately arrested Burtsev and placed him in prison, where he played cards with former police officials. Liberated in February 1918, he emigrated and resumed his publishing activities, now directed against the Bolshevik government. He also waged a campaign against Bolshevik secret agents in Europe. He spent his final years in poverty in Paris and died of blood poisoning.

Bibliography: Burtsev's main autobiographic work is *Bor'ba za svobodnuiu Rossiiu. Moi vospominaniia, 1882-1924 gg.*, 2 vols. (Berlin, 1924). On Burtsev, see Nurit Schleifmann, "The Okhrana and Burtsev. Provocateurs and Revolutionaries," *Survey*, Vol. 27 (1983), 22-40, and N.A. Sidorov and L.I. Tiutiunnik, "V.L. Burtsev i rossiiskoe osvoboditel'noe dvizhenie (po materialam TsGAOR SSSR i TsPA IML pri TsK KPSS)," *Sovetskie arkhivy*, No. 2 (1989), 56-62.

Jonathan W. Daly

BUTLEROV, ALEKSANDR MIKHAILOVICH (1828-1886). Chemist and educator. See Butlerov, Aleksandr Mikhailovich, MERSH, Vol. 6.

Additional bibliography: A.M. Butlerov, *Sochineniia*, 3 vols. (M., 1953-1958), *Nauchnaia i pedagogicheskaia deiatel'nost'* (M., 1961); Nathan M. Brooks, "Alexander Butlerov and the Professionalization of Science in Russia," *Russian Review*, Vol. 57 (1998), 10-24; Alan J. Rocke, "Kekulé, Butlerov, and the Historiography of Chemical Structure," *British Journal for the History of Science*, Vol. 14 (1981), 27-57.

BUZA, YELISEI (?-1642?). Cossack corporal, explorer.

Buza was dispatched from Yeniseisk in 1636 with orders to explore all rivers flowing into the Arctic Ocean and to impose fur tribute (yasak) on the tribes living near the shores. He at first had only about ten companions but after wintering at the Olekminsk fort (ostrog) was joined by another thirty or so. In the spring of 1637 he set off with them and in two weeks reached the mouth of the Lena River. From there in a single day he reached the mouth of the Olenek River, up which he rowed until he found Tungus camps. He remained among the Tungus throughout the winter of 1637 and collected furs from them. In the spring of 1638 Buza and his men set off across land to the Lena, reaching it at the confluence with the Moloda River. There they built two boats and sailed back to the ocean. After five days on the Arctic they found the mouth of the Yana, which they proceeded up until they found Yakut encampments. They spent the winter collecting fur tribute among the Yakuts and in 1639, when the river ice broke up, returned down the Yana. At the mouth of the river they encountered a Yukagir shaman who guided them to Yukagir lands. Buza and his men imposed the fur tribute upon the Yukagirs and lived with them for the next three years. In 1642 Buza sent a Cossack back to Yakutsk with the furs they had collected and later returned himself to report, among other things, on the large deposits of silver ore in the areas he had explored. About the further fate of Buza, as is true of most seventeenth-century explorers and yasak collectors, nothing more is known.

Bibliography: D. Sadovnikov, *Nashi zemleprokhodtsy* (M., 1874); "K russkoi istoriografii. Gerard Miller i ego otnosheniia k pervoistochnikam," *Bibliograf*, No. 1 (1889), 1-11; "Rasprosnye rechi eniseiskogo sluzhilogo cheloveka P.L. Kozlova ot 17 sentiabria 1640 goda o pokhodakh Eliseia Buzy," *Dopolneniia k aktam istoricheskim*, Vol. 11, No. 86 (1886); N.N. Ogloblin, "Vostochno-sibirskie poliarnye morekhody," *Zhurnal Ministerstva Prosveshcheniia*, No. 5 (1903), 38-62.

BYZANTINE POLITICAL THEORY. Thought about the nature of the state in the Christian Roman Empire of the East.

When the Roman Empire became a Christian state, Roman political ideas were recast in a Christian mode. Because Christians believed that history was the unfolding of God's plan, early Christians viewed the Roman Empire as created specifically to unify the Mediterranean world so that the Gospel could be preached more effectively. The conversion of the Roman emperor Constantine the Great to Christianity (c. 312) was seen as the next step in sanctifying the world. The new Christian Roman, or Byzantine, Empire, was conceived as the physical counterpart of the Christian church, the body, as it were, of which the soul was the church. The state's existence was justified by its role as protector of the church, the Christian community that was seen as essentially coextensive with the empire. Church and empire were assumed to have the same membership and the same goal, saving souls. The head of the empire was the emperor appointed by God, a fact proven by his acceptance as ruler by the church, the people of God. In the pagan Roman Empire the emperor held his positon by the consent of the army and the Senate representing the populace. In the Christian Byzantine Empire he held his post by the consent of the church, which was seen as representing the empire's citizenry.

The Christian Byzantine emperor was an autocrat. All political power in the state was his, and the only power government officials exercised was that delegated by the emperor. The emperor was not a tyrant free to do anything he chose. He had to behave as a Christian emperor or he would be thought to have lost God's mandate and would risk being replaced. Theodor Mommsen, the eminent historian and legal theorist, correctly described this system as "an autocracy tempered by the legal right of revolution." If an emperor were toppled, it was a sign that God transferred his support to the new ruler. A coup was deemed successful if the church agreed to crown the new claimant to the throne, thus proving God chose him to replace the previous ruler. In most cases the throne passed from father to son in recognizable dynasties with the successor being crowned as co-ruler in his father's lifetime.

The relationship between church and state in the Byzantine Empire is often described as caesaropapism, a system in which the state dominates the religion. But this description is only an unsuccessful attempt to distinguish the Byzantine church-state relationship from the system that prevailed in the medieval West where the pope claimed dominion over civil rulers. In fact the Byzantine ideal was one that Byzantine thinkers described as symphony, a relationship where church and state worked together because they had the same constituency and the same goals. Both institutions were mandated to create an approximation of the Kingdom of Heaven here on earth. Thus the state supported the church financially and geared its policies to spread the influence of Christianity in and beyond the empire. The church in turn preached the divine appointment of the emperor and the duty of Christians to be loyal and patriotic citizens. The reality did not always live up to the ideal. Emperors were able, for example, to call church councils and try to dictate their decisions for political purposes. They could not, however, force the members of the church to accept such decisions. In the long run it appears that the church had more staying power and eventually won in such conflicts. The emperor could appoint bishops but he had great difficulty in removing them. The church after all had the powerful weapon of excommunication from the church to wield, and an excommunicated emperor was seen as having lost his God-given right to rule.

The Byzantine emperor was in several ways a sacred figure. By the late fifth century emperors must be crowned by the patriarch of Constantinople, the head of the church in the empire, to be recognized as legitimate. At first the ceremony was a simple reenactment of the traditional Roman acclamation by the people, but soon the ritual developed into an ecclesiastical ceremony that looked very much like a clerical ordination rite. Indeed, the emperor had some rights normally restricted to the clergy, such as taking communion in the sanctuary and incensing the altar on special occasions. His ceremonial robes served as models for clerical vestments, and ecclesiastical ceremonies were inspired by imperial ceremonial, further confusing the distinction between religious and imperial power. In a society where reality was seen as a copy of ideal forms, where people viewed the Christian empire as a pale earthly copy of the Kingdom of Heaven, the emperor was viewed as occupying the place in this world that God occupied in heaven. He was a sacred autocrat and sometimes was depicted with a halo.

The Byzantine conception of the emperor enunciated by the church was of no immediate concern in Kievan Rus. The emperor was far away and of little concern to the people of Rus except as a religious figure. As God's viceroy on earth he was respected, but in the Kievan polity he had little political role to play except as patron of the Orthodox Church. The political system dominant in Rus in this period was decentralized and based on a traditional brother-to-brother succession, a far cry from the centralized dynastic monarchical system of the Byzantine Empire. Although Kievan Rus was in no real sense a vassal state to the Byzantine Empire, the leading princes carried the honorary title of archon, the designation of provincial governors in the Byzantine Empire. They put that title on their Greek seals, and Grand Prince Yaroslav the Wise of Kiev (r. 1019-1054) was depicted in the Byzantine court costume of an archon in a highly visible fresco in the Cathedral of St. Sophia in Kiev that he founded. Still, Byzantine religious tracts such as those in the Izbornik (Miscellany) of 1076, which were originally addressed to an emperor, were readdressed to Rus princes in Slavic translation, acknowledging the independent status of the Rus princes.

The concept of a sacred Orthodox emperor in Byzantium was kept alive by the church during the period of Mongol rule in Russia (c. 1240-c. 1380) and evoked considerable interest during the reign of Ivan III "the Great" of Moscow (r. 1462-1505), whose second wife was the niece of the last Byzantine emperor. No longer subservient to the Mongol emperor the centralizing grand prince of Moscow began to adopt the trappings of the Byzantine emperors, for the Byzantine Empire was conquered by the Turks in 1453 leaving the Orthodox Church without its traditional protector. Doubtless it was pointed out to the grand prince, who now styled himself tsar (caesar, emperor), that a few generations earlier a patriarch of Constantinople had warned a Muscovite prince that one could not have the church without an emperor. Because there was no longer a Byzantine emperor in Constantinople, Ivan, now an independent Orthodox ruler, assumed the mantle of protector of the church with the title of emperor. He introduced Byzantine court ritual into the Kremlin and even used the Byzantine imperial coronation ceremony for a co-ruler to appoint his grandson as his successor.

The full flowering of Byzantine political ideology in Muscovy occurred during the reign of Ivan IV "the Terrible" (r. 1533-1584). Under the tutelage of Metropolitan Makary of Moscow, Ivan was crowned by the metropolitan with the full ritual of a Byzantine imperial coronation. Various grand princely robes were assimilated to elements of Byzantine imperial costume, and Ivan IV was designated tsar and samoderzhets (emperor and autocrat) and began to employ the prerogatives of a Byzantine emperor. For example, he called councils of the Russian church and took upon himself the imperial task of announcing and enforcing their decisions. Judging from his correspondence with Prince Andrei Kurbsky, Ivan clearly saw himself as the successor to the Byzantine emperor as God-appointed moderator of the Orthodox Church. A whole cluster of literary works grew up expressing similar ideas and creating a mythic justification for the Russian rulers' imperial status and for Moscow being the Third Rome, the successor to the Orthodox empire of Byzantium.

Bibliography: Francis Dvornik, *Early Christian and Byzantine Political Philosophy*, 2 vols. (Washington, 1966), particularly Vol. 2; Gilbert Dagron, *Empereur et prêtre. Étude sur le césaropapisme byzantin* (Paris, 1995); Francis Dvornik, *Byzantine Political Ideas in Kievan Russia*, Dumbarton Oaks Papers, Vols. 9-10 (1956), 73-121; William K. Medlin, *Moscow and East Rome* (Geneva, 1952).

George P. Majeska

BYZANTINE WINE AND OLIVE OIL IN KIEVAN RUS. Wine was far more prevalent in the everyday life of the Middle Ages than it is today. Wine was needed for sacramental purposes as well as for everyday drinking. In medieval times wine was consumed by most Europeans, from peasants to monks, princes and bishops. Because water in the Middle Ages was often polluted and therefore undrinkable, people drank other beverages, including wine, to quench their thirst. The church also required significant quantities of wine for its liturgy. Aside from religious, recreational, and everyday drinking, wine was used as medicine. Grape extract and wine were made into vinegar, which was used in cooking as well as for medicinal purposes.

While the export of Byzantine wine and oil to foreign lands was prohibited by the late ninth-century Byzantine law code, the Basilika, which reiterated the same prohibition set in the late sixth-century Codex Justinianus, Greek wine and oil flowed freely to the lands of Kievan Rus from the late tenth to the mid-thirteenth centuries. The Russian Primary Chronicle recorded that already in the early tenth century Grand Prince Oleg brought wine back to Kiev from Constantinople. The Rus-Byzantine treaty of 907 indicates that Rus merchants staying in Constantinople were entitled to a six-month's supply of various foodstuffs as well as wine. When Grand Prince Sviatoslav contemplated moving his capital from Kiev to Pereiaslavets on the lower Danube, he argued that all the riches of his realm were concentrated there. In enumerating these riches, Sviatoslav specifically mentioned gold, silks, fruits, and wine from Greece. The most famous chronicle episode in reference to wine is Vladimir's reply to the Volga Bulgar embassy which tried to convert him to Islam. When the Grand Prince heard that Islam required abstinence from wine and pork, he supposedly exclaimed, "Drinking is the joy of the Rus. We cannot exist without that pleasure." Grand Prince Vladimir's conversion to Orthodoxy in 988-989 was unquestionably the single most important act that assured the constant flow of Byzantine wine and oil to the Rus lands. After the conversion the Rus found that this religion required the constant import of wine and oil for church services. As the result of the conversion and close trade ties between Kiev and Constantinople, which dated to c. 900 if not earlier, Byzantium became the main supplier of wine and olive oil to Kievan Rus.

After the conversion Byzantine wine was to be found throughout the Rus lands. Wine was provided by the princes to the needy in Rus towns. One text notes that Grand Prince Vladimir I distributed "bread, vegetables, honey, wine" and other necessities to the "ill and the poor." Other sources relate that affluent boiars who were patrons of the churches, monasteries, and nunneries in their neighborhoods provided them with wine and oil.

Recreational wine drinking also appears to have been widespread. A number of ecclesiastical sources of the Kievan era condemn excessive wine drinking. One states "For woe unto that city in which the prince is young and loves to drink wine with young councilors to the accompaniment of lyres (gusli)." In the Izbornik (Miscellany) of 1076 the Rus church tried to spell out some precepts for daily living to guide the faithful and especially the ruling circles. According to these precepts drinking wine was perfectly acceptable but should be done in moderation. Various sermons were directed to common people to warn them of the dangers of drinking too much wine and other alcoholic beverages. While sermons contain many rhetorical elements, the fact that some of them were addressed to ordinary people suggests that wine drinking was also well known among the non-elite population of Rus.

Although we find many references to wine and oil in Kievan Rus sources, little written evidence was preserved concerning wine and oil imports to Kievan Rus lands. The finds of amphorae (korchagi), large clay vessels with conical bottoms used to transport and store wine and oil, or their shards during the archaeological excavations of many Kievan Rus sites provide an invaluable supplemental source for the study of the wine and oil trade. These finds make it clear that wine and oil were imported both to the large towns and small hamlets of Rus starting in the late tenth century. By the twelfth century these imports reached significant proportions as many members of the urban elite in almost all the Rus towns had developed a taste for wine. In addition to the secular market the conversion of Vladimir and the spread of Christianity throughout the Rus lands meant that Byzantine and Rus merchants had a growing market for communion wine. To date archaeologists have unearthed shards of amphorae at more than 150 sites of the Kievan era, including towns, settlements, and cemeteries, ranging from Staraia Ladoga in the north and Tmutorokan on the south to Drogichen in the west and Gorodok on the Volga in the east. Because wine and oil were imported from the south, the greatest concentration of amphorae shards occur in southern Rus lands. By far the greatest numbers have been found in Kiev, the richest city in Rus and also one of the main commercial junctions for the transport of wine and oil to other Rus lands.

Large quantities of wine were stored in the dwellings of the Rus elite. Written sources from the Kievan period mention, in passing, the existence of princely wine cellars (medushki). On one campaign in 1146 two Davidovichi princes captured the estate of another prince which had a cellar containing wine and meat. On the same campaign these princes looted eighty amphorae of wine from the cellar of Prince Sviatoslav Olgovich. In the well-known account of the murder of Grand Prince Andrei Bogoliubsky of Suzdalia (c. 1174) the chronicler mentioned that the assassins went into Andrei's wine cellar and "having become drunk with wine, they went to the tent [to kill him]." Written sources leave little doubt that every Rus prince possessed a well-stocked wine cellar. Rus boiars were not to be outdone by princes when it came to the consumption of wine. Some boiars in the Galich lands had so much wine stored on their rural estates that a chronicler commented that the quantity "is scary to imagine." In fact, the boiars consumed so much wine that a much-loved boiar curse was "may he have little wine and oil."

In the southern regions of Kievan Rus amphorae were held in semi-subterranean cellars that had special cells or niches arranged in several parallel rows for the vessels. The relatively dry soil and warm temperatures of the south made cellars possible and necessary. Some of the princely cellars in Rus could hold as many as 120-140 amphorae. Such cellars have been discovered in Liubech and Novgorod-Seversky as well as Kiev. Cellars of individuals of more modest means, like craftsmen or merchants, such as those excavated in Old Riazan and at small villages in the Galich, Smolensk, and Riazan lands, held one or several amphorae. Since many areas of northern Rus, particularly in the northwest, had waterlogged soil, semi-subterranean wine cellars could not be constructed. In Novgorod and in other towns of northwestern Rus, wine was presumably kept above ground in barns or ice houses.

Wine was consumed from a great variety of vessels in Kievan Rus, such as cups and ladles made of wood, silver, copper, or bronze, and other vessels made of precious and semi-precious metals. Bone drinking horns and glass vessels, including wine glasses, beakers, goblets were common. The best collection of wooden vessels apparently used for wine comes from Novgorod. Since these were the cheapest vessels, they were probably most popular among the lower classes. Among elite wine drinkers glass containers were most common vessels. A great many of these containers and their fragments have been discovered in towns and settlements throughout the Rus lands.

Based on the evidence of later medieval written sources and specific types of amphorae, it appears that the production centers of nine-tenths of all amphorae found in the Rus lands were the Byzantine territories of northern Anatolia (Trebizond) and the southern coast of the Sea of Marmora (Triglia). These two areas provided most of the wine that was imported to Kievan Rus. Amphorae found in Novgorod and Novogrudok suggest that the largest exporter of wine to Rus during the Kievan period was Trebizond and its adjacent regions. Until the end of the eleventh century Trebizond and Triglian wines were shipped to Novgorod either in equal quantities or the latter dominated over the former. From the turn of the twelfth century wine imports from Triglia declined to very insignificant levels, as compared to the wine brought from Trebizond. The significant decrease in the number of amphorae brought from the area of the southern coast of the Sea of Marmora is quite logically connected with the defeats of the Byzantines by the Seljuks in the last half of the eleventh century. After the Byzantine defeat trade between the Sea of Marmora and Kievan Rus greatly declined. Since Trebizond remained loyal to Constantinople, its wine and oil trade with the north continued unmolested. Wine from Triglia disappeared from Novgorod after c. 1200 or about the time that Constantinople and the Byzantine Empire fell to Latin domination in 1204. Trebizond wine continued to be imported north into the Rus lands until the Mongol conquest.

In the eastern Mediterranean and Black Sea regions amphorae were used up to the fourteenth century when they were replaced by wooden barrels or casks (Italian voutsia, botte) which were faster, easier, and safer to handle and transport. When the trade of wine and oil came under the control of Italian merchants by the 1310s-1340s, these two commodities were increasingly sold in barrels throughout the eastern Mediterranean and the Black Sea regions. Amphorae disappeared from Cyprus, Rhodes, Tana, Caffa, Constantinople, Acre, and other cities. It has been suggested that the decline in the use of the amphora as a transport vessel was directly linked with the diminishing size of the Byzantine Empire, the limitations of the Byzantine maritime trade, the demise of the ancient centers of amphorae production, such as Egypt and Palestine, and the loss of trade to the Venetians and the Genoese who used wooden casks for transporting wine and oil. It is very likely that during the Mongol period Byzantine wine still was imported to the Rus lands but in wooden barrels which are much more difficult to trace archaeologically.

Unfortunately, until the thirteenth and fourteenth centuries literary sources do not contain information about the merchants who brought wine to the Rus lands, and the nationality of the merchants trading Byzantine wine during earlier periods is open to speculation. Since the Italians were granted special privileges in the wine trade by the Byzantines during the second half of the thirteenth century, it can be concluded that until then Greeks acted as the main, if not sole, merchants for Byzantine wine. The presence of Greek graffiti on some amphorae found in the eastern Mediterranean and the Black Sea regions as well as in Kievan Rus suggest that the wine trade was in the hands of Byzantine merchants. However, the finds of graffiti written in Old Rus or Old Church Slavonic on some Byzantine amphorae unearthed in the Rus lands suggest that some of the wine trade also was handled by Rus merchants. For instance, one amphora dating to the second-half of the twelfth century found in old Riazan is inscribed "New good wine sent to the prince [by] Bogunko." Similarly, an amphora shard dating to the Kievan period, found at a small Rus settlement along the Sula River, read "Prokupov's amphora (korchaga)." It is quite likely that Greek wine was imported by Byzantine merchants to various ports of call on the Crimea and the Taman Peninsula from wine producing areas such as Trebizond, as it was in the fourteenth and fifteenth centuries by Italian merchants. Thereafter wine was shipped further north by Rus merchants who labeled their amphorae with their names and in some cases indicated to whom the wine was destined to be sent or sold. The merchants carried wine and oil north from the Black Sea coast in river boats and perhaps also in carts. Ships were obviously preferred if they were available, since water transport was by far the cheapest and easiest.

Olive oil had even more uses than wine in the Middle Ages. It was used in cooking, medicine, anointing during religious services, lighting, and in Kievan Rus olive oil was melted together with amber to make a shellacking agent or olifa used in icon painting and jewelry-working. Consequently the commerce in olive oil also played a significant role in Byzantine-Rus economic relations. Various Kievan Rus prayer books and sermons speak about the use of olive oil for religious purposes. Some passages refer to the healing of the sick by anointing with olive oil. The Tale of the Miracles of Roman and David contains the following passage: "When he heard this, Lazor bade her [the sick woman] stand before the church doors during the liturgy, so that when they finished singing they would pray for her and anoint her with olive oil." The Kievan Caves' Paterik states, "And whenever anyone brought in a child with some illness, people would bring the child to the monastery to the venerable Feodosy, who would order Demian to say a prayer over the sick person. He at once would do so and anoint him with holy oil (maslom sviatym), and those who came to him were healed." Olive oil also was used in lamps. The Paterik clearly states that the only proper oil for lamps was olive oil, since flaxseed oil was considered improper.

Wine and olive oil constituted major components of the Byzantine-Rus trade during the Kievan era. Both commodities were used in religious services and in various other functions. It is quite possible that the Byzantine restrictions on the export of their wine and oil were lifted once Rus converted to Christianity. In other words, once Rus became a part of the so-called Byzantine commonwealth after 989-999, the Byzantines opened their markets in these commodities to the Rus. From that moment to the end of the Kievan era wine and oil were some of the most important items of Byzantine trade with Kievan Rus.

Bibliography: T.S. Noonan and R.K. Kovalev, "Prayer, Illumination, and Good Times. The Export of Byzantine Wine and Oil to the North of Russia in Pre-Mongol

Times," *Byzantium and the North. Acta Byzantina Fennica*, Vol. 8, 1995-1996 (1997), 73-96, "Wine and Oil For All the Rus'! The Import of Byzantine Wine and Oil to Kievan Rus'," *Byzantium and the North. Acta Byzantina Fennica*, Vol. 9, 1997-1998 (1999), 87-121; I.V. Volkov, "Importnaia amfornaia tara zolotoordyn-skogo goroda Azaka," *Severnoe Prichernomor'e i Povolzh'e vo vzaimootnosheniiakh Vostoka i Zapada v XII-XVI vekakh* (Rostov-on-Don, 1989), 85-100, "O proiskhozh-denii i evoliutsii nekotorykh tipov srednevekovykh amfor," *Donskie drevnosti*, Vol. 1 (Azov, 1992), 143-156, "Import iz Sviatoi Zemli? (Amfory gruppy kleima SSS v Prichernomor'e i gorodakh drevnei Rusi)," *Problemy istorii* (Rostov-on-Don, 1994), 3-8, "Amfory Novgoroda Velikogo i nekotorye zametki o vizantiisko-russkoi torgovle vinom," *Novgorod i Novgorodskaia zemlia*, Vol. 10 (Novgorod, 1996), 90-103; R.L. Rozenfel'dt, "Privoznaia keramika. Amfory i krasnoglinianye kuvshiny," *Drevniaia Rus'. Byt i kul'tura*, ed. by B.A. Kolchin and T.I. Makarova (M., 1997), 33-36.

Roman K. Kovalev

C

CABARET. Minor, multigeneric theatrical entertainment in modern Russia.

Dictionaries of the Soviet period often defined cabarets as restaurants with a small stage, or èstrada, in bourgeois countries. This attitude characterizes the shifting fate of cabaret in Russia, a competition between the supposed profiteering of minor, eclectic art forms and the grand, more honorable plans of equally grand stages. The mixed fortunes of cabaret begin at the very start of the twentieth century, when this evidently foreign endeavor coincided with the recent commercialization of native performance, the gypsy singers and circus artistes who came increasingly to urban fairs and summer restaurants with romances or choral numbers. This contest and combination of styles took place in St. Petersburg and Moscow, in the gray area between established or regally endorsed drama and a more spontaneous, amorphous mode of performance.

In 1908 a business opened in St. Petersburg with the name The Crooked Mirror (Krivoe zerkalo), replacing an unprofitable casino that previously occupied the premises. The cabaret's emphasis was to be on small, multiple presentations with a particular leaning towards satire in either musical or literary form. Given the social atmosphere of impending unrest in Russia at this time, many spoofs were directed against contemporary excess, such as ostentatious opera or the failings of a self-assured upper class.

After a couple of years success allowed the Crooked Mirror to embrace both bigger premises and a new director, Nikolai Nikolaevich Evreinov (1879-1953). Keen to dissolve the rather haughty distance between play and parterre, Evreinov offered his audiences maximum emotional involvement in all productions, so they would pass through the same experiential states as the actor, resulting in a unified monodrama. Actors often left the confines of the stage, and lighting or sound effects ignored the fourth wall, or footlights. This led to other, equally democratic projects, such as scenes from Gogol's Government Inspector, presented according to five different directorial theories, including fashionable silent cinema without any text whatsoever. With his colleague Boris Fedorovich Geier (1876-1916) Evreinov produced irreverent shows, including a love story as it might have been treated by four classic Russian playwrights.

Besides mockery of fashionable aesthetics such as decadent prose, modern philosophies and social fads like psychoanalysis also became caricatured travesties. Since these performances were couched in dramatic forms, they were both implicit and explicit challenges to the more imposing projects of Konstantin Sergeevich Stanislavsky (1863-1938) and Vsevolod Emilievich Meierkhold (1874-1940).

At the same time more literary accents were evident at The Bat (Letuchaia mysh), which originated as tomfoolery among actors from the Moscow Art Theater and opened in 1910. These get-togethers, which included Chekhov's wife, continued a domestic tradition of cabbage parties (kapustniki, pl.), a type of miniature Mardi Gras prior to the closure of theaters during Lent. Using ridicule and burlesque, personified puppets and shadow play, the Bat's synthesizing goals overlapped with the World of Art movement, which hoped to amalgamate more serious art forms. Under this influence cabaret slowly grew into a more elaborate, yet stylistically coherent event, a so-called Theater of Miniatures that paid enormous attention to decoration, interior and costume design. Song and extremely lavish costumes were notably preserved in marionette performances, in which actors and actresses dressed as tableaux vivants or toys would come alive for the time of their number, then lapse back into silent inanimacy. There are parallels here with commedia dell'arte personae that were so important for later performers such as Aleksandr Nikolaevich Vertinsky (1889-1957).

The manager of The Bat, Nikita Fedorovich Baliev (1877-1936), originally ran this thespian operation from a central Moscow cellar to which classical actors would descend, still in makeup for a late evening's misconduct. Matters went so well that Baliev left his job as a minor actor in the Art Theater and became compère of The Bat, where he enjoyed infinitely more success. He became such a celebrity that people expected to see him at the entrance to the club in formal attire, asking all customers to sign a register.

Perhaps the most famous Russian cabaret of all, The Stray Dog (Brodiachaia sobaka), opened its doors in St. Petersburg on the last day of 1911 and was soon guided to great accomplishment by compère Boris Konstantinovich Pronin (1875-1946). Here the influence of serious art was even more evident, as poets like Osip Mandelshtam, Vladimir Maiakovsky, Nikolai Gumilev, Velimir Khlebnikov, Anna Akhmatova, and Mikhail Kuzmin made regular appearances. The inclusive, accepting atmosphere of early cabarets fell often to snobbery and elitism in this nightspot, something Pronin did little to discourage. He charged less fashionable clients an exorbitant entrance fee. The club remained in business until 1916, when it was replaced by The Comedians' Respite (Prival komediantov) under the guidance of Pronin, Meierkhold and Sergei Yurievich Sudeikin (1882-1946).

The revolution also led to the closure after a few years of both The Bat and The Crooked Mirror. The former organization tried to relocate in Paris, as Chauve Souris, and many other key cabaret directors avoided trouble by moving south, to Kiev or Odessa. Baliev, taking The Bat westwards in 1920, was able for a while to entertain émigrés while increasing the amount of French-language material for local audiences. He even took the company to the United States in 1922, raising money for the new Soviet homeless with help from Al Jolson and Charlie Chaplin.

It was only during the New Economic Policy that cabaret reappeared with enthusiasm, profit and freedom. Evreinov returned, restaging a lot of his pre-revolutionary works in Moscow. Futurist poets, such as Maiakovsky, also worked from the small stage and grew fond of its confrontational immediacy. Viktor Borisovich Shklovsky (1893-1984) gave a key speech on futurism and new Soviet society in the Stray Dog, then civil war scattered cabaret performers nationwide. Warfare produced a need for mobility. Several thousand tiny troupes traveled endlessly, using satire to mock the outgoing regime and promote social renovation. The most famous of these groups was The Blue Blouse (Siniaia bluza), which performed skits, choreography, and news items.

As cabaret evanesced in the 1930s, it grew into a new form known as èstrada, a term taken from the French or Spanish for small stage. Here the Soviet regime endorsed a rubric to encompass satire, popular song, puppetry, circus acts, dancing, comedy and other minor genres. The Crooked Mirror may have been able to reopen in the mid-1920s at a different address and exist thanks to NEP until the early 1930s, but it quickly became a victim of intolerance of commerce. Comedy skits remained a major part of Soviet life when compères left for Paris, and witty, now politicized cabaret was centralized in the Moscow Theater of Satire. Spoofs developed most famously in the work of Arkady Isaakovich Raikin (1911-1987). Raised in Riga and educated in Leningrad, Raikin began his career as a compère for puppet shows, with work in circuses, theatrical miniatures, parodies and pantomimes, before winning the comedy section of the First All-Union Variety Competition in 1939. Often compared to Charlie Chaplin, his theatrical endeavors became famous nationwide, at which point the small dimensions of erstwhile cabaret and stand-up routines became the broader sweep of cinema. Raikin made his first feature film as leading man in 1954 in We Met Somewhere (My s vami gde-to vstrechalis), but even that was designed as a series of sketches, strung together as memories of a holiday in the south.

Soviet historians found the rasion d'être of new socialist light entertainment no longer within four decorated walls, nor as mockery of splendid imperial artistry. Scholars instead drew endless parallels with both the small, nomadic art forms of folk art, while discerning the usefulness of quicker genres in a quickly changing society. Folk performers once were outside society, beyond the dictates of one system, just as èstrada embraced a healthily inconstant aesthetic. A compère still held these fragments together, and here at least the Soviets gratefully acknowledged the heritage of Baliev. Rather than draw a direct parallel with cabaret Soviet èstrada became canonized within the healthier, affirmative and multigeneric traditions of the circus. The compère became a ringmaster. Like the circus, which is both unified and offered directly to the audience by a ringmaster, èstrada's compère created a meaningful whole from the initially disparate acts and intentions of any show. He also exemplified the civilizing, audience-oriented nature of the performance, as opposed to the voyeuristic stance of a typical theater audience.

Cabarets became the bigger Theaters of Estrada or music halls in Soviet cities including Moscow, Leningrad, Gorky, Rostov-on-Don, and Taganrog, yet even they suffered problems sometimes. The capital's music hall opened in 1926 and for ten years until its closure, when it was handed over to a folk troupe, it offered variety shows, unified both ideologically and aesthetically by a resident company. One of its last artistic directors strove to separate èstrada from the classical, purer genres by insisting upon a synthetic aesthetic, mixing drama, opera, ballet, operetta, songs, and circus, but the Kremlin was unimpressed. Despite being a generous sponsor for an entire decade the state began asking whether even èstrada was unavoidably bourgeois and fit for extinction, natural or otherwise. The often grotesque or foreign nature of lighter genres was very much at odds with the officially endorsed aesthetic of socialist realism. The Moscow Music Hall closed, and Leningrad's equivalent suffered the same fate. The Moscow Theater of Satire, in fact, was tellingly housed in a building that beforehand was first a circus, then a music hall, and finally an operetta theater.

Even outside such establishments erstwhile cabaret artists often suffered. Given the new, grandiose leanings of Stalinist art after the 1920s, the subjective interpretation of satire or love songs was outmoded, to say the least. Singers moved into the genre of non-satirical feuilletons for the sake of safe, political clarity and a more meaningful content. Others organized or conducted èstrada orchestras. A few tried to stay true to their earlier songs, yet they could only do so by occasionally adopting an oratorical air or makeshift sycophancy.

Variety and cabaret traditions decreased in number, affected principally by the formation in 1931 of the State Union of Music, Estrada and Circus. In an initial survey the organization found that the standards of these artists left much to be desired and so a call went out to the Writers' Union to help them out of their artistic doldrums. Even in 1940, when a large state exhibition was staged to celebrate the goals of Soviet variety, doubts persisted as to its applicability for society.

It was the Second World War that brought the greatest return of cabaret variety to Soviet society, just as it survived by abandoning its location in one particular place during the civil war. The years of international conflict required enormous enterprise from the people of the small stage. Between 1941 and 1945 èstrada singers, musicians, jugglers, puppeteers, and story-tellers gave 1,350,000 concerts, more than 473,000 of them dangerously close to the front. More than a thousand èstradniki were subsequently awarded medals, twelve of them became Heroes of the Soviet Union. Even the Red Army itself formed a song and dance ensemble within weeks of the German invasion.

To take short, witty acts from peacetime into political warfare the piano was replaced at the front with the considerably lighter accordion. Mobility was an extremely good idea, as aerial dogfights were often visible during concerts. The nation's most famous big-band on several occasions threw itself into a ditch to avoid Luftwaffe strafing. Twenty minutes later they would be playing again. In this setting the band lost its prior, stagy grandeur and became wittier once more, a trait seen in many wartime songbooks as a result. Barbed anti-fascist stanzas employed a frontline drollness that allowed musicians like Leonid Osipovich Utesov (1895-1982) to move easily from peacetime to wartime, to avoid ideology, and still meet with state approval.

There was always an antipathy in the Soviet Union towards cabaret's significance. Èstrada emphasized song, comedy, and a civic spirit more than the sarcastic, high-art elitism ultimately adopted by The Stray Dog. Soviet television after Stalin's death often included long-legged, sequined foreign dancers in its depictions of cabaret. The word cabaret kept its veneer of restaurants and foreign business. Published for the first time at the start of the twenty-first century, Communist Party rulebooks for Soviet diplomats or trade delegates stated it was explicitly forbidden to visit cabarets or brothels, to receive mail from an individual, or to take nocturnal walks without official accompaniment. The awkward significance of cabaret traditions during the Gorbachev-era glasnost was already just as manifest in problems concerning the word "variete" or variety. The term èstrada can be translated as post-cabaret variety, but after perestroika the latter often meant small-scale, nightclub, casino or restaurant performance. Performers were loath to associate themselves with variety or cabaret more than with èstrada, because of the connotations of commercialism and foreign triviality.

Performers in more liberal, popular parts of the Soviet Union such as the Baltic region were happier cultivating this new cabaret atmosphere and seeing more vacationers who desired a lounge or dinner-theater mélange. The singer, dancer, and actress Laima Vaikule (1954-) began her work in Riga cabarets and hotel lounges in the 1980s with songs by Raimond Voldemarovich Pauls (1936-), and the two of them fought hard in the Soviet press to defend variete against accusations. When hard liquor was very cheap and very available under Brezhnev, inexpensive restaurants in Latvia were some of the few places where decadent, multigeneric variete could be seen. Neo-cabaret had a very hard time shaking a reputation of frivolity and tipsiness.

This prejudice persisted. In the early 1990s, as artists traveled to America, they were disappointed to find themselves playing in nothing more than émigré restaurants and surrounded by alcohol. Disillusionment was hidden by loud expressions of feigned indifference. It was only later in the decade in Moscow and St. Petersburg that the sung, choreographed, and dramatized traditions of cabaret came back from exile amid separated, Soviet rubrics or canons and even opened in old premises with their old names once more.

Bibliography: Sharon M. Carnicke, *The Theatrical Instinct* (New York, 1989); B. Henry, *Theatrical Parody at the Krivoe Zerkalo* (Ph.D. diss., Oxford, 1997); R. Russell and A. Barratt, eds., Russian Th*eatre in the Age of Modernism* (Houndmills, 1990); Harold B. Segel, *Turn-of-the-Century Cabaret* (New York, 1987), "Russian Cabaret in a European Context" in Lars Kleberg and Nils Ake Nilsson, eds., *Theater and Literature in Russia, 1900-1930* (Stockholm, 1984); Laurence Senelick, *Cabaret Performance,* 2 vols. (Baltimore, Md., 1989-1993); Liudmila Tikhvinskaia, *Kabare i teatry miniatiur v Rossii, 1908-1917* (M., 1997); Elizaveta D. Uvarova, ed., *Russkaia sovetskaia èstrada, 1917-1929* (M., 1976).

David MacFadyen

CABINET OF MINISTERS (1731-1742). A small council active during the reign of Empress Anna Ivanovna and the regencies that immediately followed her death in October 1741.

Formally created by Empress Anna's decree of 18 October 1731, the Cabinet of Ministers arose from a kind of kitchen cabinet or grouping of high-ranking statesmen. It existed to advise the newly enthroned empress who had little experience in administrative affairs, especially as concerned Russian high politics and policy-making. Although Anna tore up the restrictive Conditions formulated by the Supreme Privy Council and declared restoration of autocracy (samoderzhavie), she obviously needed elite assistance in the actual business of governing. Hence the cabinet, a new foreign term in Russian administrative terminology, resembled in its early years the Supreme Privy Council without the latter's discredited name. That is, the cabinet was not supposed to limit the empress's absolute authority, but simply provide her with advice and assistance as required. At first it comprised veteran statesmen Chancellor Count Gavril Golovkin (1660-1734), Vice-Chancellor Count Andrei Osterman (1686-1747), and Prince Andrei Cherkassky (1680-1742). Later participants included Count Pavel Yaguzhinsky (1683-1736), Artemy Volynsky (1689-1740), Aleksei Bestuzhev-Riumin (1693-1766), Count Burkhard von Münnich (1683-1767), and Count Mikhail Golovkin (1694-1755).

Because the Cabinet of Ministers included prominent statesmen from aristocratic families it immediately assumed some status in assisting the new empress's initiation into myriad duties and concerns. Soon after its formal constitution in 1731 the cabinet seemed to have supplanted the Governing Senate, whose membership drastically contracted, as the empire's highest administrative body. But the cabinet's jurisdiction remained so undefined that soon it was flooded with all kinds of matters important and trivial, and its working membership often shrank to just Osterman and one other. In the early years Anna sometimes issued oral orders to the cabinet, then on 9 June 1735 she issued an imperial decree prohibiting acceptance or execution of oral orders not signed by her imperial majesty or her cabinet ministers, and declaring the signature of three ministers equal to that of the monarch. At the end of 1738 the empress ruled that any documents presented for her signature must be countersigned by the appropriate cabinet minister. In short, it proved difficult to distinguish the autocrat's authority from that of the cabinet, and the cabinet's functions were confused and confusing to monarch and ministers alike. Elizabeth's new government, when confronted with this dilemma, abolished the cabinet on 18 October 1731 as too reminiscent of the Supreme Privy Council and restored the Governing Senate to its former high status.

Bibliography: Evgeny Anisimov, *Empress Elizabeth. Her Reign and Her Russia, 1741-1761,* ed. and trans. by John T. Alexander (Gulf Breeze, Fla.: Academic International Press, 1995); E.V. Anisimov, *Rossiia bez Petra, 1725-1740* (SPb., 1994); A.N. Filippov, *Uchebnik istorii russkogo prava,* 4th ed. (Iurev, 1912), pt. 1; John P. LeDonne, *Absolutism and Ruling Class. The Formation of the Russian Political Order, 1700-1825* (New York, 1991); Brenda Meehan-Waters, *Autocracy and Aristocracy. The Russian Service Elite of 1730* (New Brunswick, N.J., 1982); *Rossiiskaia gosudarstvennost' v terminakh. XI-nachalo XX veka. Slovar'* (M., 2001); George L. Yaney, *The Systematization of Russian Government. Social Evolution in the Domestic Administration of Imperial Russia, 1711-1905* (Urbana, Ill., 1973).

John T. Alexander

CADASTRES IN THE RUSSIAN EMPIRE. Cadastres are lists of surveyed land parcels accompanied by each parcel's taxable value.

Prior to the existence of a regular land market assessors calculated values by capitalizing the average yearly income for a given soil type and a given crop. Assessors generally calculated income by determining the average value of the harvest of a given crop at average market prices for inputs and harvest over a certain number of years. Given the extent of the task and the sparse and unreliable nature of available data, assessors often applied values calculated for several sample parcels to parcels of like soil type and husbandry in a given area. Cadastres became an important tool for emerging absolutist monarchies in the seventeenth century as rulers attempted to roll back encroachments on crown lands and increase revenues by more systematically assessing land taxes. Many Enlightenment thinkers believed cadastres reflected the application of reason to tax collection. They also considered the idea of taxing land based on its productivity, as opposed to persons based on their membership in a given social estate, more just. Given the difficulty and expense of creating a cadastre most European cadastre projects existed mainly on paper. Even the best example of uniting statist and Enlightenment goals, the French cadastre enacted by Napoleon in 1807, took years to complete and contained many imperfections.

Cadastre work within the Russian Empire took place on a number of levels and, like that in the majority of Europe, remained an unsystematic and incomplete affair. On one level, the state enacted a General Survey (generalnoe mezhevanie) in 1765. The main purpose of the General Survey was to delineate the precise boundaries between noble and crown lands and to establish boundaries within the latter between lands assigned the local state and crown peasants. This was especially important in light of Peter III's secularization of church lands in 1762 and Catherine II's subsequent conversion of these lands to state property in 1764. Although the project's main emphasis lay in surveying, officials also used these forays into the provinces to collect a wide variety of data on the well-being and livelihood of local peasants as well as the taxes and dues levied upon them. These data proved useful for future administrators and formed the basis of V.I. Semevsky's classic study of the eighteenth-century peasanty, *Peasants during the Reign of Empress Catherine II* (Krestiane v tsarstvovanii Imperatritsy Ekateriny II, 2 vols., 1901-1903). Although it never covered the entire empire, the General Survey managed to include thirty-four provinces by the time officials brought its work to a close in 1843.

The state carried out more systematic cadastral work in the 1830s and 1840s as part of Count P.D. Kiselev's reform of the state and crown peasantry under the auspices of the Ministry of State Domains. The bulk of this work took place between 1842 and 1856 under the direction of several persons who later played key roles in the Great Reforms, such as Nikolai Miliutin and A.P. Zablotsky-Desiatovsky. Preliminary investigations revealed that, although the state assigned each peasant commune a collective tax burden based on its number of taxable males, communes attached the tax burden to a land allotment of a certain size. When communes repartitioned their land, they also repartitioned tax burdens. Kiselev thus thought it crucial to align taxes with land revenues. He hoped that the survey would allow the state to rationalize and regularize its income from dues and taxes by shifting the tax burden from persons to land and that this in turn would ameliorate the condition of peasants in areas experiencing economic difficulties.

Officials of the ministry's Department of Rural Economy collected data from state peasant communities in twenty-five provinces, classifying land holdings according to soil fertility, calculating the labor necessary for various types of cultivation, and compiling series data on local grain prices. Regional differences in the empire's rural economy stymied official hopes that calculating land income would aid reform efforts. Cadastral measures worked well in fertile black-soil areas but failed in the north and other areas where poor soils prevented land allotments from even feeding individual households. Peasant incomes in such areas were high, however, owing to peasant reliance on cottage industry and wage labor. In these areas the goals of the reform forced officials to collect data on non-agricultural incomes, thereby abandoning plans to base peasant dues on land values. Nonetheless the reforms succeeded in allotting additional land to needy peasant communities and increasing annual state revenues by six million rubles without raising the tax rate. The reform process revealed the limitations of the cadastral process. The Ministry of State Domains continued to conduct cadastral surveys of state and crown lands periodically throughout the nineteenth century but on a selective basis.

The actual value of peasant allotment land became a key issue during the serf emancipation process. The state committed itself to a landed emancipation that would compensate serf owners for the loss of land peasants received as allotments.

This commitment to compensate serf owners at some level which might provide them with capital to intensify production on the remainder of their estates, the inability to provide this compensation from the state treasury because of a banking crisis, and the resultant need to determine how much the peasants would have to pay to redeem their allotments put the question of land values center stage. The fact that the state itself would play the role of banker for the forty-nine year redemption process made its interest in the actual value of the land on which it held mortgages especially great. There were also serf owners sitting on several of the provincial committees who believed that a cadastral assessment would work to their benefit. Because of time constraints and the Ministry of State Domains' earlier experience, officials led by P.P. Semenov-Tian-Shansky dismissed the idea of determining allotment values by cadastral means. The state relied instead on what peasants currently paid, a measure it already knew. Semenov found the lack of relevant information in the emancipation process so troublesome that one of the main projects during his tenure as head of the interior ministry's Central Statistical Committee (CSC) was an inventory of the empire's arable land and its yields (Perepis pozemelnoi sobstvennosti). Provincial statistical committees began collecting and submitting data to the CSC in 1877-1878. The CSC eventually published the results in eight volumes that covered twelve geographic areas of European Russia, excluding the Don Cossack region, throughout the 1880s. The CSC carried out additional surveys in 1887 and 1905.

The empire's zemstvo institutions did extensive and detailed cadastral work from the mid-1870s until the onset of the Great War. When the state created zemstvo institutions in 1864, it also gave them the power to raise money by taxing land, forests, urban real estate, and other types of property according to its value and income. The rules that awarded the right to tax provided no instruction as to how to calculate value and income. Given the lack of specific guidelines, zemstvos used a wide variety of methods to calculate value and assess taxes, most of which worked to the advantage of the local noble landowners who dominated the zemstvos. By the mid- to late1870s a number of zemstvos, most notably those of Chernigov, Moscow, and Tver provinces, were utilizing local land surveys, important data related to soil conditions, production costs, and market prices, and using this information to construct a uniform system of taxation on a cadastral basis.

The process did not take long to become a highly political affair in several ways. Young, populist-minded people comprised the majority of those hired to carry out zemstvo cadastral work. They found such work an ideal opportunity to study the peasantry and the commune. Many also possessed specialized training in current statistical methods from the Law Faculty of Moscow University, where they studied under Professor A.I. Chuprov. When they entered the field, they did so deeply imbued with sympathies for the peasantry and a faith that their task represented an application of science to administration. The thoroughness with which they approached their work soon landed many of them in trouble with their employers. The Kherson, Chernigov, and Riazan zemstvos dramatically closed their statistical bureaus for a period of time when statisticians' field work turned up cases of outright tax evasion by noble landowners or found the local nobility to blame for the poor condition of peasant households.

The most important political issue related to the methods zemstvo statisticians employed to conduct cadastral work. Reflecting an organic view of Russia's rural economy, in line with the German historical school of economics and their own interest in the functioning of the peasant commune, zemstvo statisticians developed a method known as the household inventory (podvornaia perepis). This involved the collection of a wide variety of data for individual peasant households instead of merely collecting data for communes as a whole. This methodological choice earned the ire of some and the praise of others. Some provincial zemstvos, such as Moscow's, gave their statisticians and the heads of their statistical bureaus—for Moscow, V.I. Orlov and N.A. Kablukov—complete methodological freedom. Other zemstvos generally cared little for the method employed but chafed at the time and expense necessary to conduct household inventories. Still others insisted that the household inventory method was unnecessary, as the value of peasant allotment land could be determined simply by collecting data from neighboring noble estates. This was an opinion shared by the interior ministry, which viewed with suspicion the prospect of politically questionable statisticians touring peasant villages. Zemstvo statisticians found the latter method unacceptable because it lumped together peasants and their natural economy with nobles producing for the market. Only a study of peasant conditions of production, they argued, could yield a fair assessment of taxes.

State interest in tax reform, the continued absence of a standardized method for assessing taxes throughout the thirty-four zemstvo provinces, and pressure from the interior ministry led to the convocation of an inter-ministerial commission to review zemstvo taxation procedures. The results of the commission's work were codified by a statute of 8 June 1893 and a set of instructions published in 1894. In the discussions zemstvo statisticians received support from the finance ministry and its head, Sergei Witte. Witte insisted that the new rules require the actual investigation of properties, as opposed to extrapolating land values from data submitted by agents. The rules also legitimated the zemstvos' right to create statistical bureaus and hire statisticians. The interior ministry persisted in its attempts to keep statisticians out of the village by requiring zemstvos to obtain special permission to conduct household inventories (1887) and temporarily banning zemstvo statistical work between 1895 and 1897, ostensibly because of the planned census. The pace of zemstvo assessment work consequently slowed, and this prompted additional state review of assessment procedures. A finding of 1899 led to the contribution of state funds for zemstvo cadastral work.

V.K. Pleve's insistence that statisticians contributed directly to peasant disturbances in Poltava and elsewhere during 1902 resulted in yet another conference and the publication of new instructions in 1905. The new instructions severely curtailed statisticians' ability to conduct household inventories. To cope with these constraints zemstvo statisticians increasingly turned to sampling and compilation of data on peasant budgets. Taken together, the household inventories that characterized zemstvo cadastral work in the 1880s and the budget analyses that dominated zemstvo studies in the empire's last quarter century contributed greatly to the work of the prominent agrarian economist A.V. Chaianov and the organization and production school of economics. These studies also remain a rich source for research on the post-emancipation peasantry.

Bibliography: S.D. Rudin, *Mezhevoe zakonodatel'stvo i deiatel'nost' mezhevoi chasti v Rossii za 150 let, 19 sentiabria 1765 g.-1915 goda* (Pg., 1915); N.M. Druzhinin, *Gosudarstvennye krest'iane i reforma P. D. Kiseleva,* 2 vols. (M., 1958); W. Bruce Lincoln, *In the Vanguard of Reform. Russia's Enlightened Bureaucrats, 1825-1861* (DeKalb, Ill., 1982); Walter M. Pintner, *Russian Economic Policy under Nicholas I* (Ithaca, N.Y., 1967); Rossiia, Ministerstvo Gosudarstvennykh Imushchestv, Departament Sel'skago Khoziaistva, *Khoziaistvenno-statisticheskiia materialy, sobiraemye Kommissiiami i Otriadami uravneniia denezhnykh sborov s gosudarstvennykh krest'ian,* 2 vols. (SPb., 1857), *Istoricheskoe obozrenie piatidesiatiletnei deiatel'nosti Ministerstva Gosudarstvennykh Imushchestv, 1837-1887,* 2 vols. (SPb., 1888); D.A. Tarasiuk, *Pozemel'naia sobstvennost' poreformennoi Rossii. Istochnikovedcheskoe issledovanie po perepisi 1877-1878 gg.* (M., 1981); Rossiia, Tsentral'nyi Statisticheskii Komitet pri Mininsterstve Vnutrennykh Del, *Statistika pozeml'noi sobstvennosti i naselenykh mest Evropeiskoi Rossii po dannym obsledovaniia, proizvedennago statisticheskimi uchrezhdeniiami Ministerstva Vnutrennykh Del, po porucheniiu Statisticheskago Soveta,* 8 vols. (SPb., 1880-1885), *Glavneishiia dannyia pozemel'noi statistiki po obsledovaniiu 1887 goda,* 60 vols. (SPb., 1892-96), *Statistika zemlevladeniia 1905 g.,* 50 vols. (SPb., 1906-1907); A. Polenov, *K voprosu o podatnoi reforme. Obzor system zemskago pozemel'nago oblozheniia, 1865-1879,* 2 vols. (SPb., 1880); V.F. Karavaev, ed., *Bibliograficheskii obzor zemskoi statisticheskoi otsenochnoi literatury so vremeni uchrezhdeniia zemstv,* 2 vols. (SPb., 1906); A.A. Rusov, *Kratkii obzor razvitiia russkoi otsenochnoi statistiki* (Kiev, 1913); N.A. Svavitskii, *Zemskie podvornye perepisi. Obzor metodologii* (M., 1961); Robert E. Johnson, "Liberal Professionals and Professional Liberals. The Zemstvo Statisticians and Their Work" in Terence Emmons and Wayne Vucinich, eds., *The Zemstvo in Russia. An Experiment in Local Self-Government* (Cambridge, 1982); David W. Darrow, "The Politics of Numbers. Zemstvo Land Assessment and the Conceptualization of Russia's Rural Economy," *Russian Review,* Vol. 59 (January 2000), 52-75.

David W. Darrow

CAKSTE, JANIS (1859-1927). Latvian national leader and statesman.

Cakste was born on 14 September 1859 in Lielsesava, Kurland province, into a peasant family. He completed his primary-level education in Jelgava (Mitau), provincial capital of Kurland, and in 1882 he finished the course of studies at Jelgava Gymnasium. Cakste continued his education at Moscow University, where he studied law, graduating in 1886. He then returned to Jelgava, where he was employed for several years within the provincial prosecutor's office before working as a lawyer. He was active in Latvian associational life in Jelgava. Cakste soon expanded his activities to journalism, and from 1888 to 1906 he was publisher and editor of the Latvian newspaper Homeland (Tevija) . He also was elected to the Jelgava city council.

Cakste was elected as a deputy from Kurland province to the first all-Russian State Duma, in which he was associated with the Constitutional Democrats (Kadets). When the Duma was dissolved in July 1906 after being in session less than three months, Cakste was among those liberal and leftist deputies who gathered in the Finnish town of Vyborg to sign a manifesto calling on imperial Russia's citizens to resist the government by not paying taxes or providing army recruits. For this action Cakste was disfranchised and imprisoned for three months, as were the other signatories.

In 1915 Cakste fled the German advance into the Baltic region. In Petrograd he helped found the Latvian Refugees' Committee which, in addition to relief work among Latvian war refugees, pressed for Latvian autonomy. In Stockholm in 1916 Cakste wrote a short book titled *The Latvians and Their Latvia* (Die Letten und ihre Latvija, in German), in which he championed Latvian national autonomy. After the signing of the armistice on 11 November 1918 Latvian political leaders, with the exception of the Latvian Bolsheviks, met in Riga on 17 November 1918 and secretly formed a National Council, which elected Cakste its president. The following day the National Council declared the independent Republic of Latvia. The prime minister of the Latvian provisional government was Karlis Ulmanis, who also was the dominant political figure in interwar Latvia. In January 1919 Cakste was the primary representative from Latvia at the Paris Peace Conference.

Hostilities in Latvian areas did not end until 1920, and in May of that year Cakste was elected president of the Latvian Constitutional Convention. The first Saeima (parliament), convened in 1922, elected him the first president of Latvia. In 1925 the Saeima elected him to a second term. Cakste was a member of the Democratic Center party which, although small, was influential as it was situated between the relatively balanced Latvian political right and left. He remained in office until his death on 14 March 1927.

Bibliography: Alfred Bilmanis, *A History of Latvia* (Princeton, N.J., 1951); Andrejs Plakans, *Historical Dictionary of Latvia* (Lanham, Md., 1997), *The Latvians. A Short History* (Stanford, Cal., 1995); *Gosudarstvennaia Duma pervogo prizyva* (M., 1906); Georg von Rauch, *The Baltic States. The Years of Independence. Estonia, Latvia, Lithuania, 1917-1940* (London, 1974).

Bradley D. Woodworth

CALVINISM IN RUSSIA. The Protestant doctrinal system propounded by John Calvin (1509-1564) and developed by his followers. Calvinism was one of the most important elements of the Reformed or Presbyterian tradition, but it also influenced other Protestant Christians, such as Anglicans and Baptists.

While studying at the universities of Paris and Orleans, John Calvin embraced the Protestant principles of Martin Luther (1483-1546): the supreme authority of the Bible, justification of the sinner by grace through faith, and the priesthood of all believers. Like Luther he rejected indulgences, the cult of the saints, relics, papal claims to universal jurisdiction over the church, and the Catholic theology of the Eucharist. At the same time Calvin, and Huldrych Zwingli (1484-1531) who preceded him, sought to systematize Protestant theology and eliminate what they regarded as papist deformations of Christianity. Calvin preferred a much simpler liturgy than had Luther. The Reformed liturgy was based on the pre-Reformation preaching service or prône, not on the Latin mass. Calvin was more thoroughly iconoclastic and held to a version of the Ten Commandments that specifically forbade the making of graven images. Calvin's theology also de-emphasized the Eucharist. While Luther affirmed the real presence of Christ "in, with, and under" the bread and wine, Calvin argued that the "real but spiritual presence" of Christ was to be found in the action of partaking the Eucharist, not in its physical elements. Unlike Lutherans, who celebrated the Eucharist each Sunday, Calvinists generally partook of the Eucharist only once per month.

In 1536 Calvin moved to Geneva, Switzerland, where he further developed both his doctrinal system and a presbyterian theory of church government that has characterized the reformed tradition. For Calvin the true church was the community that properly preached the Word of God and correctly administered the sacraments. In each congregation authority was vested in an oligarchy of lay elders or presbyters. Regional synods ruled over several congregations.

Calvin promoted his ecclesiology and doctrinal system through a vigorous publication program. Calvinist churches developed in Poland and Lithuania (1557), France (1559), Scotland (1560), the Netherlands (1571), and Hungary (1576). After Calvin's death his followers continued to develop his doctrinal system, and at the Synod of Dordrecht in 1618-1619 the Dutch Reformed Church affirmed five principles that have since been associated with Calvinism: the total depravity of humanity, God's unconditional election of the saved, limited atonement (i.e., Christ died only for those whom God had chosen to save, not for all humanity), the irresistible grace of God, and the impossibility of the elect ever falling from grace. All five of these doctrines follow from the Calvinist emphasis on God's absolute sovereignty.

The history of Calvinism in Russia can be divided into three large periods. During the first period, from the late sixteenth century to 1762, Calvinism was primarily the faith of small groups of German, Dutch, Swiss, and French specialists and merchants. They lived in the capitals and trading towns of Russia. In the second period, which began with the accession of Catherine II (r. 1762-1796) to the throne and ended with the Bolshevik Revolution, two significant groups of Calvinists, Germans and Lithuanians, became part of the Russian Empire as the Russian state expanded. During the Soviet period from 1917 to 1991 Calvinists, like other Christians, experienced severe persecution, especially in the 1930s. Soviet expansion in World War II added the Hungarian and Ukrainian Calvinists of western Ukraine to the USSR. Finally, in the post-Soviet period Calvinists began to reestablish themselves and to reach out beyond their ethnic enclaves to the broader Russian community.

The earliest Calvinists to arrive in Russia were Dutch merchants who in the mid-sixteenth century gained trading concessions and established trading posts in the Kholmogory region of Russia. In the seventeenth century Dutch ties with Russia continued to increase as merchants and other specialists settled in Muscovy. In the Russian capital of Moscow the Dutch Calvinists built a wooden chapel by 1616 and hired a pastor from 1629. In 1632 Dutch iron producers and armaments manufacturers settled in Tula at the tsar's invitation. By 1649 the Dutch Reformed pastor of the Moscow church was leading occasional services, and by 1654 the Dutch merchant Peter Marselis hired a preacher from Holland. In 1660 a visiting Dutch pastor was able to preach to Reformed congregations in Arkhanglelsk, Kholmogory, Yaroslavl, and Vologda. The Dutch Reformed of Arkhangelsk called a pastor from Holland in 1660 and built a new church in 1674.

Peter the Great (r. 1682-1725) turned to Western specialists who happened to be Calvinists for help in modernizing Russia. In 1689, five years after the revocation of the Edict of Nantes, Peter issued an invitation to Huguenot refugees fleeing French persecution. One of his early mentors was Franz Lefort (1656-1699), a Genevan who fought with the Dutch against Catholic France before immigrating to Russia. Lefort had a strong influence over the young tsar and encouraged him to look to the Netherlands as a source of expertise.

Peter actively recruited other Protestants, such as Admiral Cornelius Cruys (1657-1727), to help build his new capital of St. Petersburg, which he founded in 1703. Cruys, a Norwegian Lutheran married to a Dutch Calvinist, supported Protestants of all kinds. In 1708 he built a wooden church on his property where Lutherans and Reformed could worship together. As the Protestant community grew, Lutherans and Reformed formed separate congregations divided by national origin and denomination.

There were three communities of Reformed in St. Petersburg: the Dutch, the French, and the Germans. At the request of the Dutch ambassador and some of the wealthy merchants the Dutch church obtained its own pastor from Amsterdam in 1717. The small congregation, which never exceeded 250 members, continued to meet in Cruys's house church until 1732, when it constructed a new church building on what was then the outskirts of the city on the Moika River and the main city thoroughfare, Nevsky Prospect. Rebuilt in 1831-1835, the Dutch church remained a vital part of the religious life of the capital until it was closed in 1923. Even now it is an important city landmark, the home of the A.A. Blok library.

Despite its small size the Dutch church served as an important link to the Netherlands. The Dutch community relied for its vitality on its close connection with the rusaki, Dutch merchants primarily from the town of Vriezenveen in the Netherlands who decided to try their fortunes in Russia. Dutch sailors and merchants who traveled to St. Petersburg paid a special fee to support the church, and in 1842 the church was placed under the authority of the Dutch ambassador. This special arrangement freed the pastor from following Russian religious regulations, and the last pastor of the Dutch church, Herman Pieter Schim van der Loeff who served from 1914 to 1919, used this limited freedom after the Bolshevik revolution to look after the entire Reformed community of Petrograd.

The French Reformed community of St. Petersburg also built a small one-story church in 1732, which they shared with the Germans. For over fifty years until 1788 the church alternated between French and German pastors. In 1858 the congregations separated, and the Germans completed their own building in 1865. Twenty years later the Reformed population in the Russian capital stood at only 3,838 with some 3,000 Germans and 500 French.

Despite their small numbers the Reformed communities of St. Petersburg actively articulated and lived a missionary vision. In 1818 they established a Reformed school, in 1835 an orphanage, in 1851 a diaconate for social ministry, and in 1859 a hospital. During the Russo-Turkish War of 1877-1878, the Russo-Japanese War (1904-1906), and World War I, Reformed Christians organized field hospitals for the Russian army.

Russia received a new influx of Calvinists beginning in 1762 when Catherine II invited German colonists to settle sparsely populated territories on the Volga River. Catherine promised the foreigners special privileges, including religious freedom. Although the vast majority of the Volga Germans were Lutherans, immigrants from Hesse, Switzerland, and the Palatinate created three large Reformed parishes in the settlements of Norka, Ust-Zolikha, which was also called by its German name, Messer, and Goly Karamysh, or Balzer in German. By 1864 the number of Reformed Christians in the Volga settlements had reached 38,000.

Tsar Alexander I (r. 1801-1825) continued Catherine's policy of encouraging German immigration to sparsely populated areas of the empire. In 1809 Reformed German colonists from the Palatinate and Württemberg established the settlements of Rohrbach and Worms near Odessa in the Ukraine. In the same year 100 German Reformed families founded the village of Neudorf in what is today Karmanova, Moldova. Because the Russian Empire had no Calvinist theological faculty to train pastors for these colonists, they maintained their connection to Reformed centers in Switzerland. As a result these parishes served as conduits for new theological fashions from Western Europe. For example, Johannes Bonekemper (1795-1857), a Prussian Reformed pastor trained in the missionary school in Basel, Switzerland, led a major Pietistic revival among the Germans of Ukraine from 1824 to 1848 when he served as minister in Rohrbach and Worms. Later, from 1865, Bonekemper's son Karl continued his father's work as pastor of Rohrbach. After the emancipation of the serfs in 1861 this Pietistic revival attracted Ukrainian and Russian peasants, who began to study the Bible in Russian and to adopt some elements of Protestant theology. This movement, known as shtundizm because its adepts met for a Bible-study hour (Bibelstunde, in German), was a precursor to the Russian Baptist Union that formed in 1884. Although Russian Baptists generally hold to Arminian rather than Calvinist theology, they still honor the spiritual influence of the strictly Calvinistic Bonekempers.

In the early nineteenth century this Pietistic revival and the apocalyptic expectations occasioned by Napoleon's invasion of Russia in 1812 encouraged interdenominational cooperation and unity. Alexander I permitted Protestant missionaries, including some Calvinists, to work among the indigenous peoples of the empire. From 1806 to 1825 Scottish Calvinists established a missionary colony in Karass in the Caucasus to convert Muslims to Christianity. Under the auspices of the British and Foreign Bible Society founded in 1804 Calvinist colporteurs, such as the Scot John Melville (d. 1886), sold Bibles throughout Ukraine, southern Russia, and the Caucasus. From 1814 to 1840 English Calvinist missionaries labored in Siberia to convert Buddhist Buriats. This spirit of interdenominational cooperation also led to a union of Reformed and Lutheran Christians in Arkhangelsk in 1818, but this experiment was not repeated elsewhere. The profound differences in sacramental theology and liturgical practice between Lutheran and Reformed proved too great to overcome.

Francophone immigrants also contributed to the growth of Calvinist communities in the Russian Empire. In 1822 French-speaking Swiss immigrants founded a Reformed congregation in Khabag on the Bessarabian coast. In 1843 the francophone Calvinists of Odessa established their own independent church.

The conquest of Lithuania, Poland, and Courland in 1795 brought new communities of Calvinists under Russian rule. In the sixteenth and seventeenth centuries prominent members of the Lithuanian noble Radvila family, notably Mikalojus Radvila the Black (1515-65), who served as chancellor of Vilnius, actively supported Calvinism and established Protestant printing presses, schools, and churches to preserve and spread the Evangelical Reformed faith. In the 1897 census 10,115 Lithuanians claimed the Reformed faith. Courland, much of present-day Latvia, included Calvinist churches in the towns of Libau and Mitau.

Although a distinct minority, the Calvinist Christians of the Russian Empire steadily grew from the 1760s to 1914. By 1864 there were over 60,000 Reformed Christians. Nearly 40,000 lived in the German settlements on the Volga River, another 17,000 resided in Poland and Lithuania. Thirty years later the Russian census numbered Reformed Christians at 84,337. In 1914 there were forty-five Reformed parishes in the empire, including twenty in Lithuania, eleven in Poland, three in St. Petersburg, three on the Volga, six in Ukraine and southern Russia, and three in what is today Latvia. Although most Reformed parishes were located in Poland and Lithuania, most Reformed Christians lived in the German colonies on the Volga or in Ukraine. Under the law code of 1832 only those Reformed Christians who lived in the western provinces had the right to their own synod. In most of the empire the Reformed existed as a special department under the authority of the more numerous Lutherans. This administrative measure helped to marginalize the Reformed Church in Russia.

In 1917 the Bolshevik Revolution created the first officially atheist state in history, and Calvinists, like other religious believers, faced persecution and hardship. The Volga region, where most Calvinists lived, suffered intensely during the famine of 1919-1921. New, more stringent requirements for legal registration of religious congregations enacted in 1929 led to the wholesale closing of churches. Within a year Soviet authorities dissolved all the Reformed churches remaining in the USSR with the single exception of the church in Odessa, and that church soon closed as well. When Germany invaded the USSR in 1941, Soviet authorities responded in part by deporting the Volga Germans, including Reformed Christians, to Siberia. As a small minority, Reformed Christians were especially vulnerable to the repressive measures of the Soviet state.

Soviet expansion during the Second World War brought three Calvinist communities into the USSR: the Lithuanian Reformed Church, the Sub-Carpathian Reformed Church, comprised primarily of ethnic Hungarians, and the Ukrainian Evangelical Reformed Church. By 1945 the Lithuanian Reformed Church consisted of only two pastors and twelve parishes. The Soviet government did not allow theological training for Reformed pastors, and in 1982 the last Reformed minister died. The Synod was formally reconstituted in 2001 and has its headquarters in Birzai. Today Lithuanian Calvinists number 7,000 in seven parishes.

The Sub-Carpathian Reformed Church traces its roots to a council in Berehovo in 1545 that officially adopted Calvinism as the religion of the Hungarian minority in the Carpathian mountains. By 1950 the church had 95,000 members in ninety parishes served by sixty-seven ministers. These Hungarian Reformed resisted Soviet efforts to force them into a union with the Baptists, and today their church maintains 105 congregations.

During World War II the USSR also annexed eastern Galicia, where Ukrainian Calvinists had established the Ukrainian Evangelical Reformed Church in 1925. By 1945 the church consisted of thirty congregations and fifteen ministers. Soviet authorities, alarmed by Ukrainian nationalism, severely persecuted the church and drove it underground. In 1989, under the more tolerant policies of Mikhail Gorbachev, the church reconstituted itself.

During most of its existence in Russia Calvinism was the faith of ethnic minorities. Then in 1991 a small group of Russian Calvinists created the Union of Evangelical Reformed Churches of Russia, which was officially registered in June 1992. By 1996 the Union had grown to include six congregations in Moscow, Tver, Omsk and Ufa. In 1994 a second union of Calvinist churches, the Reformed Fundamentalist Church, was registered with its headquarters in Tula, the home of the Dutch Calvinist entrepreneurs who brought the Reformed faith to Russia in the seventeenth century. The Reformed Fundamentalist Church has only seven parishes and about 2,000 members.

Reformed missionaries from other countries have sought to revive Russia's Calvinist tradition. Korean Presbyterians have been especially active. They have established over sixty congregations throughout Russia, a theological academy in

Moscow, and two seminaries in Vladivostok. Working primarily with the Russian Korean population, which numbered just under one-half million in the 1989 Soviet census, Korean Presbyterians have opened their churches to other nationalities, including Russians. The Presbyterian Church in America founded the Reformed Presbyterian Church of Russia in St. Petersburg in 2000.

Outside the Reformed Church, Calvinist theology is beginning to have a greater impact on other denominations. Unlike most Baptists in the English-speaking world the Russian Baptist movement traditionally rejected the Calvinist doctrine of the perseverance of the saints and holds that it is possible for a true Christian to lose his salvation. After studying in Britain the Russian Baptist Andrei Valtsev became a convinced Calvinist and helped to organize a Reformed Baptist Church in St. Petersburg in April 2000. Many of the American parachurch missionary agencies, such as Campus Crusade, are currently bringing a Calvinist perspective to Russia.

From the early seventeenth century Calvinism has been the religion of small ethnic minorities in Russia. In their religious practice French, Swiss, Germans, Dutch, Lithuanians, and some Balts maintained their separate cultural identities within the multinational empire. Reformed churches served as an important conduit of ideas, practices, and economic links between Russia and Western Europe. Their small numbers and minority status made Calvinist Christians more vulnerable to state persecution and pressure. Despite these dangers Reformed Christians actively engaged in education, health care, and urban missions, and have made a significant contribution to Russian cultural life. After nearly disappearing in the Soviet period, Calvinist Christians have begun to reach out beyond their traditional ethnic boundaries.

Bibliography: Hermann Dalton (1833-1913), the pastor of the German Reformed Church in St. Petersburg from 1858 to 1889, wrote the classic history of the Reformed Church in Russia, *Geschichte der reformierten Kirche in Russland* (Gotha, 1865) and compiled *Urkundenbuch der evangelisch-reformierten Kirche in Russland* (Gotha, 1889). Erik Amburger provides a useful survey in *Geschichte des Protestantismus in Russland* (Stuttgart, 1961). J.H. Hebly, *Protestants in Russia*, trans. by John Pott (Grand Rapids, Mich., 1976), and Walter Kolarz, *Religion in the Soviet Union* (New York, 1961), are also helpful. Recent studies of ethnic communities with valuable information about Calvinism include *Gollandskaia reformatskaia tserkov' v Sankt-Peterburge, 1717-1927* (SPb., 2001) and *Geschichte und Kultur der Deutschen in Russland/UdSSR* (Stuttgart, 1989). Hans Brandenburg, *The Meek and the Mighty. The Emergence of the Evangelical Movement in Russia* (New York, 1977), gives a colorful account of Calvinists in nineteenth-century Russia. C.R. Bawden, *Shamans, Lamas, and Evangelicals. The English Missionaries in Siberia* (Boston, Mass., 1985), presents a delightful history of an Evangelical mission in Russia.

J. Eugene Clay

CANON LAW, kanonicheskoe pravo or tserkovnoe pravo in Russian, concerns the application of the body of ecclesiastical regulations, or canons, that govern church life in the Eastern Orthodox Church, as in the Roman Catholic Church. Canons regulate norms of behavior and morality, ecclesiastical structure, and church discipline.

The Russian Orthodox Church inherited most of its canonical regulations from the Byzantine church, which formulated the most authoritative canons. The canons that received universal acceptance in the Orthodox Church derive from decrees of the so-called Apostolic canons, the seven ecumenical councils held during the fourth through the eighth centuries, certain local councils, and the prescriptions of particular church fathers. The decisions regarding church life and discipline made by the ecumenical councils were particularly important, for the Orthodox Church regards the ecumenical council as the only infallible authority in matters of church life and dogma. The most important council for Orthodox canon law was the Council in Trullo (691-692), which was regarded as an extension of the Sixth Ecumenical Council (Constantinople, 680) and was convened precisely to settle matters of church discipline. The Council in Trullo gave ecumenical authority to the decisions of certain earlier local councils and the disciplinary recommendations of esteemed church fathers.

At one level, canons that received ecumenical acceptance were regarded as immutable (Council in Trullo, canon 2). At another level canons apply to concrete historical circumstances of the church's life, and canonical norms changed as circumstances changed, consequently later councils modified or completely altered earlier norms. Thus canon 12 of the Council in Trullo mandated celibacy for the episcopate, in contrast to previously accepted practice. From a theological perspective, as a rule, the Orthodox Church regards the canons as expressions of immutable norms in changing historical circumstances. Their essential purpose and meaning do not alter, but their particular expressions may change in different circumstances. This approach has led to considerable disagreements with regard to how literally the canons from antiquity were to be applied in later stages in the church's history. Orthodox canon law was not law in the modern sense of the word. Rather, canons were frequently used as norms to guide in particular circumstances, especially those that concern moral and ethical issues of the laity. Canons dealing with penitential discipline, rather than setting specific penalties in accord with the offense, stress the inner disposition of the penitent; the penances were understood as medicinal rather than punitive. Some canons, such as the requirement that parish priests marry prior to ordination, were universally observed, whereas others, such as the minimum age requirement of thirty for parish priests, or canons that prohibit the transfer of bishops from one diocese to another, were routinely ignored.

Canons in the Orthodox Church deal with a variety of issues concerning the organization of the church as well as establishing norms for clergy and laity. Thus there are canons that deal with the relationship between church and state as well as the church's relationship with those it regards as heretics or dissenters. Canons establish the constitution and administration of the church and regulate the church's members—clergy, monastics, and laity. They establish rules for administering the sacraments, in particular marriage. They also deal with church property and income of clergy. Canons deal with infractions of church norms such as apostasy, schism, sacrilege, together with ecclesiastical penalties such as excommunication, deposition of clergy, and anathematization. Finally, they are concerned with judicial processes such as ecclesiastical courts. Canons thus set the norms for very important dimensions of life for both clergy and laity. While the Orthodox Church allows divorce under certain circumstances and remarriage for the widowed, for example, it upholds the norm of one marriage for the clergy. Divorced persons, therefore, are prohibited from being ordained, and widowed clergy are prohibited from remarrying.

In addition to canons deriving from purely ecclesiastical sources the church respected civil laws regarding church life enacted by the Byzantine emperors. Canons (kanones) continued to be distinguished from civil laws (nomoi), but systematic collections first compiled in the sixth century and called nomokanones set canons and civil laws side by side on particular topics. The most important of these collections were the *Synagoge in Fifty Titles*, attributed to Patriarch John Scholastikos in the mid-sixth century and the *Nomokanon in Fourteen Titles* of Patriarch Photios from the later ninth century. The latter was particularly influential. The first part of the collection was organized according to topic and summarized the relevant canons and civil laws, and the second part, called the Syntagma, contained the canons derived from councils and fathers given conciliar authority by the Council in Trullo.

Byzantine canon law developed significantly in the twelfth century through the systematic commentaries of Alexios Aristenos, John Zonaras, and Theodore Balsamon. Although earlier collections were arranged according to content, no system of canon law was ever developed in Byzantium. These commentaries evolved to resolve the complications and contradictions that arose with regard to the application of the canons. Aristenos endeavored to explain the meaning of the canons primarily through logic and linguistic analysis. Zonaras attempted to sort through the canons and reconcile contradictions. His hermeneutic was based on the principle that older canons had greater primacy and were to be followed over later rulings and particularly over civil laws. Balsamon attempted the most thoroughgoing critical explanation of contradictory passages in the canons yet often employed artificial arguments to reconcile contradictions between contemporary practice, or civil laws, and the canons.

The earliest Slavic collections of canons originated in the ninth century, and these were used by the church in Rus. The first, attributed to St. Methodius, was the *Synagoge in Fifty Titles* of John Scholastikos, and the second was the *Nomokanon in Fourteen Titles*. The most influential canonical collection for the medieval Russian church was the *Kormchaia kniga* (Pilot's Book), which consisted of an edition of the *Nomokanon in Fourteen Titles* prepared by Archbishop Sava of Serbia. Metropolitan Kirill of Kiev selected this edition for use in Russia and the church council of Vladimir in 1274, under Kirill's direction, adopted it as the official code of the church. Like the earlier nomokanones it was not a complete collection of the canons but did include both Byzantine civil laws and some of the commentaries. There were a multitude of manuscript traditions that differed significantly in content, and none became standard. The divergences created confusion, and therefore Patriarch Joseph set out to establish a single text of the *Kormchaia kniga,* which was published in 1650 and then replaced by a revised edition by Patriarch Nikon in 1653. Nikon's edition of the *Kormchaia kniga* became the first single, unified code of church law in the Russian Orthodox Church. There were many problems with it, but the Synod chose to reprint it without revisions in 1787 and again several times in the early nineteenth century. The full text of the canons, excluding the civil laws, did not appear in print in Russia until the Holy Synod published the *Book of Canons of the Holy Apostles, Holy Ecumenical and Local Councils, and Holy Fathers* (Kniga pravila sv. apostolov, sv. soborov vselenskikh i pomestnykh i sv. ottsov) in 1839.

After the conversion of Rus the question arose whether the Russian church was required to observe the imperial civil laws on church matters contained in the nomokanones. Although it continued to be under the jurisdiction of the Patriarch of Constantinople and received new regulations from the patriarch, it existed in different conditions than the Byzantine Empire and was subject to its own princes rather than to the Byzantine emperors. According to the Russian church historian Anton Kartashev, the Russian church de facto ignored Byzantine civil legislation, and the grand princes of Rus issued their own regulations concerning church matters. As a result, certain categories of laws developed that pertained only to the Russian church. Texts survive that attribute statutes to Grand Princes Vladimir and Yaroslav, although historians debate the authenticity of these statutes. Evgeny Golubinsky argued against their authenticity, whereas Vasily Kliuchevsky and Anton Kartashev argued that they were genuine but contained later additions.

The involvement of the episcopate in the juridical sphere was one area in which the Russian church developed in unique ways. In Byzantium civil judicial authorities could invite bishops to participate in legal cases involving Christian laity, particularly if the cases concerned moral issues. In Rus, contrary to Byzantium, crimes were punished largely by fines that were paid to the prince and became an important source of support for the princes. For bishops to be involved in such cases would amount to their interference in the prince's property. As a result bishops were not involved in a wide variety of cases, rather were delegated their own specific types of cases; and these types of cases developed into a special category of crimes that fell under the jurisdiction of the church with corresponding financial benefits. Those crimes that fell under the jurisdiction of the church consisted of infractions that generally were not considered sins in pagan Rus, matters relating to family life, sexual morality, blasphemy, and witchcraft. While the clergy naturally would be interested in such matters from the moral point of view, the grand princes of Rus gave them the force of civil law under the legal jurisdiction of the church. In addition to certain types of crimes certain categories of people also fell under the sole legal jurisdiction of the church, in particular the clergy, but also people who fell under the care of the church such as servants of the church, homeless pilgrims (stranniki), and those who lived in homes the church provided for the poor or for widows. The categories of infractions that fell under the jurisdiction of the church gradually broadened and came to include disputes between masters and servants, intra-family disputes between spouses or between parents and children, issues concerning adoption and illegitimate children, as well as matters concerning marriage such as divorce and degrees of consanguinity.

In addition to the canons that hold ecumenical authority for all Eastern Orthodox churches, each national Orthodox Church issues regulations dealing with the particularities of its own circumstances. Few such regulations survive from the pre-Muscovite period. The most important regulations concerning the Russian Orthodox Church stem from the Stoglav (Hundred Chapters) Council of 1551 and the Ecclesiastical, or Spiritual, Regulation of Peter the Great of 1721. The Stoglav Council dealt particularly with problems in church life, including improper performance of services, immoral behavior of clergy and laity, disorders in monasteries. The council also sought to regulate and bring unification to the order of liturgical services and performance of sacraments, as well as exercise control over ecclesiastical organizations such as hostels for the poor, schools for clergy, and iconography workshops. Scholars of the Stoglav Council note its tendency to give preference to local traditions and the demands of contemporary church life over canons with ecumenical authority.

The Ecclesiastical Regulation of Peter the Great made dramatic changes in the organization of the Russian Orthodox Church, in particular abolishing the patriarchate and establishing the Holy Synod as the governing body of the Russian Orthodox Church during the imperial period. Much of the Regulation has a programmatic character, setting forth ideal norms rather than a body of law or an institutional statute per se. Many of these ideals were realized only over the course of the eighteenth century, and others were not realized the way they were envisioned in the Regulation at all. The Regulation was particularly focused on such things as eliminating superstition, such as dubious relics or miraculous icons, detecting schismatics, requiring formal education for the clergy, establishing regular preaching and requiring regular episcopal visitations. It also established the structure and function of the Holy Synod. The Regulation, in its Supplement, stated specifically that there were weaknesses of the Russian clergy that required particular regulations. Most of this material was general and programmatic, rather than specific statutes, stating for example that candidates to the priesthood have testimony to their fitness for ordination, and that priests know properly how to treat people in confession or comfort the sick. The most infamous rule required clergy to inform on those who reveal treasonous intentions during the confessional. With regard to penance the Regulation explained that the canons were not to be applied legalistically, rather left to the judgment of the spiritual father who must take into account the spiritual state of the penitent and the circumstances of the sin. In this they appealed to church fathers and commentators on the canons such as Balsamon. The Regulation also established norms for monasticism, such as setting the minimum age for tonsure at thirty for men, and fifty or sixty for women.

As in Byzantium civil laws also regulated church life in Russia. A law of 1832, for example, stipulated that candidates for monasticism must undergo a three-year novitiate, that male candidates, except widowed parish clergy and graduates of theological institutions, must be thirty years old to be tonsured and that female candidates be forty, a more realistic age than the one set by the Ecclesiastical Regulation. Such laws took precedent over church canons and were strictly observed by the church.

Canon law was introduced as a subject of study in Russian theological institutions at the end of the eighteenth century and became an object of serious scholarly study in the nineteenth. Metropolitan Platon (Levshin, 1737-1812) introduced the subject as a course of study in the Moscow Theological Academy in 1776, focusing on interpreting the *Kormchaia kniga*. In 1798 the Holy Synod required that the subject be taught in other theological institutions. Upon reorganization of theological institutions in 1810, the study of canon law came to be regarded as a branch of theology, and Archimandrite Filaret (Drozdov, 1783-1867) established the program of study. In 1835 the study of canon law was introduced as a subject of study for law students at the university, and in 1863 independent departments (kathedra) of canon law were created in university law schools. Finally, canon law became an independent academic discipline in the theological academies in 1884.

The Russian church relied on the *Kormchaia kniga* until the first publication of the full texts of the ancient canons by the Holy Synod in 1839. The first edition included Greek and Slavonic texts, whereas later reprints contained only the Slavonic text. In 1875 the Society of Lovers of Spiritual Enlightenment published a new edition of the complete canons together with the first complete translation of the commentaries of Aristenos, Zonaras, and Balsamon. In the second half of the nineteenth century the scholarly study of the canons developed extensively in Russia. Of particular note were the textbooks of Professor Ioann Skvortsov of the Kiev Theological Academy (1848), Bishop Ioann (Sokolov) of Smolensk (1853), Professor I.K. Sokolov of Moscow University (1888), Professor I.S. Berdnikov of Kazan University (1898), and Professor N.S. Suvorov of Moscow University (1889-1890). Professors A.S. Pavlov (d. 1898), V.N. Beneshevich (early twentieth century), and S.V. Troitsky (d. 1972) contributed various important monographs and studies in canon law.

The intensive study of canon law in late nineteenth century revealed contradictions between canons or inconsistencies in their application, which raised many questions about their immutability and obligatory nature. The Church Council of 1917-1918 attempted to deal with a wide range of issues regarding ecclesiastical organization and discipline, but its work was cut short because of the Bolshevik Revolution. Some liberal parish clergy remained unsatisfied with the results of the council and these clerics, who gained control of the church administration in 1922 and were known as the Renovationists, tried to enact a series of reforms. They argued that the canons were mutable and could be revised under new circumstances. During their council in 1923 they enacted reforms that allowed bishops to marry and widowed parish clergy to remarry. The Patriarchal church rejected these reforms. Many of the questions raised at the end of the nineteenth and early twentieth centuries still await resolution.

Bibliography: The standard collection of Orthodox canons in English is Henry R. Percival, *The Seven Ecumenical Councils of the Undivided Church. Their Canons and Decrees* (New York, 1900). Important Russian texts include *The Spiritual Regulation of Peter the Great*, trans. by Alexander V. Muller (Seattle, Wash., 1972), T. Barsov, ed., *Sbornik deistvuiushchikh i rukovodstvennykh tserkovnykh i tserkovno-grazhdanskikh postanovlenii po vedomstvu pravoslavnogo ispovedaniia* (SPb., 1885), and E.B. Emchenko, *Stoglav. Issledovanie i tekst* (M., 2000). Studies include Nicholas N. Afanasiev, "The Canons of the Church. Changeable or Unchangeable?" *St. Vladimir's Seminary Quarterly,* Vol. 11 (1967), 54-68, E.V. Beliakova, "Stoglav i ego mesto v russkoi kanonicheskoi traditsii," *Otechestvennaia istoriia,* No. 6 (2001), 90-96, John H. Erickson, "The Orthodox Canonical Tradition," *St. Vladimir's Theological Quarterly,* Vol. 27 (1983), 155-67, A.V. Kartashev, *Ocherki po istorii Russkoi tserkvi* (M., 1991), Scott M. Kenworthy, "Russian Reformation? The Program for Religious Renovation in the Orthodox Church, 1922-1925," *Modern Greek Studies Yearbook,* Vol. 16-17 (2001-2002), Ia. N. Shchapov, *Vizantiiskoe i iuzhnoslavnianskoe pravovoe nasledie na Rusi v XI-XIII vv.* (M., 1978), Vladislav Tsypin, "O kanonakh s tolkovaniiami Episkopa Nikodima (Milasha)" in Nikodim (Milash), *Pravila Pravoslavnoi tserkvi s tolkovaniiami Nikodima, episkopa Dalmatinsko-Istriiskogo* (Sergiev Posad, 1996), v-xiii, and Ivan Zuzek, *Kormcaja Kniga. Studies on the Chief Code of Russian Canon Law* (Rome, 1964).

Scott M. Kenworthy

CANTEMIR, DIMITRIE (1673-1723). Moldavian prince, scholar, diplomat, and strategist.

Born in a noble family reputedly of Tatar origin, Dimitrie succeeded his father Constantin (r. 1685-1693) and his elder brother Antioch (r. 1696-1700 and 1705-1707) to the throne of the Moldavian Principality. Dimitrie himself ruled Moldavia twice briefly, in 1693 and 1710-1711. During his second reign he conspired with Peter the Great against his suzerain, the Ottoman sultan, and had to flee after the fateful battle of Stânileşti. In Petrine Russia his son Antioch became a high-ranking diplomat and one of the first authors of satires in modern Russian literature.

Young Dimitrie was brought to Constantinople as guarantee for his father's loyalty to the sultan. His forced stay in the capital from 1688 to 1691, where he studied at the academy of the patriarchate, introduced him to Islamic culture and knowledge and put him in contact with Russian and Western diplomats as he acted in the city as his brother's representative at the Porte. In the process Cantemir learned a dozen languages and became a multitalented scholar, a linguist of international repute, a historian of his own state and people as well as the Ottoman Empire, a geographer, philosopher, and ethnographer.

Convinced that the Ottoman Empire would soon fall and in fierce competition with his Wallachian colleague, Constantin Brâncoveanu, Cantemir denied the sultan's suzerainty soon after his elevation to the throne and signed a secret alliance, the Treaty of Luțk of 13 April 1711, with Peter the Great who was looking for local allies in a first Balkan campaign against the Ottoman Empire. Due to betrayal of their plans and the slow progress of the Russian army towards the Danube, the surprise attack failed, and Peter the Great found himself surrounded by far superior Turkish forces on the bank of the Prut River near Stânilești. By putting up a staunch defense and by offering bribes and strategic concessions, the tsar managed to escape with the Peace of the Prut on 12 July. Allegedly, he refused to hand Cantemir over to the sultan as a traitor and negotiated a safe-conduct, despite adverse military odds. Retreating behind the Dniester River, Peter the Great showed his gratitude to the Moldavian prince and alleviated his forced exile with the title of a Russian prince, a generous pension, major estates in southern Russia, and other privileges.

The Russian ruler came to appreciate the intelligence and insights of the erudite Moldavian, who became an important counselor and accompanied the tsar on some more successful campaigns. Apart from these political activities Cantemir involved himself in literature and science during his exile in Russia. He already had written a handful of religious and philosophical works by 1711, but his years in Russia were definitely more productive and scholarly, evidently thriving on the knowledge he acquired in Constantinople in combination with the influence of Peter's reforms. The influence of the Enlightenment is discernable in his interest in and rational argumentation on the ethnogenesis and history of his people. Cantemir acquired European fame and was honored with membership in the Berlin Academy in 1714. Cantemir died in exile at the age of fifty, shortly before Peter the Great nominated him to be the first president of the Russian Academy of Sciences. In 1935 his mortal remains were exhumed and returned to Moldavia, now a Romanian province, and reburied at the Trei Ierarhi Church in Iași (Jassy), his old capital. Both Romania and Moldova lay claim to Cantemir the statesman and the intellectual as part of their national history and cultural heritage.

Bibliography: Cantemir's major works include histories of his country and the Ottoman Empire. *The History of the Growth and Decay of the Othman Empire* (London, 1734) was published originally in Latin in 1714-1716. *An Ancient Chronicle of the Romano-Moldo-Vlachs* (Bucuresti, 1999) was published first in Romanian as *Hronicul vechimei a romano-moldo-vlahilor* in 1722. The travelogue *A Description of Moldavia* (Bucuresti, 1976) appeared as *Descrierea Moldovei* in 1716. Cantemir's roman à clef on local politics, *A Hieroglyphic History* (Bucuresti, 1977), appeared in 1705 as *Istoria ieroglifica.* In 1971 Anatol Codru directed a documentary on the life of Cantemir in Chișinâu. On the events of 1710-1711, see Wim P. van Meurs, "Dimitrie Cantemir as Strategist," *Romanian Civilization,* Vol. 7, No. 2 (1999), 3-12. On the scholar Cantemir and his thought, see *Ein bedeutender Gelehrter an der Schwelle zur Frühaufklärung. Dimitrie Cantemir, 1673-1723* (Berlin, 1974). For comprehensive biographies, see his son's postscript in *Dimitrie*

Cantemir. Historian of Southeast and Oriental Civilizations (Bucuresti, 1973), or Virgil Cândea, *Dimitrie Cantemir, 1673-1723, 300th Anniversary of his Birth* (Bucuresti, 1973). On Cantemir's *Nachleben*, see Wim P. van Meurs, *The Bessarabian Question in Communist Historiography. Nationalist and Communist Politics and History-Writing* (Boulder, Colo., 1994), Chapter 6.4.

Wim P. van Meurs

CAPITAL PUNISHMENT IN RUSSIA AND THE SOVIET UNION. According to the eleventh-century law code, Russkaia pravda, capital punishment was applied among the Eastern Slavs for property crimes. Homicide by contrast usually was punished by means of blood feuds, which generally resulted in members of the victim's clan killing the suspected culprit. The law codes of the fifteenth and six-teenth centuries (sudebniki) expanded the range of capital offenses to include killing one's lord, sedition, and crimes against the church.

Criminal punishments in medieval and early modern Europe, from the Atlantic to the Ural Mountains, were brutal. Into the eighteenth century convicted criminals were sometimes tortured, mutilated, ripped to pieces, and then burned. Russia's law code of 1649 (Sobornoe ulozhenie), which listed over sixty capital offenses, prescribed especially cruel methods of capital punishment, including burning alive, choking with molten metal, and burying alive. Tens of thousands were executed during the reign of Ivan IV yet, despite its small population, more people were executed in England, more than 150,000 during the reigns of Henry VIII and Elizabeth I alone. Peter the Great's Military Statute (artikul voinsky) of 1715 prescribed death for 122 crimes. English criminal law defined some two hundred capital offenses as late as 1819.

In some regards Russia appears to have been at the forefront of the Enlightenment trend toward making criminal punishments more humane. A decade before the publication of Beccaria's *On Crimes and Punishments* (Dei delitti e delle pene, 1764) Empress Elizabeth strictly limited the legal scope of capital punishment. Perhaps twenty thousand people were executed summarily during the suppression of the Pugachev rebellion, and some convicts died each year from wounds inflicted by knouting in Russia until the practice was abolished in 1845. For the next seventy years only about a dozen people were executed on court orders in Russia. In England and Wales, by contrast, the yearly number of executions as late as the first decades of the nineteenth century was just under one hundred. Similarly, public executions were abolished in England in 1868 and in Russia in 1881, but in France only in 1939.

Russia's penal code of 1845 prescribed sentences of death only for violent attacks on the sovereign, for conspiring against the state order, for treason, or for breach of quarantine. Unlike in most of western Europe such grave crimes as murder, rape, armed robbery, and arson were not capital offenses. In practice the regular courts during imperial Russia's final century condemned to death only a very small number of people. More active in this regard were the military courts, which were speedier, more likely to convict than the regular courts, and issued harsher sentences. Most of the fifty death sentences issued in Russia from 1845 to

1875 were handed down by military courts. Twenty of the sentences were carried out. The military statute of punishments allowed for the application of capital punishment to civilians only under exceptional circumstances. Nearly all of those executed organized or sought to organize armed insurrections. Seven of them were military personnel. During the same interval, by contrast, 620 criminals in France, 271 in Prussia, 360 in England and Wales, and 1,325 in the United States were executed by sentence of the courts.

The outbreak of revolutionary terrorism in the 1870s, the widespread unwillingness of judges and juries to condemn defendants apparently guilty of criminal attacks against government officials, and the impossibility of removing liberal judges provided justification for selectively reabrogating the rights of Russian subjects, expanded by Alexander II's Great Reforms of the 1860s, and reasserting the powers of officialdom. The assassination of a senior official prompted the adoption of a law of 9 August 1878 permitting the systematic transfer of cases involving violent attacks on government officials to military courts, which were guided by the harsh laws of wartime. The liberal publicist N.I. Faleev called the law of 9 August the "cornerstone of future security measures" ("Rossiia pod ohkranoi," 5). An attempt on the life of Alexander II on 2 April 1879 caused him to empower governors general to transfer to courts-martial any persons whose actions were deemed potentially harmful to public order and tranquility. Finally, the security law of 14 August 1881, adopted following the assassination of the emperor, allowed the interior ministry, upon obtaining the consent of the Ministry of Justice, to transfer to military courts specified state-crime cases, as well as cases of violent resistance to, or physical attacks against, administrative officials in their line of duty. In regions declared in a state of reinforced security (usilennaia okhrana), governors general had the right to transfer to military courts any case deemed important to preserving order.

Even so the annual number of executions in Russia before 1906 remained quite modest. Thus from 1876 to 1905 Russian military courts issued 484 death sentences, most for civil crimes like murder and banditry, all of which were carried out. In the same period twelve people were executed for political crimes after trial by the Senate. In all in these three decades roughly 500 people were executed in Russia, compared to 405 in England, 260 in Prussia, and 620 in France, although those nations had populations one-fourth to one-third the size of Russia's. These figures exclude executions in those countries' colonial possessions. During the period from 1892 to 1906 nearly five hundred people were sentenced to death each year in British India. The execution rate was even higher in the United States, which between 1880 and 1905 had 2,743 executions, despite having a population half the size of Russia's.

Many government officials opposed the death penalty on principle. Jurists on an interdepartmental commission chaired by Deputy Justice Minister E.V. Frisch argued in 1881 against applying capital punishment to political and religious criminals, and the officials who drafted the criminal code of 1903 expressed their principled opposition to capital punishment in general, although the State Council preserved the death penalty in both cases. In the courtroom itself it seems that judges issued ever milder sentences as the 1905 revolution approached. Even during turbulent 1905 the leniency of judges and prosecutors was striking. Not a single person was executed in Russia from 1 January to 6 October 1905, when a soldier was put to death for attempting to kill an officer. The year had begun famously with Bloody Sunday when troops fired on a peaceful demonstration and killed two hundred.

Beginning in 1906, however, the number of executions in Russia rose dramatically. During the three years from 1906 through 1908 as many as 2,215 people were executed by military-court sentence, or five per million population annually, a rate three times higher than for the same years in the US. Nonmilitary courts put no one to death in those years. To this figure one must add more than one thousand people killed by punitive expeditions from December 1905 into 1906 and one thousand more executed by military field courts. This was terrible carnage, a shocking deviation from the path Russia had followed until those years. One would be remiss not to compare this massive slaughter to other revolutionary situations, such as the terrible repression of the Paris Commune in the final week of May 1871, when troops massacred as many as twenty thousand communards. France's population at that time was only about one third of Russia's in 1905. Thus, the French government in quashing the Commune killed proportionately six times more people, and in a much shorter period, than Russia's did in suppressing the revolution of 1905. Both episodes appear to be gross aberrations brought about by the desperation of governments struggling to survive in the face of broad-based popular disorder. Indeed, the number of executions in Russia decreased to 129 in 1910 and to 25 in 1913. That figure compared very favorably with those of the major European countries. In 1913 in Prussia there were twenty-two executions in a population of forty-three million. In England and Wales there were about thirteen in a population of thirty-six million, and in France approximately nine in a population of thirty-nine million.

An important reason for the decline of executions in Russia was public opposition. Most telling, on 19 June 1906 the first Duma voted without a single dissenting vote to abolish capital punishment. Although the bill never became law owing to the dissolution of the Duma, Russian intellectuals, public figures, clergymen, and professionals continued to agitate vehemently for an end to the death penalty. Even the justice minister admitted publicly that capital punishment should not be used to punish civil crimes, at a time when civil and political crime were blending together in something like an orgy of criminality.

It seems the execution rate did not increase dramatically during the World War, although summary executions by military authorities were presumably more frequent. Capital punishment was abolished in all its forms, even for desertion, on 1 March 1917, even before Nicholas II abdicated. On 12 July as military discipline broke down, the Provisional Government restored capital punishment at the front.

Upon coming to power in October the Bolsheviks abolished capital punishment but then authorized summary executions in February 1918 with oversight by the

Cheka, when German troops attacked Russia. In June the government decreed that revolutionary tribunals could resort to capital punishment at their discretion. Hundreds were executed summarily even before the declaration of the Red Terror in early September. This policy, which coincided with the Russian Civil War (1918-1920) and by which both the Cheka and revolutionary tribunals were authorized to issue death sentences, resulted in killing at least fifty thousand people. Capital punishment was repealed in January 1920 except in Ukraine then restored again in May. At this time, moreover, revolutionary tribunals were specifically empowered to order the immediate execution of individuals to forestall the possibility of appeal. Summary executions continued in 1921 during the suppression of rebellions in Kronstadt and in the countryside. Although the security police were empowered in early 1922 and again in late 1922 summarily to shoot bandits, which meant rebels of various kinds, the incidence of capital punishment fell dramatically in the following years, down to 1,748 death sentences in 1924 and 880 in 1926, only half of which were actually carried out. Despite the frequent use of capital punishment the criminal codes of 1922 and 1926 stressed the provisional character of capital punishment and reduced the number of capital offenses, and periodical amnesties commuted a large number of death sentences to various periods of incarceration.

The incidence of capital punishment increased dramatically beginning in the 1930s. During much of that decade hundreds of thousands people were shot extrajudicially and almost completely arbitrarily, at least 681,692 in 1937 and 1938 alone according to a report prepared for the Communist Party leader Nikita Khrushchev in 1956. The number of executions fell to 2,600 in 1939 and 1,600 in 1940, then rose to over 30,000 in the first two years of the war, before dropping to 3,000-4,000 annually in the postwar years. Capital punishment was abolished again in 1947 then restored once more in 1950. The criminal code of 1960 specified twenty-four capital offenses, although in practice most death sentences were issued for murder or other violent crimes. In the 1960s an average of 500 to 1,000 people were executed annually in the Soviet Union. In the 1970s the yearly number of executions fell to the low hundreds. The incidence diminished further in the 1980s at just one hundred sentenced to death in 1989. In 1992 President Boris Yeltsin created a commission on pardons to evaluate the appeals of convicts, including those sentenced to death. In that year only one person was executed in the Russian Federation. Within a few years the number of executions began to rise again, reaching eighty-six in 1995. In August 1996 President Yeltsin imposed a moratorium on executions as a precondition for admission to the Council of Europe. Since 1997 no one has been executed in Russia. In January 1997 a new criminal code, which lowered the number of capital crimes to five, entered into force in the Russian Federation. In June 1999 Yeltsin pardoned the remaining several hundred prisoners on death row. Nevertheless the death penalty remains legally in force, and the prosecutor general's office proposed in 2002 to rescind the moratorium and to apply the death penalty vigorously.

Bibliography: Jonathan W. Daly, "Criminal Punishments and Europeanization in Late Imperial Russia," *Jahrbücher für Geschichte Osteuropas,* Vol. 47 (2000), 341-62, "On the Significance of Emergency Legislation in Late Imperial Russia," *Slavic Review,* Vol. 54 (1995), 602-29; William C. Fuller, Jr., "Civilians in Russian Military Courts, 1881-1904," *Russian Review,* Vol. 41 (1982), 288-305; M.N. Gernet, *Smertnaia kazn'* (M., 1913); J. Arch Getty, Gabor T. Rittersporn, and Viktor N. Zemskov, "Victims of the Soviet Penal System in the Pre-War Years. A First Approach on the Basis of Archival Evidence," *The American Historical Review* , Vol. 98 (1993), 1017-1049; Peter Liessem, "Die Todesstrafe im späten Zarenreich. Rechtslage, Realität und Öffentliche Diskussion," *Jahrbücher für Geschichte Osteuropas,* Vol. 37 (1989), 492-23; Alexander S. Mikhlin, *The Death Penalty in Russia,* trans. by W.E. Butler (London, 1999); O.B. Mozokhin, "Vnesudebnye polnomochiia VChK" in *Istoricheskie chteniia na Liubianke, 1998 god. Rossiiskie spetsluzhby na perelome epokh, konets XIX veka-1922 god,* ed. by A.A. Zdanovich, M.N. Petrov, and V.N. Khaustov (M., 1999); A.A. Piontkovskii, *Smertnaia kazn' v Evrope* (Kazan., 1908); Donald C. Rawson, "The Death Penalty in Late Tsarist Russia. An Investigation of Judicial Procedures," *Russian History,* Vol. 11 (1984), 29-52; Pieter Spierenburg, *The Spectacle of Suffering. Executions and the Evolution of Repression. From a Preindustrial Metropolis to the European Experience* (Cambridge, 1984); Saul Ushevich, *Smertnye kazni v tsarskoi Rossii. K istorii kaznei po politicheskim protsessam s 1824 po 1917 god,* 2nd ed. (1933); S.N. Viktorskii, *Istoriia smertnoi kazni v Rossii i sovremennoe ee sostoianie* (M., 1912); N.I. Faleev, "Rossiia pod okhranoi. Istoricheskii ocherk," *Byloe,* No. 2 (1907).

Jonathan W. Daly

CARNIVAL IN RUSSIA. The Russian carnival encompasses folk theater and its allied traditions of theater of the boulevard, the theater of the carnival (balagan), street and fun fair (guliane) and trade fair (yarmarka).

The carnival can be seen as the native tradition of performance in Russia and as an alternative to European theater. Prior to the introduction of Western theater by Ivan the Terrible and Peter the Great, the Russian Orthodox Church was vociferously opposed to both theatrical performance and to itinerant folk performers (skomorokhi) who wandered from village to village. The folk celebrations staged in honor of the seasons and such liminal events as funerals, weddings, and rites of passage into adulthood were seen by the church as evidence of demonic possession, devil worship, and paganism and, in a sense, competition to the pomp and pageantry of the Orthodox mass.

In the Middle Ages the unsavory nature of the carnival and its performers was commented upon by many of the chronicles of the time. Skomorokhi were described as pagans who tempted the faithful with their profane songs and were in the service of the devil. In broadsheets and other contemporary sources the performers were often depicted as half human/half goat musicians usually performing with bears and other trained animals. Adam Olearius, the German diplomat who visited Russia in 1630, wrote that the carnival was a vulgar, riotous collection of musicians, dancers, and puppeteers obscenely cavorting through the fairground. The customs of these carnivals, which included puppet shows, clowning, face painting, masquerade, crowning a king of fools, and bear taunting, identified the events as a marginally acceptable practice that allowed its participants to act outside the behavioral norms of the society.

Spring planting celebrations, harvest festivals, and Lenten carnivals were opportunities for people to sing, dance, and stage plays, such as The Boat (Lodka) and Tsar Maksimilian and his Disobedient Son Adolf (Deistvo o tsare Maksimilian i ego nepokornom syne Adolfe), which were performed both in organized performances by professional performers and in impromptu gatherings. These folk performances were almost never performed from a written text. Variations of story, different dialog, even a different ending were common. Motifs, half-remembered lines, and melodies from folk performances pop up in the cultural contexts of urban street fair, having become a part of the discourse that creates common culture. Thus, the reference to a boat in a Petrushka puppet show coupled with a familiar melody played by the hurdy-gurdy is a reference to Stenka Razin's murder of his true love to insure the loyalty of his compatriots and prompts viewers to understand the correct context for Petrushka's savage beating of his bride. The carnival became a means of transmitting the oral culture of the lower classes. Given the widespread illiteracy of peasants and urban workers, the carnival was a means of maintaining and transmitting the traditions and shared experiences of the people.

In general the lower classes were controlled strictly by the tsarist government and by the church, even so the authorities gave carnivals and street fairs more freedom both in repertoire and in the behavior of the visiting crowd. These holiday events allowed the lower classes to release their aggression and dissatisfaction in a relatively harmless fashion. The lack of censorship is reflected in the types of entertainment favored: thieves' songs, obscene rhymes, peepshows, travelogues, exhibitions of oddities, and so forth. It was only after the Revolution of 1917 that the carnival was restricted and its content subjected to governmental censorship.

Trade fairs, such as the Nizhnyi Novgorod yarmarka, were cultural events with performances, art exhibitions, architectural constructions, and music. The surrounding community provided less wholesome entertainment, including taverns and gambling houses. These fairs took on the characteristics of self contained cities with banks, theaters, markets, and restaurants lasting for the duration of the fair. The government also staged fairs so that the common people could celebrate national events. In 1913 Nicholas II staged a large fair in St. Petersburg in honor of the tercentenary of the Romanov House. This fair ended in tragedy with the death of hundreds of revelers crushed in a riot.

Throughout history the effect of the carnival is evident on popular art forms such as broadsheets (lubki), Petrushka, peasant theater, and naive art. It provided viable alternatives for the creation of radically new art forms as opposed to the imported values of Western art and literature. The carnival tradition with its wealth of folk sources provided contemporary artists and performers with a view other than the opinion held by most members of elite Russian society that traditional Western theater was superior to its folk counterpart. The various attempts to create a national theatrical style were plagued by charges of slavish imitation of Western sources. It was only with a return to the native traditions of Russia that a unique style developed.

A progression can be traced from Alexander Pushkin, who in the 1820s and 1830s was concerned with creating a reading public as the basis for a national literature, through Vissarion Belinsky in the 1840s, who first framed the question "Does Russia have a literature?" and on to On the Reasons for the Decline and on New Trends in Contemporary Russian Literature (O prichinakh upadka i o novikh techeniiakh sovremennoi russkoi literatury, 1893), in which Dmitry Merezhkovsky claimed that Russia failed in its quest to create a literature based on the Western model. The bias against folk theater was yet another manifestation of the drive toward Westernization instituted by Peter the Great and nurtured by Catherine the Great, who wrote several plays during her reign, on one hand, and the resistance of the Russian Orthodox Church to displays of so-called pagan ritual on the other. By imposing the European standards of high and low culture on performances, the official hierarchy ignored or even discouraged the study of the popular culture of the skomorokhi, the puppet theater, the puppet mysterium (vertep), and even rituals involving death and marriage. It was only in the nineteenth century that the folk tradition became the subject of intense study by the Slavophiles, who saw folklore as the true source of literature and art characteristic of Russia and were determined to use culture for a nationalist political agenda.

By the end of the nineteenth century the resurrection of the folk tradition was part of an evolving process of inclusion of carnival in the art, music, and theater of the time. Modest Mussorgsky's Khovanshchina (1880, new arrangement by Nikolai Rimsky-Korsakov, 1886) and Boris Godunov (1874, new arrangement by Nikolai Rimsky-Korsakov, 1896) borrowed heavily from the folk melodies and motifs of the fair to evoke the historical and cultural atmosphere of Russia. Rimsky-Korsakov used folk melodies and carnival throughout his own works, prominently featuring the folk theater in the prologue to The Snow Maiden (Snegurochka, 1880). The modernists were even more enchanted with the carnival and its exuberant spirit of freedom. Alexander Blok wrote Balaganchik (1906) as a protest against the overly aestheticized tendencies of symbolism that he felt lost touch with the true nature of the Russian people. Igor Stravinsky's ballet Petrushka (1911), with Alexandre Benois' designs for sets and costumes, represented a complete appropriation of the low culture of carnival. The futurists drew upon this tradition by elaborating the theories of the symbolists and transforming their ideas into actual works. It is only with futurism that the influence of the marginalized folk genres became not merely affectation but a driving force for the creation of a new art form. The futurists accepted even the "dirt and refuse" of Belinsky's Russia that the symbolists were unwilling to allow into their literature. Such previously unacceptable topics as graffiti, dirty words, advertising, the vulgarity of peasant tales and songs, and scatological humor became a vital element of art and literature, allowing the folk sensibilities of the peasant to invade the temple of high art. The influence of the folk genre, both directly through the research of folklorists and indirectly in the ideas of the symbolists, is prominent in the works of the futurists. This manifestation of popular culture was especially pronounced because of the relationship between folk performance and futurist performance as a synthesis of theater with life.

The study of carnival and popular culture was freighted with political considerations under communist rule as is demonstrated in studies of the subject, most notably *Petrushka* by Catriona Kelly and Douglas J. Clayton's *Pierrot in Petrograd*. Folk tales, heroic epic, and folk dramas were important to the communist regime both as representations of the creative and therefore legitimate acts of the working class and as the stirrings of revolutionary struggle against the nobility. Often folk theater was used by the communist elite (Narkompros, Proletkult) as a vehicle for propaganda and for legitimizing the new government by explicitly linking it to the folk tradition. Even the scientific language of ethnography did not escape the political process. The terms populiarnaia kultura and folklorny teatr assumed the added ideological baggage of Marxist ideas of evolution and enlightened consciousness. The intermixing of traditions and genres was increased greatly by technological reproduction and transmission which essentially brought folk culture into wide distribution and transformed spontaneous performance into codified texts.

It was in the context of the highly politicized discourse of Marxism that Mikhail Bakhtin began to study carnival as the inversion of all normal standards of behavior. His ground-breaking study of the grotesque, *Rabelais and His World* (Tvorchestvo Fransua Rable i narodnaia kultura srednevekovia i Renessansa), which Bakhtin wrote in the 1930s but was able to publish only in 1965, was at once a study of carnival as a revolutionary alternative to the rigorous controls of society and a critique of the tightly controlled authoritarianism of Stalin's Russia.

Bibliography: Mikhail Bakhtin, *Rabelais and his World* (Bloomington, Ind., 1984); J. Douglas Clayton, *Pierrot in Petrograd* (Montreal, 1993); Catriona Kelly, *Petrushka. The Russian Carnival Puppet Theatre* (Cambridge, 1990); Albert Konechnyi, ed., *Peterburgskie balalgany* (SPb., 2000); Barbara Lönnqvist, *Xlebnikov and Carnival* (Stockholm, 1979); Iurii Lotman and Boris Uspenskii, *New Aspects in the Study of Early Russian Culture. The Semiotics of Russian Culture*, trans. and ed. by Anna Shukman (Ann Arbor, Mich., 1984); Neia Zorkaia, *Na rubezhe stoletii. U istokov massogo iskusstva v Rossii 1900-1910 godov* (M., 1976).

Mark Konecny

CARPATHIAN MOUNTAINS. One of the major mountain ranges of Central Europe.

The Carpathians extend for approximately 1,000 miles (1,610 km) in an arc-shaped formation through the countries of Slovakia, the Czech Republic, Poland, Ukraine, and Romania. The width of the Carpathian Mountain system varies with the greatest width corresponding to the highest mountain peaks along the Slovak-Polish border and in the Transylvanian region of Romania. The Carpathian

Mountains are not a single unified mountain system but are made up of several geologically unique regions. In the northern extent of the mountain range, in southern Poland, the Carpathians are referred to as the Beskids and the Low and High Tatra mountains. In northern Romania the Carpathians are known as the Transylvanian Alps. The highest point in the Carpathian Mountain range is Gerlachovsky Stit at 8,711 feet (2,665 m) in Slovakia.

Although the Carpathians are generally considered to be younger than the Alps, most geologists consider the Carpathians to be an extension of the Alpine mountain system. The Carpathians are the result of mountain thrusting and folding of the Earth's crust. The mountain range is a series of three parallel structural ranges with the inner range being the youngest, made up of Tertiary volcanic rocks formed less than fifty million years ago. The range also displays a geographic variation in age, the youngest regions of the Carpathians being located in the southeast and the oldest in the west.

The Carpathian Mountains link the Alps with the Balkan Mountains. In the western regions of the range the Danube River separates the Carpathians from the Alps. The Alps and the Carpathians only connect at two points, along the Bakony Mountains near the city of Vac, just north of Budapest, and at the Leitha Mountains to the south of Vienna. The Danube River also separates the Carpathians from the Balkan Mountains at Orsova on the Romanian-Yugoslavian border. In all other locations plains surround the Carpathians. They include the great Hungarian Plain to the southwest, the lower Danube Plain to the south, and the European Plain to the north.

Many rivers of Central Europe rise in the Carpathians. Most of them are tributaries of the larger rivers of Central Europe. Due to their central location and elevation the Carpathians form the northern boundary for the Black Sea watershed and the southern boundary for the Baltic Sea watershed. Approximately 90 percent of the water runoff in the Carpathian Mountains runs into the Black Sea. The mountains provide water to several important watersheds in the region, including the Danube, the Vistula and the Oder rivers.

Earthquake activity is not uncommon in the eastern Carpathian region. This is both the result of the mountain building activities of the region and the collision of the Eurasian and the African plates. Both Ukraine and Romania have been victimized by seismic activity as a result of these processes, and chronic destructive earthquakes are common in the region. Most of these earthquakes are concentrated in the Vrancea region of Romania. During the latter part of the twentieth century Bucharest was subjected to three earthquakes over 6.5 on the Richter scale. Earthquakes under magnitude 5 happen on an almost yearly basis.

Glaciation has not been a major influence on most of the Carpathian region due to their relatively low elevation. Only in the highest regions, which were covered by glaciers, are cirque lakes and waterfalls common features due to glacial erosion.

Transportation through the Carpathians is not a major challenge. Several low passes facilitate movement. The Jablunka Pass at 1,970 feet (600 m) is one of the most important. It is the principal route between Silesia and Hungary and the route of the Breslau-Budapest railway. The Delatyn or Kdrosmezo Pass (3,300 feet, 1,006 m) is also referred to as the Magyar route, suggesting its possible past as a path of migration to the region.

The Carpathian region is dominated by a continental climate, a consequence of its distance from the Atlantic Ocean and the proximity of the Alps, which produce a rain shadow on the Carpathians, keeping the moist air of the Atlantic away from the region. The rain shadow effect is also influenced by elevation. The lower basins of the Carpathian region are especially dry. Some areas receive less twenty-four inches (61 cm) of rain in a year. At the highest points in the mountain system the amount of rainfall increases up to a maximum of seventy inches (180 cm).

Temperatures in the Carpathian region are also influenced by altitudinal zonation but not at a consistent rate. Temperature inversions, where cold air is below warm air, are not uncommon for the region. One of the major influences on this pattern of temperature inversion is again the Alps, which tend to limit the amount of warm maritime air reaching the lower regions of the Carpathians.

The biogeography of the Carpathians is quite varied. The distribution of plant life is influenced by the altitudinal variations within the region. Oaks and elms dominate the lowest regions of the Carpathians. As altitude increases, beech trees replace the oaks and elms. Spruce trees and dwarf pines dominate the next two altitudinal regions in the Carpathians. At the highest altitude mountain pastures are the dominant plant regime.

Animal life is also diverse throughout the Carpathian region. Throughout the forested regions of the Carpathians live bears, wolves, lynx, deer, and boars, which have a major influence on the economy of the region. Chamois and marmots live in the highest regions of the Carpathians.

Many natural hazards characterize the Carpathian Mountain regions and influence the population and landforms. Earthquakes are probably the most dramatic. Another major natural hazard is flooding. The waters of the rivers of the region are augmented during the spring and summer by melting snow. At times these floods have reached catastrophic proportions. The floods of March 2001, for example, damaged extensive areas of Hungary and Ukraine, forcing the evacuation of over two hundred villages. The financial costs were also burdensome. The Hungarian government spent over US $1,000,000 a day to fight the Tisza floods in 2000, leading to massive budget cuts in all government ministries.

Human activities have had an adverse effect on the environment in the region. Logging is a major issue in the Carpathians where deforestation may destroy the habitat for the imperial eagle. Industrial pollution is another major concern. Tropospheric ozone concentration has increased throughout the Central European region. One of the most dramatic environmental disasters was the contamination of the Tisza River with cyanide in 2000. The spill was the result of spring floods causing overflow of a waste pond at the Aurul gold mine in Baia Mare, Romania. The cyanide had a catastrophic effect on the wildlife of the region, termed an aquatic Chernobyl by European environmental groups.

The history of human settlement in the Carpathian region has been extensively studied. Archeologists have found evidence of Paleolithic settlements in the caves of the region. During the late Neolithic age the population of the Carpathian Basin made wide use of copper. Copper artifacts were not unique to one culture, rather were of inter-regional character.

Migration of nomadic populations played an important role in peopling the Carpathian region. In the thirteenth and fourteenth centuries nomadic shepherds from what is now Romania moved throughout the Carpathian region. Some eventually settled in the southern regions of the Carpathian Mountains.

The distribution of sedentary populations is strongly influenced by topography. Isolation caused by extreme topography has produced a wide diversity of nationalities. The northern slopes of the Carpathian region are dominated by Poles. Czechs populate the west and Slovaks the center. A large Hungarian population dominates the southern region. In the east the Ukrainians populate the northern section of the eastern Carpathians, while Romanians predominate in the southern sections. Germans and Hungarians are important components of the population on the Transylvanian Plateau. In the extreme southwestern region of the Carpathians there are Serb settlements.

The diversity of settlement has long contributed to conflict based on competing and overlapping claims of territorial homelands. One of the best known of these claims was the German demand for the Sudetenland that led to the Munich Pact. Another sizable German population, the Carpathian Germans of Slovakia, numbered approximately 130,000 at the start of World War II. While the Reich government in Berlin was especially concerned with the Sudeten Germans, they saw German groups throughout Southeastern Europe as important to the expansion of the Reich and to the germanization of this area. They were tied to the German state, accepted funding for German schools, churches and political movements, and provided increased motivation for German involvement before and during World War II.

The Hungarians are another significant minority throughout the Carpathian region, where approximately 90 percent of the Hungarian population lives. A large number of Hungarians live in regions outside the Hungarian state. Hungarians are the second largest expatriate population in Europe behind only the Russians in total number of nationals living as members of a minority group. A major cause of their dispersion was the Treaty of Trianon in 1920, which divided their population among five different countries. Since then the issue of Hungarian minorities, who have long complained about their treatment and participated in irredentist movements, has been a significant problem. Similar tensions among other ethnic groups is common in the Carpathian region.

Within Ukraine the Carpathian Mountains act as a boundary between the Transcarpathian Administrative Region (Zakarpatska Oblast) and the rest of Ukraine. The Zakarpatska Oblast is also known as Ruthenia, Carpathian Ukraine or Subcarpathian Ruthenia. The major cities of this region include Uzhhorod, the capital, Mukacheve and Khust. Several groups have ruled this region even in recent history.

Until World War I Hungarians, who acted as absentee landlords, dominated the region. After World War I the Khust Ukrainian Congress voted for union with Ukraine but backed away from this position when Ukraine was absorbed into the USSR. The population of the region then voted to join the newly created state of Czechoslovakia as an autonomous region. This lasted until the Munich Pact brought extensive German influence to Czechoslovakia and greater autonomy to the region. This freedom was short-lived as Hungary soon annexed the region. The Hungarian occupation lasted until 1944 when the Soviet army and local forces seized the Transcarpathian region. In 1945 the region was ceded to the USSR and in 1946 was given its current name.

The majority of the population of the Transcarpathian region is Ukrainian with Hungarian, Russian and Slovakian minorities. The region is well endowed with natural resources, including coal, marble, limestone, and timber. The region also supports some agriculture, including production of wheat, corn, tobacco, and potatoes.

The economic geography of the Carpathian region is focused on extractive industries and tourism. Farming, livestock raising, especially sheep herding, and logging are major economic activities. Oil and natural gas exist in the Carpathian Mountains, and natural gas has become a potential growth industry for the region. Several countries hope to exploit natural gas for their own use and for export.

Tourism has become an important growth industry in the Carpathian Mountains, and hunting is an important aspect of it. It is estimated that one set of red-deer antlers can bring US $10,000 into the Polish economy. Wild boar is another important trophy animal hunted in the Carpathians. One of the major problems with hunting in the region has been the prevalence of predators. Polish deer hunters blame wolves for declining deer populations.

Ecotourism also has become an important source of economic development in the region. The relative isolation of the area offers a major draw for hikers and campers, especially in Romania. Skiing is an important growth industry in the region, and resorts have become important for the Romanian economy. The Romanian government created an Agency for Mountainous Regions in 1990 to promote rural tourism as a means of economic development in mountainous areas. Rural tourism is advertised to the international community as a method of sustainable tourism. National identity, an unspoiled environment, and traditional culture are important factors in promoting such tourism.

The post-communist era in the Carpathian Mountain region has brought revaluation and redevelopment. Several political issues have been particularly important. The division of Czechoslovakia into the Czech Republic and Slovakia is but one of the most visible. Other ethnic issues have also been important, including the Hungarian minority issue. Economic considerations have been significant. The redevelopment of economic systems away from the Soviet model has caused many problems. Unemployment has been high as noncompetitive industries are restructured. Even so, the transition from the Soviet model has allowed the countries of the Carpathian region to look at other economic opportunities, such as tourism. One of the greatest legacies of the Soviet era has been environmental crises. Both industrial and residential pollution have negatively affected the Carpathian environment. From cyanide pollution to tropospheric ozone concentration to deforestation the Carpathian environment has been degraded. This creates a dilemma for the governments of the region. The growth of the tourist industry depends on a pristine environment while other industries require the exploitation of that environment.

Bibliography: Louis L. Lote, ed., *Transylvania and the Theory of Daco-Roman-Rumanian Continuity* (Rochester, N.Y., 1980); Karoly Kocsis and Eszter Kocis-Hodosi, *Hungarian Minorities in the Carpathian Basin* (Toronto, 1995); Joanna Sofaer Derevenski, "Rings of Life. The Role of Early Metalwork in Mediating the Gendered Life Course," *World Archaeology*, Vol. 31, No. 3 (2000), 389-406; Valdis O. Lumans, "The Ethnic German Minority of Slovakia and the Third Reich, 1938-45," *Central European History*, Vol. 15, No. 3 (1982), 266-296; Iu.A. Ermolenko and S.M. Stoiko, *Karpaty glazami liuboznatel'nykh. Kraevedcheskie ocherki* (L'vov, 1980); O.S. Vialov, ed., *Istoriia geologicheskogo razvitiia Ukrainskikh Karpat* (Kiev, 1981); Boguslaw Bobek and Kajetan Perzanowski, "Carpathian Mountain Predators," *Earthwatch. The Journal of Earthwatch Institute*, Vol. 13, No. 4 (1994), 81.

Richard L. Wolfel

CARTOGRAPHY AND MAPPING IN RUSSIA TO 1914. Early western images of the world included some essential Russian elements. The Don River, for example, was one of three water bodies that divided the medieval circular Christian tripartite world, centered on Jerusalem, in which Asia occupied the upper half. One indentation in the surrounding ocean was the Caspian Sea. Ptolemy's *Geographia* and its various revisions perpetuated information about the Russian lands from such classical authors as Pliny, Strabo, and Isidore well into the sixteenth century, when Matthew of Miechow ventured that the Ryphei and Hyperborei montes exist merely on paper and in the imagination of cosmographers. That the great rivers of European Russia rose not in these mountains but from a common area in the plains of central Russia was first expressed cartographically in Baron Sigismund von Herberstein's map of 1546.

As with many other nations, the earliest cartographic records belong not to outsiders but to the indigenous people. In the precontact period these records tended to be more cosmographical than geographical. After contact with outsiders they tended to be the reverse. In the Russian case roving hunters and traders, looking to establish trade contacts with native people, sought geographic information about the land and its resources. Unfortunately, many of the documents created in these contact situations were drafted on perishable materials so that few survived. While their existence is attested to by reliable witnesses, evidence also suggests that geographic and cartographic knowledge was part of a vernacular tradition which meant that few documents were needed by the native peoples themselves.

By the late fifteenth century the Tatar yoke was lifted and many Russian principalities were absorbed into Muscovy in a unified and centralized state. These conditions fostered the development of cartographic work in order to strengthen economic relations among the regions and to support various economic, developmental, military, and political purposes. Since many of these hand-drawn records have been lost, much recent research has focused on inferring their existence, context, and form. In general, the Russian maps of this period were in manuscript form, characterized by rich geographic content and place names embedded within a dense network of rivers and water bodies, and were given their place by travel distances between settlements. Most often these maps were accompanied by a descriptive text and were little influenced by scientific progress being made in the West. They were produced in several different administrative offices such as the Landed Estates Office, the Foreign Office, and the Defense Chancellery (razriad).

Specific evidence of these maps can be found in various lists, inventories, and descriptions going back to the late fifteenth century and to the reigns of Ivan III (r. 1462-1505) and Vasily III (r. 1505-1533). The most famous of these was the Book of the Great Draft, or sometimes Great Drawing (Kniga Bolshomu chertëzhu). The Bolshoi chertezh, drawn at the end of the sixteenth century, showed the Muscovite state as far as the Ob River and its boundaries with its neighbors. Subsequently its authors, draftsmen Afanasy Mezentsov and Fedor Nekvasin, produced other chertezhy (pl.) of the Russian state. When the maps were lost in a great fire in Moscow in 1626 the draftsman were ordered to make a new chertezh. That same year a chertezh of the Ukrainian and Cherkassian cities from Moscow to the Crimea was produced. The Kniga Bolshomu chertezhu described both of these maps.

Useful light has been shed on the Bolshoi chertezh by maps drawn when a Russian agent abroad or a foreigner's trip to Russia was involved. Most notable were the maps of Ivan Liatsky, which were published by Sebastian Munster in 1544, by Herberstein in 1546, by Battista Agnese in 1550 on the basis of information obtained from Dmitry Gerasimov on an embassy to Italy, by Anthony Jenkinson in 1562, and by Hessel Gerritsz in 1613. Study of these maps, which covered most of European Russia, established the Russian provenance of much of their content and helped Europeans to replace Ptolemaic ideas with increasingly more accurate images of the sources of its five great rivers.

Russia's conquest of Siberia, beginning with Yermak's conquests in the Ob basin, was accomplished mostly by 1639. As a result a great number of route maps were collected in Tobolsk, the regional capital. Their quality reflects the variable talents of the soldiers, traders, and adventurers who led these expeditions across a vast and poorly known continental interior and to the Arctic and Pacific coasts. Two results of the accumulation of all this material was a chertezh of Siberia in 1667 produced under the supervision of Siberian governor Petr Ivanovich Godunov and a chertezh of 1673 of all Siberia down to the Chinese and Nikan empires.

Subsequently Semen Yulianovich Remezov collected many other maps and over the next two decades copied them into draft books, three of which have survived.

His work is considered to be exemplary of a system of recording and compiling new geographic information developed earlier in European Russia. From these maps the Russians now had a faithful and detailed cartographic description of Siberia and its complex network of rivers, water features, settlements, and of many aspects of the environment. Remezov's city plans are a rich source of street layout and architectural details of existing and lost buildings.

At the turn of the eighteenth century progress in Russian mapping activities centered on the dynamic initiatives of Tsar Peter the Great (r. 1689-1725). Peter's first important act in this respect was to establish in Moscow in 1701 a navigation school intended to train students in mathematics and civil and marine sciences. From this school were to come the first surveyors and geodesists to develop the scientific bases of Russian cartography and to carry out systematic surveys across the empire. Peter also brought printers and engravers to Russia allowing new maps to be engraved and printed in Russia.

An important figure at this time was Ivan Kirilov who as secretary of the Senate organized and directed the government's work of the graduate geodesists in the first crucial decades and who between 1724 and 1734 produced the first comprehensive collection of maps of Russia. After his death in 1737 Kirilov's work was taken over by Vasily Nikitich Tatishchev (1686-1750), an administrator and statesman with active interests in geography, history, mining, and mintage. He helped systematize and improve the accuracy of gathering descriptive information of outlying regions with a 198-item questionnaire. Upon Russian expansion into Kazakhstan and Central Asia, Tatishchev and Petr Ivanovich Rychkov (1712-1777) organized the Orenburg Expedition to gather geographic information about the region and its peoples.

After its founding in 1739 the Geographical Department of the Academy of Sciences received field reports from various scientific expeditions sent across the empire and thus was a major center of general mapping. Significant for this work were the contributions of foreign scientists invited to Russia to work on various projects and who stayed for many years. Notable among them was Joseph Nicolas Delisle who came to Russia in 1726 to occupy the chair of astronomy, geography, and navigation at the academy and to prepare a general map of the Russian Empire. His plan was to construct first a solid triangulated grid based on astronomical observations so that the required regional sheets would fit together correctly. Over the next sixteen years work proceeded, sometimes without Delisle's help or involvement. In 1745 the academy's *Atlas of Russia* finally appeared. It was made up of thirteen sheets at 1:1,527,000 for the Urals and European Russia and six more for Siberia at 1:3,360,000. A two-sheet general map at 1:8,400,000 was included.

Delisle's contributions to this effort and to the work of the academy are universally recognized. Unfortunately he has been a source of some controversy because his plan of triangulating the entire empire was unachievable at a time when maps were badly needed and because he made copies of many of the new maps that came to the academy and sent them back to France. When he left Russia, he used these materials to publish, among others, a map of the Northern Pacific in 1750. This map revealed secret results of Bering's second expedition and the relationship of eastern Siberia to western North America before the Russians were able to do the same in 1754.

Delisle was one of a number of distinguished scientists working at the academy, including Mikhail Vasilievich Lomonosov (1741-1765), Gerhard Friedrich Müller (1751-1765), and Stepan Yakovlevich Rumovsky (1756-1812). The academy also helped the naval authorities in drawing, engraving and printing charts of various rivers, lakes, seas and oceans, and maps of the sources of ship timber. The surveys, initiated by both the academy and the navy, were carried out by the Admiralty College under the command of a naval officer. To assist in this, advanced students at the Navigation School in Moscow spent their last years in St. Petersburg specializing at the Naval Academy which opened in 1715.

The Academy of Sciences was responsible for a great variety of other maps. These ranged from maps for travel by members of the imperial family and other sovereigns and dignitaries to maps for calendars (mesiatseslovy). The latter were often original maps illustrating scientific articles of general interest. By the end of the century the academy's Geographical Department had lost its importance for general mapping and was abolished.

By mid-century the initiatives of Peter and the leadership and work of Kirilov, Tatishchev, Delisle, and others established a sound scientific basis for Russian cartography. Trained geodesists with written instructions were now specifically assigned to expeditions such as the First Kamchatka Expedition (1725-1730) and the Great Northern Expedition (1733-1743), both led by Vitus Bering and Aleksei Chirikov, and to the General Survey of Russia which began in 1766. The century's second half saw other expeditions across the Northern Pacific, including those of Petr Krenitsyn, Mikhail Levashev, Grigory Shelikov, Iosif Billings, and Gavriil Sarychev. These expeditions established the priority of Russian mapping of this region.

During this same period there was need to establish precisely the boundaries between crown lands and private lands granted to privileged land-owners for performing specific tasks for the state. A special Land Surveying Expedition was established in the Senate for this work. This survey was to produce maps at an array of scales, atlases, and economic notes for the thirty-five provinces. The scales ranged from survey units at 1:8,400 to district maps at 1:42,000 to atlas plates at 1:84,000 or 1:168,000. When completed early in the nineteenth century the survey provided the country with a most comprehensive and detailed record for economic development and administration and in many ways represented the fulfillment of Peter's dream of bringing Russian scientific achievement to a level with, or surpassing, that of Western Europe. The founding of the Depot of Maps in 1797 marked the beginning of the military topographic service. Its charge was to produce extensive topographical surveys in the western frontier provinces and compilation of small- and medium-scale maps. Toward that end the *Hundred Sheet Map* at scale 1:840,000 was produced in the period 1801 to 1804. It was the first detailed, multi-sheet (107) map to encompass all of European Russia and the Caucasus. In 1822 a second agency, the Corps of Military Topographers, with an attached school, was established. Throughout its 100-year history it had a complement of some 500 men. With the much smaller Military Topographical Depot these offices carried out all the basic astrogeodetic, topographical, and cartographic operations of the state for the next century. This focus is related to the increasing complexity of the mapping process, the scientific understanding required, and concurrent needs for more highly trained and specialized personnel.

In 1822 the corps was attached to the General Staff and the Military Topographical Depot to promote better functioning as the state's topographical mapping service in peacetime and in mapping behind the army in time of war. The first director of the corps was the surveyor and cartographer Fedor Fedorovich Shubert (1789-1865). By his initiative maps of the provinces at scales 1:168,000 and 1:210,000 and for the whole of European Russia at 1:420,000 were compiled and engraved intermittently up to 1839 when some sixty sheets were published.

Shubert was followed by Major General Petr Aleksandrovich Tuchov who initiated in 1845 a 1:126,000 topographic map program for western European Russia to replace the maps at 1:168,000 and 1:210,000 scales. By 1863, 435 sheets were published. As the Shubert maps were now quite outdated, a new *Special Map of European Russia* at scale 1:422,000 was initiated. It was designed for military planning but it also met the demands of Russian society for good, detailed maps. By 1872 all 152 sheets were compiled and some were being printed and sold. By 1903 the series had expanded to 167 sheets and was the basis for many special purpose maps by other agencies and institutions. Given the very high scientific and technical expertise applied to this series, it retained its practical value well into the Soviet era.

One important name associated with this program was Ivan Afanasievich Strelbitsky, who was first commissioned to produce the *Special Map*. Another area of his expertise was cartometry, the branch of cartography dealing with precise measurement. Strelbitsky's various measurements of the size of Russia brought him recognition, awards at home and abroad, and a commission from the International Statistical Congress in The Hague to make such measurements for all the countries of Europe.

There is also a rich history of atlas making in Russia, beginning with the several collections noted above, especially those of Semen Remezov. The world's first river atlas, Cruys' *Atlas of the Don River and Black Seas*, was printed in Amsterdam in 1704. The first atlas published in Russia was Kiprianov's *Atlas of the World* in 1713. A twenty-seven sheet *Atlas Compiled for the Benefit and Use of Youth* was published by the academy in 1737. With increasing numbers of trained personnel and greater quantities of information being gathered, the number and variety of atlas products increased dramatically. They were created for such varied purposes as navigation, schools, military history, and travel.

After the emancipation of the serfs in 1861 a rapidly growing capitalistic system created the need for more sophisticated thematic mapping. As a result a large number of complex atlases were produced by both governmental and public institutions. They covered many topics such as the railway system, agriculture, woodlands, the environment, geology, meteorology, and a great variety of economic activities and statistical measures. In 1899 the *Atlas of Finland*, then still a grand duchy of Russia, was produced. Distinguished by its exceptionally full and varied content, it became the model by which most countries in the twentieth century produced their own national atlases. In 1914 the *Atlas of Asiatic Russia* was created to assist in the application of agrarian policy and development of the natural riches of this vast area newly accessible by the trans-Siberian railroad that was completed in the first years of the twentieth century.

Bibliography: Leo Bagrow, *A History of the Cartography of Russia up to 1600*, ed. by Henry W. Castner (Wolfe Island, Ont., 1975); Leo Bagrow, *A History of Russian Cartography up to 1800*, ed. by Henry W. Castner (Wolfe Island, Ont., 1975); Samuel Baron, "The Lost Jenkinson Map of Russia (1562). Recovered, Redated and Retitled," *Terrae Incognitae*, Vol. 25 (1993), 53-65; *Essays on the History of Russian Cartography, 16th to 19th Centuries,* selected and trans. by James R. Gibson (Toronto, 1975); Leonid Arkadievich Gol'denberg, *Semen Ul'ianovich Remezov* (M., 1965); Elena Alekseevna Okladnikova, "Traditional Cartography in Arctic and Subarctic Eurasia" in J. Brian Harley and David Woodward, eds., *The History of Cartography*, Vol. 2, Book 3 (Chicago, Ill., 1998), 329-349; Boris Petrovich Polevoy, "A History of the Cartography of Russia up to 1800," trans. by James R. Gibson, *The Canadian Cartographer*, Vol. 13, No. 2 (1976), 167-173; Boris Petrovich Polevoy, "Siberian Cartography of the 17th Century and the Problem of the 'Great Draught,'" trans. by James R. Gibson, *The Canadian Cartographer*, Vol. 14, No. 2 (1977), 85-100; Alexey Vladimirovich Postnikov, *Russia in Maps. A History of the Geographical Study and Cartography of the Country* (M., 1996), "Russian Traditional Cartography of the Seventeenth Century and the Importance of Semen Ulyanovich Remezov and His Drawing Books of Siberia," *Portolan* (2002), 17-33; Boris Aleksandrovich Rybakov, *Russkie Karty Moskovii, 15 nachala 16 veka* (M., 1974); Fyodor Anisimovich Shibanov, *Studies in the History of Russian Cartography,* Part 2, trans. by James R. Gibson (Toronto., 1975); Mikhail Alekseevich Tsvetkov, "Cartographic Results of the General Survey of Russia, 1766-1861," trans. by James R. Gibson, *The Canadian Cartographer*, Vol. 6, No. 1 (1969), 1-14.

Henry W. Castner

CARTOONS. Animated cinema in Russia, 1912- .

Animated cinema began before the Russian Revolution when the famous silent movie director Aleksandr Alekseevich Khanzhonkov (1877-1945) invited the Polish puppeteer Władyslaw Starewicz (1882-1965) to Moscow in 1911. His first, somewhat grim stop-action film, The War of the Stag Beetles and the Capricorn Beetles, was released 26 April 1912. Other features followed over the next two years, ranging between 440 and 941 feet (134-287 m) in length. By 1918 Starewicz made over sixty films. Soviet historians concluded in subsequent years that the production of genuinely socialist cartoons began slightly later, in 1922, when the first Experimental Animation Workshop was formed, part of what later became the All-Union State Institute of Cinematography (VGIK). Instigating a revolutionary style the early film China on Fire (Kitai v ogne) narrated capitalist mistreatment of industrious Chinese peasants which once led to an uprising. A rather long feature running about 3,280 feet (1,000 m) or fifty minutes, it employed hinged two-dimensional figures against a three-dimensional backdrop, which commentators later explained were not a means to reduce the budget of a protracted venture, rather respectful replicas of en face and profile portraiture in Chinese graphic arts. Animated cinema faced other, more technical problems. Old cameras, often stolen from pre-revolutionary museums, typically were used only for short, freeze-frame films of no more than 197 feet (60 m) or three minutes. Longer projects were extremely complex, yet the authorities knew that brief, cheaper productions would never foster long-term audience interest.

Matters began to stabilize by 1925 when studios were organized in both Moscow and Leningrad. This slowly helped to advance a consciously Soviet type of children's cartoon, both national in form and socialist in content. A typical product of this time was Senka the African (1927), based on a story by the famous author Kornei Ivanovich Chukovsky (1882-1969), who also wrote Scrubadub (Moidodyr), a comic strip tale of talking washtubs. Senka, seated on a zoo bench, dreams about exotic flying animals. This purportedly vacuous yet popular entertainment was felt by some to be detrimental to correct communist education.

Similar concerns were difficult to address on a nationwide scale because studios in provincial or far-flung parts of the Soviet Union had as yet little or no contact with one another. As trepidation grew in the 1930s over what exactly was proper socialist animation, some form of aesthetic or organizational centralization became inevitable. It appeared finally in 1936 with the creation of the Soviet state cartoon studio Soiuzmultfilm. By declaration of the State Directorate for Cinema and Photographic Industries, the central Moscow film studio Mosfilm merged with another major Moscow studio Mezhrabpomfilm, and the resulting association was housed in real estate owned by the directorate itself. Still creation of this entertainment center did little to ameliorate the situation even in Leningrad. Lenfilm was paying no particular attention to cartoons. In Kiev meager resources meant that early, entertaining artistic animation was, for a while, completely abandoned. The nation's collective response to American animation was thus relatively slow, despite the exciting theory behind the work of Lev Konstantinovich Atamanov (1905-1981) and his most famous character, Kliaksa, an amorphous, active hero born in 1934 of inkpots and blessed with the ability to change shape frequently.

Soviet film developed further in the 1930s towards the integration of children's animation, structuring the social future, and folklore, interpreting or canonizing the past. These plans were delayed because of the swift and unexpected evacuation of Soiuzmultfilm during World War II. Everything moved to Samarkand and many artists saw active service. After the war a decree was issued by the Soviet Ministry of Cinematography in 1948 to accelerate and propagate cinematic cartoons. Bureaucrats concurred that folklore offered answers to many postwar ideological questions and was attractive to animators as a union of invisible magic and visible nationalism. This logic of ever-new, traditional performance developed even during the war, especially in the work of Zinaida S. (1900-1983) and Valentina S. (1899-1975) Brumberg. Their cartoons of Pushkin's Tale of Tsar Saltan (1943) and Gogol's The Lost Letter (1945) drew much from Ukrainian local color and tales of jolly peasantry.

Ethnography was apparent in films by Ivan Petrovich Ivanov-Vano (1900-1987), such as the folkloric Little Hump-Backed Horse (1947), which received lavish official praise. The film's artists abbreviated but did not modernize its text, choosing to save novelty for witty, wholly visual elements taken from folk painting, architecture, ceramics, and carvings. Soviet animators soon began to interweave innovative fantasy, ostensible reality, and civic relevance by working with so-called éclairs, using a rotoscope and tracing the outlines of live footage onto celluloid, producing line drawings that delineated color fields. These techniques were frequently used between 1950 and 1955, applied best in Pushkin's Tale of the Fisherman and Fish (1950). After a brief period of high appreciation the techniques were criticized for reducing reality to external elements, slavishly emulating photography, and losing all vital magic (skazochnost). After similarly composed cartoons like The Frog Princess and Chekhov's Kashtanka, the éclair technique was criticized for its naturalism.

The enduring problem of photography versus fancy was important in Atamanov's lengthy and supernatural Golden Antelope (Zolotaia antilopa, 1954), based upon a series of Indian folktales. Though the film makes considerable use of traced live-action scenes, its great success was its creation of a new, positive hero, a young Indian boy who saves a coin-producing magic antelope from the evil grasp of a local raj. Anatomically accurate human figures were at least presented against a backdrop of a more fluid, indistinct jungle with which that figure harmonized.

A related step towards slightly less objective representation came in 1952 when Soiuzmultfilm opened an independent division of puppet and freeze-frame films. Six puppet or stop-frame works were released around the Soviet Union in the 1950s, but they were also accused of naturalism, of looking needlessly real. One of the strangest films ever produced in the Soviet Union, Moody Julie (Yulia-kaprizulia), clearly shows this problem, using almost frighteningly realistic puppets to tell the tale of a sullen young girl. Julie bawls at the slightest excuse and, just as Lewis Carroll's Alice, almost drowns an entire park when water shoots from her eyes faster than from a garden hose.

A subsequent solution, and in some ways the key cartoon of the era of the Thaw, came in 1962 from Fedor Savelievich Khitruk (born 1917) as The Story of a Crime (Istoriia odnogo prestupleniia). Its groundbreaking style reflected the aesthetics of the UPA studio in America, which successfully challenged Disney's predominant, profitable aesthetic with a simple animation style. Khitruk's film is based upon flat, two-dimensional chromatic blocks in accelerated, jerky motion to depict not dogma but the social difficulties of nervous bodies, overworked cars and other troubled forms.

By 1970-1971 the socialist art form of cartoons was confident enough thanks to its purposeful innovation to bless critical studies with titles like *The Art of Animation Yesterday, Today, and Tomorrow*. The characters and styles of past classics like The Snow Queen (Snezhnaia koroleva, 1957) or Winnie the Pooh (Vinni-Pukh, 1969) were constantly echoed even in an atmosphere of multiple styles. This development paradoxically was described as a dialectic leading to states not easily translated into language. Words often were replaced by heartfelt images, sounds and noises. Cartoon backdrops over time likewise faded to neutral colors. Audio elements regularly became mere indicators of depth and perspective, for example, with echo, all in order to circumvent naturalistic excess.

Artists and journalists paid great attention to various imperceptible, smaller forms of being, and the minor, peripheral, and provincial origins of non-Russian animators were used to plot this art form's healthy, multidirectional distribution across the entire nation. At this time the public heard more often of projects throughout the USSR, among them the first Armenian cartoons (Lev Atamanov), establishment of Georgia's Goskinrom or subsequent Gruziia-film (Vakhtang Bakhtadze), Kievan movies (Ippolit Lazarchuk and Fedor Khitruk), wartime evacuee efforts in distant, dusty Samarkand (Mstislav Pashchenko), and the work of female artists (Valentina and Zinaida Brumberg). This diversity was due to the initial leniency of the sixties and was characterized by an ethical aspect of social, non-judgmental inclusion. The small, fluffy stop-frame figure Cheburashka embodied current notions of non-verbal, charitable sentimentality best of all. He arrives in Russia in a slightly stiff state, squeezed into a box of foreign oranges, then slowly his and his fellow puppets' large eyes blink, their mouths slightly alter shape during speech, and body parts grow more flexible as they interact.

A clearer civic spirit reappeared in 1980 in connection with the sports atmosphere of Moscow's 1980 Olympic Games. Journalists wrote endlessly of socialist animation as embodying three parallel types of movement: mechanical, physical, and emotional. In a grand, tellingly entitled collection of 1983, *The Wisdom of Fantasy* (Mudrost vymysla), this new and exciting state of affairs was assessed in a timely analysis of Soiuzmultfilm, now producing 80 percent of its work for children. The authors concluded that the studio's childish, emotional expressions of unrest might even be credited with the creation of a novel time and space. Everyday life was reconstituted on the screen and offered as an affective alternative to the shambles of Soviet political existence. It was at this time that Yury Borisovich Norshtein (1941-) made his masterpiece Tale of Tales (Skazka skazok), the metaphysical tale of a lost wolf cub amid the cruelty of World War II and modern, quotidian heartlessness.

Another Soviet classic embodies these metamorphoses, the film in 1986 by Natalia Golovanova (1942-), A Boy Like Any Other (Malchik kak malchik). A series of russet line-sketches on a similarly colored, fawn wash, the feature tells of a boy's fantasies as he moves through a busy city, shown to us initially in hectic split-screen. When he passes through the urban sprawl and out into the countryside, he is gradually isolated with a few blades of grass, plants change into faces, then become various objects. Proceeding beyond dualistic thought film makers believed that, once animation was reduced to these essences, multifaceted variety was subsumed into the structure of a celluloid frame, of polyphonic space itself.

Just prior to perestroika natural multiplicity found its greatest significance in animated film by advocating ways to interact with the environment and actively work upon it. A strange imperative resulted. Disappear with humility into the variegated environment and adopt a meaningful stance by meaning less and less, maybe absolutely nothing. One artist now defined selfhood expressed not as bold, dogmatic cinema, rather as a butterfly combining active decisions, the flap of wings, and the humbling feel of shifting outside forces, the buttressing of the wind. Artists theorized increasingly about cartoons as gestures, not words, as expressions both active and passive. A good example of their variety is found in wordless puppet films of the 1980s, such as The Door by Nina Ivanovna Shorina (1943-), portraying unspoken social problems of increasing frustration caused by a faulty door at the entrance to an apartment building, quandaries orchestrated to the sounds of Chaikovsky.

The first major history of animation published after perestroika, *The World of Cartoons* (Mir multfilma), came at a time when Soiuzmultfilm was releasing over thirty films a year and employing more than five hundred people in multiple attempts to capture or express the full range of affective forces and gesturing faces. The study held that in Cheburashka, for example, one enters just "this most intricate world of human feelings" mapped on puppets' faces, "thanks to the wise and thoughtful skill of a director" (61). The goal of younger filmmakers was now the "harmony of [manifold] emotional and intellectual sources" (76). Soviet cartoons now made "impressive new discoveries in the most traditional genres" of the canon, such as the very funny Journey of an Ant by Eduard Vasilievich Nazarov (1941-). Here, with beautiful fluidity in depiction of wind-blown trees, an ant is carried far away into foreign territory, where swarms of minor figures cross the screen at any given moment: worms, other ants, grasshoppers, bugs, and fleas. Speech is reduced to the expression of emotion as heartfelt noise, such as squeaks, grunts, and whistles.

As the Soviet Union came to a close and Soiuzmultfilm was ravaged by market pressures, the greatest heroes or godfathers of animation, such as Ivan Ivanov-Vano and Fedor Khitruk, continued their traditional improvisation, their ability to make native animals fly or change shape. Khitruk paraphrased Norman McLaren, saying once again as animation began another dialectical negation that the most important thing was not the content of cinematic frames, but the humbling silences between them, the relation of frames to one another, which creates movement.

A non-violent challenge was mounted successfully against or parallel to the grand narratives of Soviet times. Commentators even celebrated the fact that Moscow was no longer the center of the profession, outdone now by studios in Armenia, Uzbekistan, Sverdlovsk, Kiev, Belarus, Georgia, Kazakhstan and Kyrgyzia. This state of liberation, dissolving, or dissipation, it was felt, began many years ago. The supposedly monumental, wholly political changes of perestroika were less eventful, if not meaningless. Changes of equal consequence occurred long ago in animation, and prompted films based upon inquiry into current social experience or sympathy. Exclusive politics became the socializing inclusiveness of a non-judgmental art form.

Viacheslav Mikhailovich Kotenochkin (1927-2000), the mastermind behind Russia's most popular cartoon series, Just You Wait! (Nu, pogodi!), formulated this well. The series consisted basically of wordless chase sequences between a ragged wolf and an innocent hare. In 1999 whenever he asked children at public engagements if they wished to see some cartoons, they invariably screamed with delight. This enthusiasm was hard to maintain at the end of the century, given the funding problems suffered by cartoon festivals such as Krok in Ukraine or the Little Golden Fish in Moscow. Much animation, the victim of market forces, gravitated towards computer media, advertising, or television work, rather than feature films. Nonetheless, the Oscar in 2000 awarded to The Old Man and the Sea by Aleksandr Konstantinovich Petrov (1957-) and the huge success of the web-based Masiania cartoons in 2002 offered some hope for the future.

Bibliography: Sergei V. Asenin, ed., *Mudrost' vymysla* (M., 1983), *Mir mul'tfil'ma* (M., 1986), *Mul'tiplikatsiia sotsialisticheskikh stran kak sotsial'no-esteticheskii fenomen* (M., 1989); Dmitrii N. Babichenko, *Iskusstvo mul'tiplikatsii* (M., 1964); Giannalberto Bendazzi, *Cartoons. 100 Years of Cinema Animation* (Bloomington, Ind., 1994); Ivan P. Ivanov-Vano, *Kadr za kadrom* (M., 1980), *Ocherk istorii razvitiia mul'tiplikatsii* (M.,1967); Viacheslav M. Kotenochkin, *Nu, Kotenochkin, pogodi!* (M., 1999); Jay Leyda, ed., *Eisenstein on Disney* (London, 1988); Ion Popesku Gopo, *Fil'my, fil'my, fil'my* (Bucharest, 1963).

David MacFadyen

CATHERINE I (1683?-1727). Wife of Peter the Great and empress of Russia. See Catherine I, MERSH, Vol. 6.

Recent scholarship and commentary have allotted greater attention to Catherine I, the Livland Zolushka (Cinderella), both as person and public figure. Doubts persist over her origins and year of birth. All agree that she was not Slavic but Germanic, Scandinavian, or Latvian and that she could not write although she spoke German, Swedish, Russian, and Polish. Her strong influence on Peter I has been attributed to extrasensory powers, perhaps a fancy way of interpreting female wiles and native shrewdness. Certainly she proved extraordinarily fertile with some ten or twelve offspring, only two of whom reached adulthood, Anna (1708-1728) and Elizabeth (1709-1761). Energy and endurance enabled her to accompany Peter on several campaigns and journeys abroad, and she displayed impressive muscular strength.

She and Peter may well have married secretly years before their public wedding of 1712, which struck English envoy Charles Whitworth as "one of the surprising events in this Wonderful age" (Whitworth, xx-xxi). Her rising visibility coincided with evolution of the europeanized court in the last fifteen years of Peter's reign. One manifestation was establishment of the Order of Saint Catherine in 1714, the sole knightly order for women in imperial Russia with its motto "For Love and the Fatherland." She was publicly praised for exemplary courage in the Pruth campaign, when "Without Regard to the Imbecility and Tenderness of her Sex...in that Critical Juncture She behaved herself not like a Woman but a Man, wherefore our whole Army will witness, and can testify to our whole Empire" (Cracraft, 442-443). As she often served as an intercessor for the powerful and the common folk, her positive image was fortified by association with Saint Catherine of Alexandria and the Virgin Mary. Amiable and sociable, she frequently appeared in public in gala dress, dancing and drinking. Whitworth called her "the famous Czarina" and "this memorable woman." Later he saw her succession as "one of the most Extraordinary Incidents in all History" (xx-xxi). Nobody could have predicted that her brief reign would be the first installment of virtually continuous female rule till 1796, an era of "Russian matriarchate" (Pushkareva) as personified by the series of "Amazon autocratrixes" (Alexander).

Catherine shared Peter's rough and ready humor, teasing him in later life as old man, just as he had called her old girl (muder, matka). She wore Amazon dress during public celebrations in 1722-24. At her coronation in Moscow on 7 May 1724 she was lauded as a peer of Semiramis of Babylon, Tamara of the Scythians, and Penthesileia of the Amazons. The scandal surrounding her relationship with courtier William Mons remains controversial. Some defend her against rumors of adultery, whereas others repeat tales of conspiracy with Menshikov to poison Peter in revenge for Mons's execution. Her brief reign may be rationalized as an overdue relaxation after prolonged Petrine stress. It saw a continuation of Europeanization, an active foreign policy, marriages with European dynasties, and consensus government via the Supreme Privy Council. Chudo's parody dubs her "a Lithuanian whore; not to be confused with Catherine the Great, who was German" (Chudo, 181). She deserves more respect.

Bibliography: John T. Alexander, "Favourites, Favouritism and Female Rule in Russia, 1725-1796" in Roger Bartlett and Janet M. Hartley, eds., *Russia in the Age of the Enlightenment. Essays for Isabel de Madariaga* (London, 1990), 106-124, "Amazon Autocratrixes. Images of Female Rule in the Eighteenth Century" in Peter I. Barta, ed., *Gender and Sexuality in Russian Civilisation* (London, 2001), 33-54, "Catherine I, her Court and Courtiers" in Lindsey Hughes, ed., *Peter the Great and the West. New Perspectives* (London, 2001), 227-249; E.V. Anisimov, "Ekaterina I" in A.N. Sakharov, ed., *Romanovy. Istoricheskie portrety, 1613-1762,* Vol. 1 (M., 1998), 340-374, *Rossiia bez Petra* (SPb., 1994), *Zhenshchiny na Rossiiskom trone* (SPb., 1998); V.S. Beliavskii, "Zolushka na trone Rossiiskom" in *Na Rossiiskom prestole, 1725-1796* (M., 1993), 5-64; V.I. Buganov, "Ekaterina I," *Voprosy istorii,* No. 11 (1994), 39-49; Alicia Chudo and Andrew Sobesednikov [Gary Saul Morson], eds., *And Quiet Flows the Vodka, or When Pushkin Comes to Shove* (Evanston,

Ill., 2000); James Cracraft, ed., *For God and Peter the Great. The Works of Thomas Consett, 1723-1729* (New York, 1982); Janet M. Hartley, *Charles Whitworth. Diplomat in the Age of Peter the Great* (Aldershot, 2002); Lindsey Hughes, *Peter the Great. A Biography* (New Haven, Conn., 2002), *Russia in the Age of Peter the Great* (New Haven, Conn., 1998); Natalia Pushkareva, *Women in Russian History from the Tenth to the Twentieth Century*, ed. and trans by Eve Levin. (Armonk, N.Y., 1997); Charles Whitworth, *An Account of Russia As It Was in the Year 1710* (Strawberry Hill, 1758).

John T. Alexander

CATHERINE II "THE GREAT" (1729-1796). Empress of Russia, 1762-1796. See Catherine II, MERSH, Vol. 6.

Additional Bibliography: John T. Alexander, *Catherine the Great. Life and Legend* (New York, 1989), *Bubonic Plague in Early Modern Russia. Public Health and Urban Disaster* (Baltimore, Md., 1980), "Catherine II (Ekaterina Alekseevna), 'The Great,' Empress of Russia" in *Dictionary of Literary Biography*, Vol. 150, *Early Modern Russian Writers, Late Seventeenth and Eighteenth Centuries*, ed. by Marcus Levitt (Detroit, Mich., 1995), 43-54; Isabel de Madariaga, *Russia in the Age of Catherine the Great* (London, 1981), *Catherine the Great. A Short History* (New Haven, Conn., 1990), *Politics and Culture in Eighteenth-Century Russia. Collected Essays of Isabel de Madariaga* (London, 1998); Simon Sebag Montefiore, *Prince of Princes. The Life of Potemkin* (London, 2000); Simon Dixon, *Catherine the Great* (London, 2001); E. Hübner, et al. eds., *Russland zur Zeit Katharinas II. Absolutismus, Aufklärung, Pragmatismus* (Cologne, 1998); A.B. Kamenskii, *"Pod seniiu Ekateriny." Vtoraia polovina XVIII veka* (SPb., 1992); O.A. Omel'chenko, *"Zakonaia monarkhiia" Ekateriny II. Prosveshchennyi absolutizm v Rossii* (M., 1993); Claus Scharf, ed., *Katharina II. Russland und Europa. Beiträge zur internationalen Forschung* (Mainz, 2001).

John T. Alexander

CATHOLICISM IN RUSSIA. See Catholicism in Russia, MERSH, Vol. 6.

Study of this topic has flourished in the last thirty years, attention being directed mostly to outstanding figures about whom there already existed a body of knowledge. This is primarily the result of the availability of sources outside the Soviet Union as well as the many individuals traveling between Russia and western Europe. Changes in recent decades in Russia have made publication on forbidden or sensitive topics easier there and facilitated archival access.

The Greek monk Maxim (1470-1556, canonized 1988) was brought to Russia in 1515 to help improve the intellectual quality of the Orthodox Church. It was not known at the time that he had lived for a time in Italy where he was a member of the Dominican Order. He was able to introduce some western ideas to Russia, but as a consequence he suffered a prolonged period of incarceration. Maxim may be viewed as a prototype, copied in succeeding ages. The Jesuit Antonio Possevino (1533?-1611) planned to convert Russians living in Poland-Lithuania to Catholicism and then to go on to Russia proper. Nothing much came of his efforts, but he did have discussions with Ivan the Terrible of which he left an account. Whether Dmitry the Pretender (1582-1606), the brief occupant of the Russian throne, was himself a convert or merely persuaded the Polish King Sigismund III (r. 1587-1632) that he might become one is disputed. Rumors to this effect helped bring about his over-throw and the elimination of Jesuits and others from Poland, who joined him in Moscow. In the reign of Aleksei Mikhailovich (r. 1645-1676) an attempt to rec-oncile the churches was undertaken by the Croat priest Juraj Krizhanich. Of his sixteen years in Russia fifteen were spent in Siberia. He is remembered as a pioneer panslav and linguist.

The takeover of much of Poland-Lithuania by Catherine the Great resulted in Catholic priests becoming Russian residents. A result of the French Revolution was the appearance in Russia of emigre priests and active Catholic laymen. Their involvement in education led to the founding of schools as well as to the efforts of individuals as teachers and tutors. Their presence also resulted in a number of conversions, including some well known, such as that of Sofia Svechina (1782-1857) whose conversion was due in some measure to conversations with the Sar-dinian ambassador, Joseph de Maistre. Emigres had much to do with the conversion of Countess Rostopchina and her sisters and daughters. These conversions and some among the students at the Jesuit College in St. Petersburg led to a backlash, the expulsion of the Jesuits in 1816, and the withdrawal of Count de Maistre soon after.

Other Russians were converted abroad. Prince P.B. Kozlovsky (1783-1840) was converted in Rome, probably in 1803, as was Princess Zinaida Volkonskaia (1792-1862) in 1829. Kozlovsky was a friend and correspondent of Maistre, whose comments on Russia may have originated in discussions with the prince. Kozlovsky developed ideas similar to those of Petr Chaadaev (c. 1794-1856) and communicated his criticisms of Russia to the Marquis de Custine who incorporated them into his famous account of Russia in 1839. Others who converted abroad include the former ambassador in Vienna Prince A.K. Razumovsky and the Decembrist M.S. Lunin. Somewhat surprising was the deathbed conversion of the head of the police, General Count Benkendorf (1781-1844). Because of continuing prejudice against converts many chose to live abroad, including S. Svechina and Princess Volkonskaia. Sve-china is credited with a number of conversions, particularly that of Prince Ivan S. Gagarin (1814-1882), nephew of her sister. Gagarin gave up his post in the Russian embassy in Paris and in 1843 entered the order of Jesuits. He was very influential, launching the still extant periodical Etudes, publishing widely and making available early editions of some of Chaadaev's and de Maistre's writings. Another Russian priest influenced by him was Paul Pierling, whose book on Gagarin, completed in 1914 but published only in 1996, was the last of many of his studies of Catholicism in Russia.

The dramatic events of the twentieth century saw regions of the tsarist Russian Empire, such as Poland and the Baltic States, become independent, fall under Soviet control again after World War II, and become independent again as the Soviet Union collapsed. These areas are nowadays more easily studied as discrete states. However persecution, particularly in the later Stalin period and especially of Uniates, meant that Siberia was for a time a special region of Catholic concentration. Changes initiated under president Mikhail Gorbachev led to some relaxation. Gorbachev himself met Pope John Paul II in 1989 and in 1991, and a Catholic diocese was established in Novosibirsk to look after Siberia as a whole. The pope's activities were regarded by the Moscow patriarchate as intrusive. His invitation to a synod in Rome was declined and his proposal to visit Russia regarded with suspicion. Relations remain tense.

Bibliography: A major recent publication is Ekaterina Nikolaevna Tsimbaeva, *Russkii Katolitsizm. Zabytoe proshloe rossiiskogo liberalizma* (M., 1999). Jack V. Haney, *From Italy to Muscovy. The Life and Works of Maxim the Greek* (Munich, 1973); M.V. Sinitsyna, *Maksim Grek v Rossii* (M., 1977); A.J. Langeler, *Maksim Grek* (Amsterdam, 1986); Walter Delius, *Antonio Possevino und Ivan Grozny* (Stuttgart, 1962); Hugh F. Graham, ed. and trans., *The Moscovia of Antonio Possevino, S.J.*, (Pittsburgh, Penn., 1977); A. Possevino, *Istoricheskie sochineniia o Rossii XVI v.* (M., 1983); T. Eekman and A. Kadic, eds., *Iuraj Krizanic (1618- 1683). Russophile and Oecumenic Visionary* (The Hague, 1974); John M. Letiche and Basil Dmytryshyn, *Russian Statecraft. The Polytika of Iurii Krizhanich* (Oxford, 1985); Daniel L. Schafly, "The Rostopchins and Roman Catholicism in Early 19th-century Russia" (Ph. D. diss., Columbia University, 1972); Marthe de Hedouville, *Les Rostopchine* (Paris, 1984); G.R. Barratt, *M.S. Lunin. A Catholic Decembrist* (The Hague, 1974); Lucjan Suchanek, "Les Catholiques russes et les procatholiques en Russie dans la premiere moitie di XIXe siecle," *Cahiers du monde russe et sovietique*, Vol. 29, Nos. 3-4, 1988; J.M.P. McErlean, "Catholic, Liberal, European. A Critic of Orthodox Russia, the Diplomat Prince P.B. Kozlovskii (1783- 1840)" in C.E. Timberlake, ed., *Religious and Secular Forces in Late Tsarist Russia* (Seattle, Wash., 1992), "Catholics in Tsarist Russia," *Modern Encyclopedia of Religions in Russia and the Soviet Union,* Vol. 5 (Gulf Breeze, Fla.: Academic International Press, 1993); Bastien Miquel, *Joseph de Maistre. Un philosophe a la cour du Tsar* (Paris, 2000); Maria Fairweather, *The Pilgrim Princess. A Life of Princess Zinaida Volkonsky* (London, 1999); Clotilde Giot, "Jean Sergueievitch Gagarin, premier jesuite russe et artisan de 1 'union des Eglises (1814-1882)" (Doctoral thesis, Université de Lyon III, 1993); Jan Joseph Santich, "The Role of the Jesuits in the Westernisation of Russia, 1596-1656" (Ph.D. diss., University of California, Berkeley, 1992); A.R. Andreev, *Istoriia ordena Iezuitov. Iezuity v Rossiiskoi imperii, XVI-nachalo XIX veka* (M., 1998); Alexis U. Floridi, *Moscow and the Vatican* (Ann Arbor, Mich., 1986); Pedro Ramet, ed., *Christianity under Stress.* Vol. 2, *Catholicism and Politics in Communist Societies* (Durham, N.C. 1990); A.Walicki, "Catholicism in the Eastern Church in Russian Religious and Philosophical Thought," *Soviet Union*, Vol. 15, No. 1 (1988); Oxana Antic, "New Structures for the Catholic Church in the USSR." *Report on the USSR*, Vol. 3, No. 21 (24 May 1991), 16-19.

John M.P. McErlean

CATOIRE, GEORGY LVOVICH (1861-1926). Russian composer and musical theorist of French descent.

Georgy Lvovich Catoire (Kataur) was born in Moscow 27 April 1861 and died there 21 May 1926. In 1875 he began to study piano with Karl Klindworth who encouraged him to study the works of Richard Wagner. Catoire joined the Wagner Society in 1879 and attended a festival at Bayreuth in 1885. He graduated from Moscow University with a degree in mathematics in 1884, thereafter devoted his life to music. In 1885, on the advice and encouragement of Petr Chaikovsky, he went to Berlin where he continued his studies with Klindworth and took composition lessons with Otto Tirsch, then later with Philippe Rufer. Upon his return to Russia a few years later he pursued private lessons in counterpoint from Anatoly Liadov and composition with Nikolai Rimsky-Korsakov in St. Petersburg. When he returned to Moscow, he continued to teach himself composition and consulted with Anatoly Arensky and Sergei Taneev, who became a good friend. In 1916 Catoire was appointed professor of composition at the Moscow Conservatory, a post he held until his death in 1926. As a composer Catoire takes Chaikovsky as his point of departure. The influence of Wagner is also clearly apparent, as is that of Frédéric Chopin, César Franck, and later Claude Debussy.

For the last nine years of his life, as a teacher of theory and composition at the Moscow Conservatory, Catoire became increasingly involved in questions and issues of musical theory. He used the theoretical concepts of music theory established by Hugo Riemann, Ebenezer Prout, and François Gevaert as his own starting point. Among the concepts are the idea of chord function, the hierarchy of systems, and a general approach to formal analysis. This interest resulted in two seminal works. In *The Theoretical Course of Harmony* (1924) he based his conclusions on works from the late nineteenth century and discussed tonality and chord structure from a broad perspective. In his incomplete and posthumous *Musical Form* (1926) Catoire challenged and expanded some of the arbitrary aspects of rhythmic theory pioneered by Riemann and pointed to the existence of mixed and transitional types of musical forms.

More importantly, he was the first Russian theorist to adapt Riemann's approach for pedagogical purposes. In doing so, Catoire laid the foundations of a theoretical pedagogy in Soviet music. In part because of the lack of music textbooks in the Soviet Union during the 1930s Catoire's methods were widely adopted. According to Ellen Carpenter, "his treatment of form as a manifestation of 'artistic content' as well as of purely formal delineations and functional (dialectic) properties, rendered his approach acceptable to Marxists" (293).

Among Catoire's pupils were Dmitry Kabalevsky, Viktor Bely, Leonid Polovinkin, and Vladimir Fere.

Works: Symphony, opus 7, 1889; Symphonic Poem, opus 13, 1899; Piano Concerto, opus 21, 1909; Rusalka, opus 5, 1888; Romances, opus 29, 1915, and opus 32, No. 3, 1916; Piano Trio, opus 14, 1900; Violin Sonatas, opus 15, 1900, and opus 20, 1906; String Quartet, opus 16, 1901; String Quartet, opus 23, 1909; Piano Quintet, opus 28, 1914; Piano Quartet, opus 31, 1916.

References: V. Beliaev, *G. Katuar* (M., 1926); S. Evseev, "Georgii L'vovich Katuar," *Sovetskaia Muzika*, No. 5 (1941), 48-57; E.D. Carpenter, "The Contributions of Taneev, Catoire, Conus, Garbuzov, Mazel, and Tiulin" in G.D. McQuere, ed., *Russian Theoretical Thought in Music* (Ann Arbor, Mich., 1983), 273.

Gregory Myers

CAULAINCOURT, ARMAND AUGUSTIN LOUIS, MARQUIS DE (1773-1827). Duke of Vicenza, French ambassador to Russia from 1807-1811 under Napoleon Bonaparte, memoirist of the Napoleonic regime.

Caulaincourt was born into an old French noble family with a strong military background and joined that family tradition at a young age, entering the royal cavalry at age fourteen and serving in the republican French army in the Vendée and southern Germany. It was likely Charles Maurice Talleyrand who brought the young Caulaincourt to Napoleon's attention, resulting in his first diplomatic assignment, a mission in St. Petersburg in 1801. In 1803 he participated in the kidnapping of the Duke d'Enghien, whose subsequent execution haunted Caulaincourt's reputation for the rest of his life. In 1804 the emperor forbade Caulaincourt to marry Madame de Camsy, a prohibition that was only lifted in 1814. Despite these incidents Caulaincourt was one of Napoleon's most dedicated followers, and his memoirs are one of the most valuable primary sources of the Napoleonic period.

In 1807 Napoleon appointed Caulaincourt ambassador to Russia. It was in this capacity that the French diplomat grew to respect Alexander I. Caulaincourt tried to maintain peace between the two nations, speaking frankly with Napoleon about Alexander's unwavering determination to hold his ground. He relayed Alexander's warning, "I shall not be the first to draw my sword, but I shall be the last to sheathe it," as well as his comment that in the event of a French invasion he would retire to Kamchatka rather than sign a treaty unfavorable to Russia. Caulaincourt's straightforwardness distinguishes him from many others in Napoleon's entourage. By all accounts he was one of the only men to speak honestly with Napoleon even when the truth was unpleasant.

Despite Caulaincourt's warnings Napoleon was undeterred and decided to invade Russia in 1812. Caulaincourt, as grand master of the horse, accompanied Napoleon and was in charge of efficient transportation of headquarters. His memoirs give a vivid portrayal of the deprivations of Napoleon's armies in Russia, the burning of Moscow, and the grim retreat of the French troops.

Upon the conclusion of that ill-fated invasion Napoleon appointed Caulaincourt foreign minister, where he served through the emperor's abdication in 1814 and again during the Hundred Days. During these final years Caulaincourt struggled to negotiate peace as the French representative at a number of failed conferences. Faithful to the end, Caulaincourt desperately tried to negotiate a deal that would allow Napoleon to keep his throne. His memoirs are particularly interesting in their descriptions of the final days at Fontainebleau and Napoleon's abdication, and are the only reliable account of Napoleon's attempted suicide. Upon Napoleon's final defeat the victors allowed Caulaincourt to retire to his estates where he compiled the memoirs that would eventually were published in 1933.

Bibliography: Caulaincourt's memoirs have been published as *Memoirs of General de Caulaincourt, Duke of Vicenza*, ed. by Jean Hanoteau, 3 vols. (London, 1930) and *With Napoleon in Russia*, ed. by George Libaire (New York, 1935). See also Jean Tulard, *Dictionnaire Napoleon* (Paris, 1987), Edward A. Whitcomb, *Napoleon's Diplomatic Service* (Durham, N.C., 1979), and Harold Nicholson, *The Congress of Vienna* (New York, 1946).

Lee A. Farrow

CAVIAR. The processed salted roe of sturgeon.

The world's finest caviar comes from the Caspian Sea where until recently several species of sturgeon thrived. These include the giant beluga (Huso huso), the osetra or Russian sturgeon (Acipenser guldenstaadtii), and the sevruga or stellate sturgeon (Acipenser stellatus). Sturgeon feed on the rich organic matter found in the Caspian's mildly saline water. Twice a year, in spring and fall, they head north to spawn, primarily in the vast delta of the Volga River and in the Ural River of Kazakhstan.

The eleventh-century Russian Primary Chronicle tells of up to ten thousand fishermen descending yearly on the Volga to fish its teeming waters. So valuable were sturgeon that the thirteenth-century court of Grand Prince Yaroslav Vsevolodovich in the sovereign state of Novgorod had a special sturgeon master to oversee the procurement, preparation, and serving of sturgeon. Preparation involved not only the flesh, but also many of the sturgeon's innards from the spinal marrow to the roe.

The Russians most likely learned to process fish eggs with salt from Greek traders along the Black Sea coast, but it wasn't until the Mongol occupation that a caviar industry developed in Russia. The Mongols trapped the sturgeon when they came into the rivers to spawn, driving stakes into the river bottom to form weirs. The early Russians speared the fish, but the Mongols developed a system of floating hooks that could catch many fish at once by their tails. By the fourteenth century the sturgeon fishing industry on the Volga was thriving, centered in the city of Astrakhan at the mouth of the river. The availability of excellent local salt helped to further trade.

In 1556 Ivan the Terrible routed the Mongols from Astrakhan, and Russia gained control of the fisheries. A century later Tsar Aleksei Mikhailovich (ruled 1645-1676) issued an edict regulating the caviar trade and imposing a government tax on all sales. By this time the sturgeon stocks were already being depleted. When Peter the Great ascended the throne, he forbade the use of the floating hooks, though compliance was difficult to monitor. Fishermen still used log fences for weirs and dragged cotton nets through the water to catch fish. The sharp scutes (spiny plates) on the sturgeon frequently tore the nets, which were replaced by sturdy monofilament only in the late nineteenth century.

By today's standards the numbers of sturgeon caught even in the eighteenth century were vast. At the height of the spawning season up to 250 belugas an hour were caught, yielding up to 80,000 fish a year. Beluga sturgeon can weigh over two thousand pounds (909 kg), though such specimens are rare today. Since a female sturgeon carries up to 15 percent of her weight in eggs, that translates into a yield of three hundred or more pounds (roughly 136 kg) of eggs from a single fish. The abundance of eggs and the fact that caviar was sanctioned by the church as appropriate for the many fast days of the Russian Orthodox year meant that aristocrats and commoners alike could enjoy the salted roe. Russians considered sturgeon caviar the finest, but they also enjoyed salted roe from fish such as burbot, white salmon, pike, carp, and grayling. Only the legendary golden caviar was reserved exclusively for the tsars. Although this caviar has still not been definitively identified, it most likely consisted of eggs that would have produced albino sturgeon.

Making caviar requires both skill and speed, as the fish eggs are fragile and perishable. The egg sac must be extracted by hand. The roe is gently pushed through a sieve to separate it from the membrane, then mixed with brine. Ideally it is kept cold during processing, generally at 28° to 32° F (-1.7° to 0° C), to maintain freshness. Salting helps to preserve the roe and lowers the temperature at which the eggs will freeze. The best fresh caviar, which contains roughly four percent salt, is known as malossol. In modern times a small amount of borax is also added to yield a slightly sweeter taste and reduce the need for salt. Borax-treated caviar cannot be sold in the United States at present.

The flavor and quality of caviar depend on the type of sturgeon from which the roe is taken and the way it is handled. The fish should still be alive when the eggs are removed so that harmful enzymes aren't released. Only in the late twentieth century did Igor Burtsev, a scientist at the Russian Federal Research Institute for Fisheries and Oceanography, develop a method for milking sturgeon so that the fish could be returned live to the water to begin a new cycle of egg production. Many connoisseurs consider beluga roe the best because the eggs are the largest and most subtle in flavor. But most Russians prefer a stronger taste, choosing instead osetra or sevruga roe. Osetra roe is dark golden in color and of medium size. The eggs of the sevruga are dark grey to black and quite small. Many Russians prize the especially strong flavor and texture of pressed caviar (paiusnaia ikra), eggs that have been pressed into a concentrate the consistency of thick jam.

Over the centuries foreign visitors to Russia commented on the Russians' love of sturgeon roe and their neglect of the fish's excellent flesh. Traveling from Holland in the mid-seventeenth century, Jan Struys found that Russians used caviar as lavishly as the Dutch used butter and noted that only a small amount of the fish itself was salted for use among the peasantry. In 1671 Samuel Collins, the English physician to Tsar Alexei Mikhailovich, published an account of his sojourn in Russia that included a chapter on caviar and its preparation. He was appalled at the waste of the sturgeon flesh, which he considered a delicacy.

Medieval Russians usually seasoned their caviar with pepper, chopped onion, vinegar, and oil. Often they ate it hot. After extracting the fresh roe they would sprinkle it with salt and pepper, dust it with flour, fry it, often still in the egg sac, and serve it with an onion, cranberry, or saffron sauce. Pressed caviar was particularly well regarded. Sometimes it was chilled, cut into slices, and flavored with an herb vinegar or mustard sauce. For the Muscovite dish kalia, pressed caviar was cut into thin rounds then placed in an earthenware pot with chopped onion, pepper, pickles, pickle brine, and water. This mixture was steamed in the Russian stove with additional pepper added on serving.

By the mid-nineteenth century, due to diminishing fish stocks, the finest sturgeon caviar was a dish for the wealthy and a symbol of luxury. In an 1897 book on domestic economy, *Home and Housekeeping*, Marie Redelin suggests serving caviar on toast points or mounded in a pyramid and decorated with lemon wedges with croutons on the side. Nineteenth-century culinary fashion also called for slicing pressed caviar and serving it in a napkin as serviette caviar (salfetochnaia ikra). The saltiness of the roe makes it a perfect accompaniment to vodka or champagne, and in fact recent studies have shown that caviar contains acetylcholine, which increases alcohol tolerance.

Caviar was transported overland in linden barrels from the Caspian region to Moscow and St. Petersburg. For the tsar and other wealthy consumers live sturgeon were transported in carts and later in special railway cars with tanks so that the eggs could be harvested on site for optimal freshness. Russia also exported a great deal of caviar. From the accounts of Giles Fletcher, who traveled to Russia in 1588, we know that French and Dutch merchants, along with some English, were already shipping caviar to Italy and Spain. Adam Olearius on an embassy to Russia in the 1630s noted that hundreds of barrels of caviar were sent to Italy. In the seventeenth century Tsar Aleksei Mikhailovich granted monopoly trade rights to foreigners, including the Englishman John Osborne and a Hamburg merchant named Belkins.

By the late nineteenth century the Russian caviar trade was booming. In 1896 Russia exported 5,616,000 pounds (2,555,280 kg) of salmon caviar and 828,000 pounds (376,740 kg) of sturgeon caviar, primarily to Europe. Then production began to fall due to over-fishing, and a nascent caviar industry arose in the United States based on the Atlantic sturgeon found in the Hudson and Delaware rivers. Soon these waters, too, were over-fished, and by 1913 on the eve of Russia's entry into World War I Astrakhan was again the center of the world caviar trade.

Russia's entry into World War I and the chaos of the Revolution of 1917 and ensuing Civil War provided a respite for the sturgeon, whose depleted stocks began to recover. After the revolution the Soviet government brought the Astrakhan fisheries under state control and created fishing collectives. Recognizing caviar as a lucrative export product, in 1920 the Soviets signed an exclusive agreement with the Petrossian brothers to ship Russian caviar to Paris. Other export agreements soon followed. Except for the massive hydroelectric dam built at Volgograd (Stalingrad), which effectively diminished the sturgeons' spawning grounds by two-thirds, governmental controls actually helped preserve the sturgeon during the Soviet period. Limits were placed on fishing, hatcheries were built, and money was spent on sturgeon research. After the collapse of the Soviet Union the caviar trade became a free-for-all, with profit the driving motive and no thought given to ecology. The result is that all varieties of Caspian sturgeon are now endangered, and the huge beluga sturgeon is nearly extinct.

The problems facing the Russian caviar industry are manifold. As a landlocked sea the Caspian endures extreme hydrologic variations. Between 1900 and 1977 its water level fell by nearly ten feet (3 m), diminishing its productive area by almost 1,200 square miles (3,122 sq. km). This decrease led to a loss of important feeding grounds and made the water more saline. Although the waters of the Caspian have been rising again since 1978 and should continue to do so for several more decades, the stocks of commercially important fish, including various types of sturgeon, have been much depleted by the region's altered ecology. This problem is compounded by the Caspian's other natural source of wealth, namely oil, whose exploitation yields even greater profits than fishing. Concentrations of residual oil have caused a severe decline in the growth rate, maturation, and reproductive capacity of the native sturgeon. Burdened also by the unchecked inflow of agricultural and waste waters, the Caspian can no longer clean itself, and plankton, the sturgeon's major source of food, cannot photosynthesize as effectively.

An even greater problem is poaching, which presently is a cutthroat business. Throughout the 1990s official caviar production fell off drastically, even as illegal catches continued to rise. Government figures show a 90 percent decline in the legal trade between 1994 and 1995. Most of the sturgeon poaching takes place not in Russia proper, but in its former autonomous republics, especially Dagestan. Illegal harvesting costs Russia vast sums in lost revenue. The government has responded by sending in OMON, its special forces, to battle the poachers. International environmental organizations such as TRAFFIC similarly have become involved in trying to staunch the illegal flow. Much of the poached caviar is of inferior quality, and foreign importers are now wary of caviar originating in Russia, with the result that Russia is no longer the world's largest exporter of caviar. That honor now goes to Iran.

Geneticists in the Volga region continue to work on creating a new, heartier, species of sturgeon, based on the success of the bester, a cross between the beluga and sterlet developed in 1952. The bester can produce eggs every two years, making it a good choice for aquaculture. Scientists are also experimenting with farm-raised sturgeon, particularly in the Caspian waters belonging to Kazakhstan. Still, the prospects for the sturgeon look dim, especially for the great beluga, which has managed to survive since prehistoric times.

Bibliography: The most recent and thorough account of the caviar trade is Inga Saffron, *Caviar. The Strange History and Uncertain Future of the World's Most Coveted Delicacy* (New York, 2002). On Caspian sturgeon and early caviar production see A.A. Bakhtiarov, *Briukho Peterburga. Ocherki stolichnoi zhizni*

(SPb., 1888). Further useful information on caviar is in travelers' accounts: Samuel Collins, *The Present State of Russia* (London, 1671), ch. 27, Adam Olearius, *The Travels of Olearius in Seventeenth-Century Russia*, trans. and ed. by Samuel H. Baron (Stanford, Cal., 1967); Ia.Ia. Struis, *Tri puteshestviia*, trans. by. E. Borodina (M., 1935), orig. pub. 1676 in Amsterdam. On the ecology of the Caspian see Lisa Speer, et al., *Roe to Ruin. The Decline of Sturgeon in the Caspian Sea and the Road to Recovery* (New York, 2000). On the illegal caviar trade see A. Vaisman and V. Gorbatovsky, eds., *Wild Animals and Plants in Commerce in Russia and CIS Countries* (M., 1999). For culinary information consult Susan R. Friedland, *Caviar. A Cookbook with 100 Recipes. A Guide to All Varieties* (New York, 1986).

Darra Goldstein

CELMIŅŠ, HUGO (1877-1941). Latvian statesman, agronomist.

Celmiņš was born to a peasant family in Lubāna, Livland province of Russia. A specialist in dairy farming and cattle-breeding, he was educated at an agricultural secondary school in Mogilev, the Baltic Polytechnical Institute (1899-1903), and in Switzerland at the University of Bern (1913-1914). In the years before World War I he held various positions with the Riga Central Agricultural Society and with the Ministry of Agriculture and State Domains in Petrozavodsk and Riga. He was active as a journalist during this period as well, writing for the Latvian nationalist daily Baltic Messenger (Baltijas vēstnesis) in 1906 and serving as chief editor of The Baltic Agriculturalist (Baltijas Lauksaimnieks) from 1907 to 1913. Celmiņš also saw duty as a junior officer in the Russian army during the Russo-Japanese and First World wars and in the newly formed Latvian army during his country's independence wars.

The postwar era witnessed Celmiņš' emergence as a prominent figure in Latvian politics. Elected to the National Constitutional Convention, which governed the country from 1920 to 1922, and then to the parliament (Saeima), he served as prime minister (1924-1925 and 1928-1931), minister of agriculture (1920-1921 and 1924-1925), minister of education (1923-1924) and minister of foreign affairs (1925 and 1930-31). He was later mayor of Riga (1931-1935) and Latvian ambassador to Germany (1935-1938). Latvia's first independence period ended with the Soviet occupation of 1940. The communist authorities, who moved quickly to destroy the Latvian political elite, soon arrested Celmiņš and deported him to Siberia, where he perished.

During Latvia's brief parliamentary era Celmiņš was a major force in the Agrarian Union (Zemnieku Savienība), a moderately conservative party with close ties to farm organizations and the cooperative movement. A system of proportional representation produced a parliament of one hundred members divided among as many as twenty-seven parties, none of which ever held a majority. The result was a series of often fragile coalitions mostly headed by the Agrarian Union, the country's second largest party after the Social Democrats. As minister of agriculture Celmiņš presided over the sweeping agrarian reform of 1920, which was one of the most important pieces of legislation implemented by the Latvian government. For centuries the Latvians lived under the rule of Baltic German aristocrats, a few hundred of whom still owned nearly half the arable land when the country won its independence. Celmiņš and his colleagues saw the reform as a way to ameliorate rural poverty, to strengthen the political and economic position of ethnic Latvians vis-a-vis their former masters, and to immunize the rural proletariat against communist propaganda emanating from Moscow. The result was the expropriation of large landholdings without compensation and their redistribution in the form of small farms to Latvian agricultural workers and military veterans.

Celmiņš' role in the national leadership ended with the triumph of his Agrarian Union colleague and rival, Kārlis Ulmanis. The early 1930s were a turbulent time in Latvian politics, as the local impact of world depression and a threatening international situation combined to encourage the rise of domestic extremism and to destabilize parliamentary life. In 1931 Ulmanis, who served as head of government three times during the 1920s, engineered the collapse of Celmiņš' governing coalition in order to propel himself back into power. Celmiņš subsequently won election to the Riga mayoralty, but Ulmanis' coup of May 1934 brought an authoritarian regime which dissolved all political parties and suspended elected local governments as well as the national parliament. The dictatorship held Celmiņš in disfavor, permitting him to remain in office until the end of his original term, then replacing him with an Ulmanis loyalist. Celmiņš' appointment to Berlin effectively removed him from the local scene. In 1938 he retired to private life.

Bibliography: Ādolfs Klīve, *Latvijas neatkarības gadi* (New York, 1976); Edgars Dunsdorfs, *Kārla Ulmaņa dzīve* (Stockholm, 1978); Andrejs Plakans, *The Latvians. A Short History* (Stanford, Cal., 1995); Georg von Rauch, *The Baltic States. The Years of Independence, 1917-1940* (Berkeley, Cal., 1974); Ādolfs Silde, *Latvijas vēsture, 1914-1940* (Stockholm, 1976).

Anders H. Henriksson

CENSORSHIP IN THE RUSSIAN EMPIRE. See Censorship in the Russian Empire, MERSH, Vol. 47.

Additional Bibliography: V.G. Chernukha, *Pravitel'stvennaia politika v otnoshenii pechati 60-70-ye gody XIX veka* (L., 1989); G. Doktorov, "Reforma tsarskoi tsenzury," *Kontinent*, No. 36 (1983); Iu.I. Gerasimova, *Iz istorii russkoi pechati v period revoliutsionnoi situatsii kontsa 1850-kh gg.* (M., 1979); *Tsenzura v Rossii. Istoriia i sovremennost'. Sbornik nauchnykh trudov.* Vyp. I (SPb., 2001).

Daniel Balmuth

CENSUSES IN RUSSIA, THE SOVIET UNION, AND POST-SOVIET STATES. See also Censuses in Russia and the Soviet Union, MERSH, Vol. 6.

Prior to Peter I (r. 1682-1725) population counts were infrequent. They generally consisted of enumerations of hearths or households for fiscal purposes. Records exist of tax censuses in Novgorod and Kievan Rus and of population counts associated with Tatar tribute levies in the thirteenth century. After the fourteenth century rulers concerned themselves less with population counts than with land surveys. For reasons associated with population dislocation and movement as well as increasing revenue needs, the Muscovite state again counted people in the seventeenth century. These household censuses were restructured and regularized by the introduction of the poll tax in 1719. Between 1719 and 1721 authorities undertook the first of what would be ten so-called revisions (revizii). The sole purpose of these population counts was to enumerate males subject to the poll tax and conscription. The state expected social/class estate (soslovie) institutions to keep lists of their own members. Prior to 1918 the Russian Orthodox Church also kept accounts of births, deaths, and marriages (metricheskie knigi). The lack of population data necessary for undertaking local projects, such as sanitation, health care and education, led many towns, provinces, and zemstvos to undertake local population counts in the nineteenth century. Prior to 1897 officials could gauge the magnitude of the empire's population only by gleaning figures from many sources.

By the time of the last, tenth, revision in 1857-1858 the practice of partial population enumeration was already obsolete. As academician and statistician P.I. Keppen noted, such partial censuses failed to provide "either material for scientific conclusions, or other bases for the discussion of many legal and administrative questions that require information on the distribution of the entire population by age, social estate, religion, family position, tribe, literacy, occupation, and ability to work" (RGIA, f.1290, o.10, d.5, 1.1). Keppen's reasoning reflected the continued march of cameralist thinking within the empire's bureaucracy and the rise of statistical thinking that permeated Europe in the nineteenth century.

The International Statistical Congress, a body organized to promote increased and standardized statistical work throughout the world, began creating a standard census form at its first meeting in 1853. Subsequent congresses, which included representatives of the Imperial Russian Geographic Society beginning in 1857, continued this work. In 1860 the Imperial Russian Geographic Society called on all interested parties to submit census plans for a juried contest. At the same time the state reorganized the collection of statistical data in the empire by creating a Central Statistical Committee within the interior ministry. In spite of these measures P.P. Semenov-Tian-Shansky, the head of the Central Statistical Committee, and other officials of the Great Reform era made little progress toward carrying out a complete census of the empire. The largest obstacle preventing a general census was the finance ministry, which shied from the costs associated with a census and insisted that the existing system of revisions was necessary for the collection of the poll tax.

The military reform of 1874 provided a compelling reason to conduct a complete census of the entire population. For the first time in the empire's history all twenty-one-year-old males, regardless of social estate, were subject to conscription. The new system required that the government have some idea of how many males were eligible for service each year. Existing revisions only accounted for part of the draft-age population. Between 1878 and 1882 the government attempted to register and count those subject to military service by compiling family lists (semeinye spiski). For the taxable estates this was done by extrapolating from lists compiled as a part of the Tenth Revision. Other estates were asked to submit the information voluntarily. The government calculated the size of the taxable population for 1874 as a base year by multiplying figures from the Tenth Revision by the rate of population growth. This put the entire process on an imprecise footing, especially as provincial statistical committees carried out the revision, calculated the rate of population growth, and extrapolated differently for each province. Initial inaccuracies multiplied with each passing year because lists were corrected only for families having draft-age sons. Imperial defense thus provided a key argument in favor of conducting a general census.

The abolition of the poll tax in 1886 removed the finance ministry's continued need for an estate-based population count and its greatest objection to conducting a general census. A series of commissions began work on a census project. The State Council finally passed a census law on 5 June 1895. Because it conducted its own enumerations, the law exempted Finland from the census completely. Those charged with drafting the census law also believed the largely nomadic populations of several regions in the steppe, Central Asia, and the Far East were too uncivilized to be counted by the same rules as other population groups, so the census statute exempted these areas from standard census rules.

After compiling a list of inhabited places, the Main Census Committee distributed the first census forms in November and December of 1896. The final date for enumerators to verify the forms was 28 January 1897. Enumerators recorded persons on census forms by household according to individuals' own indications or those of the head of household. The census law prohibited enumerators from requesting any form of official documents as verification of identity. Over 100,000 enumerators took part in the census. They came from all walks of life, from peasants to princes, and managed to count more than 127 million persons in the dead of winter with few problems. Although one scholar notes a nearly 30 percent undercount of some Siberian peoples, the error was probably much smaller and was not the result of lack of effort. Parts of the population, notably some Old Believers, members of religious sects, Jews, Tatars, and Bashkirs tried to avoid being counted or resisted being counted as the law dictated. Nonetheless the census count itself was a success. Less successful, from the standpoint of the Central Statistical Committee, was the use of Herman Hollerith's punch card machines for tabulating census data. The process of entering the raw data onto cards and running them through the machines proved to be substantially more time consuming and costly than originally projected. As a result, several proposed data comparisons were abandoned and it took nearly a decade to finish publishing census results.

Administrators used preparations for a second census to conduct an agrarian census in 1916 and an urban census in 1917. The main interest of both lay in identifying provisioning resources and needs, as well as enumerating men, livestock and other materials of importance to the war effort. The Bolsheviks carried out another partial census in 1920. This was the first census managed exclusively by professional statisticians. Collected data related to nationality was especially important to the new regime as it formulated its nationality policy (korenizatsiia).

Due to the Civil War census officials were not able to count the population in Belarus, the Crimea, Transcaucasus, the Far East, or Central Asia. The census also missed substantial portions of Ukraine and parts of the Volga, North Caucasus, and Siberian regions. Statisticians estimated that this resulted in an undercount of approximately 28 percent. Their extrapolation yielded a population count of just over 137 million persons.

The first complete Soviet census took place in 1926. The explicit goal of the census was the collection of data necessary for formulating the First Five Year Plan. The 1926 census still stands as the most comprehensive population count conducted on Soviet territory. The age data was especially rich and created an opportunity to construct life tables for the populations of Ukraine, Belarus, and the European areas of the RSFSR. An unprecedented period of preparation preceded the census, including a period of formal training for enumerators. The Council of People's Commissars issued a decree guaranteeing the confidentiality of census information in hopes that it would increase the accuracy of the count. In addition to standard population data the census collected information on housing resources, taxes, and new construction. A greatly expanded number of nationality choices also reflected the development of the policy of korenizatsiia. The census recorded a total population of 147 million.

The census planned first for 1930 and then for 1935 was postponed to 1937, when as might be expected it became highly politicized. The results came under immediate fire in the Communist Party Central Committee and were not published until after the fall of the USSR. The reported reason for invalidating the results was the method by which census officials verified household lists in order to avoid double-counting persons absent from their place of legal residence on the day of the census. Several other considerations contributed to the census' suppression. This was the only Soviet census to contain a question on religion, based on the 1936 constitution's guarantee of religious freedom, and officials possibly found these figures embarrassing. A more likely explanation is that throughout the mid-1930s Gosplan published a projected population of 180 million based in part on population growth rates from the mid-1920s. These projections appeared in official Soviet publications and in foreign statistical publications as well. Furthermore, in a speech of 1935 Stalin proclaimed that the success of socialist construction could be seen in a doubling of the urban population since the last census. The results of the population count of 1937 not only failed to demonstrate these claims but fell far short of them. Results indicated a total population of only 162 million, and a doubling of the urban population took place not by actual migration but due to the reclassification of many rural inhabited places as towns. Whatever the case there is reason to believe that the 1937 count reflected the embarrassing loss of population due to collectivization and the resultant famines in Ukraine and parts of the Volga region. All those in charge of census operations at the center were soon arrested.

The recount of 17 January 1939 took place under circumstances designed to achieve more favorable results. Gosplan's original projection disappeared from census discussions, and Viacheslav Molotov (1890-1986) oversaw census operations.

All census officials and enumerators received extensive training and went to the field only after passing competency exams. A propaganda campaign encouraged public participation by appealing to socialist competition between census districts under the slogan "Don't miss [counting] a single person!" Officials made special efforts to count the homeless and the unregistered residents of urban areas, that is, those living there illegally. In addition officials conducted for the first and only time in Soviet censuses special population counts of persons on active military duty and persons incarcerated within the GULAG system. When initial returns still appeared unsatisfactory, authorities issued a rebuke to local census officials for their lack of diligence. Whereas the Tambov census inspector discovered only four persons missed on his first tour, this number increased to 287 after he received the rebuke. Researchers note that such incidents were common.

The 1939 census again mirrored changes in Soviet nationality policy. The number of recognized nationality and ethnic groups declined from the 194 recognized in 1926 to 97. The census officially recorded a population of 170.5 million persons. Although not much of a difference from the 162 million counted in 1937, this figure nearly halved the gap between the 1937 census figure and the original Gosplan projection. Internal communications among census officials, Molotov, and Stalin reveal an actual count of 167.3 million persons. The addition of 3.2 million persons, taken in the aggregate, is not especially significant, yet there are indications in the regional breakdown of additions that officials attempted to soften population shortfalls in critical areas. For example, the official population figure for the German Volga Republic, which was devastated by collectivization and famine, exceeded the actual count by nearly 10 percent. Furthermore, officials adjusted regional census totals to conceal other sensitive information. Ostensibly to avoid giving away military secrets, nearly half of the 2.1 million soldiers on active duty appeared in the census not at their place of deployment but among the population of their home regions. Officials also redistributed nearly 760,000 inhabitants of the GULAG system from their places of incarceration to their pre-arrest locales. In the case of the Komi ASSR redistribution reduced the total official population by 23 percent and the male population by nearly a third. In spite of such redistribution prisoners still constituted the majority of the official population in many areas. Although scholars agree that the census generally offered an accurate count of the population, they also suggest that researchers approach the data with care. Census officials planned to publish the results in seven volumes over the course of 1939-1940, but except for comparative tables in publications of the 1959 census results they were not published until after the Soviet Union's demise.

The first Soviet post-war census took place in January 1959. Its organization and administration became standards for all subsequent Soviet censuses. Census preparations included a congress of statisticians and representatives of various scientific, economic, and governmental institutions interested in census results. The congress devoted a substantial amount of time to devising and debating the content of the census form and the rules governing the form's completion. A 1957 trial census of approximately one million inhabitants from a variety of locales provided data for the discussions. A massive propaganda campaign that included public lectures, exhibits, newspaper articles and broadcasts on both radio and television aimed at encouraging cooperation with enumerators. Pointed instructions to enumerators requiring them to record answers as given by respondents and forbidding census officials from asking respondents to produce any sort of official documents reflected the developing thaw in Soviet society. At the same time the new census procedures centralized census administration on the local level. The Central Statistical Administration in Moscow added a permanent department to supervise this and subsequent censuses.

Events again led census officials to deviate from a decennial schedule. Some suggest that officials delayed the planned 1969 census until 1970 in order that it coincide with the centennial of Lenin's birth. Technical difficulties associated with a trial census in 1967 stand as another possible explanation for the postponement. The technical issues stemmed from Soviet statisticians' decision to use sampling in the census. Sampling remains a contentious issue among census-takers throughout the world, and there is no reason to suppose that it was any less so in the Soviet Union. The use of sampling in the 1970 census characterized census taking for the remainder of the Soviet Union's existence. All respondents completed a form consisting of eleven basic questions. Census officials modified the question on age from the 1959 census to include year and month of birth. They hoped that this more precise age data would reduce the data distortion that occurred as a result of rounding ages to the nearest half year. The main form also asked for more detailed information on second languages and reasons for temporary absence from respondents' places of legal residence. Every fourth household completed three other forms designed to collect information related to the occupational structure of the population and on commuting. The occupational questions asked for additional data on persons employed in private agriculture and on the previous occupations of pensioners. The government never published results from the questions on commuting. The results of the 1970 census revealed a number of important milestones in the demography of the Soviet Union, including an expansion of the number of cities with a population greater than one million from three in 1959 to ten and an increase in the urban population to more than 50 percent of the total, from 48 percent in 1959 to 56 percent in 1970. The census registered a total population of nearly 242 million.

The 1979 census again made use of a 25 percent sampling procedure. It also, for the first time in Soviet census taking, made extensive use of computer systems. The census consisted of sixteen questions. All respondents completed the first eleven questions. Several disputes about the census form and changes in census questions reflected broader issues in Soviet society. Some argued for changing the census category native language (rodnoi yazyk) to conversational language (razgovornyi yazyk) and omitting the qualifier fluently (svobodno) from the question on second languages. These changes never made it into the final census form. They may have reflected an increasing party emphasis, enshrined in the new Brezhnev constitution, on the idea that the Soviet system had created a Soviet people (sovetskii narod) and thus rendered nationality an increasingly meaningless category. A proposal to include Soviet nationality as a category did not make the final census form.

For the first time since 1926 the census again registered marital status by type. The census form dropped the question on literacy, a reflection of Soviet achievements in that area. Enumerators were instructed to make a special notation if they encountered an illiterate person. The census also gave up soliciting data on reasons for temporary absences from legal residences and dropped questions on commuting from the 25-percent sample forms. This apparently reflected a certain resignation to the fact that, in spite of the registration and passport system, the Soviet population was relatively mobile. The 25-percent sample form also expanded the section on private employment to ask respondents why they were not employed in social production, a question that perhaps also reflected a certain amount of resignation and exasperation. Although the Central Statistical Administration published preliminary census results by administrative unit in April 1979, additional data from this census appeared only sporadically in the journal Vestnik statistiki until collected and published in 1984. None of these publications included age data for the population, in spite of specific attempts to collect better age data in the 1970 and 1979 censuses. Such an omission possibly reflected embarrassment over the age structure and longevity of the population, that is, that the population was not healthy in terms of fertility and mortality. A more substantial publication of 1979 census data appeared only in 1989-1990. The census registered a total population of just over 262 million persons.

The conduct of the 1989 census reflected many of the changes taking place under perestroika. Census authorities carried out an extensive dress rehearsal for the 1989 census in 1987. Unlike previous test censuses, officials used this rehearsal to make adjustments to the understandability of census questions for enumerators and respondents alike and to test new computer technology related to processing and interpreting census data. The test run also provided an opportunity to verify street names and dwelling address numbers and provide on-the-job training for enumerators. The census questionnaire administered 12-19 January 1989 continued to make use of the 25-percent sampling procedure for some questions but also contained a significant expansion in the number of questions asked. The total number of questions rose from sixteen to twenty-four. Each respondent provided answers to twelve basic questions. The form also contained a question on place of birth as a means of understanding migration patterns. Reflecting the Soviet government's attempts to address practical complaints about Soviet life, seven additional questions aimed at soliciting information on housing conditions. Census officials hoped that such data would enable the state to make good on a resolution of the Twenty-Seventh Party Congress calling for the provision of a separate apartment or dwelling for every Soviet family by the year 2000. Census officials also asked mothers belonging to the 25-percent sample to indicate the total number of children born to them and the number of those children still alive.

The volume of published data from the 1989 census substantially exceeded that of any of the other Soviet censuses taken after 1926. The ten volumes of published data provided information on a total of nearly 287 million inhabitants. This marked more than a nine percent increase in the population since 1979. The highest growth rates, ranging from 22 percent to 34 percent, belonged to the republics of Central Asia. Total urban population increased by 25.2 million over that of 1979 to 188.8 million persons. Natural growth accounted for 14.6 million of the increase and the rest was due to migration from rural areas. The growing urban population inhabited 2,190 cities, of which fifty-seven had populations greater than 500,000 and twenty-three had populations exceeding one million. The census results also indicated that the gap between numbers of males and females continued to narrow from its high of 20.7 million in 1959 to 15.7 million in 1989. The bulk of the gap, owing to a higher male death rate and the continued demographic effects of the events of the first half of the twentieth century, existed among those over the age of thirty.

Plans for the first post-Soviet censuses in the new states of the former USSR emerged under the auspices of the Commonwealth of Independent States in the mid-1990s. Most countries agreed to adhere to United Nations census guidelines in terms of census scheduling and the collection of basic data. Monetary constraints and political instability made it difficult for most states to conduct censuses as scheduled in either 1999 or 2000. Nonetheless, all former republics of the USSR except Moldova completed censuses by the end of 2003. Moldova is slated to conduct a census in 2004. Turkmenistan's 1999 census counted only a five percent sample of the population. To the extent that they are available, the results of these censuses reflect many of the demographic trends that emerged in the late Soviet period. The populations of the Central Asian republics continued to increase, in the Tadjik and Kyrgyz cases by nearly 20 percent. Kazakhstan stands as the lone exception in the region. Its population declined by nearly eight percent between 1989 and 1999 largely due to the emigration of Russians and Ukrainians. Censuses of the Baltic states, Ukraine, Belarus, Georgia, Armenia, and Azerbaijan also indicated a loss of population from emigration and declining birth rates. According to preliminary 2002 census results, the Russian Federation appears to be the main beneficiary of emigration from these other states. Census officials predicted a total population for the Russian Federation of 143 million. Early returns indicated a final figure closer to 145 million, four million of which emigrated to the Russian Federation since 1989. The population total reflected a decline of two million persons since the demise of the USSR, but was smaller than that anticipated by census officials. The politics of national identity were very prominent in Russia. Cossacks agitated and won the right to be listed in the census as a separate nationality, and ethnic Tatar leaders campaigned for all Tatars to drop regional identifications they believed allowed others to divide the Tatar nation.

Bibliography: Ralph S. Clem, ed., *Research Guide to the Russian and Soviet Censuses* (Ithaca, N.Y.,1986); Rossiiskii Gosudarstvennyi Istoricheskii Arkhiv (RGIA), fond 1290 (Ministerstvo Vnutrennykh Del), opis' 10 (Pervaia Vseobshchaia

Perepis' Naseleniia Rossiiskoi Imperii); Rossiia, Tsentral'nyi Statisticheskii Komitet pri Ministerstve Vnutrennykh Del, *Ocherk razvitiia voprosa o vseobshchei narodnoi perepisi v Rossii. Ministerstvo vnutrennikh del. Tsentral'nyi Statisticheskii Komitet. 20 fevralia 1890 g.* (SPb., 1890), 3-4; Federal'naia Arkhivnaia Sluzhba Rossii and Rossiiskii Gosudarstvennyi Arkhiv Ekonomiki, *Vsesoiuznaia perepis' naseleniia 1937 goda* (Woodbridge, Conn., 2000); Rossiiskaia Akademiia Nauk, *Vsesoiuznaia perepis' naseleniia 1939 goda. Osnovnye itogi. Rossiia* (SPb., 1999); V.B. Zhiromskaia, "Vsesoiuznye perepisi naseleniia 1926, 1937, 1939 gg. Istoriia podgotovki i provedeniia," *Istoriia SSSR*, No. 3 (1990), 84-103; USSR, Tsentral'noe Statisticheskoe Upravlenie, *Chislennost' i sostav naseleniia SSSR. Po dannym Vsesoiuznoi perepisi naseleniia 1979 goda* (M., 1984); Goskomstat SSSR, *Itogi Vsesoiuznaia perepis naseleniia 1979 goda. Statisticheskii sbornik*, 10 vols. (M., 1989-90); "On the preliminary results of the 1989 All-Union census of the population," *Current Digest of the Soviet Press*, Vol. 41, No. 17 (1989), 17-23. This is a complete translation of articles from *Izvestiia*, 28 April 1989, 1-3 and *Pravda*, 29 April 1989, 2. Gosudarstvennyi Komitet SSSR po Statistike, *Itogi vsesoiuznoi perepisi naseleniia 1989 goda*, 12 vols. (Minneapolis, Minn., 1992-1993); Karen Bronshteyn, *The 1989 USSR Census. A Bilingual (Russian/English) Companion Guide to the Microfiche Edition* (Minneapolis, Minn., 1994); Azarbaycan Respublikasi Dövlat Statistika Komitasi, *Azarbaycan Respublikasi ahalisinin 1999—cu il siyahiya alinmasi 1999* (Baku, 2001); Kyrgyz Respublikasynym Uluttuk Statistika Komiteti, *Main Results of the First National Population Census of the Kyrgyz Republic of 1999* (Bishkek, 2000), *Population of Kyrgystan. Results of the First National Population Census of the Kyrgyz Republic of 1999 in Tables. Publication II* (Bishkek, 2000), *Regiony Kyrgystana. Itogi pervoi natsional'noi perepisi Kyrgyzskoi Respubliki 1999 goda*, 8 vols. (Bishkek, 2001); Qazaqstan Respublikasynyng Statistika Zhonindegi Agenttigi, *Kratkie itogi perepisi naseleniia 1999 goda v Respublike Kazakhstan* (Almaty, 1999), *Istochniki sredstv sushchestvovaniia naseleniia Respubliki Kazakhstan. Itogi perepisi naseleniia 1999 goda v Respublike Kazakhstan* (Almaty, 2000); Latvia, Centrala Statistikas Parvalde, *Latvijas 2000. Gada tautas skaitisanas rezultati. Statistikas datu krajums* (Riga, 2002); Lithuania, Statistikos Departamentas, *Gyventojai pagal lyti, amziu, tautybe ir tikyba* (Vilnius, 2002); Eesti Riiklik Statistikaamet, *2000. Aasta rahva ja eluruumide loendus* (Tallin, 2001); Belarus', Ministerstva Statystyki i Analizu, *Itogi perepisi naseleiia Respubliki Belarus' 1999 goda*, 6 vols. (Minsk, 2000-2002); Susan B. Glasser, "Russia Starts to Take Its Measure. First Post-Soviet Census Aims to Quantify Social Change," *The Washington Post*, 10 October 2002; Fred Weir, "What You Won't Find Out from Russia's Census," *The Christian Science Monitor*, 17 October 2002; *Osnovnye itogi vserossiiskoi perepisi naseleniia 2002 goda*, 14 vols. (M., 2004).

David W. Darrow

CENTRAL ASIA, ANCIENT AND MEDIEVAL (to 1700). The term "Central Asia" is today most commonly used to refer to the region consisting of the ex-Soviet states of Uzbekistan, Tajikistan, Turkmenistan, Kirgizstan, and Kazakhstan, the territory circumcribed bys borders established during the Soviet Union's great delimitation of the states in the 1920s. As such, this term carries modern political, cultural, and geographical connotations that significantly detract from its precision in historical discussions. For the purposes of this entry the term Central Asia refers to the area roughly delimited by the pastoral-nomadic Qipchaq (Kipchak) steppe in the north, the Tien Shan mountain range in the east, the Caspian Sea in the west, the Qara Qum (Kara Kum, Black Sand) desert in the southwest, and the Hindu Kush mountain range in the southeast.

Central Asia has an extreme continental climate. Temperatures in the plains commonly exceed 122°F (50°C) in the summer months and are correspondingly cold in the winter. In the north, in the vicinity of the Aral Sea, the mean temperature in January is a mere 11°F (−11.8°C), compared to 76° F (26°C) in July. Mean temperatures measured at Termiz, in the south, are significantly warmer, 89°F (31.5°C) in July and 35°F (1.7°C) in January.

The severe summer heat and arid climate have made water a commodity of primary importance in Central Asia, and since about 1000 B.C. agriculture in the region has depended upon irrigation. Canals channel water from the few rivers that carry the annual snowmelt from the mountain ranges in the southern and eastern parts of the region. The two major rivers of the region are the Amu Darya (Greek Oxus, Arabic Jayhun) and Syr Darya (Greek Jaxartes, Arabic Sayhun). The Amu Darya, the larger of the two, originates in the Pamir and Hindu Kush mountain ranges and flows for roughly 1,550 miles (2,495 km) until it empties into the Aral Sea. In the past the more northerly Syr Darya, which emerges from the Fergana Valley swollen with the snowmelt from the surrounding mountains, flowed nearly 870 miles (1,400 km) to the Aral Sea. Since the 1970s, because a dramatic increase in the amount of water taken for irrigation, it has failed to reach the sea.

Archeological evidence provides the greatest insight into the pre-Islamic history of Central Asia. This evidence suggests the presence of settlements in the region already in the fourth millennium B.C. and the development of Iron Age communities by the beginning of the first millennium B.C. The ethnic identity of the aboriginal inhabitants of Central Asia remains a matter of speculation, as they disappeared from the historical record in the first half of the second millennium B.C., replaced by or incorporated into the Indo-Iranian tribes who moved into the region from southern Russia. By the first millennium B.C. these tribes emerged as the dominant ethnic group across both sedentary Central Asia and the steppe.

The historical record becomes clearer following the conquest of the localized, sedentary polities of Central Asia by Cyrus, the founder of the Persian Achaemenid Empire. According to the account delivered by Herodotus, Cyrus was killed in Central Asia while fighting the Indo-Iranian Saka (Scythian) tribal confederation in 530-529 B.C. Despite this loss, Achaemenid control over the region continued. Just a few years later the Persian Empire stretched northward from the celebrated capital of Emperor Darius I at Persepolis (Persis, near modern Shiraz) to the steppe empire of the Sakas. Darius ruled over the provinces of Bactria, now northern Afghanistan and Tajikistan, Soghdia (the bulk of sedentary Central Asia, including the Zarafshan River Valley and the Farghana Valley), and Khwarezm (Choresmia, the fertile region along the banks of the Amu Darya south of the Aral Sea). The Persians' administrative capital in Central Asia appears to have been the Soghdian city of Marakanda, modern Samarkand, from which the Achaemenid religion (Zoroastrianism), culture and the use of the Aramaic script spread across the region.

Bactria emerged as the primary administrative center of Central Asia following the Central Asian campaigns of Alexander the Great in 329–327 B.C. Under Alexander and his Hellenic Seleucid successors Mediterranean trade with China and India passed through Bactria, and it was in this period that the east-west Silk Road trade first rose to prominence, carefully protected by numerous Greek garrison towns. Soghdian merchants took advantage of their intermediary position in this exchange and developed a network of merchant diaspora communities located in strategic commercial centers across much of Eurasia. From this time the movement of merchants, precious metals, and material goods along the Eurasian caravan routes continued to grow even as political control in Central Asia passed from the Seleucid rulers to a succession of invading tribes from the north. This included the Parni, who moved through Central Asia and became the Hellenized rulers of Parthia in the third century B.C., the Sakas in the second century B.C., and soon after them the Yüeh-chih, as referred to in the Chinese sources, who pushed the Sakas further south.

Very little information is available regarding even important political events in Central Asia in this period of nomadic domination. In the early decades A.D. political control over Central Asia shifted to a splinter branch of the Yüeh-chih that had broken southeastward, settled, and established the Kushan Empire. They were centered in Bactria and held expansive territory on both sides of the Hindu Kush. Western demand for such luxury goods as silks and spices increased markedly during the early Roman Empire, and the eastward movement of Roman specie in exchange for goods from China and India provided a strong foundation for the emerging Kushan state and their Soghdian vassals. It should be emphasized that cultural influence did not move solely from the west to the east. In the second century the later Kushans are known to have promoted the Indian religion of Buddhism, which spread westward along the trade routes traversing the Hindu Kush and across the Amu Darya, where it found a receptive audience in Soghdia. In Central Asia the second century was a period of considerable development in terms of manufactured goods, irrigation agriculture, architectural technology, and the arts, much of which exhibited a strong Indian influence.

By the end of the third century the Persian rulers of the Sasanian Empire (226-651) had decisively extended their control over Kushan territories in Central Asia, including Bactria, Khwarezm, and Soghdia. The Sasanian rulers considered themselves the heirs of the more ancient Persian Achaemenid tradition, and they were determined to purge Greek influence from their realm. The Sasanians promoted the Achaemenid religion of Zoroastrianism, and the state dialect of Persian (Dari) began to replace local languages in Central Asia.

In the late fourth century Sasanian control over Central Asia was interrupted by an invading confederation of Indo-European nomadic tribes, generally referred to by the simplified designation of the Huns. Some sources call them Chionite, possibly a derivative of the earlier Hiung Nu. The local rulers of Khwarezm, Soghdia, and Bactria dismissed their Sasanian overlords to make alliances with these steppe tribes in an effort to ensure the safe movement of goods and people across the steppe. From the mid-fifth century the Huns migrated in large numbers into India, displaced by the Hephthalites, a confederation of Altaic tribes from the east, possibly mixed with Indo-Europeans. There is some indication that a portion of the early Hun tribes was simply absorbed by the Hephthalites. By the beginning of the sixth century, Altaic tribes were the dominant population of the steppes, and the Hephthalites were in a protracted struggle with the Sasanians for sovereignty over Central Asia.

The Hephthalite political presence in Central Asia ended with the rise of the Turk Qaghanate (552–659, 682–741, commonly referred to as the First and Second empires), which emerged from the Altai Mountains to exert control over a vast domain extending from the Urals to Mongolia. Already in the 560s Turkic tribes in collaboration with the Sasanians invaded the Hephthalite domains in Central Asia. The Hephthalites were quickly defeated, and their territory was divided between the Turks and the Persians. This Turko-Persian alliance was short-lived, however, as commercial interests quickly led the Turks to turn against the Persians in favor of their western rivals, the Byzantines. The Turks moved further south and occupied the Soghdian city-states to the north of the Oxus, beginning the long process of Turkic migration into Central Asia. This process was slowed in the mid-seventh century by the westward expansion of the Chinese T'ang Dynasty (617-906) and more directly in the early eighth century by the arrival in Central Asia of a conquering force of Arab Muslim armies.

The Arab conquests eastward began shortly after the death of the Prophet Muhammad in the year 632. In 637 the Caliph 'Umar (634–644) led the Arabs to victory over the Sasanians at the celebrated Battle of Qadisiyya, resulting in the conquest of the Persian capital of Ctesiphon and the expulsion of Sasanian authority from Iraq. The last Sasanian emperor, Yazdagird III, fled eastward to the oasis of Merv, where he was killed in the year 651. In the next three years Arab armies extended their control over all of Persia up to the Amu Darya.

With the rise of the Umayyad Caliphate (661–750) and the Arab conquest of Central Asia the historical record becomes much clearer, although our understanding of the early Arab expansion into the region remains largely dependent upon information provided by later Islamic historians and geographers. The general image presented by these sources is that the Arabs began running raids into the wealthy Soghdian city-states from their outpost in Merv in 673. The actual Arab conquest of Central Asia did not begun until 705, when the Caliph Abu al-'Abbas

(705–715) appointed Qutayba bin Muslim to be the governor of the eastern Iranian province of Khurasan. Qutayba led the Arab armies to place Bukhara under siege in 709 and first attacked Khwarezm in 712. Despite Central Asian appeals for assistance, the Turk Empire proved unable to protect their Soghdian vassals. Still, internal struggles in the Umayyad Caliphate kept the Arab armies from establishing a firm hold over Central Asia until after the 'Abbasid revolution (749–750). In 751 the Arab armies met and defeated the expansionist T'ang Chinese at the Battle of Talas, north of Tashkent, henceforth limiting T'ang territorial claims to the lands east of the Tien Shan. Islamic rule would not reach eastern Central Asia for another seven centuries.

Beginning in the eighth century, the Arab sources refer to Central Asia by the geographic designation Mawarannahr ('Ma wara al-nahr'). The etymologies of the terms Mawarannahr, that which is beyond the river in Arabic, and its earlier Greco-Latin counterpart Transoxania, the land beyond the Oxus, illustrate their reference to the territory to the north and east of the Oxus River (Amu Darya) and distinguish that province from the eastern Iranian province of Khurasan. Even following the Mongol conquests of the thirteenth century, the Amu Darya was chosen to delimit the boundaries of the territories to be held by the Mongol Il-Khans in Persia and the Chaghatai Khans in Mawarannahr. Considering this, the eminent Russian orientalist V.V. Bartold has rightly suggested that the term Mawarannahr was coined specifically to refer to the more sedentary territory beyond the Amu Darya and that it became associated with Islamic civilization.

The territory of Mawarannahr included the civilized, that is, more sedentary lands across the Amu Darya, a region that was held in contradistinction to the almost exclusively pastoral-nomadic steppe to the north, known to the medieval Perso-Arabic authors as Turkistan. It is likely that on the eve of the Arab conquests the designation Turkistan was applied to both the sedentary and pastoral lands to the north of Iran, Turks having populated these areas from the sixth century. The Arab conquests pushed the nomadic Turkic tribes northward, leaving the ethnically heterogeneous sedentarists, Turks and Persian-speakers, to be placed under the administration of the caliphate. With the designation of the sedentary lands as Mawarannahr, the name Turkistan became commonly applied only to the pastoral-nomadic steppe lands further to the north. It was not until the nineteenth century that the association of Turkistan with the pastoral-nomadic steppe was to change permanently, with the Russian colonization of large portions of sedentary Central Asia and the tsarist colonial administration's designation of these possessions as the governate-general (guberniia) of Turkestan, or the Turkestan Territory (Krai).

The final geographical term to be discussed here is Turan. In the ancient period sedentary Iranian peoples distinguished their agricultural civilization (Iran) from the pastoral-nomadic steppe (Turan), which was also populated by Iranians. It is not surprising that the implication of this word changed with the vicissitudes of history, and subsequent authors owe their understanding of the word to the meaning espoused by Firdawsi (c. 940–1020), the eastern Iranian author of the epic poem The

Book of Kings (Shah-nama). Firdawsi presents the Turkic tribes, by that time the dominant steppe population, as the inveterate enemy of the Iranians, and refers to them as Turanians. In later centuries the meaning of this term changed again as large numbers of Turkic peoples migrated southward, settled in Central Asia, and increasingly became the dominant population of the entire region. By the late medieval era people both internal and external to the region commonly employed Turan to designate sedentary Central Asia.

For the Arabs the name of the province was Mawarannahr, and it was placed under a series of Arab regional governors in the early years of the 'Abbasid Caliphate (750–1258). Consolidation of caliphal control over the region was difficult at first but was considerably advanced as the aristocratic landlord class (dihqan) gradually adopted Sunni Islam. In the ninth century Central Asia produced its first Islamic ruling family, the Samanids (819-1005), an Iranian dihqan dynasty from the upper Oxus valley near Termiz. In 875 political expediency led the caliph to recognize the Samanids, originally subordinate to the Arab governors of Khurasan, as the official rulers of both Mawarannahr and Khurasan. A decline in caliphal authority soon left the Samanids largely independent of outside intervention, although it should be stressed that they maintained their allegiance to Sunni Islam and dutifully continued to rule in the name of the caliph. The Samanids earned a reputation as enlightened rulers, and their period is considered to be one of economic prosperity and great support for Islamic literature and scholarship. The Samanids' greatest legacy was their synthesis of Islam with Persian language and culture. This greatly facilitated the process of islamicization across Central Asia and laid the foundation for Central Asia, especially the Samanid capital of Bukhara, to emerge as a center of Islamic civilization. There is some evidence that missionary activity under the Samanids even promoted the expansion of Islam into the steppe.

The Samanids were able to prosper at least partly because of their success at maintaining a well-fortified frontier against their nomadic neighbors to the north. They used their fortresses as much to provide Muslim troops with staging points for frequent raids into the pagan steppe as to provide defense from nomadic incursions. These raids afforded the Samanids and their Abbasid benefactors an unlimited supply of Turkic slaves (Persian ghulam, Arabic mamluk), a commodity in high demand due to the Turks' legendary military prowess. As internal conflict and economic crises weakened the Samanid dynasty at the end of the tenth century, they no longer could maintain a firm barrier against the steppe, and political control over Mawarannahr moved permanently from Iranian hands to successive waves of in- vading Turks.

The Turkic Muslim Qarakhanid tribes had been encroaching on Samanid territory for decades when they entered Bukhara in 999 and extinguished the teetering Samanid dynasty in 1005. The arrival of the Qarakhanids begins the long process of turkicization of sedentary Central Asia, as Turkic-language speakers eventually either subsumed most Iranian-speaking Tajiks or relegated them to the mountainous periphery of the upper Oxus valley. Meanwhile, the Samanids' Turkic military slave-generals had fled Mawarannahr in the year 977, established their own dynasty, the Ghaznavids, and extended their control over Iran and Khurasan. The greater Samanid realm was thus divided in two. The Qarakhanids maintained control over Mawarannahr and the other areas to the north of the Oxus, while the Ghaznavids controlled the areas to the south. This arrangement did not last long. Another group of Muslim Turks from the steppe, the Seljuks (1040–1194), pushed the Ghaznavids out of Khurasan in 1040, extended their control as far west as Iraq and Syria, and overran the Qarakhanids in Mawarannahr in the 1070s. The Seljuks quickly fragmented into a number of smaller sultanates, although they remained dominant in Central Asia until 1141, when they were displaced by another invading nomadic force, the Buddhist Qarakhitai, who had been driven out of northern China. Islamic rule was returned to the region just a few decades later by a local aristocratic dynasty, the Khwarezmshahs, who emerged from their position as hereditary governors of Khwarezm and vassals to the Qarakhitai to extend their control southward into Khurasan. By 1210 the Qarakhitai had been pushed back into the steppe areas of eastern Kazakhstan (Semireche), and the Khwarezmshahs had established themselves as the independent rulers of Central Asia and Iran.

It was in this period that the Mongol ruler Temujin, known since 1206 by the title of Chingis Khan (Genghis Khan or Oceanic Ruler), unleashed the full force of his Turko-Mongol troops against the sedentary population of Central Asia. In 1209 the Uighur rulers of Sinkiang willingly submitted to Mongol rule, and the Mongol troops quickly extended their conquests further to the west, annexing the Qarakhitai realm in Semireche in 1218. In that same year Chingis Khan sent 450 Muslim merchants to the neighboring Khwarezmshah's frontier outpost at Utrar, where the local governor accused them of spying for the Mongols, executed them, and confiscated their goods. Chingis Khan responded by sending three ambassadors to the Khwarezmshah 'Ala al-din Muhammad (r. 1200-1220) to demand retribution. This embassy met with little success, and in 1219 Chingis Khan disengaged his troops from their war in northeastern China in order to give the Khwarezmshah his full attention. As the Mongol horde approached, 'Ala al-din Muhammad fled to an island in the Caspian Sea, where he died in 1220. The Mongols sacked and demolished the cities of Central Asia, and by 1223 they had extended their control over Mawarannahr, Khurasan, and Khwarezm.

Following the death of Chingis Khan in 1227 the Mongol Empire was divided among the royal family into four appanages (ulus). Chaghatai, the second oldest son and most fervent supporter of the Chinggisid law code (the yasa), was granted the central steppe area in the Ili River valley, and he eventually enlarged his domain to include Mawarannahr and Sinkiang. Islamic civilization continued under Chaghatai rule, although it did so in a considerably less advanced position. The Mongols' destruction of formerly great Islamic centers of learning across the region was compounded by Chaghatai's hostility toward the religion, which left regional governors scrambling to protect the Muslim population rather than working to advance Islamic civilization. This began to change with the conversion of the

Chaghatai Khan 'Ala al-din Tarmashirin to Islam in the year 1326, although he was deposed and killed eight years later for having forsaken the yasa of Chingis Khan. The Mongols of the Chaghatai Khanate may not have been ready to embrace an Islamic ruler, but Islamic law (shariah) soon replaced the yasa in Central Asia.

In the mid-fourteenth century Timur (1336–1405), also Timur the Lame or Tamerlane, a young Muslim noble of the increasingly influential Turkic Barlas tribe, was appointed to the position of assistant to the Chaghatai governor of Mawarannahr. The young upstart quickly shook off his overlord and by 1370 had established his authority over the Chaghatai domains in Mawarannahr. His military exploits were nearly constant from this period, and he was rarely found in his celebrated capital of Samarqand. Between 1372 and 1388 Timur consolidated his control over Khwarezm, and he continued his conquest and pillaging westward, making several expeditions into Iran, Anatolia, Transcaucasia, and the Golden Horde territories of modern Russia. In 1398 Timur's armies crossed the Hindu Kush and sacked Delhi, bringing back incredible wealth and some 12,000 slaves, many of whom were put to work as laborers on his grandiose construction projects in Samarqand. Timur died in 1405 in Utrar on his way to campaign against Ming China. It is telling that, despite his unquestionable position of authority, legitimacy in this period remained entrenched in Chingisid tradition. Thus, Timur initially propped up a puppet khan from the Chingisid lineage, he claimed only the modest title of Commander (amir), and he earned the relational title Son-in-Law (guregan) by marrying a number of Mongol princesses.

Timur's was the last great nomadic empire of the steppe. As the invention of gunpowder weapons became increasingly universalized in the fifteenth and sixteenth centuries, larger and wealthier agrarian gunpowder empires were able to neutralize the military advantages that had for so long been associated with the nomads' mobility and fabled archery skills. Timur's heirs, less destructive than their progenitor, focused their efforts more on consolidating their control and rebuilding Central Asia and Iran than on conquest, and historians commonly refer to Central Asia's fifteenth century as the Timurid Renaissance. This was the era of such literary figures as the poets 'Abd al-Rahman Jami and Mir 'Ali Shir Nava'i, the celebrated painter Bihzad, and the austere Naqshbandi Sufi Sheikh Khwaja Ahrar, under whose leadership the Central Asian Sufi orders and Sunni Islam in general returned to an elevated position in Central Asian society. Timurid control over Central Asia lasted until the end of the century, when Uzbek tribes from the Golden Horde migrated into Mawarannahr under the leadership of Shaybani Khan and forced Babur (1483–1530), the last of the Timurid ruling clan (and a Chingisid on his mother's side), to depart his recently acquired ancestral capital of Samarqand and flee to Kabul. After many years of hardship, in 1526 Babur emerged victorious over the Lodi Afghan ruler of the Delhi Sultanate and established his own Timurid dynasty in India, the Mughal Empire.

Bibliography: Zahir al-Din Muhammad Babur, *Babur-nama. Memoirs of Babur*, ed. and trans. by Annette Beveridge (Delhi, 1989); V.V. Bartold, *An Historical*

Geography of Iran, trans. by Svat Soucek and ed. by C.E. Bosworth (Princeton, N.J., 1984), *Turkestan Down to the Mongol Invasion*, trans. and rev. by V.V. Bartold and H.A.R. Gibb (London, 1928); Ibn Battuta, *The Travels of Ibn Battuta, A.D. 1325–1354*, trans. by H.A.R. Gibb, 3 vols. (New Delhi, 1993); "Central Asia," *Encyclopaedia Iranica*, ed. by Ehsan Yarshater (London, 1982-); "'Mâ warâ' al-nahr" and "Tûrân," *Encyclopaedia of Islam*, ed. by M.Th. Houtsma, et al., 4 vols. (Leiden, 1913–1936); "Turkistân," *Encyclopaedia of Islam*, new edition, ed. by B. Lewis, Ch. Pellat, and J. Schacht (Leiden, 1954-); Richard Frye, *Bukhara. The Medieval Achievement* (Costa Mesa, Cal., 1997), *The Golden Age of Persia* (London, 1975), *The Heritage of Central Asia* (Princeton, N.J., 1996); H.A.R. Gibb, *The Arab Conquests in Central Asia* (London, 1923); Peter Golden, *An Introduction to the History of the Turkic Peoples* (Wiesbaden, 1992); René Grousset, *The Empire of the Steppes. A History of Central Asia*, trans. by Naomi Walford (New Brunswick, N.J., 1970); 'Ata-Malik Juvainî, *Ta'rîkh-i Jahân Gushâ. The History of the World-Conqueror*, trans. by J.A. Boyle, 2 vols. (Cambridge, Mass., 1958); Juzjani, *Tabakât-i Nâsirî, A General History of the Muhammadan Dynasties of Asia, including Hindûstan from A.H. 194 (810 A.D.) to A.H. 658 (1260 A.D.) and the Irruption of the Infidel Mughals into Islâm*, trans. by H.G. Raverty, 2 vols. (London, 1881); Beatrice Manz, *The Rise and Rule of Tamerlane* (Cambridge, 1989); V. Minorsky, trans., *Hudûd al-'Âlam. The Regions of the World* (Karachi, 1980); David Morgan, *The Mongols* (Oxford, 1986); Narshakhi, *Ta'rîkh-i Bukhârâ. The History of Bukhara*, trans. by R.N. Frye (Cambridge, Mass., 1954); G. Le Strange, *The Lands of the Eastern Caliphate* (Cambridge, 1905); Denis Sinor, ed., *The Cambridge History of Early Inner Asia* (Cambridge, 1990); Tabari, *The History of al-Tabari*, 39 vols. (Albany, N.Y., 1985-); A.Z.V. Togan, *Ibn Fadlan's Reisebericht* (Leipzig, 1939).

Scott C. Levi

CENTRAL ASIA, IMPERIAL RUSSIAN (1700-1917). Central Asia was home to distinct but interrelated pastoral and settled cultures and economies as Russian troops approached in the eighteenth century. Nomadic Turkic tribes of the Kazakh confederation, which arose as a successor to the Mongol empire, dominated on the steppe lands. The confederation was divided into three tribal federations, or hordes (zhuz), the Greater, Middle, and Lesser, each led by a khan. All practiced a pastoral economy based on mixed livestock and functioned according to kinship relations, clans holding separate winter feeding grounds. A traditional but flexible body of judicial customs, the adat, governed Kazakh society. Relative stability among the Kazakh tribes led them into greater trade relations with their oasis neighbors to the south in the seventeenth century. In the southern regions near the Caspian Sea Turkmen tribes carried out a pastoral lifestyle in a desert environment.

A period of decentralized appanage rule followed the collapse in 1598 of the Shaybanid dynasty in oasis Central Asia. As the regional economy improved, three khanates emerged, intent on centralizing power. Khiva to the west, stretching to the Caspian Sea, and Bukhara, surrounding the cities of Bukhara and Samarkand, were joined in the eighteenth century by the khanate of Kokand, which was centered around the Fergana Valley. Dominating the ruling classes were descendants of another post-Mongol Turkic political confederation, the Uzbeks. Each khanate ruled over a number of other groups, from Persian-speaking Tajiks to pastoralist Kazakhs and Turkmen, as well as Jewish communities and Armenian and Tatar diaspora. Urban residents of the khanates were known as Sarts, and grouped themselves according to kin, background, or economic activity in distinct neighborhoods (mahalla). Islam played an important role in local culture, although the political power of the clergy, the ulama, waxed and waned. In the oasis countryside irrigated agriculture and fertile loess soil produced harvests of grain, fruits and cotton. Artisanal work and extracted minerals along with these agricultural products invigorated the bazaar economy of Central Asia, whose trade with regional neighbors and Russia grew consistently in the decades preceding the Russian conquest. Yet growing friction between the khanates as well as with neighboring nomadic tribes engendered frequent military conflict that hindered economic development.

Diplomatic contacts between Russia and Central Asia date from the sixteenth century. Russian tsars and Central Asian leaders looked to each other to expand their respective economic opportunities and political influence from Europe to as far east as China and India. Russian interest in Central Asia intensified under Peter the Great. Intrigued by rumors of potential riches as well as by its strategic location, Peter dispatched numerous envoys and expeditions to the region, sometimes with disastrous results. In 1717 Khivans killed Prince Aleksandr Bekovich-Cherkassky (?-1717) and hundreds of his armed party. But other Central Asian leaders looked upon Russia as a potential partner. Devastating raids from the north and east by Oirat and Kalmyk tribes and poor relations with the khanates precipitated efforts by the khan of the Lesser Horde Kazakhs, Abulkhayr (?-1748), to seek assistance from Russia as it expanded deeper into the steppe. In 1730 the Russian foreign office accepted Abulkhayr's pledge to serve the tsar in exchange for protection against external enemies. For the first time Russia became directly involved in the complex politics of Central Asia.

Construction on the Kazakh steppe of the fort of Orenburg in 1735 signaled tsarist expansionist goals. Orenburg was built not only to anchor a new fortification line, but to encourage economic activity and future Slavic colonization. Russia also hoped to increase its interaction with the Kazakhs, who were seen as potential allies. Some Kazakhs sought to exploit the Russian presence to support their own position against rivals within their hordes, surrounding tribes, and the khanates.

Russians and Kazakhs entered into a complex colonial relationship. Russians initially practiced tactics of control used with other steppe tribes. Tribal leaders willing to offer loyalty received payments and promises of aid against enemies. As Russians constructed forts across the region, land emerged as another important incentive. Pledges of cooperation from tribal leaders sometimes allowed crossing imperial fortification lines to graze their herds on quality land. Territorial competition intensified as Cossacks and Slavic settlers penetrated more deeply into the steppe. Kazakhs who were denied access to sufficient feeding ground led frequent raids and rebellions against their own leaders who had submitted to Russian control in the late eighteenth century.

Russian officials devised numerous strategies to civilize the Kazakhs. Enlightenment notions of progress conditioned the Russian view of the nomadic people as backwards but also as children who could be transformed into loyal citizens. Policy initiatives to meet goals of control and civilization during the Catherinian era fell victim to continuing chaos in the steppe. Governor-General Baron Osip Igelstrom's plan in 1787 to abolish the title of khan in favor of elected councils as a means to introduce western political concepts and stabilize steppe unrest lasted only three years. By 1790 Russian officials returned to earlier policies of supporting khans who pledged loyalty, yet lack of land continued to spark unrest. In 1801 Tsar Paul (r. 1796-1801) signaled recognition of the plight of Kazakh tribes by his creation of an entirely new unit, the Inner Horde, which was given sufficient land behind Russian fortification lines to sustain its pastoral economy. Yet the Russian desire remained ultimately to settle the steppe and introduce agriculture among the Kazakhs.

In 1822 Governor-General of Western Siberia Mikhail Speransky (1772-1839) promulgated the Regulations on the Siberian Kirgiz, designed to shift the Kazakhs gradually but firmly towards sedentarism. The regulations imposed on the region a colonial administrative structure, restricted nomadic migrations, and introduced Russian notions and practices of law and order. Speransky encouraged Kazakhs to occupy posts in his extensive bureaucracy in the hope they would become vehicles for Russian influence. Elections replaced Kazakh methods of choosing leaders that privileged knowledge and wisdom. The regulations, nonetheless, allowed the continuation of Kazakh customary law, the adat, and did not establish immediate measures to force settlement.

Unrest over continuing infringement upon their land-use patterns in addition to increased taxation sparked a major rebellion of Middle Horde Kazakhs, led by Kenesary Qasim (1802-1847), against the Russian regime in 1837. The revolt, which lasted nine years, saw armies as large as twenty thousand oppose tsarist forces and allowed Kenesary to rule over significant portions of the steppe. Russian determination to retain control of the region was underlined by the dispatch of extra troops to suppress the uprising and the decision to establish a separate governor-generalship for the steppe in 1844.

Russian advances towards the khanates began in the early 1860s. Relations between St. Petersburg and the leaders of Bukhara, Khiva, and Kokand had deteriorated. The khanates refused demands to end discriminatory trade practices on Russian merchants and to liberate Russians sold as slaves. In 1839 a mission to Khiva to force submission to these conditions once again ended in a thorough Russian defeat with only one-third of the five-thousand strong contingent returning. Tsarist determination to enforce its will upon the khanates strengthened in the

1860s. Minister of War Dmitry Alekseevich Miliutin (1816-1912) argued that the region provided ideal ground for an offensive operation following the Russian humiliation in Crimea. Victories against weaker khanates would unsettle the British who, like Russia, were employing spies and envoys in the Great Game for influence in Central Asia. Adding to its empire would affirm Russia's position as a great European state and allow it to participate in the great civilizing mission of the era. Advocates for expansion also pointed to the drastic increase in cotton prices as a result of the US Civil War. Conquest of Central Asia, the major supplier of cotton to Russia, would assure a steady and cheap supply of the vital commodity. Both the ministries of foreign affairs and finance vigorously opposed potential expansion, however, fearing a hostile British reaction and increased costs while the country was attempting to rebuild in the era of the Great Reforms.

Russian frontier commanders, meanwhile, were making their own advances into the oases. Realization of their superiority over poorly-trained and armed Central Asian troops as well as a desire for prestige and advancement motivated these attacks, which they justified as preventing anarchy on the frontier. In 1863 Mikhail Grigorovich Cherniaev (1828-1898) defied orders from his superiors and seized the Kokandian city of Suzak. Further military campaigns followed, and Cherniaev advanced towards the central trading city of the khanate, Tashkent, which had a population of approximately eighty thousand. Each conquest received approval from Tsar Alexander II (1818-1881), whose desire for military glory now led him to support, albeit tacitly, a forward policy.

Cherniaev's conquest of Tashkent with 1,951 troops on 17 June 1865, coming against official orders, proved a decisive moment in Russian expansion. After significant debate the tsar in April 1867 made the city the capital of the new province of Turkestan, appointing as governor-general Konstantin Petrovich von Kaufman (1818-1881). Kaufman was given extraordinary powers to deal with neighboring khanates without requiring approval from St. Petersburg, signaling an aggressive phase of expansion of Russian power southwards.

Victory at Tashkent with the loss of only twelve soldiers solidified views of Russian military dominance. Leaders of the Central Asian khanates, previously sheltered from direct contact with powerful rivals, did not significantly alter military equipment or tactics over the eighteenth and nineteenth centuries. They relied on exploiting the rivalry between Great Britain and Russia in the region to allow them to keep their independence, whereas the British government made no formal objections to Russian military campaigns in Central Asia in the 1860s. Despite worries of an imminent Russian move towards India, British leaders limited their desired sphere of influence to Afghanistan. Some argued that Russian expansion would exercise a civilizing influence, calming their own northern frontier.

Tsarist forces continued military operations following the conquest of Tashkent. Kaufman seized the city of Samarkand from the emirate of Bukhara in May 1868 and forced its emir, Muzaffar al-Din (?-1885), to sign a convention favorable to Russia in exchange for keeping his throne. In 1873 a joint operation of forces from

Orenburg and Tashkent defeated the khan of Khiva. To minimize administrative cost and prevent large-scale uprisings against Russian forces Kaufman preferred to rule these khanates indirectly. In 1875 a rebellion in Kokand against the Russian-backed leader Khudayar (?-1886) pushed Kaufman to conquer the region. After victory came reprisals. Tsarist forces wiped out many winter feeding grounds of local nomads who participated in the uprising and annexed the region as the district of Fergana within the province of Turkestan.

Russian forces now turned to the Turkmen tribes. Turkmen raids, particularly around the Caspian port of Krasnovodsk, which Russia annexed in 1869, legitimized another round of conquests. Turkmen tribes exhibited effective resistance, resulting in approximately three hundred Russian deaths around the fortress of Geok-Tepe in 1880-1881. Tsarist troops in turn murdered thousands of civilians in their eventual victory. Only when Russian forces came against British interests in northern Afghanistan after the conquest of Merv in 1884 was expansion halted. Borders between the two empires were settled in 1895 after a final round of tsarist expansion in the Pamir mountains.

Russian rule in Central Asia was shaped by the Steppe Commission, appointed after the conquest of Tashkent. Charged to study the region and develop an appropriate administration, the commission offered several initiatives that were adopted by the tsar in April 1867. Among the most important of these, in addition to the formation of the province of Turkestan, was the decision to unite civil and military functions in the figure of the governor-general. Officials at lower levels also discharged both responsibilities, leaving no counterweight to the power of regional military commanders. The commission did recognize the different customs and modes of life of the peoples of the region and determined that non-political affairs were to be left in the hands of local elites. Yet tsarist officials remained free to deem political any act in which they desired to intervene.

When Russian conquest ended by 1895, Turkestan consisted of five regions (oblasti, pl.): Syr-Daria including Tashkent, Fergana, Samarkand, Semirechie, and Transcaspia. The steppe governor-generalship contained four regions: Akmolinsk, Semipalatinsk, Uralsk, and Turgai. A governor ruled each region, which in turn was divided into districts (uezdy, pl.), presided over by a commandant. Along with these Russian-ruled territories remained the semi-independent khanate of Khiva and the emirate of Bukhara.

As in the steppe, the Russian administration in Turkestan attempted a form of indirect rule, allowing a degree of self-government for local villages, tribes, and cities. Nonetheless the introduction of elections to choose native leaders and representatives to the imperial authorities altered politics and social relations. Power and authority in Central Asia rested not on institutional arrangements but upon personal bonds, prestige, and kinship hierarchies. Victors in elections proved in cases to be those most adept at manipulating electoral procedure, often with the assistance of Russian authorities. Structures of power eroded and opportunities for exploitation increased, as certain elected officials, now on the colonial payroll, employed the support of overlords to rule in the interests of their kin group or to levy additional fees on their constituents. Other elected leaders worked to negotiate with official-dom to gain maximum advantage for their areas in an unequal colonial relationship.

Corruption was pronounced among tsarist officials in Central Asia. Activities ranged from embezzlement of official funds to the extraction of supplemental taxes to outright extortion. Soldiers and settlers commonly beat the local population in order to steal goods, including animals of nomadic herders and supplies of local businessmen. The region quickly gained a reputation across the empire for its culture of corruption, provoking the dispatch of several investigatory commissions from St. Petersburg.

Russian intervention in the region had a significant impact on Bukhara and Khiva. Muzaffar requested and received the support of tsarist forces to put down unrest and consolidate power in the eastern reaches of the emirate. Tax burdens on Bukharan peasants mounted as the emir no longer feared internal opposition. In Khiva governor-generals supported pro-Russian elements in the khanate, favoring the Uzbek ruling classes against the Turkmen tribesmen of the region.

Another major concern of the tsarist administration in Central Asia was the exploitation of local resources. Governor-General Kaufman's primary interest involved the development of cotton. In 1871 he dispatched agronomists to Texas to investigate means of improving cotton production. The resulting refinement of suitable strands of American cotton for growth in Central Asia dramatically improved yields. Assisted by local policies that offered credits, distributed seeds at low costs, and set favorable taxation rates, cotton production exploded, growing fifteenfold in the 1880s alone. National tariffs against cotton imports also spurred growth. Yet this expansion did not engender structural change in the countryside. After initial failures of large cotton farms, Russian and Central Asian entrepreneurs began to work as intermediaries, advancing credit and purchasing supplies from peasant farmers. Peasants as a result were now dependent upon global market prices and tied into a never-ending cycle of debt. Despite these problems by the turn of the century the colonial economy of Central Asia met expectations of becoming a major reservoir of cotton for the tsarist state.

Other products important to the regional economy included tobacco, silk, and dried fruits. Later the extraction of minerals, including coal, oil, and gold, became a focus of the colonial regime. The construction of railways through the region, although undertaken for military imperatives, greatly aided the colonial economy. The first line was constructed from the Caspian port of Krasnovodsk in 1881, reaching Samarkand in 1888 and Tashkent ten years later. Trade between the metropole and periphery dramatically increased as a result, but goods still had to cross the Caspian Sea to reach European Russia. In 1906 a direct line was completed between Tashkent and Orenburg with connections to central Russia.

Governor-General Kaufman and his successors intervened selectively in Central Asian culture. Islam played a complex role in the lives and thoughts of the local population. Among nomads Islamic tenets, introduced by itinerant Sufi priests, were accepted and syncretized into Kazakh customary practices and law. In the settled areas the clergy (ulama) existed alongside political authorities and enforced Muslim law, the sharia. Kaufman sought to control the political and legal aspects of Islam in society. He introduced an electoral system for Islamic judges and abolished the position of the leading religious official (sheykh-ul-Islam) and chief legal guardian (qazi qalan) in Tashkent. Such acts coexisted with a general policy of disregard (ignorirovanie) of Islam in local cultural life. Kaufman and his successors believed that Islam, perceived by them as inherently backwards, would decay as the indigenous population learned more European ways. Missionary activity was forbidden so as not to provoke a defensive reaction among adherents of a religion the Russian authorities feared. Colonial officials nonetheless maintained decent relations in many cities with the ulama, which they viewed as a force for stability.

Gradual efforts to apply western ideals of civilization to the population focused on the transmission of a Russian education to select residents, particularly children and youth of the elite. Russian Orientalist intellectuals introduced numerous incarnations of hybrid Russian-native schools in both the steppe and oasis regions. The numbers of students remained extremely low despite efforts to requisition the sons of native elites for these schools. Local elites nonetheless adopted at their own pace aspects of Russian education and European culture which they deemed useful.

More intrusive than the colonial state in Central Asia were Russian settlers. Increasing numbers of Slavic peasants moved into the steppe in the 1850s, many without official permission. They ignored the designs of colonial officials, which foresaw a planned, measured colonization of Central Asia. Numerous efforts to direct settlement, particularly towards the border regions with China where Slavic peasants could serve as a bulwark of expansionism, enjoyed only limited success. Peasants seized land across nomadic migratory lines, intensifying unrest among local tribes. In the oasis areas arriving settlers crowded the new, urban Russian areas built alongside important cities, particularly the capital Tashkent. Their presence destroyed the image of privilege and power of the colonizer that colonial officials hoped to transmit through construction of straight, tree-lined streets and imperial European architecture.

A massive wave of colonization began in the 1890s. Famine and disease in European Russia pushed hundreds of thousands of peasants towards Central Asia. Colonial officials complained bitterly of unauthorized arrivals, but by the late 1880s central officials viewed colonization of Asian Russia as a solution for perceived peasant overcrowding in the metropole. In 1896 St. Petersburg established a Resettlement Administration (Pereselencheskoe upravlenie) to prepare laws and locate territory to accommodate Slavic colonists. Census results in 1911 counted 1,543,505 Russians in the steppe and 406,607 in Turkestan. The volume forced local officials to infringe increasingly on the lands of the local populations, particularly pastoralist feeding grounds. Many nomads were forced to transform their land-use patterns, building permanent settlements on their winter pastures and adopting a semi-nomadic form of life. The most impoverished became landless laborers, and many moved to the cities.

Colonization and other effects of colonial rule precipitated resistance. In 1892 official efforts to interfere in the cultural and medical practices of the local population, ostensibly to counter the impact of a cholera epidemic, met with opposition. Anger at orders regulating burial practices and treatment of corpses culminated in a march of the local population to the headquarters of the city commandant of Tashkent on 24 June. Russian settlers and soldiers responded by killing approximately one hundred demonstrators and native bystanders. Following the incident much of Turkestan was placed under emergency rule. In May 1898 a growing tax burden and worsening economic conditions played a role in an uprising in the Fergana Valley. The Sufi priest Muhammad 'Ali Ishan (?-1898) led a crowd that killed twenty-two Russian troops in Andijan as part of a larger movement intending to restore the khanate of Kokand. Russian troops quickly crushed the uprising, executed its leaders, and forcibly resettled entire villages. Resistance nonetheless continued at a lower level, and attacks on individual colonial officials increased in subsequent years.

Central Asian reaction to the Russian presence involved more than simple resistance. Better transport routes as a result of the conquest provided economic opportunity for a sophisticated business class. Central Asians owned 85 percent of the rough-processing cotton plants in the region. A new middle class of intermediaries who brought the crop from the countryside to the plants, known as the chistachi, also prospered. Russian settlers employed these developments as evidence of their more gentle brand of colonialism, even complaining that Central Asians had profited more than they from colonizing.

Colonial rule also generated new intellectual currents among Central Asians. Foremost among these were the new-method thinkers or jadids. At the turn of the century a generation of young intellectuals, building on movements elsewhere in the Islamic world, sought to renovate their society and overcome apparent European dominance through the acquisition of knowledge. At the center of their plans were new-method schools, which incorporated subjects not taught in the traditional Islamic system, including mathematics, geography, and foreign languages. Jadid thinkers, a diverse group, advocated progress and charged indigenous elites, in particular the ulama, with perpetuating backwardness in local society in order to maintain influence. Supported by liberal commercial elites, Jadids opened hundreds of schools across the region, but their influence was limited to urban areas, and even there their numbers paled in comparison to those in the educational system of the ulama.

Tsarist policies and settler actions during the First World War exacerbated colonial inequalities. By late 1915 the tsarist state imposed fixed procurement prices for Turkestan cotton and steppe livestock well below market rates. Central Asian Muslims, although exempt from the draft, were charged a debilitating 21 percent war tax. Colonial officials and settlers levied their own additional taxes and requisitioned hundreds of thousands of animals and food products from the local population. Such requisitioning occurred even as food supplies to the region virtually ceased by 1916. Central Asia by virtue of the emphasis on cotton lost its self-sufficiency in food, and drought conditions led to increasing hunger.

On 25 June 1916 colonial officials received an order from Tsar Nicholas II (1868-1918) to draft 250,000 Central Asians for rearguard service, thereby freeing Slavic troops for the front lines. News of the draft announcement sparked immediate resistance. On 4 July a riot in the city of Khojent resulted in the deaths of dozens of tsarist officials and sparked incidents of violence across Turkestan. In the steppe and Semirechie region along the border with China, Central Asian pastoralists, their numbers reaching 30,000, attacked the large Russian settler population. Central officials dispatched sixteen companies of troops to Central Asia to defeat the uprising. The resulting repression resulted in unknown thousands of deaths and drove 300,000 nomads from their traditional grounds. Many of them fled to China. Artillery leveled entire villages, killing thousands more before the rebellion dissipated, and the draft, in a much reduced fashion, began in September.

Most notables in Central Asian society, including jadids, liberal intellectuals, and Muslim clerics, never embraced the rebellion, believing success impossible against superior military force. Yet indigenous elites had grown increasingly disillusioned with the imperial regime. Initial hopes of greater participation in central policies faded following the elimination of Turkestan from elected representation in the State Duma in 1907. Harsh punitive measures in 1916 ended beliefs that imperial Russia represented a force for stability or progress in Central Asia. Rationing policies favoring the settler population, introduced during the winter of 1916-1917, sparked further anger as starvation threatened. A wide spectrum of Central Asian elites began to consider autonomy or outright independence from their colonial overlords necessary for equality, freedom, peace, and development of the region as the tsarist regime collapsed in February 1917.

Bibliography: On the peoples of the region, see Elizabeth E. Bacon, *Central Asians under Russian Rule* (Ithaca, N.Y., 1966), Edward A. Allworth, *The Modern Uzbeks. From the Fourteenth Century to the Present. A Cultural History* (Stanford, Cal., 1990), and Martha Brill Olcott, *The Kazakhs* (Stanford, Cal., 1995). A study of the initial Russian conquest is Michael Khodarkovsky, *Russia's Steppe Frontier. The Making of a Colonial Empire, 1500-1800* (Bloomington, Ind., 2002). David MacKenzie explores the importance of unauthorized advances on the frontier in "Expansion in Central Asia. St. Petersburg vs. the Turkestan Generals, 1863-1866," *Canadian Slavic Studies*, No. 3 (1969), 286-311. N.A. Khalfin argues that economic motives played a primary role in *Prisoedinenie Srednei Azii k Rossii (60-90-e gody XIX v.)* (M., 1965). On relations between Russia and Great Britain, see Mohammed Anwar Khan, *England, Russia, and Central Asia. A Study In Diplomacy, 1857-1879* (Peshawar, 1969). Still useful overviews of the imperial period are Richard A. Pierce, *Russian Central Asia, 1867-1917. A Study in Colonial Rule* (Berkeley, Cal., 1960) and Seymour Becker, *Russia's Protectorates in Central Asia. Bukhara and*

Khiva, 1865-1924 (Cambridge, Mass., 1968). For an early Soviet view that condemns colonial officials and settlers, see P.G. Galuzo, *Turkestan-Koloniia. Ocherk istorii Turkestana ot zavoevaniia russkimi do revoliutsii 1917 goda* (M., 1929). A recent publication that lauds the actions of leading tsarist generals is Evgenii Glushchenko, *Geroi imperii. Portrety rossiiskikh kolonialnykh deiatelei* (M., 2001). A recent look at important facets of imperial rule from Kaufman's policies to the 1916 revolts is Daniel Brower, *Turkestan and the Fate of the Russian Empire* (London, 2002). More specialized studies that expose important aspects of colonial rule on the Kazakhs include Thomas Winner, *The Oral Art and Literature of the Kazakhs of Russian Central Asia* (Durham, N.C., 1958) and Virginia Martin, *Law and Custom on the Steppe. The Kazakhs of the Middle Horde and Russian Colonialism in the Nineteenth Century* (Richmond, Eng., 2002). For two excellent works on the new intellectual currents emerging from the colonial idiom and their impact on oasis society, see Hélène Carrère d'Encausse, *Réforme et Révolution chez les Musulmans de l'Empire Russe* (Paris, 1966), and Adeeb Khalid, *The Politics of Muslim Cultural Reform. Jadidism in Central Asia* (Berkeley, Cal., 1997). See also Serge A. Zenkovsky, *Pan-Turkism and Islam in Russia, 1905-1920* (Cambridge, Mass., 1960). On the Russian settler community, including information on the Cholera Riot of 1892, see Jeff Sahadeo, "Creating a Russian Colonial Community. City, Nation, and Empire in Tashkent, 1865-1923" (Ph.D. Diss., University of Illinois, 2000). On Russian settlers, see as well A.I. Ginzburg, *Russkoe naselenie v Turkestane, konets XIX-nachalo XX veka* (M., 1992). Revolts in Fergana are analyzed in Beatrice Forbes Manz, "Central Asian Uprisings in the Nineteenth Century. Ferghana under the Russians" *Russian Review*, Vol. 46 (1987), 261-281. On the revolt of 1916, see Edward Dennis Sokol, *The Revolt of 1916 in Russian Central Asia* (Baltimore, Md., 1954).

Jeff F. Sahadeo

CENTRAL ASIAN FORUM. An organization intended to promote cooperation among governments, business, and non-governmental organizations in the Central Asian region. Previously known as Central Asian Union (1990-1994) and Central Asian Economic Union (1994-2000).

Representatives of Kazakhstan, Kyrgyzstan, Tajikistan, Turkmenistan and Uzbekistan established the Central Asian Union (CAU) during an informal meeting in Alma-Ata (renamed Almaty) on 23 June 1990. The CAU was initially intended to promote cultural, political, and economic cooperation within the region and to coordinate a common stand in negotiating their relations with the Soviet central government during the revision of the Soviet Union Treaty. On 14 August 1991 the heads of the Central Asian states formally established an Inter-republic Consultative Commission with its center in Ashgabad, Turkmenistan. In response to the unilateral Belarus-Russia-Ukraine agreement on dissolution of the USSR on 8 December 1991, the Central Asian states jointly supported establishment of the Commonwealth of Independent States (CIS). Intensive informal negotiations between the former Soviet republics finally led to the signing of the Almaty Declaration in December

1991, which endorsed mutual acceptance of existing borders, denunciation of any territorial claims on each other, and guaranties of ethnic minorities' rights. In early 1992 negotiations within the CAU framework were crucial in formulation of a joint stand on security relations with post-Soviet Russia and other members of the CIS and in signing of the CIS Security Treaty (Dogovor o kollektivnoi bezopasnosti) during the CIS security summit in Tashkent in May 1992.

Between June 1992 and April 1994 the CAU was largely inactive, as Tajikistan and Turkmenistan left the organization due to changes in their domestic and foreign policy environments. It was further undermined by the unilateral introduction of the Kyrgyz currency, the som, in May 1993, which led to a customs war on the borders between the republics and also negatively affected regional economic cooperation. In April 1994 Kazakhstan and Uzbekistan re-launched the union as the Central Asian Economic Union (CAEU). Kyrgyzstan joined the organization in the same year. The CAEU members established several inter-governmental institutions. This included the Inter-government Executive Committee, Central Asian Bank, Council of Prime Ministers, the Council of Defence Ministers, and various others. In early 1998 Tajikistan formally applied for membership in the CAEU and was accepted as a full member. These steps allowed an increase in intra-regional trade of about 15 to 20 percent. The CAEU collapsed in late 1998, when Kyrgyzstan independently negotiated its entry into the World Trade Organization (WTO). Consequently the region faced a new cycle of conflicts over custom duties, import tariffs, cross-border trade, border delimitation, the presence of military anti-personnel and anti-tank land mines, and entry-visa regimes. In 1999 security arrangements within CAEU were further undermined because Uzbekistan unilaterally decided to leave the CIS Security Treaty and to join GUAM, an organization that unites Georgia, Ukraine, Azerbaijan and Moldova. Meanwhile Kazakhstan, Kyrgyzstan and Tajikistan decided to extend the CIS Security Treaty for five years. The Central Asian republics nonetheless continued cooperation in security issues and sent their troops to the Central Asian Peacekeeping Battalion military exercises, which were conducted under US and NATO sponsorship. See also Central Asian Peacekeeping Battalion, SMERSH, Vol. 5.

In January 2001 the CAEU was reconstituted as the Central Asian Forum (CAF). The new institution was intended to promote greater coordination and informal talks between government institutions, businesses, and regional non-governmental organizations. According to CAEU-CAF, between 1991 and 2001 its members signed more than 250 treaties and agreements aimed at simplifying regional trade, movement of goods, and services. However, significant differences in the members' approaches to economic and political reforms and in their foreign policy orientations undermined regional cooperation within CAF. In 2001 negotiations over removal of customs and border controls within the region were halted, and CAF members introduced entry visas for citizens of Kyrgyzstan and Tajikistan, thus ending CAF's visa-free travel regime. In 2001-2002 the leaders of the member countries agreed to continue regular meetings to discuss regional problems and to resolve differences on such issues as the environment, population movements, defense policy, cultural exchange and regional cooperation in development of transportation infrastructure. In 2002 and 2003 the Central Asian republics in cooperation with several donor organizations discussed development of several major multi-million-dollar investment projects for modernization of the regional transportation infrastructure.

Bibliography: R. Abazov, "Forces of Integration and Disintegration in Central Asia in the Post-Cold War Era" in Ertan Efegil, ed., *Geopolitics of Central Asia in the Post-Cold War Era. A Systemic Analysis* (Haarlem, 2002); Bartlomiej Kaminski, ed., *Economic Transition in Russia and the New States of Eurasia* (Armonk, N.Y., 1994); Boris Rumer and Stanislav Zhukov, eds., *Central Asia. The Challenges of Independence* (Armonk, N.Y., 1998); *Sbornik dokumentov i materialov po voprosam ekonomicheskoi integratsii respublik Kazakhstana, Kyrgyzstana, i Uzbekistana* (Almaty, 1995); Kasymzhomart Tokayev, *Diplomatia Respubliki Kazakhstana.* (Astana, 2001).

Rafis Abazov

CENTRAL ASIAN PEACEKEEPING BATTALION. Also known as Centrasbat. A peacekeeping unit jointly established in 1996 by Kazakhstan, Kyrgyzstan, Uzbekistan, and Tajikistan, which joined in 1998.

Centrasbat has no fixed number of solders and officers. Its size fluctuates according to operational needs and contributions from the members. The idea of developing military cooperation between the Central Asian states was initiated in 1992 at the beginning of the civil war in Tajikistan and establishment of the Commonwealth of Independent States' Security Treaty. Some time and a number of steps were needed to realize the project.

In 1992-1993 Kazakhstan, Kyrgyzstan, and Uzbekistan sent their defense units to Tajikistan to stabilize the situation there, but they disagreed over their objectives and the nature of military cooperation, such as whether a joint military unit should be created. Not until December 1995 did the Central Asian leaders agree on the forms of their cooperation and establish a Joint Council of Defense Ministers within the framework of the Central Asian Economic Union. In December 1996 the council worked out an agreement on establishment of the Centrasbat. The unit's main objective was to promote cooperation and coordination between member countries' defense forces in case of emergency, militant incursion, or other needs. It was intended that the participating countries would jointly finance Centrasbat's logistical support and military exercises.

In 1997 the United States' Atlantic Command decided to sponsor the first joint military exercise to include Centrasbat and American troops. In August-September 1997 Centrasbat personnel underwent training at Fort Bragg, North Carolina, and on 15 September 1997 forty Central Asian and 500 US troops parachuted into Kazakhstan. For the US it was the largest airborne operation on the territory of the former Soviet Union, and for the Central Asian republics it was the first operation on their soil with US participation. To further develop the potential of such joint exercises it was decided to continue them on an annual basis with NATO troops participating, sponsored primarily by the US. The main objectives of the exercises were to maximize the interoperability of the participating troops in actions against militant or terrorist groups and to improve their ability to conduct peacekeeping and humanitarian operations. It was also decided that further joint exercises should be conducted within the framework of NATO's Partnership for Peace program. In 1998 Russian and Turkish forces teamed with Centrasbat and US troops in joint military exercises on the territory of Kazakhstan and Kyrgyzstan. In May 1999 the Centrasbat annual multi-national exercises were conducted for the first time in a training seminar format at the US Central Command Center at Tampa, Florida. In September 2000 Centrasbat exercises took place in Kazakhstan, focusing on peacekeeping and humanitarian assistance in the field, although Kyrgyzstan and Uzbekistan were unable to participate because of militant incursions from Tajikistan into their territories.

In 2001-2002 the US-led war on international terrorism and against the Taliban regime in Afghanistan contributed to some changes in the format and operational tasks of Centrasbat. In 2001 Centrasbat exercises were conducted in Ramstein, Germany, as a command post headquarters exercise. It is expected that Centrasbat is to play an increasing role in developing the Central Asian regional security architecture after the beginning of the US-led war on international terrorism.

Bibliography: Martha Olcott, *Central Asia's New States. Independence, Foreign Policy, and Regional Security* (Washington, 1995); Ustina Markus and Daniel Nelson, *Brassey's Eurasian Security Yearbook* (Washington, 2000).

Rafis Abazov

CENTRAL ASIAN RAILROAD. Built 1880-1888, running from Krasnovodsk through Samarkand and Tashkent.

The tsarist Russian government built the Central Asian Railroad in stages between 1880 and 1888, with subsequent extensions, primarily for strategic purposes and in tandem with tsarist expansion into the Bukharan emirate. Its history reflects the nature of Russian imperialism in that region.

The earliest proposals, put forward in the 1850s to the 1870s, were to build a railroad along the caravan route between Orenburg and Tashkent to facilitate trade between Russia and Central Asia. Turkestan Governor-General K.N. von Kaufman seconded these proposals to help secure Russian control over the territory. Fiscal crises, bureaucratic inertia, and the army's doubts about the relevance of railroads led to inaction on the matter. The failure of military engagements with the Teke Turkomans in 1879 gave new life to the project, but along a more southerly route extending from Uzun-Ada on the Caspian Sea to Kizil-Arvat, hence the original name, the Trans-Caspian Military Railroad. Then and thereafter the route, which eventually ran from Krasnovodsk through Ashkhabad, Merv, and Samarkand to Tashkent and Andizhan, was selected according to the needs of the moment rather than following any preconceived plan for the annexation of the region. Other factors in the selection of the route involved the proximity of the railroad to the Afghani border at a time of Great Game competition with British forces coming out of India and the desire to tap the agricultural resources of the Fergana Valley. Russian delicacy in handling relations with the emir of Bukhara accounts for the decision to build the railroad south of that city, where inhabitants referred to locomotives as Satan's wagons before getting used to them. Including all branch lines, the railroad was eventually 1,550 miles (2,495 km) in length.

Several foreigners, including Fernand de Lesseps of Suez Canal fame, failed in their bids to build the railroad. Construction instead was placed in the hands of General M.N. Annenkov, the officer responsible for military transport within the war ministry. Annenkov succeeded in completing the first section of the railroad rapidly despite being faced with sandstorms, fuel, timber, and water shortages, and attacks by hostile natives. He dealt with these problems by planting desert shrubs along the route to hold the sand in place, building embankments to lift the track off the desert floor, shipping petroleum from Baku and wood from Russia, regularly running water cars along the route, and dispatching Cossacks to defend the line. Laborers were in short supply and were either recruited from military engineering battalions or imported from Russia and Azerbaijan. A hundred-mile stretch through the Karakum desert was the first railroad line to be laid across sand dunes anywhere, and Annenkov won international renown and a medal from the tsar for his accomplishment. But extreme weather conditions continued to play havoc with the track, and most experts at the time considered the line to be shoddily built, a result of the government's instruction to build as cheaply and fast as possible. The overall per mile cost of the railroad compared favorably with the Trans-Siberian but was rather high compared to privately constructed roads.

The first section of the railroad was built too late to be used as intended, for the capture of Geok Tepe had already taken place by that time. But the railroad laid the groundwork for the Russian colonization of the Bukharan emirate. Administration of the railroad was led by the Russian diplomat N.V. Charykov, who negotiated to win the tsarist government permission to build the line in the first place. Construction and operation resulted in the influx of Russian civilians and soldiers and establishment of several Russian towns, including New Bukhara, now Kagan. Russian, Armenian, and Jewish businessmen appeared in greater numbers than ever before and soon came to dominate the Uzbek economy. They imported Russian manufactures, exported cotton, built cotton mills, and founded metalworking factories to supply the railroad. All industrial workers were Russians. Bypassing Bukhara until the emir had a branch line constructed in 1900-1901, the railroad precipitated that city's economic decline while revitalizing commerce in Samarkand and other towns along the route.

Because of its role in the Russian colonization of Central Asia the railroad inspired projects with similar purposes in other parts of Asia, including the Trans-Siberian and Chinese Eastern railroads. Its success also bred proposals for extension of the rail network elsewhere in Turkestan, including the Orenburg-Tashkent line, which was completed in 1906, and links to the Trans-Siberian, most of which were not built until Soviet times.

Bibliography: Edward Allworth, ed., *Central Asia. A Century of Russian Rule* (New York, 1967); Seymour Becker, *Russia's Protectorates in Central Asia* (Cambridge, Mass., 1968); Steven G. Marks, *Road to Power. The Trans-Siberian Railroad and the Colonization of Asian Russia* (Ithaca, N.Y., 1991); A.M. Solov'eva, *Zheleznodorozhnyi transport Rossii vo vtoroi polovine XIX v.* (M., 1975); J.N. Westwood, *A History of Russian Railways* (London, 1964); W.E. Wheeler, "The Control of Land Routes. Russian Railways in Central Asia," *Journal of the Royal Central Asian Society* (October 1934), 585-608.

Steven G. Marks

CENTRAL BUREAU OF MOSLEM ORGANIZATIONS OF THE RUSSIAN COMMUNIST PARTY (1918-1921). Leading organ of Muslim communists of the new Soviet state.

In June 1918, when a gathering of Muslim communists of the Russian Federation (RF) met in Kazan, they decided to organize a separate Muslim communist party and elected a central committee to represent the interests of the Muslim population. The Central Committee of the Russian Communist Party (Bolsheviks, RCP(b)) condemned this decision and organized the first Congress of Muslim Communists of the RF.

The congress was held in Moscow in November 1918 with approximately sixty delegates in attendance, representing Muslim communists of the lower Volga region, the Caucasus, and Central Asia. This congress declared the central committee of Muslim communists formed in June disbanded and condemned nationalist and separatist tendencies as harmful for the unity of the communist cause. They decided instead to organize the Central Bureau of the Muslim Communists of the RCP(b). The newly elected central bureau unanimously accepted the rule of the RCP(b) and guidelines of its program. The congress also decided to organize a Central Muslim War Collegium and Muslim bureaus in districts and regions (uezdy and oblasti, pl.). The purpose of the bureaus was to conduct communist propaganda and agitation among local populations, to increase a number of Muslim communists, and to translate the regulations and programs of the RCP(b) into local languages.

In March 1919 the Central Bureau of the Muslim Communists of the RCP(b) was renamed the Central Bureau of the Communist Organizations of the Peoples of the East. The name change was prompted by the establishment of the Third Communist International and prospect of proletarian revolutions in the near future in eastern nations such as China, Afghanistan, Persia, and Turkey. The new central bureau published its own journal, The Red East (Krasnyi vostok).

The Second Congress of the Communist Organizations of the Peoples of the East was held in Moscow from 22 November to 3 December 1919 on the initiative of the central bureau of the Peoples of the East. The Congress was attended by seventy-one voting and eleven non-voting delegates. On the opening day Lenin delivered a report on the current situation. The resolution adopted after his report was intended to serve as the basis for further work in the Muslim regions and countries of the East. The congress outlined the tasks of the party and the government in the Eastern countries and elected a new central bureau.

In January 1920 the central bureau was renamed again, becoming the Central Bureau of the Turkic Peoples. This time the change was caused by the perceived need to strengthen party work among the Turkic peoples of the RF, especially in Central Asia, and to encourage the anticolonial revolution in Turkey. In May 1921 the Central Bureau of the Turkic Peoples was dismissed by order of the Organizational Bureau of the Central Committee of the RCP(b), which declared the central bureau's international mission accomplished.

Bibliography: "Tsentral'noe Biuro Musul'manskikh Organizatsii RKP(b)" in *Bol'shaia Sovetskaia Entsiklopediia*, 50 vols., Vol. 46 (M., 1954), 537; M.A., Saidasheva, *Lenin i sotsialisticheskoe stroitel'stvo v Tatarii, 1918-1923* (M., 1969); "Pis'mo TsK RKP(b) vsem partiinym komitetam i politorganizatsiiam o rabote sredi narodov vostoka (21.02.1920)" in *KPSS v rezoliutsiiakh i resheniakh s"ezdov, konferentsii i plenumov TsK*, 16 vols., Vol. 2 (M., 1970), 147; T. Davletshin, *Sovetskii Tatarstan. Teoriia i praktika leninskoi natsional'noi politiki* (London, 1974); *Kommunisticheskaia Partiia Kazakhstana. Spravochnik* (Alma-Ata, 1990); Alexandre Bennigsen and S. Enders Wimbush, *Muslim National Communism in the Soviet Union. A Revolutionary Strategy for the Colonial World* (Chicago, 1979); Alexandre Bennigsen and Chantal Lemercier-Quelquejay, *Les Mouvements Nationaux chez le Musulmans de Russie. Le Sultangalievisme au Tatarstan* (Paris, 1960); Helene Carrere d'Encausse, *The Great Challenge. Nationalities and the Soviet State* (New York, 1992); Shoshana Keller, *To Moscow, Not Mecca. The Soviet Campaign against Islam* (Westport, Conn., 2001).

Irena Vladimirsky

CENTRAL CHILDREN'S THEATER. Founded in 1936, renamed the Russian Academic Youth Theater in 1992.

In March 1936 the Central Committee of the Communist Party and the Council of People's Commissars established the Central Children's Theater (Tsentralny detsky teatr), which was meant to serve as a model for the artistic, pedagogical, and political functioning of Soviet theaters for children and youth. The official purpose of children's theater was to help shape the aesthetic and ideological education of future Soviet citizens. The theater was housed on Sverdlov Square, now Theater Square, in a newly renovated building that formerly accommodated the Second Moscow Art Theater. It was adjacent to the famous Maly and Bolshoi theaters. Natalia Ilinichna Sats (1903-1993) was its first artistic director. In the late 1980s the Central Children's Theater focused increasingly on a repertory of classics in order to attract new audiences and escape the stigmas from the past. In 1992 it changed its name to the Russian Academic Youth Theater (Rossiisky akademichesky molodezhny teatr, RAMT).

The Central Children's Theater was officially hailed as an entirely new theater, but the core consisted of the troupe of Natalia Sats's Moscow Theater for Children. It opened with a production depicting contemporary Soviet school life. Serezha Streltsov, written by schoolteacher and pedagogue, V.A. Liubimova, was taken directly from the repertory of the Moscow Theater for Children. While the play seemed ideologically correct and emphasized discipline, respect, and conformity, it was proscribed in 1937. According to the administration of theaters of the all-Union Committee on the Arts, the play contained "slander against the Soviet school and schoolchild, and a perverted interpretation of the feeling of duty and comradeship among youth" (Sosin, 178). Shortly afterwards Natalia Sats was exiled as an enemy of the people. In the short time she was director she attracted some famous figures, among them Sergei Sergeevich Prokofiev (1891-1953), who composed the music for Peter and the Wolf, which premiered in the theater on 5 May 1936.

The theater employed 375 people, including an orchestra of twenty-eight. As the official state theater for children it functioned on the basic principles of Soviet children's theater established by Aleksandr Aleksandrovich Briantsev (1883-1961) and Nikolai Nikolaevich Bakhtin (1866-1940) at the Leningrad Theater of the Young Spectator (Lentiuz), founded in 1922. The Central Children's Theater consisted of an artistic and a pedagogical section, which jointly decided the repertory. It offered a variety of productions, including contemporary plays, classics, historical plays, and fairy tales. It geared its productions towards three age groups: seven to nine, ten to thirteen, and fourteen to seventeen years old.

During WWII the Central Children's Theater evacuated to the city of Kuzbass but remained in operation. It returned to Moscow in 1943. Following the general trend in theater for children and youth, the post-war years were characterized by patriotism and collective thought as a dominant theme, inspired by Stalin's theories of the non-antagonistic contradictions. This led to two basic problems in the theater, a lack of conflict and an absence of comedies.

The heyday of the Central Children's Theater came during the Thaw period (1953-1964). Noted scholar and literary advisor of the Moscow Art Theater, Anatoly Mironovich Smeliansky (b. 1942), claims that the revival of the Russian stage after the death of Stalin began in the Central Children's Theater, which offered a creative outlet for some of the most famous theater practitioners of the post-Thaw period.

Georgy Aleksandrovich Tovstonogov (1915-1989), head of the Bolshoi Drama Theater in Leningrad from 1956 until his death, began directing at the Central Children's Theater in 1949 with Somewhere in Siberia (Gde-to v Sibiri). Tovstonogov came from Tbilisi, Georgia, where he staged productions for the Russian Theater of the Young Spectator (TIUZ). Tovstonogov turned the Bolshoi Drama Theater into one of the strongest Russian companies of the post-Stalin period and trained and influenced some of the most innovative contemporary directors in Russia.

Oleg Nikolaevich Efremov (1927-2000), founder of the Sovremennik (Contemporary) Theater and artistic director of the Moscow Art Theater from 1970 until his death, acted at the Central Children's Theater from 1949 to 1956 and occasionally directed. With students from the Moscow Art Theater he founded his own theater, the Sovremennik, in 1957. It was the first theater in decades that was not dictated from above but formed by and for the artists themselves.

Anatoly Vasilevich Efros (1925-1987), director of several theaters, among others the Malaia Bronnaia, the Lenkom, the Moscow Art Theater, and the Taganka, joined the Central Children's Theater from 1954 to 1964. Efros was one of the most independent and innovative directors during the Soviet regime.

Maria Osipovna Knebel (1898-1985), actor, director, and teacher, trained in the Second Moscow Art Theater Studio of Michael Chekhov (1891-1955) and was a member of the Moscow Art Theater from 1924 to 1950. She was removed from the Moscow Art Theater in 1951 and placed at the Central Children's Theater. In 1955 she became the theater's artistic director, remaining until 1960 and returning from 1966 to 1968. Knebel's teachings, particularly her approach to the classics, and her books on the methods of Konstantin Sergeevich Stanislavsky (1863-1938) as modified by Michael Chekhov have influenced directors at the Central Children's Theater into the twenty-first century. At the Central Children's Theater Knebel pushed for an innovative repertory, focusing on the psychological struggles of young protagonists.

In 1955 Knebel and Efros staged the highly controversial play Three Went to the Virgin Lands (My v troem poekhali na tselinu) by Nikolai Fedorovich Pogodin (1900-1962) at the Central Children's Theater. The play was inspired by Pogodin's own trip to the Virgin Lands, and attempted to give a true picture of what he witnessed, not hiding the complexities and difficulties of cultivating those virgin territories. It was received with mixed reviews, criticized for its questionable educational values, hasty writing, and lack of observation. The Communist Party newspaper Pravda called it a big mistake to include this play in the repertory, and it was banned soon after opening.

The plays of Viktor Sergeevich Rozov (b. 1913) were more successful. With Anatoly Efros directing and Oleg Efremov in the leading parts, seven plays by Rozov premiered at the Central Children's Theater between 1949 and 1960. Rozov's plays featured young protagonists with which both actor and audience could easily identify. The productions were primarily attended by young people at first, but more and more adults appeared in the audience. The partnership of Efros, Rozov, and Efremov was not only the basis for the theater's success during the Thaw, it was formative for the three artists' subsequent careers.

By the end of the Thaw Knebel was forced to leave the theater, and Efros and Efremov chose to leave to pursue their own careers, taking the plays of Viktor Rozov with them. The Moral Code of the Builder of Communism, which was included in the 1961 program of the Communist Party and adopted that year by the theater, laid out the principles of conduct expected of all members of the communist social order. These included devotion to the cause of communism, love of the socialist homeland, conscientious labor for the good of society, intolerance of violations of the public interest, and an uncompromising attitude to injustice, parasitism, dishonesty, and careerism. The Central Children's Theater entered a period of stagnation, returning to its pre-Thaw practices. During the 1960s and 1970s the Central Children's Theater remained officially the foremost theater for children and youth. Official documents and reports did not reflect the gradual decline of the quality of productions and actors, but these became apparent in the period of openness (glasnost).

In 1980 Aleksei Vladimirovich Borodin (b. 1942) was appointed artistic director. Borodin recruited some young actors and began to create a repertory troupe in which the new generation could learn from the older generation and the older could draw energy from the younger. In 1985 the theater produced a controversial, contemporary play, dealing with gangs, peer pressure, and youth loneliness. Pitfall, Size 46 Medium (Lovushka #46, rost vtoroi) by the journalist Yury Shchekochikhin revived memories of the days of Efros, Efremov, and Rozov.

Glasnost brought the problems of theater for children and youth to stage front. At stake was the official function and place of an art form, which from its inception was closely connected to the political doctrine of the Soviet regime. Borodin adapted to the ideological shifts by focusing on a repertory of foreign and Soviet classics with a humanistic philosophy. Asserting that youth theater is first and foremost theater, and thus art, he presented classical literature as the best way to prepare a future audience for the Bolshoi and the Maly. The pedagogues of the theater agreed, maintaining that youngsters only had to look outside for contemporary issues. From the pedagogues' perspective the Central Children's Theater did not so much alter its course as to reinforce the already existing trend to increase productions geared to slightly older audiences.

While the theater's artistic and educational direction remained virtually unaltered by the changing material circumstances of the late 1980s and early 1990s, the theater did change its name in 1992. The former Central Children's Theater, as it is commonly referred to, became the Russian Academic Youth Theater (RAMT) in an attempt to escape the confines of children's theater. At the same time the theater struggled to maintain its reputation in the 1990s with new productions for mixed audiences or adults as well as in productions for children. Financial problems forced it in 1996 to give up its small stage to the Bolshoi Theater and to rent out a large part of their building to private businesses, including a woodworking shop and a photocopying shop.

As the theater entered the twenty-first century, the tide again began to turn. In the late 1990s the theater abolished its pedagogical section, a crucial component for a theater for children and youth under the Soviets. The teaching section was restored in 2000. RAMT did not forget that it was the foremost professional state-supported theater for children and youth in the USSR. The young audience may be what makes RAMT unique and builds a loyal audience. The popularity of its children's and family productions, both older ones such as Dream to be Continued (1986) by Sergei Vladimirovich Mikhalkov (b. 1913) and newer ones such as Pollyanna (1996), show that RAMT fills a niche as one of the few state-subsidized professional theaters for children and youth. In 2003 RAMT is still one of the largest theaters for young audiences in the world with over 100 actors and 200 other personnel.

See also Children's Theater, SMERSH, Vol. 5.

Bibliography: The most important Russian sources on the Central Children's Theater are Alexandra N. Gozenpud, *Tsentral'nyi detskii teatr, 1936-1961* (M., 1967), and the sixtieth anniversary publication *Na Teatral'noi Ploshchadi, sleva ot*

Bol'shogo (M., 1996). General sources on Soviet children's theater include Aleksandr A. Briantsev, *Vospominaniia, stat'i, vystupleniia, dnevniki, pis'ma* (M., 1979), and Lenora G. Shpet, *Sovetskii teatr dlia detei* (M., 1971). See also the autobiographies of Nataliia I. Sats, *Deti prikhodiat v teatr* (M., 1960) and *Novely moei zhizni* (M., 1972). In English see the Ph.D. dissertations of Gene Sosin "Children's Theater and Drama in the Soviet Union, 1917-1953" (Ph.D. diss., Columbia University, 1958) and George Shail "The Leningrad Theater of Young Spectators" (Ph.D. diss., New York, University, 1980). See Anatoly Smeliansky, *The Russian Theater after Stalin* (Cambridge, 1999) for a first-hand account of the Russian theater in general. For a more comprehensive history of Soviet and Russian theater for children and youth, with a special focus on the developments in the Central Children's Theater /RAMT, see Manon van de Water, *I Will Grow Up! A Cultural History of Ideological Coercion and Artistic Innovation in Moscow Theaters for Young People, 1917-2000*, to be published by the University of Wisconsin Press in 2004.

Manon van de Water

CENTRAL MUSIC SCHOOL (1932-). Tsentralnaia Musikalnaia Shkola, known by its abbreviated name Tsemsha. Provides training for musically talented children at Moscow's Chaikovsky State Conservatory.

The Moscow conservatory was founded by Nikolai Rubinstein, the well-known pianist and conductor, in 1866. Over the years its more famous professors have included Petr Chaikovsky (1840-1893), Sergei Taneev (1856-1915), Vasily Safonov (1852-1918), Mikhail Ippolitov-Ivanov (1859-1935), Nikolai Miaskovsky (1881-1950), and Dmitry Shostakovich (1906-1975). The conservatory moved into its current quarters, best known for its acoustically splendid, 2,000-seat Grand Hall, in 1901. It was renamed in honor of P.I. Chaikovsky in 1940. The conservatory currently comprises seven departments, which specialize in piano, orchestral studies, vocal studies, choral conducting, composition, history and theory of music and ethnomusicology, and the history and theory of music performance. Since 1993 the conservatory has included the Studio for New Music Ensemble, founded by composer Vladimir Tarnopolsky (1955-). The conservatory's library boasts one of the richest collections of books and music in Russia.

The Central Music School was founded within the conservatory in 1932 by Aleksandr Goldenveiser (1875-1961) and Genrikh Neigaus (1888-1964) as a place where young prodigies could study with the conservatory's best teachers. Surprised by their young pupils' amazing receptiveness, the professors soon had them rehearsing pieces normally reserved for their most senior students. Goldenveiser, who had been at the conservatory since 1906, remained with the program until 1961. Lazar Berman (1930-), the renowned pianist, considered Goldenveiser a brilliant teacher who introduced students to the spirit of the music. Neigaus came to teach piano at the conservatory in 1922. A talented performer, once called the poet of the pianoforte, Neigaus was a great teacher who strove to create an intellectual and romantic school of pianism. His most famous pupils, both graduates of the Central Music School, were Sviatoslav Rikhter (1915-1997) and Emil Gilels (1916-1985).

Other famous musicians who attended the Central Music School were Leonid (1924-1982) and Oleg (1946-1990) Kogan, Tatiana Nikolaeva (1924-1992), Gennady Rozhdestvensky (1931-), Mikhail Pletnev (1957-), Vladimir Ashkenazy (1937-), Vladimir Spivakov (1944-), Lazar Berman, and Nikolai Lugansky (1972-). Dmitry Paperno (1929-), a brilliant pianist who was a witness to the golden age of the piano at the conservatory, describes the rich musical life of Moscow along with the brutal repression of the Stalin years in his memoir, *Notes of a Moscow Pianist*.

The Central Music School remains today one of the most sought after institutions for musical training in Russia and the world. The teaching methods that produced so many great musicians have changed little over the years.

Bibliography: L. Ginzburg, ed, *Moskovskaia konservatoriia, 1866-1966* (M., 1966); N.V. Tumaninoi, ed., *Vospominaniia o Moskovskoi konservatorii* (M., 1966); V. Tereshchenko, *Tsentralnaia muzykalnaia shkola* (M., 1962); Natal'ia Andreevna Mironova, *Moskovskaia konservatoriia. Istoki, vospominaniia i dokumenty, fakty i kommentarii* (M., 1995); Klavdiia Viacheslavovna Uspenskaia and Iuliia Andreevna Rozanova, *Moskovskoi konservatorii 100 let* (M., 1966); Iurii Keldysh, *Sto let Moskovskoi konservatorii* (M., 1966); E. Alekseeva and G.Pribegina, eds., *Vospominaniia o Moskovskoi konservatorii* (M., 1966); G.Pribegina, ed., *Moskovskaia konservatoriia, 1866-1991* (M., 1991); V. Berezin, ed., *Ispolnitel'skie i pedagogicheskie traditsii Moskovskoi konservatorii. Sbornik statei* (M., 1993); *Musical Education in the USSR* (M., 1986); Daniel Robert Remeta, "Music Education in the USSR" (Ph.D. diss., UCLA, 1976); Victor Joseph Burner, *Concerto. A Musical Sojourn in Moscow. A Guide to the Moscow Conservatory* (Pasadena, Cal., 1995); Dmitry Paperno, *Notes of a Moscow Pianist* (Portland, Oregon, 1998). The ninety-eight-minute video "Russia's Wonder Children," directed by Irene Langemann and produced by Wolfgang Bergmann for First Run/Icarus Films, shows some remarkable archival material from the era in which the USSR aimed to demonstrate its cultural superiority to the world.

Pieter J. Mulder

ČERNIUS, JONAS (1898-1977). Prime minister of Lithuania (30 March 1939-22 November 1939).

His Common Work (Vieningo Darbo) government lasted for eight months, from the day after the Nazi seizure of the port of Klaipėda until the Soviet ultimatum for establishment of Red Army bases in Lithuania following the Ribbentrop-Molotov pact.

Jonas Černius was born 6 January 1898 to Kazys and Grasilda Černiauskai, a Lithuanian couple residing in Zuntė, a suburb of Kupiškis in Panevėžys County. He attended gymnasium at Panevėžys, and joined the Lithuanian army on 27 February 1919 when he was twenty-one years old. During the War of Independence (1918-1920) he served in the Third Lithuanian Battalion and fought the Bolsheviks at Daugava when the army was defending the country on three fronts, against the Red Army in the east, Polish troops in the south, and undischarged German soldiers known as the Bermont troops in the north.

After the war Černius took advanced military technical courses at the Technical Faculty of Kaunas University, the Higher School of Military Engineering in Brussels (1926-1929), and the École Supérieure de Guerre in Paris (1930-1932). He was appointed to command of the Lithuanian Army's technical staff in September 1932. When Stasys Raštikis(1896-1985), a graduate of the German Military Academy, became supreme commander of the Lithuanian army, Černius was appointed as deputy on 1 January 1935.

Černius was an exemplary commander who implemented important reforms in the army, strengthening and modernizing its practices. He was awarded the Grand Duke Vytautas Magnus Cross and the rank of brigadier general on 23 November 1937. President Antanas Smetona (1874-1944) appointed him prime minister in 1939 as independent Lithuania faced its most serious crisis. He previously belonged to no political party but quickly earned the title General of Hope by attempting to unite Lithuania's major political parties, inviting representatives of Christian Democrats (Krikščionys Demokratai), People's Party (Liaudininkai), National Party (Tautininkai), and Social Democrats (Socialdemokratai) into a coalition government as a response to the loss of Klaipėda.

Černius followed his president's policy of strict neutrality closely, and his government therefore refused to comply with German suggestions that Lithuania respond to the Polish military evacuation of Vilnius, when the army moved to defend Poland's western borders, by taking the city into its possession. At the same time he opened the frontier with Poland to Jewish refugees fleeing Nazi occupation.

It was unfortunate that his government's internal divisions were exacerbated by disagreements about agricultural reforms. He was accused of being overinfluenced by the supreme commander of the army, and a decision to abandon subsidies to the main daily newspaper Lietuvos Aidas attracted sharp criticism from the ruling Nationalist (Tautininkų) Party. The government was finally forced to resign after its acceptance of the Soviet ultimatum, which required Red Army military bases to be established on Lithuanian territory.

Černius returned to the army, taking command of its First Division ground forces. When the Soviet occupation began on 21 June 1940, he was given the Twenty-Ninth Territorial Command of the Soviet Army (1940-1941), becoming probably the only high-ranking Lithuanian officer to avoid internment in the Soviet gulags. He soon abandoned Soviet military service and returned to Kupiškis where he worked as the director of a local mill. When the Red Army returned to Lithuania in 1944, he and his family fled along with other educated Lithuanians to Germany.

His life as an emigre was not easy. In the summer of 1947 the family arrived in England where he worked on farms. In spring 1948 they reached New York. He was employed as a laborer in New Jersey when the United American Lithuanian Relief Fund (Bendras Amerikos Lietuvių Fondas, BALF) invited him to join its advisory staff. From 1951 he worked as an engineer with General Motors at Flint, Michigan and did not miss a day's work in twelve years before retiring in 1963. In 1973 he and his wife Veronika moved to be near his son Vytautas in Claremont, California. He died there of cancer on 3 July 1977 and is buried in sight of the Pacific Ocean in Los Angeles.

The usual interpretation of his period as prime minister is that the biggest challenge to his government was the need to find an effective defense strategy against Soviet aggression, and that its attempt to swim in a rocky river without overturning the boat was an unavoidable failure. There is however an alternative school of thought advanced by Colonel Kazys Škirpa (1895-1979), Lithuania's envoy in Berlin (1938-1940) and prime minister in the provisional government of 1941, which interprets Černius' government's rejection of the German proposal that it should annex the Vilnius region as its fatal mistake. Škirpa argued that Lithuania's subsequent assignment to the Soviet zone of influence was a result of this refusal, which permitted the Red Army to occupy the region without any resistance.

Bibliography: J. Černius, "Didžiųjų įvykių išvakarėse," *Kardas*, Nos. 1-2 (1997), 8-9, 38; "Didžiųjų įvykių išvakarėse," *Kardas*, Nos. 3-4 (1997), 25, "Didžiųjų įvykių išvakarėse," *Kardas*, Nos. 7-8 (1997), 10-11; V. Černius, "Sūnus apie Tėvą - B. Gen. J. Černių," *Kardas*, Nos. 5-6 (1996), 8-9, "Sūnus apie Tėvą - B. Gen. J. Černių," *Kardas*, Nos. 7-8 (1996), 6; V. Jankauskas, "*Nepriklausomos Lietuvos Generolai,*" Vol. 1 (Vilnius, 1998), 216-227; A. Šova, "Brig. Gen. Jonas Černius. Gyvenimo ir darbo etapai. Prisiminimai apie ginklo draugą," *Kardas*, Nos. 3-4 (1996), 6-7; "Jonas Cernius (1898-)," *Encyclopaedia Lituanica*, ed. by Simas Suziedelis, Vol. 1 (Boston, 1970), 490-491; "Neutrality of Lithuania. Independence to Be Defended," The Times (London), 6 April 1939.

Darius Furmonavičius

CHABUKIANI, VAKHTANG (1910-1992). Dancer, choreographer, and teacher.

Vakhtang Chabukiani left his native Tiflis (Tbilisi), Georgia, for Leningrad in 1926 to study classical dance at the mecca of Soviet ballet training, the Leningrad Choreographic Institute. He assimilated the ballet's academic syllabus in only three years, began performing at the State Academic Theater of Opera and Ballet (the former Mariinsky, later the Kirov Ballet) in 1929, and became a soloist in that celebrated company two years later. Chabukiani's career foreshadowed that of Rudolf Nureyev. Both provincials came to Leningrad with little training, mastered classical dancing with unprecedented speed, then refashioned male dancing in their own images. As a member of the Kirov troupe Chabukiani danced leading roles in the company's traditional repertory and created lead roles in a number of the increasingly ideological ballets the troupe presented in the 1930s, including Golden Age, Fountain of Bakhchisarai, The Flames of Paris, and Partisan Days. Chabukiani's performances of the male solos in the Kirov's classical repertory remain controversial. He reworked the male variations of the greater share of nineteenth-century ballets to showcase his fiery technique, though these emendations had the unintended effect of effacing much of the original choreography for those roles, which is now long forgotten.

While still a dancer with the Kirov Ballet, Chabukiani choreographed Mzechabuki in Tiflis in 1937. The work was restaged for the Kirov the following year as Heart of the Hills, with music by Andrei Balanchivadze, the brother of George Balanchine. That ballet played an important role in the development of ballet in Georgia and marked a new direction in the history of Soviet ballet. It was one of the first to incorporate elements of native dance traditions, of Georgia in this case, into a grandly-scaled classical work. Chabukiani's Gorda (1950) became, like Heart of the Hills, a national monument, although several of Chabukiani's most important ballets found their sources in world literature. Laurencia, in 1939, was based on Lope de Vega, and Othello in 1957 on Shakespeare.

Until his retirement from dancing in 1968 Chabukiani danced the male lead in every ballet he produced. He served as balletmaster of the Paliashvili Theater of Opera and Ballet in Tiflis from 1941 to 1973 and directed the Tiflis Choreographic Academy from 1950 until 1973. Over the course of his long career he amassed an arsenal of Soviet prizes, including the title People's Artist in 1950. Chabukiani's technique was described as dazzling in the 1930s and 1940s, yet the abundant film record of his dancing reveals a deeply flawed technique. The passion and fire for which Chabukiani was once renowned nonetheless continue to enchant.

Bibliography: Marie-Francoise Christout and John Percival, "The View from Tbilisi," *Dance and Dancers* (February 1967), 20-24; "Four Russian Dancers of Today," *The Dancing Times* (October 1941), 12-14; Vera Krasovskaia, *Vakhtang Chabukiani* (L., 1956); Gennady Smakov, *The Great Russian Dancers* (New York, 1984).

Tim J. Scholl

CHAGALL, MARC ZAKHAROVICH (1887-1985). Painter, theater designer, and stained glass artist.

The eldest of nine children, Chagall was born Moisei Shagal in Vitebsk on 7 July 1887 into a traditional Jewish family. His parents supported his aspiration to become an artist by sending him to the local art academy where he studied under Yehudah Moiseevich Pen (1854-1937) between 1905 and late 1906. Chagall received solid training in the technical aspects of painting from Pen, but he soon rejected his academic artistic style in favor of a more modernist style.

Despite the fact that he did not have permission to stay in the capital, Chagall moved to St. Petersburg in late 1906 and managed to stay there by occasionally clerking for a lawyer and retouching photographs. In 1907 Chagall was accepted by the art school of the Society for the Encouragement of the Arts, thus securing a residence permit. He enrolled in the Zvantseva School from 1909-1910, during which time he studied with Lev Bakst (1866-1924) of Ballet Russe fame and Mstislav Valerianovich Dobuzhinsky (1875-1957), who was primarily known as a graphic artist. While studying and working in St. Petersburg Chagall developed his expertise in representing the human figure, as well as an interest in native Russian sources such as the icon and folk print as inspiration for modern art.

Chagall moved to Paris in 1910, bringing with him technical proficiency and a modernist conceptual language that developed during the next four years in France. He changed his name to the more European sounding Marc and also changed the spelling of his last name. Chagall established contacts with important people in the Parisian art world as well as the Russian art world in Paris. His intimates included the famed critic Guillaume Apollinaire (1880-1918) and poet Blaise Cendrars (1887-1961), as well as Russian artists Nadezhda Andreevna Udaltsova (1885-1961) and Alexander Porfirevich Archipenko (1887-1964). His works were included in important modern art exhibitions, including the 1912 Salon d'Automne and Salon des Independents. He also sent some paintings to be included in the landmark Donkey's Tail (Oslinny Khvost) and Target (Mishen) exhibitions in Moscow alongside his Russian contemporaries. His experience as an outsider informed his paintings done in Paris, especially Self Portrait with Seven Fingers which depicts multiple realities coexisting: his Jewish identity, Russian homeland, French modernist painting styles.

Although Chagall projected the image of an outsider to the French artistic scene, his art from this period bears the marks of significant developments in the French art world, including cubism, and orphism. During this first Paris period Chagall developed his visual vocabulary, on which he drew for the remainder of his career. These themes and images included nostalgic views of the Russian village and biblical imagery from the Old and New Testaments. Chagall did not consider himself a Jewish artist and was interested in exploring all themes that constituted his concept of modern life. For example, Chagall's exploration of Christian themes, as in Golgotha (1912), can be seen as an interest in the general issue of symbolic transformations and personal suffering. Moreover, painting religious themes, and Christian themes in particular, placed Chagall firmly in the tradition of Western painting and sculpture.

Chagall left Paris in spring 1914 for a short visit to Berlin and then traveled to Vitebsk to attend his sister's wedding. While he was in Vitebsk, the First World War broke out, and he was unable to return to Paris as he had planned. During his unexpected stay in Vitebsk Chagall's work took on a more subdued, less visionary quality, especially the street scenes of Vitebsk. In autumn 1915 Chagall moved with his new wife Bella to Petrograd and began regularly exhibiting with the major artistic groupings of the time, including Target, Donkey's Tail and World of Art. Chagall was given a sinecure in the office of War Economy so he could avoid active duty during the war. Between 1915 and 1917 Chagall established his reputation in Russia as an important modern artist, and his works were sold in Russian galleries. This period saw an increased interest in Jewish art and Chagall, along with Jewish colleagues including Natan Isaevich Altman (1889-1970) and El (Eleazar) Lissitsky (1890-1941), sought to create a particularly Jewish modern art. The increased interest in Jewish art was the result of archaeological expeditions in Eastern Europe, which were unearthing artifacts from Jewish history, and the activities of the Jewish Society for the Encouragement of the Arts, founded in 1916, which was regularly exhibiting and commissioning art from Jewish artists.

Chagall's vision of modern Jewish art was heavily informed by East European Jewish folk life, especially as it was represented in the stories of Sholem Aleichem

(1859-1916) and Mokher Sefarim Mendele (1835-1917). In particular Chagall created fictional worlds in which animals and humans are intimately connected and Jews live in small villages, segregated from others. By the time Chagall was working, however, most East European Jews lived in towns or cities, and their lives had little to do with raising livestock. His paintings are evocative of a fantastic world, yet constitute a critique of this world.

Chagall was in Petrograd during the Bolshevik Revolution and was personally charged by Anatoly Vasilievich Lunacharsky (1875-1933), the commissar of enlightenment, in September 1918, to return to Vitebsk and become commissar of arts for the Vitebsk region. Chagall's duties included administration of all artistic life in the region, encompassing the fine arts, music and theater. He also taught at the Vitebsk School of Art. Chagall's allegiance to the Bolsheviks has been the subject of debate. Most likely, Chagall was appointed to this position because he was energetic, had a good reputation in Russia and the west, and was not opposed to working for the Bolsheviks. Chagall attracted other art teachers to Vitebsk during winter 1918-1919, including his former teacher Dobuzhinsky, Vera Mikhailovna Yermolaeva (1893-1938), and El Lissitsky. During Chagall's tenure as commissar of arts he was primarily occupied with administrative duties and seems to have produced little except for a few designs for large scale murals to be displayed during public celebrations and holidays.

A number of factors contributed to Chagall's decision to leave Vitebsk in November 1920, including a conflict with Kazimir Severinovich Malevich (1878-1935), whose charisma and personal authority attracted students away from Chagall, and an invitation to decorate the interior of the newly-opened Jewish Chamber Theater in Moscow. Already the designer of costumes and stage sets for the State Jewish Theater in 1919, Chagall moved with Bella to Moscow in 1920 and began work on the murals for the theater's interior, the highlight of which is a twenty-six-foot-long (8 m) mural entitled Introduction to Yiddish Theater. The mural represents a summation of Chagall's themes and visual and conceptual vocabulary up to that time. It challenged boundaries between realism and abstraction, the religious past and the secular present, and it made the upheaval of modern Jewish life in Eastern Europe a central theme. The figures float above the ground against an abstract background. They include a klezmer band and actors dressed as Hassidic Jews in phylacteries doing acrobatics. Text and image are intertwined to create a complex, seemingly irrational atmosphere that dissolves the boundaries between theater and real life. Chagall envisioned the mural as a work of art in its own right that he sincerely hoped audiences of all faiths would admire.

Chagall took full advantage of the brief interlude of support for Jewish cultural institutions during the early Soviet period. Between 1920 and 1922 he was commissioned for additional stage and costume designs at the Jewish Chamber Theater as well as at the Theater of Revolutionary Satire in Moscow. He continued to paint, and these new works were exhibited alongside other Jewish artists seeking a distinctly modern Jewish art. Chagall also assisted in the organization of the First Russian Exhibition that opened in Berlin in 1922.

Chagall emigrated at that point to Berlin, and then in 1923 he settled in Paris and began regularly exhibiting his work in Europe and New York and fulfilling important commissions, such as illustrations for *Dead Souls* and the Bible. Russian village themes and scenes continued to dominate his work throughout the 1920s and 1930s, as did his fascination with the interaction between animals and humans, Christian themes, harlequins, and the circus. His visionary works were condemned as degenerate by the Nazis, and his works were burned in Mannheim, Germany, in 1933. Chagall's art achieved little recognition in Russia during most of the Soviet period, although his work was exhibited once in 1928 in an exhibition of French art.

Chagall became a French citizen in 1937 but was forced to leave France in 1941 during the Nazi occupation. He accepted an invitation by the Museum of Modern Art in New York to live and work in the United States, where he remained until 1948. During this period Chagall applied for US citizenship but was denied on grounds that he might be a Soviet sympathizer. While in the United States Chagall collaborated with choreographers in designing sets and costumes for the ballets Aleko and Firebird and had retrospective exhibitions at the Museum of Modern Art in New York and the Art Institute of Chicago.

After his return to France in 1948 Chagall was continually occupied with fulfilling monumental commissions. The most important of these included designs for stained glass windows at Hadassah Hebrew University Medical Center in Jerusalem, stained glass windows for the Cathedral at Metz, the ceiling of the Paris Opera House, windows at the United Nations in New York, and mosaics and tapestries for the Knesset building in Jerusalem. He also experimented with ceramics, continued his work with lithography and etching, and traveled and lectured extensively around Europe. Between 1948 and 1970 there were fifteen major retrospective exhibitions of his work, and he was awarded numerous prizes and honorary degrees including those from Brandeis University and the University of Glasgow.

Because of his work on stained glass windows Chagall was recognized as the foremost stained glass artist of the twentieth century. He continued to paint as well, focusing on themes from the Old Testament. These paintings from the 1950s and 1960s were collected in the Musée National Message Biblique in Nice, France.

In 1973 Chagall was invited back to the Soviet Union as part of his official rehabilitation. His visit coincided with an exhibition of lithographs at the Tretiakov Gallery in Moscow and marked the first time Chagall returned to the Soviet Union since 1922.

The last years of his life were occupied by fulfilling commissions for book illustrations, mosaics and windows. Until his death in 1985 at the age of 98 Chagall worked on lithographs for *The Odyssey* and *The Tempest*, and designed stained glass window for the Art Institute in Chicago. In 1977 Chagall was awarded the Grand Cross of the Legion of Honor by the French government.

With the large posthumous retrospective in Russia in 1987, Chagall's reputation in the Soviet Union as a great artist was re-established, prompting a flurry of books and articles devoted to him, especially the years he spent in Russia.

Chagall's works are found in collections worldwide including The Tretiakov Gallery in Moscow, The Russian Museum in St. Petersburg, The Tate Museum in London, and the Museum of Modern Art in New York.

Bibliography: Sidney Alexander, *Marc Chagall. A Biography* (New York, 1978); Marc Chagall, *My Life* (New York, 1994); Susan Compton. *Chagall. Royal Academy of Art Exhibition Catalog* (London, 1985); A. Efros and Ya. Tugenkhold, *Iskusstvo M. Shagala* (M., 1918); Benjamin Harshav, "The Role of Language in Modern Art. On Texts and Subtexts in Chagall's Paintings," *Modernism/Modernity*, Vol. 1, No. 2 (April 1994), 51-87; Aleksandr Kamensky, *Chagall. The Russian Years, 1907-1922*, trans. by Catherine Phillips (London, 1989); Franz Meyer, *Marc Chagall. Life and Work* (London, 1962); Aleksandra Shatskikh, "Chagall and Malevich in Vitebsk. A History of Their Relations," *AICARC. Bulletin of the Archives and Documentation Centers for Modern and Contemporary Art,* Nos. 27-28 (1989), 7-10.

Pamela J. Kachurin

CHAGATAI (1185?–1242). Mongolian prince, first ruler of Chagatai ulus. Also spelled Chagatay, Cagatay, Cagatay, and with an initial "j" or a "d," correctly Ca'adai, the Middle Mongolian form of his name. See also Chagatai Ulus, SMERSH, Vol. 5.

Chagatai was the second son of Chingis Khan (Cinggis-qan, 1167?-1227) and eventually received a patrimony or ulus in what is now northern Kazakhstan, western Turkistan and Afghanistan. He was noted for his severity and conservatism and adherence to the most traditional of Mongolian lifestyles, something which brought him into conflict with the agents of the Mongolian central authority under Khan Ögödei (r. 1229-1241), who were trying to tax rather than pillage the cities of the region of Bukhara and nearby areas. Chagatai's conservatism in turn had a major impact upon his successors, who gradually became rulers of an independent khanate based upon his ulus and who were among the less assimilated of all Mongolian rulers of successor states. Not a great deal is known of his life. Chagatai did participate in the early steppe wars of unification and in the first assaults on China and in the siege of Otrar (1220), apparently in the pursuit of Jalāl al-Dīn (r. 1221-1231), but did not return east with his father after 1225. He is known to have supported Ögödei, and not Joci, when the issue of succession came up.

Bibliography: W. Barthold, *Turkestan Down to the Mongol Invasion*, trans. by Mrs. T. Minorsky (London, 1977); Michal Biran, *Qaidu and the Rise of the Independent Mongol State in Central Asia* (Richmond, England, 1997); Paul D. Buell, "Sino-Khitan Administration in Mongol Bukhara," *Journal of Asian History*, Vol. 13, No. 2 (1979), 121–151.

Paul D. Buell

CHAGATAI LANGUAGE. Turkic literary language.

The Chagatai language was the Turkic literary idiom of western Turkistan and later Moghul India that emerged primarily under Tamerlane (1336-1405) and his successors and persisted as a literary language until comparatively recently.

Although it takes it name from the Chagatai ulus, the Mongol successor state that established itself in western Turkistan and nearby areas during the thirteenth century, there is nothing Mongolian about the language other than loan words. See also Chagatai Ulus, SMERSH, Vol. 5. This is entirely understandable since the Chagatai ulus itself quickly became heavily turkicized, and there is no evidence that Mongolian was used there for long even as an administrative language.

Chagatai resembles modern literary Uzbek in grammar, vocabulary, and morphology and is thus sometimes called Old Uzbek, although this is not strictly correct. Chagatai was only one of the roots from which modern Uzbek derives. Important Chagatai writers include the Moghul emperor Bābur (r. 1483-1530) and Alī-Šīr Navā'ī (1441-1501), who almost single-handedly turned Chagatai into a major literary language and preferred vehicle for literary efforts of every sort, especially poetry. The latter's encyclopedic *Bāburnāma* is a rich source for the material culture of Moghal India and living evidence for the great cultural refinement of its rulers. The development of the Chagatai language is divided into three periods: an early or pre-classical period, when the language was literally the language of the Chagatai ulus and its successor states; a classical period, the age of Navā'ī and Bābur, down to about 1600; and a post-classical period that was imitative rather than original, with the writings of Navā'ī setting the style and continuing until the beginning of the twentieth century.

Bibliography: János Eckmann, *Chagatay Manual* (Bloomington, Ind., 1966); Peter Jackson and Laurence Lockhart, *The Cambridge History of Iran,* Vol. 6, *The Timurid and Safavid Periods* (Cambridge, 1986); Thomas W. Lentz and Glenn D. Lowry, eds., *Timur and the Princely Vision. Persian Art and Culture in the Fifteenth Century* (Los Angeles, Cal., 1989).

Paul D. Buell

CHAGATAI ULUS (1260-1344). Mongolian successor state.

The Chagatai ulus was the successor state, i.e., patrimony, or khanate ruled by the family of Chagatai, second son of Chingis Khan (Cinggis-qan). Its first independent ruler was a woman, Ergene-qatun, who was regent for her son Mubārak Shāh (r. 1266) at the time of Khan Möngke's death in 1259 and the subsequent permanent breakdown of Mongolian unity. Ergene was the widow of Qara-Hüle'ü, the grandson and successor of Chagatai as head of his ulus. Although trying to avoid involvement in the civil war that followed, Ergene was deposed by Ariq-böke (?-1266) who appointed Alghu (r. 1260-1265 or 1266) in her place. Not to be outdone, Ergene then married Alghu and both began to support the claims of Qubilai as Khan Möngke's successor. This quickly resulted in conflict with Qaidu, Qubilai's other Central Asian competitor.

After Alghu's death Mubārak Shāh ruled briefly before being deposed by Baraq (r. 1266–1271), Chagatai's great-grandson. Baraq was Chagatai ulus ruler when the Talas Covenant of 1269 was agreed to whereby the various interested parties, namely Baraq himself, Qaidu, and Möngke Temür (r. 1267-1280) of the Golden Horde, agreed to a division of revenues from sedentary Transoxania, which was to become immune to tribal expropriations and continue under the rule of former imperial agent Mas'ūd Beg (?-1280s), who was in the employ of the Chagatai rulers. The agreement also governed the setting aside of specific pastures for Baraq and Qaidu, a bone of contention between the two.

By this time the dominant force was Qaidu who heavily defeated Baraq at Herat on 22 July 1270 in a dispute over the very revenues that Baraq, Qaidu, and Möngke Temür had agreed to divide equitably the previous year. As a consequence the Chagatai ulus came almost completely under the control of Qaidu, who appointed a series of puppet rulers to see to his interests. The most important of these was Du'a (r. 1282–1307), a son of Baraq, whom Qaidu was forced to support in the interests of dynastic legitimacy. Although Du'a actively supported Qaidu in his wars against Qubilai and his successors, the rulers of khanate China or the Yuan Dynasty (1260-1368), Du'a simultaneously built up his own power and the power of his ulus. Thus Du'a was able to reestablish the Chagatai ulus as a fully independent khanate following the death of Qaidu in 1301. Even during the period of Qaidu's dominance the Chagatai ulus managed to maintain active disputes with the Golden Horde over various tribal areas in the north, and with the Ilkhanate or Iran, over Khurāsān.

After Qaidu's death it was Du'a who became the dominant ruler, and it was Du'a who decided who was to be Qaidu's successor among his sons. Later Qaidu's own ulus virtually disappeared with Du'a the principal beneficiary. Dua's successor was his son Könchek (r. 1308), but following Könchek a succession struggle broke out with intervention by Chapar, the new ruler of Qaidu's former and much reduced domains. Finally the warring parties agreed upon Esen Buqa (r. 1309–1318), the brother of Kebek (r. 1309) who ruled after Könchek, although Könchek (r. 1318-1326) resumed the throne after Esen Buqa's death. By this time the Chagatai ulus was in rapid decline as its surviving Mongol elite, now thoroughly turkicized, had more and more difficulty in maintaining itself amidst a crowd of competing locals.

Kebek's successor after a short succession dispute was Tarmashirin (r. 1326–1334), the last effective Chagatai ruler. Tarmashirin, despite his Buddhist name, became the first of his house to accept Islam, making the Chagatai ulus the last of the Mongolian successor states to convert to a major religion. All the successor states except Mongol China, which took up Tibetan Buddhism, converted to Islam. Tarmashirin's conversion, although it strengthened his position in his sedentary domains, which may have been the main reason for his conversion in the first place, undermined his rule with his tribal supporters and weakened his house in the end. Tarmashirin's successors became little more than local bandits as a result, and the future lay with a new generation of more powerful, local Turkic rulers. The most famous of these to emerge, after a series of battles between competing tribal groupings, was Tamerlane (1336–1405), who was not Mongol and whose only connection with the old Chagatai ruling house was through marriage to a Chagatai princess.

Bibliography: W. Barthold, *Turkestan down to the Mongol Invasion*, trans. by Mrs. T. Minorsky (London, 1977); Michal Biran, *Qaidu and the Rise of the*

Independent Mongol State in Central Asia (Richmond, England, 1997); Paul D. Buell, "Sino-Khitan Administration in Mongol Bukhara," *Journal of Asian History*, Vol. 13, No. 2 (1979), 121–151.

Paul D. Buell

CHAIKIN, VADIM AFANASIEVICH (1886-1941). Journalist, publisher, political radical in Turkestan.

Chaikin was born in a village in Kursk province. His family background remains unknown. His older brother Anastasy lived as honorary citizen and wealthy apiarist in Andijan in Fergana Valley, Turkestan province. Chaikin never married and dedicated his life to the creation of a democratic Russia.

Chaikin attended high school (gymnazium) in Ufa, where he joined the Socialist Revolutionary Party in 1904. In 1905 he agitated among Ufa's students and allegedly took part in an assassination attempt on the governor. Three years later he was arrested in Kursk province for agitating among the peasants and convicted to five years exile in Yakutia. After his term in exile he moved to Turkestan, where he worked as a journalist.

In Turkestan Chaikin became one of the few members of the Russian community who cooperated with native Muslim liberal activists, the Jadids. He championed their cause to turn Turkestan's natives into full-fledged citizens of a democratic Russia. In 1916 he moved to Andijan to live with his older brother. Together with the Jadid lawyer Ubaydulla Khojaev (1886-1938) he founded the Andijan Publishing Company and edited the Russian-language newspaper The Voice of Turkestan (Turkestansky Golos). This was the only newspaper with a leftist orientation in Turkestan at the time, and it covered issues pertaining to the Muslim community. The company planned to issue a Turkic-language counterpart, but it never appeared in print.

After the February Revolution Chaikin became a leading member of Turkestan's provincial soviet, a member of the All-Russian Central Executive Committee of Soviets and a deputy to the Constituent Assembly. In July 1917 the Provisional Government appointed him to head the Turkestan Commission, but resistance from Tashkent railroadmen forced him to reject the offer. Chaikin opposed the putsch initiated by Tashkent's railroadmen and soldiers in September 1917 and Turkestan's Soviet government, established in November. He was forced to leave first Turkestan and then Soviet Russia and moved to Menshevik-ruled Georgia. In 1919 he headed the exile Committee for a Turkestanian Constituent Assembly together with Jadid activist Mustafa Choqay (1890-1941). The Soviet government and Stalin personally accused him of cooperating with English interventionist forces.

Chaikin eventually returned to Soviet Russia and Moscow. In 1922 he tried to mediate between the Soviet government and leaders of the armed resistance movement against Soviet power in Central Asia. From 1924 onward Chaikin spent his time in prisons, concentration camps, and exile in Suzdal, Viatka, Tashkent, and Orlov, charged with counterrevolutionary activities in underground Social Revolutionary organizations. When he was not incarcerated in these years, he worked as a journalist and historian. The last order for his arrest was issued on 22 November 1937. He was sentenced to death on 8 September 1941. He was posthumously rehabilitated on 26 July 1990.

Bibliography: Chaikin prepared a large number of works on the history of the Russian Revolution, but only one appeared in print: V.A. Chaikin, *K istorii rossiiskoi Revoliutsii, 1904-1921 gg.*, Vol. 1, *Kazn' 26 Bakinskihh Komissarov* (M., 1922). The only biographical sketch of Chaikin is in Rustambek Shamsutdinov, *Istiqlol yolida shahid ketganlar* (Tashkent, 2001), 118-143 (in Uzbek). In English, some information may be found in Adeeb Khalid, *The Politics of Muslim Cultural Reform. Jadidism in Central Asia* (Berkeley, Cal., 1998), Chap. 7.

Gero Fedtke

CHAIKOVSKY, PETR ILICH (1840-1893). Commonly spelled Peter Ilych Tchaikovsky. Widely known and popular composer.

Chaikovsky was the most celebrated and best known Russian composer in Europe and the United States. He was born in 1840 in Votkinsk some 600 miles (966 km) east of Moscow into a family with a notable tradition of military service. His father Ilia, at Petr's birth, had a prestigious state appointment and a large house. Petr had a twin brother, Modest, with whom he exchanged many letters and shared experiences, another brother, and a sister. Tutored by an attentive governess, Petr could read in French and German by age six. He was a tender and hypersensitive child.

After retiring in 1848 Ilia brought the family to Moscow. The following year the family moved again to St. Petersburg, where the boys attended a large, fashionable primary school. Petr attended the School of Jurisprudence in St. Petersburg from 1852 to 1859, a rare constant in a frequently changing way of life. His aunt Ekaterina instructed him in piano, taking him through all of Mozart's Don Giovanni, which was the first work to make a deep impression on him. Chaikovsky later wrote that Mozart was his first musical inspiration and made him love music above all else. Petr completed his first musical composition in 1854. By age fifteen he decided tentatively on a musical career and began serious piano lessons with Rudolf Kündinger, a young German pianist.

In 1854 his mother, Aleksandra, died of cholera, dealing young Petr a shattering blow. Officially, Chaikovsky died of the same disease in 1893. Chaikovsky's childhood was externally happy but full of turmoil. He experienced increasing personal problems that stemmed mainly from his homosexuality and developed into a neurotic adult with acute psychological and emotional problems.

Upon graduation from the School of Jurisprudence in May 1859 Chaikovsky entered the civil service at the bottom rank. Appointed to the justice ministry in 1859, he served three years as assistant to the head of an administrative department while he engaged in a lively but vapid social life that apparently included minor heterosexual amours. He widened his social circle by playing the piano for dancing and improvising polkas and waltzes. In 1861, he recalled, when his musical talent was discussed at home one evening, his father assured him it wasn't too late for him to become a professional musician. In July 1861 he made his first trip abroad, working as a translator. He enjoyed Paris greatly but ended deeply in debt.

Returning to Russia late in 1861, Chaikovsky began studying musical theory and decided to become a composer. His musical activities centered in the Russian Musical Society, founded two years earlier by Anton Rubinstein. When the St. Petersburg Conservatory opened in 1862 with Rubinstein as its director, Chaikovsky enrolled. He soon resigned from state service and supported himself by giving lessons in piano and musical theory. Although he still lacked confidence as a composer, his overture, The Storm (1864), revealed that he had talent. He graduated from the conservatory in January 1866 and began to teach at the newly formed Moscow Conservatory. The move separated him from family and friends, but at the conservatory he met Nikolai Kashkin and Nikolai Rubinstein, Anton's brother, who became his lifelong friends.

Meanwhile Chaikovsky worked on his First Symphony, Winter Dreams, which was first performed in February 1868 in Moscow, directed by Nikolai Rubinstein. It was a success, although fifteen years passed before it was performed again. Chaikovsky later wrote that his First Symphony was in many ways immature, but he felt it had more substance than many of his other more mature works. That year he also composed his first opera, Voevoda, which was destined for a checkered career. In Moscow he met Mily Balakirev, center of the so-called Mighty Five. For the next two years Balakirev's Russian nationalism deeply influenced Chaikovsky's creative life. Then, fearing absorption by Balakirev's nationalist school, he took a middle position between it and pro-Western elements.

In 1868 Chaikovsky fell passionately for Désirée Artôt, an opera singer and actress, the only woman who roused his sexual feelings, but she married a Spanish baritone. He retained his admiration for her as a performer. After a European trip in summer 1870 he resumed work at the conservatory. In February 1871 Chaikovsky completed his First String Quartet which was soon performed most successfully. By then Chaikovsky was living in his own three-room Moscow apartment, which he found better for composing than quarters he had shared with Nikolai Rubinstein. In April 1872 he completed the opera Oprichnik. He wrote his brother Modest that the opera was so bad that he fled from rehearsals to avoid hearing a single note. Its St. Petersburg premiere was nonetheless his first genuine popular triumph. Based on episodes from Ivan the Terrible's reign and more nationalist than Voevoda, it represented an advance in his operatic skills, yet subsequently it was rarely performed. By 1872 Chaikovsky considered his conservatory duties too time consuming. Tired and distraught, he looked forward to change.

Chaikovsky regarded his Second Symphony, completed in 1872, his best composition in terms of form. No work of his was more favored by the Mighty Five. First performed in Moscow in February 1873, its revised version of 1880 embodied his fullest identification yet with the Five's nationalism. Because it included themes from three Ukrainian folk tunes, it was called the Little Russian. That same year

Chaikovsky embarked on four years as a music critic. His last articles reported on Richard Wagner's Ring cycle at the Bayreuth opera house's opening. While he most admired music by Mozart and Beethoven, Wagner bored him and he despised the compositions of his nationalist compatriot, Modest Musorgsky. During 1873 Chaikovsky composed the Snow Maiden ballet, based on a tale by A.N. Ostrovsky. By then his feelings of depression and personal isolation were intensifying and becoming more frequent.

At the beginning of Chaikovsky's crisis years, 1874-78, he began teaching piano to nine-year-old Sergei Taneev, who became an outstanding pianist and composer, a lifelong friend, and a valued critic. Taneev later completed a number of Chaikovsky's unfinished works. In December 1874 Chaikovsky played his newly completed First Piano Concerto for Nikolai Rubinstein, who castigated it as worthless and unplayable. Rubinstein criticized what he called many trite, awkward passages and recommended the concerto be scrapped or completely revised. Chaikovsky reacted angrily and refused to change a single note. The German pianist, Hans von Bülow, admired the concerto and performed its public premiere. Chaikovsky dedicated the work to him. Edward Danreuther, who performed it at London's Crystal Palace, proposed improvements in the piano parts that Chaikovsky incorporated in the full score published in 1879.

In 1875 Chaikovsky completed his rather repetitive Third (Polish) Symphony, his least satisfactory symphonic work. Next he composed swiftly his Third Quartet which was very popular but, he wrote Modest, he feared he was beginning to repeat himself and was unable to find new ideas. At Chaikovsky's death the Third Quartet was played in tribute to him. That winter he worked on his Swan Lake ballet. Initial performances were inferior, and it was withdrawn from the repertoire in 1883. Swan Lake was next performed in St. Petersburg only in 1894, this time with brilliant success. A fine version at St. Petersburg's Mariinsky Theater in 1895 inaugurated its advance towards great popularity. Swan Lake's universal appeal was based on its tale of young lovers trapped by inexorable external forces. No tragic ballet has surpassed it in combining atmosphere, feeling, and movement with a highly stylized dance idiom.

Chaikovsky's personal crisis deepened in 1875 with bouts of violent fever and deadly melancholy which induced him to take a cure at Vichy, France. In the summer of 1876, his sympathies aroused for embattled Balkan Slavs, he composed a Slavonic March that was wildly acclaimed at its initial performance. Then in an uncertain and tormented mental state he composed Francesca da Rimini, an orchestral work whose Moscow performance in 1877 was an immense hit.

His crisis years climaxed in 1877 with a traumatic, ill-considered, brief marriage to lonely and mentally disturbed Antonina I. Miliukova, who proclaimed her love for him in many letters. Chaikovsky told her he did not love her but would be a staunch friend, then unwisely asked if she wished to marry him. She consented. Their marriage was over in fact by October 1877, but separation and divorce proceedings dragged on for many years. Antonina later died in an insane asylum.

In January 1878 Chaikovsky completed his Fourth Symphony. It was first performed by Rubinstein in February at a Russian Musical Society concert. The Fourth Symphony was a true piece of emotional autobiography, including new elements such as the theme of fate. Simultaneously, Chaikovsky was working intensively on the opera Evgeny Onegin, based on a play by Aleksandr Pushkin. Chaikovsky's style was shifting toward the cultural world of the drawing rooms and salons of St. Petersburg, but the theme of fate surfaced there too. Of all his works this was the most prodigal in musical riches. The love theme, though the most obvious, was not the chief one. Subsequently, composers Igor Stravinsky and Sergei Prokofiev emphasized Onegin's Russianness. Stravinsky considered Chaikovsky Russia's greatest opera composer and Evgeny Onegin the most intrinsically Russian opera.

Outside his close family ties Chaikovsky's most important emotional involvement was with Madame Nadezhda von Meck, a wealthy widow. Although they deliberately avoided personal meetings, their platonic love was reflected in a thirteen-year correspondence that fill three large volumes and reveal Chaikovsky's inner self. He confided more openly to her about his attitudes and creative processes than to anyone else. In response to his request for financial aid, she swiftly agreed to subsidize him regularly.

Soon after his appalling marriage Chaikovsky returned to composing regularly, with as much technical finesse although perhaps less creative spirit. Not until the Manfred Symphony of 1885 did he regain his full powers. He chose to spend long periods abroad while in Moscow people gossiped about his breach with Antonina. He found some joy in befriending a handicapped boy, Kolia, and an eleven-year-old boy singer, Vittorio, whom he found extraordinarily beautiful.

In May 1878 Chaikovsky began a violin concerto, inspired by Eduard Lalo's Symphonie espagnole. Initially it was severely criticized even by Madame von Meck. The finale's main theme was athletic, Russian, and most successful. This concerto reflected a brief phase of inward calm, during which Chaikovsky was surrounded by the young violinist Iosif I. Kotek, Kolia, and his brother Modest in congenial surroundings. His growing reputation as a composer did not help him confront his personal problems. Once back home he devised a divorce strategy and a financial settlement with his alienated wife. When he was under stress, he smoked and drank heavily and avoided composing. He told Rubinstein that he would not stay at the conservatory beyond December.

After Chaikovsky left the conservatory, he spent much of 1878-1885 wandering. His sister Sasha's residence at Kamenka, Ukraine, was the closest thing he had to a home until 1885 when he took a house at Maidanovo outside Moscow. He retreated into a solitary existence, seeking only the love of family and close friends. Chaikovsky's morale was briefly restored by fine accommodations in Florence, Italy, arranged by Madame von Meck. There he composed part of his First Suite and a new opera, The Maid of Orleans. Chaikovsky based the opera on Friedrich Schiller's play, Die Jungfrau von Orleans, as he sought to enter the international operatic scene. It was first produced in 1881 at the Mariinsky Theater and enjoyed modest success, but The Maid of Orleans soon dropped out of the Russian repertoire. Bored by inactivity in Kamenka, Chaikovsky composed his Second Piano Concerto in October 1879. It premiered in Moscow in May 1882 with his friend Taneev as soloist. Taneev found the first two movements too long and second rate. Nonetheless, it was a work of considerable significance and virtues.

Nikolai Rubinstein made the initial suggestion for Chaikovsky's famous 1812 Overture which commemorates Russia's victory over Napoleon. Some music for it was drawn from his Voevoda. More than one critic has complained that after its solemn and impressive opening the Overture's development is inadequate, the recapitulation perfunctory, and the piece as a whole too bombastic. Nevertheless it remains one of the most performed and enjoyed of Chaikovsky's compositions.

Shocked by Alexander II's murder in March 1881, Chaikovsky joined the reactionary Holy Brotherhood to defend the new emperor against terrorists. He was devoted to Alexander III and became a longtime favorite of the new tsar who reacted rather negatively to the Mighty Five. For the tsar's coronation Chaikovsky composed a march and a cantata for which he was generously rewarded. About that time he also composed Serenade for Strings, which he described as a heartfelt piece. It was performed soon after its completion by Nikolai Rubinstein at the Moscow Conservatory. The Serenade's first public performance in St. Petersburg under the direction of E.F. Napravnik also proved most successful.

Chaikovsky's seven peaceful months at Kamenka in 1880 contrasted sharply with hectic rounds in both Russian capitals. A new production of Evgeny Onegin at the Bolshoi Theater satisfied the composer, and The Maid of Orleans' premiere in February 1881 won plaudits from performers and the audience. Chaikovsky wrote at the time that he enjoyed his fame and worked hard to keep it, but his nights were troubled and often sleepless as his music gained increasing currency. Late that year he composed a piano trio as a tribute to recently deceased Nikolai Rubinstein. First performed privately in March 1882, the trio achieved much popularity in his lifetime and was played in memorial concerts for the composer.

In 1882 Chaikovsky worked on a new opera, Mazepa, based on the life of a Ukrainian opponent of Peter the Great. Both Moscow's Bolshoi Theater and St. Petersburg asked to produce it, revealing Chaikovsky's fully established reputation as a composer. Mazepa premiered in Moscow in February 1884 very successfully, although César Cui, a Mighty Five rival, claimed that Chaikovsky's creative powers were deteriorating. Mazepa, while representing a resurgence of the national element in Chaikovsky's music, failed to win a significant place in Russia's opera repertory.

Chaikovsky again left for Europe in 1884. Returning with renewed creative energy, he composed the five-movement Third Suite which involved a further exploration of melodic and orchestral possibilities and marked Chaikovsky's return to large-scale variation form. Its first performance in St. Petersburg in January 1885 was the greatest success yet scored by a Russian symphonic work. The press in both capitals was unanimously favorable.

During 1885 Chaikovsky composed the massive Manfred Symphony, based on a work by George Byron. When Balakirev proposed a second time that the story be set to music, Chaikovsky agreed to compose it. Buying a copy of Byron's *Manfred*, he read it in Davos, Switzerland and worked on it at Maidanovo, completing it in September 1885 as a four-movement symphony, which he dedicated to Balakirev. It was the most extensive orchestral piece he had yet written. Chaikovsky liked its first movement best and considered Manfred his best symphonic work. Before the end of 1886 it was performed three times in or near St. Petersburg and in New York. Even Cui praised it, especially the first movement.

Despite his emotional problems and physical decline Chaikovsky composed some outstanding works during his final years. At Maidanovo he instituted a routine he observed for the rest of his life when at home. He wanted no one near him while composing, and after 1885 he refused to show his new works to anyone. At Maidanovo he composed his eighth opera, The Enchantress, based on I.V. Shpzinski's play. Its first performance in November 1887 was quite successful, but subsequent performances left audiences dissatisfied. Chaikovsky complained that he had never worked harder on an opera and was stung by the critics' attacks. He defiantly expressed his faith in it and refused suggestions for revision. Its twelfth performance in 1888 was the last until 1902.

During 1888 Chaikovsky scored great triumphs as an international conductor. In February the Berlin Philharmonic devoted an entire program to his music, and he conducted two concerts of his own music in Prague. Modest recorded this as his brother's highest point of worldly fame, but to Chaikovsky's dismay the Russian press virtually ignored his triumph. In March he conducted parts of two concerts in Paris, was lionized by the public, and gave many press interviews.

That June Chaikovsky completed his monumental Fifth Symphony. It and his Hamlet Overture premiered in November. Both scored triumphs with audiences but were criticized by the press. Cui dismissed the Fifth as a routine work marking a further decline in Chaikovsky's creative powers. Chaikovsky also completed six songs dedicated to his former flame, Désirée Artôt, and greatly enjoyed renewed closeness with her although after 1889 they never met again.

Late in 1888 Chaikovsky undertook a second international tour, conducting his Fifth Symphony and Second Piano Concerto in Prague, and scored a personal triumph with his Onegin. In December he conducted more concerts in the Russian capitals and was reconciled with the Mighty Five.

In 1889 he completed his Sleeping Beauty ballet, achieving a closer integration of patterned physical movement with the mainly dramatic, organizing it into well shaped musical movements. Sleeping Beauty was staged in the Imperial Theater of Alexander III who relished its affirmation of monarchical grandeur. Chaikovsky spent early 1889 abroad giving concerts, the middle months in creative work, and the final ones in administrative work and concert-giving in Moscow and St. Petersburg. Pressures on him to conduct were greater than ever.

During 1889 Chaikovsky composed an opera, The Queen of Spades, using Modest's libretto which was based on Pushkin's famous short story. It premiered that December in a brilliant, well received performance. It was first performed outside Russia in Prague in October 1892. The most fully integrated of Chaikovsky's operas and the most gripping, it was more uneven than Onegin. It lacked a truly sympathetic character, revealing the composers' emotional preoccupations. Next to Onegin, the Queen became his most frequently performed opera in Russia.

During 1892 Chaikovsky composed a sextet, Souvenir de Florence, his final multimovement work except for the Sixth Symphony. That year he received a final letter from his benefactress Nadezhda von Meck, who had lost her fortune. Her subsidies ceased. The end of their relationship was a severe blow to Chaikovsky, who then destroyed his opera, Voevoda. It was later reconstructed from the orchestral material.

Learning of his sister Sasha's death, Chaikovsky at first intended to cancel a planned tour to the United States in 1891, then undertook it and kept a detailed diary of the whole trip. He was impressed by American hotel accommodations and emphasis on material comforts. His fame in the United States was already immense. It seemed that in America he was far better known than in Europe. He was amazed at his fine reception arranged by conductor Walter Damrosch to open New York's Carnegie Hall and by lavish American hospitality. Suffering from fatigue and neuralgia after a series of New York concerts, he had to cancel several conducting commitments.

In 1891-1892 he worked on the opera Iolanta and his final ballet, The Nutcracker, based on a tale by E.T.A. Hoffman. On their first few nights both were given to full houses. In January 1893 they were withdrawn after eleven performances, not to be given again in Chaikovsky's lifetime. The Nutcracker story was trite, the most inconsequential of Chaikovsky's mature theatrical pieces, and its dramatic structure the least satisfactory. Nonetheless, his music for Act I was a splendid achievement, insuring the work's lasting success and fame. Nutcracker was Chaikovsky's equivalent of Mozart's Magic Flute, childlike, controlled, elegant, and enchanting. Chaikovsky had a genius for melody that was essential for ballet as well as enormous talent for orchestration. In Swan Lake he broke from the confining mold of ballet tradition with a revolutionary work. In Sleeping Beauty he created the greatest nineteenth-century ballet. By contrast Nutcracker seemed at the time to be the saddest case among his mature works. Given its subsequent enormous popularity, it is surprising that it was not performed again in Russia until 1919, whereas Iolanta had fourteen more performances after Chaikovsky's death.

By 1891 Chaikovsky was worried by aging and weariness. During his remaining two and a half years he experienced deepening gloom despite growing personal success. Invitations to conduct his own and others' works multiplied along with ovations and honors. In those final two years he scored Nutcracker, completed his Sixth Symphony, composed a one-movement Third Piano Concerto, eighteen piano pieces, and six songs. In May 1892 he settled into a large, comfortable house in Klin near Moscow. Avoiding further foreign tours, he conducted several concerts in Odessa, including his Queen of Spades, in January 1893 to thunderous applause.

Chaikovsky sketched his great Sixth Symphony early in 1893 and scored it during the summer. He signed the completed manuscript on 31 August, noting that he was very proud of it and regarded it as his best work. Many music critics agree. The Sixth contained the most articulate first movement he ever wrote. The name Pathétique was chosen at Modest's suggestion after the premiere. Chaikovsky's biographer, David Brown, calls it the most original symphony since Beethoven's Ninth. The composer conducted its premiere after his return from London and Cambridge, where he received an honorary doctorate. He died nine days later.

The circumstances surrounding Chaikovsky's death remain controversial. Until recent years Modest's version was generally accepted as authoritative. Chaikovsky drank unboiled water, contracted cholera, and died soon after. However, cholera's incubation period is normally much longer, and seemingly refuting the cholera thesis, Chaikovsky's body was displayed at Modest's apartment freely open to visitors. Most now conclude that he committed suicide by poison. According to a Soviet account, Chaikovsky was threatened with disaster after Duke Stenbok-Fermor accused him of sexually violating his young nephew. N.B. Jacobi then convened Chaikovsky's school friends who urged him to commit suicide. We may never know the truth.

As news spread of Chaikovsky's death, hundreds paid their respects at Modest's apartment. The funeral service was held in the packed great Kazan Cathedral of St. Petersburg, an unprecedented honor for a commoner. Imperial family members attended, and Chaikovsky's music was sung by the Imperial Opera chorus. Alexander III allegedly declared, "We have many dukes and barons, but only one Chaikovsky" (Brown, Vol. 4, 487). He was buried in St. Petersburg with fellow composers M.I. Glinka, A.P. Borodin, and M.P. Musorgsky.

Bibliography: In English the best and most complete biography and musical analysis is David Brown, *Tchaikovsky. A Biographical and Critical Study*, Vol. 1 (1840-1874), Vol. 2 (1874-1878), Vol. 3 (1878-1885), Vol. 4 (1885-1893) (London, 1978-1991). Other leading English-language studies on Chaikovsky include G. Abraham, ed., *Tchaikovsky. A Symposium* (London, 1945), Edwin Evans, *Tchaikovsky* (London, 1978), Edward Garden, *Tchaikovsky* (London, 1973), John Gee, *The Triumph of Tchaikovsky* (New York, 1960), A. Orlova, *Tchaikovsky. A Self Portrait* (Oxford, 1990), John Warrack, *Tchaikovsky* (London, 1973), and E.O. Yoffe, *Tchaikovsky in America. The Composer's Visit in 1891* (New York, 1986).

In Russian some of the most important primary and critical works include N.A. Alekseev, et al. eds., *Chaikovskii i zarubezhnye muzikanty. Izbrannye pisma inostrannykh korrespondentov* (L., 1970), G. Dombaev, *Tvorchestvo P.I. Chaikovskogo* (M., 1958), E. Frid, ed., *M.A. Balakirev. Vospominaniia* (L., 1962), N. Kashkin, *Vospominaniia o P.I. Chaikovskom* (M., 1896), and A.A. Orlova, ed., *M.A. Balakirev. Perepiska s P.I. Chaikovskim* (L., 1962).

Key documents by Chaikovsky include P.I. Chaikovskii, *Dnevniki* (M.-P., 1923), *Muzikalno-kriticheskie stati* (M., 1953), *Perepiska s N.F. von Meck*, 3 vols. (M.-L., 1934-36), *Pisma k blizkim* (M., 1955), and *Polnoe sobranie sochinenii, literaturnye proizvedeniia i perepiska* (M., 1953).

David MacKenzie

CHAMBER OF MAGISTRATES. See Burmisterskaia Palata, SMERSH, Vol. 5.

CHANCELLERY OF CONFISCATION (1730-1782). Kantseliariia konfiskatsii. Government institution in imperial Russia charged with the collection of debts.

First proposed in 1729, the Chancellery of Confiscation was created in St. Petersburg by an edict (ukaz) of 27 June 1730. Three years later a branch office was opened in Moscow. In subsequent years the Chancellery of Confiscation gradually assumed the responsibilities of other government debt-collecting agencies, uniting with the Arrears Chancellery (Doimochnaia kantseliariia) in 1736 and by 1741 becoming the most important debt-collecting agency in the realm.

According to the instructions laid out in the ukaz of 1730, the Chancellery of Confiscation was created to eradicate treasury losses and to facilitate the orderly confiscation and sale of movable and immovable property. Thus the chancellery's primary function was confiscation of movable and immovable property for arrears and political crimes and appropriation and management of escheated property. The chancellery was to manage property acquired by these means until it was either reclaimed or sold. Eighteenth-century legislation reveals that the chancellery also was responsible for levying fines against individuals guilty of certain offenses, such as submitting false petitions in legal disputes.

Although the Chancellery of Confiscation suffered from significant shortcomings and was ultimately abolished in 1782, it exerted considerable influence during its fifty-two years of existence. An examination of the chancellery's voluminous journals and records reveals a pattern of daily meetings which dealt with a variety of matters, from the extraction of debts and the location of a delinquent debtor's heirs to the establishment of time periods for debts to be paid and the sale of confiscated property. These records demonstrate the actual execution of such orders, listing confiscated movable and immovable property, and sometimes the name of the purchaser and the price paid. Often confiscation involved items of the most personal nature, including belts, trousers, silk stockings, ties, scarves, ladies' gloves, shirts, hats, and winter boots. Although it appears that most nobles suffered confiscation as a result of debt, there are notable examples of confiscation as a result of the turning tide of favoritism, including the Lopukhins, the Dolgorukys, and the cases of Artemy Volynsky and Alexander Ivanovich Rumiantsev. Even the director of the Chancellery of Confiscation, Platon Ivanovich Musin-Pushkin, was not exempt. In 1740 when he fell from favor, his estates were confiscated.

The existence of the Chancellery of Confiscation and the various recorded instances of confiscation have raised the question of the frequency and purpose of this government sanction. Several historians suggested that Russia's rulers undoubtedly recognized the close connection between property rights and political freedom and sought to use this link to their own advantage. In this way the state was able to undermine the formation of a noble corporate identity. Others have questioned the frequency of confiscation and argue against such an interpretation.

Bibliography: "Kantseliariia konfiskatsii" in Brokgauz-Efron, *Entsiklopedicheskii Slovar'*, Vol. 14, 342-343; I.E. Andreevskii, "Kantselariia konfiskatsii, 1729-1780 gg.," *Russkaia starina*, No. 6 (1881), 167-186; Lee A. Farrow, "Inheritance, Status and Security. Noble Life in Eighteenth-Century Russia" (Ph.D. diss., Tulane University, 1998).

Lee A. Farrow

CHARITY AND PATRONAGE IN KIEVAN RUS (c. 994-1210). Charity and patronage played significant social, economic, political, and religious roles in Kievan Rus. Men and women, princes and princesses, monks and bishops, individual merchants and merchant corporations, and street communes, i.e., people living on the same street, provided charity and patronage in Kievan Rus. The earliest recorded reference to a charitable deed in Kievan Rus is found in the Russian Primary Chronicle in reference to Grand Prince Vladimir I who, after bestowing a tithe to the newly founded Church of the Holy Virgin (Desiatinnaia) in Kiev in 994-996, "made a great festival on that day for the boyars and elders of the people, distributing also much largess to the poor." Soon after Vladimir I donated food, 300 units (var or berkovtsy) of mead, and 300 grivnas to the poor when celebrating the consecration of the Church of Sacred Transfiguration in Vasiliev. After returning to Kiev Vladimir proceeded to donate money, drink, and food to the poor and had carts deliver bread, meat, fish, fruits, mead, and kvas to the infirm and the sick who could not walk to his palace. One of the most famous Kievan teachings concerning charity is found in the Testament of Vladimir Monomakh in which he urged his sons to be charitable to the church as well as to the common people. Aside from preaching good deeds Vladimir Monomakh was involved in the patronage of the first Rus saints, Boris and Gleb, when he decorated their coffins with silver, gold, crystal beads, and other costly objects.

One of the main forms of charity and patronage in Kievan Rus involved the construction of patron (ktitor) churches, monasteries, and nunneries. Many of these building projects were commissioned by the Rus princely families, the ruling elite, and members of the high clergy. For example, Iaroslav the Wise, who commissioned the construction of the Cathedral of St. Sofia and the Church of the Annunciation over the Golden Gate in Kiev, also founded the Monastery of St. George and the Nunnery of St. Irina and funded them from his treasury. In 1086 Grand Prince Vsevolod founded the Church of St. Andrew in Kiev and built next to it a nunnery where his daughter, Yanka, was the abbess. In 1089-1090 the Greek Metropolitan Ephraim funded the construction of the churches of St. Michael, St. Theodore, and St. Andrew, and a stone bathhouse (bania) in Pereiaslavl. In Novgorod, Poliuzhaia, the daughter of the mayor (posadnik) of Novgorod, founded the nunnery of St.

Euthemia in 1197, and two years later the wife of the prince of Novgorod founded the Nunnery of the Nativity.

In addition to funding construction projects, patrons also provided for their decoration. For example, Archbishop Nifont of Novgorod painted the porches and ornamented the entire exterior of St. Sofia in 1144. Six years later he covered the roof of the church with lead and its outer walls with plaster. In 1196 Archbishop Martury of Novgorod commissioned Olisei Grechin to paint frescos at the Church of the Holy Mother of God. Andrei Bogoliubsky, the prince of Vladimir-Suzdal principality, constructed a church in Bogoliubovo and decorated it with gold, precious stones, pearls, icons, and various ornaments. In 1155 after transferring the icon of the Holy Mother of God, originally brought to Rus from Constantinople, from Vyshgorod to Vladimir, he decorated it with more than thirty grivnas of gold as well as silver, precious stones, and large pearls. Many other such examples are found in Kievan Rus sources.

In contrast to much of the rest of Kievan Rus, where most of the churches were founded by the princely families and members of the high clergy, in Novgorod private individuals were responsible for constructing many of the local churches and abbeys. In 1115 Voigost, a wealthy merchant, founded the Church of St. Theodore of Tyre in the Slavno quarter of Novgorod. The first reported privately funded monastery in Novgorod, St. Anthony, was established by Antony Rimlianin sometime before 1119. During 1135-1136 Irozhnet, probably another merchant, founded the Church of St. Nicholas, the patron saint of merchants. A number of wooden churches were constructed in the 1140s, but the Novgorodian chronicle does not report on the social backgrounds of their patrons. Because the churches were made of wood it can be assumed that their patrons were of modest means, not princes or the high clergy. In 1156 a merchant corporation involved in international trade constructed the Church of the Holy Friday. Three years earlier the Dormition or Arkazh Monastery was constructed by a wealthy Novgorodian, Arkady, who became its first abbot. A church dedicated to the Trinity was founded in 1165 by another group of merchants, and two years later Sadko Sytinich, probably a wealthy Novgorodian merchant, funded the reconstruction of the already existing stone Church of SS. Boris and Gleb. In 1176 Moisei Domanezhich, a wealthy Novgorodian, sponsored the construction of the Church of Decollation of John the Baptist. A group of people living along St. Luke Street in Novgorod jointly commissioned the construction of a stone Church of SS. Peter and Paul in 1185.

There are other examples of church construction by private individuals in Novgorod during the Kievan period, where the large number of privately constructed churches can be attributed to Novgorod's greater autonomy from the Rus princes' influence. Church construction by private individuals was not limited to Novgorod however. The Paterik of the Caves Monastery mentions a person from Kiev who constructed a church for himself and commissioned seven icons to be painted for its iconostasis. Individuals privately funded the construction of churches in several other Rus towns.

Private donations also played a crucial role in subsidizing the economic needs of the church, monasteries, and nunneries. Gifts of money, food, goods, and kormlenie (lit. feeding or the permission to collect foodstuffs or other capital from private lands for maintenance) supported at least some, if not all, of the non-princely monasteries and nunneries in Kievan Rus. The monks of the Kievan Caves Monastery, a non-princely monastery, received money, grain, wine, olive oil, kormlenie, and other gifts from princes and other wealthy individuals. Kliment, a Kievan boyar, for example, donated a gospel and two gold grivnas for making a crown for an icon to the Caves Monastery. Yury, the prince of Suzdal, was no less generous when he donated 500 grivnas of silver and 50 of gold to decorate the coffin of Feodosy of the Caves Monastery. Prince Gleb Vseslavich and his wife over the course of their lives gave the Caves Monastery 100 grivnas of gold, 700 grivnas of silver, and five villages with serving people. In other cases one finds that monks themselves provided gifts to monasteries. For instance, Isaac, a former merchant from Toropets, distributed his wealth to monasteries and the poor upon becoming a monk at the Kievan Caves Monastery. Monk Varlaam willed to the Caves Monastery icons and other church necessities which he bought with his own money in Constantinople. A number of sources note cases of individuals distributing their wealth to churches, monasteries, and the needy, such as orphans, widows, and paupers, before taking monastic vows.

Donations to the church by private individuals also existed in other parts of Rus. Several birch-bark texts from Novgorod speak of the patronage of monasteries and nunneries by wealthy individuals. In text No. 605 one finds the mayor (posadnik) of Novgorod donating mead or honey to a monastery and No. 657 mentions an individual giving money to the St. Barbara Nunnery. A monk thanks his patrons for their material support and sends them his blessings in birch-bark text No. 503.

A number of Kievan-period wills and testaments from Novgorod speak of funding monasteries. Sometime between 1192 and 1210 a wealthy Novgorodian who became a monk donated land, villages, cattle, peasants, fishing and hunting rights, and the produce of the lands to the Khutyn Monastery. An article in the Pravda Russkaia (The Russian Justice) dealing with the proper procedures for dividing an inheritance when a will was not written states that some money was to be given to the church "to remember the deceased's soul in prayers." Kievan-era synodicals, lists of people for whose souls monks or priests were to pray, have been found in Novgorod and Smolensk written on birch-barks. The people listed in these synodicals apparently provided some form of support to the church.

Charitable acts often accompanied the deaths of individuals. For example, at the death of Vladimir I in 1015 Sviatopolk distributed largess to the people of Kiev. Prince Rostislav, after the death of his father, Grand Prince Viacheslav of Kiev, in 1154 distributed all of his father's valuables in the form of cloth, gold, and silver, except for a cross, to monasteries and prisons and to the poor in Kiev. He also left money for a memorial church service to his father and for candles and communion bread. On occasion, when people feared death, they promised to perform charitable deeds. Before going to battle against the Polovtsians in 1103, for instance, the Rus princes and their solders vowed before God and the Virgin to give food, alms to the poor, and other gifts to monasteries.

In return for donations the monks of the Kievan Caves Monastery provided a free hospital to the ill and lodgings and food to the poor. Demian, a monk and presbyter at the Caves Monastery, offered prayers and applied ointments to the sick. Agapit, another monk at the monastery, cured the sick with herbs and potions and refused to take fees for his services. Other monks at the monastery distributed their wealth to the poor. Similar conditions existed at other Rus monasteries. In the Life of Avraamy of Smolensk, for example, one finds people giving to monk Avraamy "what he needed, and he quickly distributed any surplus to widows and paupers, keeping only what sufficed for his needs." There is little question that monasteries and nunneries in other Rus towns also provided for the welfare of the poor with a portion of donated capital. The tradition of providing for the poor by monasteries remained very strong well into the Mongol and Muscovite periods. In the early sixteenth century care for the poor by monasteries became the central counter-argument of the Josephites to the non-possessors, who denounced monastic wealth in lands and property.

In Kievan Rus charitable contributions and patronage also subsidized the private parish clergy of patron (ktitor) churches. In Novgorod archaeologists unearthed a residential yard of the second half of the twelfth century that belonged to a priest-icon painter, Olisei Grechin (d. 1231). His yard was located near the Church of St. Basil Paria where he preached. The yards of his patrons, the powerful Nesdych-Miroshchinych boyar clan, stood near Olisei's and the church. A great number of shards of imported Byzantine amphorae, used to carry wine and olive oil, were found at the priest's yard. The wine was undoubtedly used by Grechin for administering communion to his boyar patrons at the church. The olive oil was also used in services for lighting lamps and anointing, and a part of it went into his icon painting to shellac the icons and mix the oil paints. As at the Kievan Caves Monastery, this wine and oil was provided by wealthy patrons. Grechin's patrons also commissioned him to paint icons of their patron saints and to pray for their relatives from the synodicals written on birch-barks, many of which were found in his yard. In this way wealthy Novgorod boyars provided their private churches with wine and olive oil for church services and gave the clerics material support as well as a place to live and a means of employment.

Performing charitable acts was not restricted to the members of the monastic clergy. A number of other types of charitable acts are found in the sources. In 1231 Spiridon, the archbishop of Novgorod, "put a common grave by the Church of the Holy Apostles" and hired an individual to transport and bury the corpses of 3,030 people who died during a severe famine that year. On occasion, references are found to people giving money or goods to those in need. For instance, in birch-bark No. 293 found in Novgorod the author of the text, who has lost everything because he was in jail, appeals to the addressee for money so that he may go on a pilgrimage.

The Kievan Caves Paterik tells of secular individuals who sometimes paid ransoms for Rus captives who were unable to pay for their own release.

Monasteries and nunneries in Kievan Rus functioned as one of the main institutions for redistributing wealth down the socio-economic ladder. Wealthy members of the Rus elite donated money and other forms of capital to monasteries and nunneries which in turn passed some of the wealth to the needy. The ruling elite profited from this patronage in several ways. The private churches and abbeys sometimes became their supporters against their political opponents among the princes or boyars and clergy. Material support of the church and the clergy also brought a means of relieving social tensions by offering the masses some economic and spiritual maintenance. Through their generous and pious acts of charity, which made their names known, the economically well-off but non-ruling members of society, such as merchants, could advance socially. In this way charity and patronage in Kievan Rus also provided social mobility to the newly-rich members of society. The already wealthy and powerful competed with each other for greatness, fame, and piety. Undoubtedly, they also hoped that their charitable deeds had true religious significance and provided merit to help them enter Heaven in the afterlife.

Bibliography: The Russian Primary Chronicle, trans. and ed. by S.H. Cross and O.P. Sherbowitz-Wetzor (Cambridge, Mass., 1973); "The Testament of Vladimir Monomakh," ibid., 206-215; *The Kievan Chronicle (Hypatian)*, trans. and comm. by L.L. Heinrich (Ann Arbor, Mich., 1978); *The Chronicle of Novgorod, 1016-1471*, trans. by R. Michell and N. Forbes (Hattiesburg, Miss., 1970); *The "Paterik" of the Kievan Caves Monastery*, trans. by M. Heppel (Cambridge, Mass., 1989); "Life of Avraamii of Smolensk" and "Tale of the Miracles of Roman and David" in *The Hagiography of Kievan Rus'*, trans. by P. Hollingsworth (Cambridge, Mass., 1992); A.A. Zalizniak, *Drevnenovgorodskii dialekt* (Moscow, 1995); A.A. Zalizniak and V.L. Ianin, "Vkladnaia gramota Varlaama Khutynskogo," *Russian Linguistics*, Vol. 16 (1993), 185-202; *Pravda Ruskaia* in *The Laws of Rus'—Tenth to the Fifteenth Centuries*, trans. by D.H. Kaiser (Salt Lake City, Utah, 1992); R. Zguta, "Monastic Medicine in Kievan Rus' and Early Muscovy" in *Medieval Russian Culture* (Berkeley, Cal., 1984); N. Dejevsky, "The Churches of Novgorod. The Overall Pattern," ibid.; B.A. Kolchin, A.S. Khoroshev, and V.L. Ianin, *Usad'ba novgorodskogo khudozhnika XII v.* (M., 1981); A.S. Khoroshev, *Tserkov' v sotsial'no-politicheskoi sisteme Novgorodskoi feodal'noi respubliki* (M., 1980). See more on charity and patronage in Novgorod and the English translation of related birch-bark texts in Th.S. Noonan and R.K. Kovalev, "Prayer, Illumination, and Good Times. The Export of Byzantine Wine and Oil to the North of Russia in Pre-Mongol Times," *Byzantium and the North, Acta Byzantina Fennica*, Vol. 8, 1995-1996 (1997), 73-96; and "Wine and Oil For All the Rus'! The Import of Byzantine Wine and Oil to Kievan Rus'," ibid., Vol. 9 (1999), 87-121.

Roman K. Kovalev

CHARITY IN IMPERIAL RUSSIA. See Philanthropy and Welfare in the Russian Empire, 1861-1917, MERSH, Vol. 51.

Additional Bibliography: Direction Générale de l'économie locale du Ministère de L'interieur, *L'assistance publique et privée en Russie* (SPb., 1906); Alla Iur'evna Gorcheva, *Nishchenstvo i blagotvoritel'nost' v Rossii. Rossisskii zhurnal kak istochnik svedenii o sotsial'nykh prioritetakh obshchestva* (M., 1999); Kantselariia po uchrezhdeniiam Imperatritsy Marii, *Sbornik svedenii o blagotvoritel'nosti v Rossii, s kratkimi ocherkami blagotvoritel'nykh uchrezhdenii v S. Peterburge i Moskve* (SPb., 1899); Anna Kletsina and Oleg Leikind, *Blagotvoritel'nost' v Rossii. Sotsial'nye i istoricheskie issledovaniia* (SPb., 2001); I.K. Labutin, *Kharakter khristianskoi blagotvoritel'nosti* (SPb., 1899); Adele Lindenmeyr, "From Repression to Revival. Philanthropy in Twentieth-Century Russia" in *Philanthropy in the World's Traditions*, ed. by Warren F. Ilchman, Stanley Katz, and Edward L. Queen II (Bloomington, Ind., 1998), "Voluntary Associations and the Russian Autocracy. The Case of Private Charity" in *The Carl Beck Papers in Russian and East European Studies* (Pittsburgh, Penn., 1990); Sergei Dmitrievich Martynov, *Predprinimateli, blagotvoriteli, metsenaty. Stroganovy, Tretiakovy, Morozovy, Guchkovy* (SPb., 1993); V.V. Menshikov, *Pomogi blizhnemu! Blagotvoritel'nost' vchera i segodniia. Sbornik* (M., 1994); I.S. Pisarenko, *Sbornik soobshchenii i dokladov. Vserossiiskaia Nauchno-prakticheskaia konferentsiia "Blagotvoritel'nost' i sotsial'no-ekonomicheskaia politika Rossii. Traditsii i sovremennost'* (Kaluga, 1997); T. Pokotilova, *Blagotvoritel'nost' v sotsial'noi istorii dorevoliutsionnoi Rossii* (M., 1997); Galina Nikolaevna Ulianova, *Blagotvoritel'nost' moskovskikh predprinimatelei, 1860-1914* (M., 1999); Pavel Vasilevich Vlasov, *Blago-tvoritel'nost' i miloserdie v Rossii* (M., 2001).

Jennifer Hedda

CHARYKOV, NIKOLAI (1855-1930). Russian ambassador to the Ottoman Porte and exile politician.

Charykov belonged to a wealthy, noble Russian family. He was born on the family's estate, Grigorevka, on 20 January 1855. During his boyhood in Moscow he had a German tutor for three years. At age eleven he was sent to Scotland, where he learned English. In August 1869 he left Edinburg for St.Petersburg. After graduating from the university there in 1875 he entered the Russian foreign service. During the Russo-Turkish War of 1877-1878 he volunteered as a Life Guard Hussar and fought in Bulgaria against the Turks. He then returned to the foreign service, where he enjoyed a successful diplomatic career. In 1881 Charykov carried dispatches to ambassadors in Berlin, Paris and London. Between 1883 and 1889 he was active in Central Asia. In 1889 he went to Paris and from there moved to Constantinople as first secretary of the Russian embassy. In 1893 he was appointed councillor of the Russian embassy in Berlin. After three years he was sent to Sofia. In 1897 he was promoted to minister-resident and sent to the Holy See in Rome, where he stayed for three years. He served in several Balkan states until 1905, when he was appointed to The Hague.

When his classmate and friend A.P. Izvolsky became minister of foreign affairs in 1907, Charykov became his political assistant and, because of his knowledge of the Balkans and the Ottoman Empire, in 1909 he was appointed ambassador to Constantinople. Charykov presented his letter of credentials to Sultan Mehmed V (Reshad) in early August and told the sultan that his main duty was to strengthen friendship between Russia and Turkey. His order to the Russian consulates in Turkey to treat Turkish citizens with respect and to observe Turkish financial regulations made a good impression and received favorable coverage in the capital's newspapers. Charykov had a particularly friendly relationship with the newspaper Tanin and its editor Huseyn Javid Bey and enjoyed good connections to many other influential personalities in Constantinople.

Charykov believed that international relations could be strengthened through economic ties as well as through politics. To that end he sponsored a Russian industrial exhibition on board the *Emperor Nicholas II* which visited Constantinople in 1910. When war between Turkey and Italy broke out in 1911, Turkish authorities prohibited passage through the Dardanelles to foreign merchant vessels, and many Russian merchant ships were stuck in Constantinople. Russian grain exports dropped 43 percent in 1911 as a consequence. Charykov wrote to Prime Minister Said Pasha on 12 October 1911 suggesting among other things that Russia might protect the Turkish straits when foreign powers threatened Turkey and help preserve the status quo between Balkan states and the Ottoman government. In return he asked that Constantinople permit the passage of Russian naval vessels through the Turkish straits.

When he hadn't received any response from Ottoman authorities by 27 November 1911, Charykov addressed another almost identical memorandum to the new prime minister Asym Bey. Turkey was not confident about Russia's intentions, and Asym Bey secretly informed London.

On 8 December 1911 the official Turkish response was given to Charykov. Turkey would not allow free passage of Russian warships through the straits in peace or wartime. This was a serious setback to Charykov. The Russian government claimed that he acted without the permission of St. Petersburg and soon recalled him. Charykov's diplomatic career was ended to save face in St. Petersburg. He retired to his family's estate, Bogdanovka, near the Volga River in Samara province. Following the Bolshevik Revolution, Charykov emigrated in 1919 to Constantinople, where he stayed with his wife until his death in 1930.

Bibliography: N.V. Tcharykov, *Glimpse of High Politics Through War and Peace 1855-1929* (New York, 1931); A.N. Kurat, *Türkiye ve Rusya* (Ankara, 1990), 156-171.

Nadir Devlet

CHASHNIK, ILIA GRIGOREVICH (1902-1929). Suprematist painter, graphic artist, and designer.

Chashnik was born at Liutsin, Latvia. His parents soon moved to Vitebsk, where he grew up. He was apprenticed to a watchmaking workshop, where he had his first drawing lessons at the age of eleven. Later he began to study under Yuri (Yehuda) Pen (1854-1937) around 1917. Interested initially in Jewish artistic traditions, Chashnik changed his orientation dramatically when, after a trip to Moscow, he returned to Vitebsk in 1919 to study with Marc Chagall (1887-1985) and then Kasimir Malevich (1878-1935) in the People's Art School, along with El Lissitzky (1890-1941), Ivan Puni (1892-1956), and other experimentalists. Under Malevich's overpowering influence he became a passionate and total convert to suprematism.

In 1920 Chashnik was a founding member of UNOVIS (Affirmers of New Art), along with other Vitebsk students of Chagall and Malevich. He took part in all the exhibitions of the UNOVIS group, fully sharing its collectivist ethos. Along with Lazar Khidekel (c. 1904-1986) he edited the only number of the journal Aero, under the UNOVIS imprint. He became increasingly interested in ideal architectural ensembles, which he tried to create along suprematist lines. With Malevich he worked on the development of arkhitektons and planits, three-dimensional suprematist compositional projects, somewhere on the borderline between architecture and sculpture.

After receiving his Vitebsk diploma in June of 1922 Chashnik followed Malevich to Petrograd to work in the State Institute of Artistic Culture. He soon began producing suprematist designs for textiles and especially for ceramics at the State Porcelain Factory in Leningrad (1922-1924) in close collaboration with Nikolai Suetin (1897-1954). Characteristically, Chashnik and Suetin attempted to grasp the structural laws which they believed would enable them to produce a universal decorative harmony rather than searching for artistic originality. Chashnik's mature work sought to combine the cool, balanced geometry and economy of suprematist design with a certain coloristic dynamism. He defined non-objectivity as the highest state of consciousness and the color black as the ultimate expression of non-objectitivty. As it was for his master, Malevich, suprematism was a religion for Chashnik, and he spoke often of it in such terms.

Chashnik contributed to the 1923 Exhibition of Petrograd Artists of All Tendencies and to the 1925 International Exposition of Decorative and Modern Industrial Arts in Paris. He worked with Malevich at the Institute of Decorative Art, and in the final phase of his career he taught at the State Institute of Art History in Leningrad (1926-1929) along with Malevich, Suetin, and various young architects, among them Aleksandr Nikolsky (1884-1953). He died of appendicitis at the age of twenty-seven. His close colleague Suetin laid a ribbon on his grave reading simply and fittingly "to an artist of the new art."

Bibliography: Victor Arwas, ed., *The Great Russian Utopia* (London, 1993); *Ilya Chashnik and the Russian Avant-Garde. Abstraction and Beyond* (Austin, Tex., 1981); Susan Tumarkin Goodman, *Russian Jewish Artists in a Century of Change* (Munich, 1995); Irina Karasik, comp., *V kruge Malevicha. Soratniki, ucheniki, posledovateli v rossii 1920-kh-1950-kh godov* (SPb., 2000); Nina Lobanov-Rostovsky, *Revolutionary Ceramics* (New York, 1990); John Milner, *A Dictionary of Russian and Soviet Artists* (Woodbridge, England, 1993); N.Yu. Semenov, ed., *Russkoe iskusstvo. Illiustrirovannaia entsiklopediia* (M., 2001); Angelica Zander

Rudenstine, ed., *Russian Avant-garde Art. The George Costakis Collection* (New York, 1981); Dmitrii Vladimirovich Sarabianov and A.S. Shatskikh, *Malevich* (M., 1993); *The Suprematist Straight Line. Malevich, Suetin, Chashnik, Lissitzky* (London, 1977).

Abbott Gleason

CHEBRIKOV, VIKTOR MIKHAILOVICH (1923-1999). Chairman of the USSR Committee of State Security (KGB), 1982-1988, and voting member of the Communist Party of the Soviet Union (CPSU) politburo from 1985 to 1989.

Chebrikov, an ethnic Russian and son of a factory worker, was born in the Ukrainian city of Dnepropetrovsk. In 1940 he entered the Dnepropetrovsk Metallurgical Institute, but World War II interrupted his studies. During 1941-1946 he served in the Soviet Army, starting as a private, rising through the positions of platoon leader and company commander, and ending his service as chief of staff and deputy commander of a battalion. He joined the CPSU in 1944. In 1950 he graduated from the Dnepropetrovsk Metallurgical Institute and began working as an engineer in G.I. Petrovsky Metallurgical Plant in Dnepropetrovsk.

During 1951-1967 Chebrikov held various Communist Party positions, starting with head of a department of the Leninsky District Party Committee (raikom) in Dnepropetrovsk. Afterward he became a secretary, then first secretary of Leninsky raikom. During 1955-1958 Chebrikov was the leading party official at the Dnepropetrovsk Metallurgical Plant, secretary of the plant party committee and party organizer of the CPSU Central Committee for the plant. From 1958 until 1959 he served as second secretary of the Dnepropetrovsk City Party Committee (gorkom). During 1959-1961 he moved up to head of a department of the Dnepropetrovsk Region Party Committee (obkom). He then served as Dnepropetrovsk gorkom first secretary until 1964. In that year he became a secretary of the Dnepropetrovsk obkom, and from 1965 until 1967 he was Dnepropetrovsk obkom second secretary.

Throughout much of his career in the Soviet leadership Chebrikov belonged to the wing of the country's political establishment known as the Dnepropetrovsk Mafia, consisting of Politburo members and CPSU secretaries whose career origins included service in the Dnepropetrovsk party organization. Prominent members included Leonid Ilich Brezhnev, first secretary (1964-1966), then general secretary (1966-1982) of the CPSU central committee; Andrei Pavlovich Kirilenko, a member of the CPSU central committee presidium (1962-1966) and politburo (1966-1982) and a CPSU central committee secretary (1966-1982); and Vladimir Vasilievich Shcherbitsky, first secretary of the Ukrainian Communist Party (1972-1989) and a CPSU politburo member (1971-1989).

In 1967 Chebrikov moved from the Dnepropetrovsk party organization to the USSR KGB, becoming head of the personnel administration of that organization. This appointment was widely regarded as part of a move by Brezhnev to undercut the influence in the KGB of his political rival and fellow Politburo member Aleksandr Nikolaevich Shelepin. In 1968 Chebrikov was made a deputy chairman of the KGB. He served later (January-December 1982) as a first deputy chairman.

In December 1982, a month after Brezhnev's death, Chebrikov became the KGB's chairman. The following year he received the military rank of army general, a four-star general. During the tenure of the pro-reform Mikhail Sergeevich Gorbachev as CPSU general secretary (1985-1991), Chebrikov's political star flared briefly, then steadily waned. In 1988 he relinquished the KGB chairmanship to Vladimir Aleksandrovich Kriuchkov.

Chebrikov held positions in leading Communist Party organs and Soviet legislative bodies during his time in the KGB. He became a candidate member of the CPSU central committee in 1971 and a full member in 1981. He gained non-voting or candidate membership in the CPSU central committee politburo in December 1983 during Yury Vladimirovich Andropov's brief tenure as CPSU general secretary, and voting membership in April 1985 shortly after Gorbachev became general secretary. After losing the KGB chairmanship in 1988, Chebrikov became a secretary of the CPSU central committee. From 1988 to 1989 he was chairman of the central committee's Commission on Legal Policy. He was elected a member of the USSR Supreme Soviet, the country's ceremonial legislature, in 1974, 1979, and 1984. He lost his membership in the politburo and secretariat at a central committee plenum on 20 September 1989 and shortly thereafter retired on a pension.

In the spring of 1989 Chebrikov became one of 2,250 members of the USSR Congress of People's Deputies (CPD), the country's first national legislature to be composed in large part of members who won their seats in competitive elections. Chebrikov was among the CPD's 750 appointed members who gained their seats as the hand-picked designees of various official political, social, or academic organizations. His sponsoring body was the Communist Party of the Soviet Union. He continued to hold CPD membership after his retirement on a pension. In the CPD he voted in March 1990 against a proposal to exclude the words "Communist Party of the Soviet Union" from Article 6 of the draft USSR Constitution then under legislative consideration, in effect voting to defend the CPSU's constitutional political preeminence. On other legislative issues he maintained a strongly anti-reform voting record.

According to Russian press reports, during the years following the collapse of the Soviet Union in 1991, leaders of the Russian security service occasionally consulted with Chebrikov. He also gave occasional interviews to the Russian media. When he died, those attending his mourning service included Premier of the Russian Federation Sergei Vadimovich Stepashin and head of the presidential administration Aleksandr Stalievich Voloshin.

In 1980 Chebrikov received a State Prize. He was awarded the title Hero of Socialist Labor in 1985. Other awards included two Orders of Lenin, two Orders of the Red Banner, three Orders of the Red Banner of Labor, the Order of Aleksandr Nevsky, the Order of the October Revolution, the Order For Services to the Fatherland, several lesser medals, and the title Honorable Worker of State Security.

Bibliography: "Biograficheskie Spravki," *Ezhegodnik Bol'shoi Sovetskoi Entsiklopedii, 1987* (M., 1987); *Deputaty Verkhovnogo Soveta, 9-ii Sozyv* (M., 1974), *10-ii Sozyv* (M., 1979), *11-ii Sozyv* (M., 1984); Masha Akhmanova, Iana Babinskaia,

Tania Kuriatnikova, Lena Lunts, Liza Stepanova, "Sostav rukovodiashchikh organov Tsentral'nogo Komiteta Kommunisticheskoi Partii, Politbiuro (Prezidiuma), Org-biuro, Sekretariata TsK (1919-1990 gg.)," *Izvestiya TsK KPSS*, No. 7, 1990; Michael McFaul and Nikolai Petrov, eds., "Deputaty 1989, 1990 i 1993 gg. i ikh reitingi," *Politicheskii al'manakh Rossii, 1995* (M., 1995); "General Chebrikov vozvrashchae-tsia v stroi," *Moskovskii Komsomolets*, 24 January 1996; Aleksandr Khinshtein, "Tri bukvy, kotorye znaet vsia strana," *Moskovskii Komsomolets*, 20 December 1996; *Narodnye Deputaty SSSR* (M., 1990); "In memoriam. Skonchal'sia byvshii predsedatel' KGB SSSR" *Nezavisimaia Gazeta*, 3 July 1999; *Vneocherednoi Tret'ii S"ezd Narodnykh Deputatov SSSR Prilozhenie k biulleteniu*, No. 4 (M., 13 March 1990).

Gregory J. Embree

CHEBYSHEV, PAFNUTY LVOVICH (1821-1894). Mathematician, founder of the St. Petersburg school of mathematics.

The eldest son of a noble family, Chebyshev was born on the family estate, Okatovo, in Kaluga province on 4 May 1821 and was tutored privately at home in Moscow. A slight limp prevented him from preparing for a military career. In 1837 he enrolled at Moscow University, studied mathematics with N.D. Brashman, and graduated in 1841. In 1846 Chebyshev defended his master's thesis and moved to St. Petersburg University as an adjunct, the equivalent of an assistant professor. His 1849 doctoral thesis, Theory of Congruences, won a Demidov Prize from the Academy of Sciences. At the university Chebyshev was promoted to extraordinary (1850) and then ordinary professor of mathematics (1860). He also held the chair of applied mathematics at the St. Petersburg Academy of Sciences, rising there from adjunct (1853) to extraordinary (1856) and ordinary (1859) membership.

Reserved and absorbed in his studies, Chebyshev lived a relatively uneventful life. In 1852 he traveled for several months in Europe, mostly in France, with a commission to study various collections of machines and mechanisms, and made the acquaintance of leading French mathematicians. After the Crimean War Chebyshev and his younger brother, an artillery professor, worked at the Artillery Committee, where he advised the army on applications of probability theory and on transition to rifled barrels. He was active on the Academic Committee of the Ministry of Enlightenment, designing curricula and supervising textbooks for secondary education. In his teaching Chebyshev was disciplined and correct towards students. His lectures ended exactly on time even if a derivation remained unfinished. Once a week he held open house for discussions with interested students. He is also remembered as the founder of the St. Petersburg mathematical school, which became one of the world's leading centers of research in pure and applied mathematics. About a dozen of his disciples achieved distinguished careers in science. Some, in particular A.A. Markov and A.M. Liapunov, made great contributions themselves.

Chebyshev's greatest accomplishments encompassed several branches of mathematics. He first attracted international attention in 1849-1852 for his studies on number theory, regarding the distribution of prime numbers. Chebyshev proved that the number of prime numbers not exceeding a certain number x is close to x / ln x. In calculus he studied whether the integrals of certain irrational functions can be expressed as algebraic or logarithmic functions. His discoveries include the textbook solution (1853) for the integration of the binomial differential x^m (a + b $x^n)^p$ dx, where m, p, and n are rational numbers. He also advanced Abel's theory of elliptic integrals.

Some of his most famous results were in probability theory, of which he may be regarded one of the founding fathers. On the basis of the Chebyshev inequality he produced a rigorous demonstration of the general law of large numbers (1866), from which the theorems of Poisson and Bernoulli followed as special cases. He investigated conditions under which the distribution of the sum of independent variables converges to the normal distribution and sketched (1887) the proof, subsequently completed by A.A. Markov, of the generalized central limit theorem of Moivre and Laplace. The results produced by Chebyshev and his students made the theory of probability a respectably rigorous mathematical theory and justified its applications to mathematical statistics, opinion polls, and the natural sciences.

Chebyshev believed that the main problems for mathematics in his time were formulated by human practices, and indeed practical problems inspired many of his most fundamental investigations. Special attention to applied mathematics became a distinctive tradition in the St. Petersburg school. This was reinforced by their location in the nation's capital and connections with the government, military and naval industries The problem of the hinge mechanism, or transformation of rotational into rectilinear movement, as in steam engines and other machines, inspired Chebyshev to lay the foundation for the general theory of approximation of functions by polynomials with the goal of minimizing deviations (1854). This work developed further into the theory of interpolation and the method of least squares (1855-1875) and the theory of orthogonal Chebyshev polynomials (1859). Chebyshev studied concrete devices such as the Watt parallelogram and himself designed a number of mechanisms, including the Chebyshev parallelogram (1868), the wheelchair, and mechanical calculators (late 1870s). The improvement of artillery fire and cartographic precision motivated other mathematical works of Chebyshev during 1850s and 1860s.

After his retirement from the university in 1882 Chebyshev continued publishing his research and working with students. He suggested to Liapunov the problem of stable ellipsoidal forms in rotating and gravitating liquid. Investigating the Chebyshev problem brought Liapunov years later to his famous theorems on the stability of motion. In recognition of Chebyshev's great contributions many prestigious scientific societies of Europe, including the Institut of France, the Royal Society of London, and the Berlin Academy, elected him a foreign or honorary member. He died after a brief illness in St. Petersburg on 26 November 1894. Chebyshev never married, although he did support an illegitimate daughter without recognizing her officially. Living frugally and investing in real estate, he bequeathed his brother an impressive inheritance of about 600,000 rubles.

Bibliography: A.N. Krylov, *Pafnutii L'vovich Chebyshev. Biograficheskii ocherk* (M.-L., 1944); *Nauchnoe nasledie P.L.Chebysheva*, 2 vols. (M.-L., 1945); V.E. Prudnikov, *Pafnutii L'vovich Chebyshev, 1821-1894* (L., 1976); A. Wassilieff, *P.L.Tschebyschef und seine wissenschaftliche Leistungen* (Leipzig, 1900); A.P. Youschkevitch, "Chebyshev, Pafnuty Lvovich," in *Dictionary of Scientific Biography*, ed. by Charles C. Gillispie, Vol. 2 (New York, 1970), 222-232.

Alexei B. Kojevnikov

CHECHENS. The largest ethnic group in the northern Caucasus.

According to the 1989 Soviet census the Chechens numbered 956,879 at the time of the USSR's collapse. Chechnia is currently part of the Russian Federation, but it has fought for independence from Russia intermittently since 1991. The Chechens are related to neighboring Ingush, whose population numbers 237,438, and together form a people who call themselves the Vainakh. The Chechens also call themselves the Nokchi. The term Chechen is an ethnonym given to them by the Russians that derives from a conquered village known as Chechen Aul. The Chechens are an indigenous Caucasian people who have lived in the valleys and foothills of the northeastern Caucasus Mountains for millennia as grain farmers and sheep and cattle herders. Their homeland is made up of the forested mountainous highlands of the northeastern Caucasus and lowlands below the Terek River. Many Chechens were forcefully settled in the lowlands during the Soviet period.

The Chechen language belongs to the Northeast branch of the Caucasian language family and is unrelated to Indo-European languages. Unlike many other non-Russian ethnic minorities in the Russian Federation, the Chechens have largely avoided russification and 97 percent claim Chechen as their first tongue, although most speak fluent Russian as well. The Chechen language is written in the Cyrillic alphabet assigned to them during the Soviet period.

The traditionally animistic and pagan Chechens and neighboring Ingush people converted to Sunni Islam between the seventeenth and nineteenth centuries under the influence of missionaries from the neighboring mountainous Muslim region of Dagestan. As did many peoples in the northern Caucasus, the Chechens adopted a tolerant mystic form of Islam known as sufi Islam that blended their pre-Islamic beliefs with mainstream Sunni Islamic beliefs. The Chechens tended to belong to the moderate Naqshbandi and Qadiri sufi orders and engaged in such sufi practices as making pilgrimages (ziyarets) to the sites of the tombs of sufi sheiks, the use of amulets to protect themselves from harm, and performing religious songs and dances (zikrs) to reach unity with the maker. Their form of tolerant frontier Islam displayed none of the puritanical streak found amongst fundamentalist Wahhabi Muslims in Saudi Arabia.

Historically the Chechens were formed into clans known as teips and these united during times of trouble or invasion to form greater alliances known as tukhums. The various tukhums then united under their respected elders to defend their home villages and nation (kaam) from external attacks. Islam provided another unifying factor, urging the Chechens and related Ingush to defend their mountainous country from non-Muslim invaders. Muslim religious leaders from neighboring Dagestan were often able to mobilize the Chechens and Ingush with calls of jihad (holy war) to defend their lands from outsiders, including the invading armies of tsarist Russia.

The Chechens first began to clash with the Russians and their Cossack frontier forces when the latter began to expand into the north Caucasus flank during the late eighteenth and early nineteenth centuries. Such leaders as the legendary mountain guerrilla leader Imam Shamil, a Dagestani belonging to the Avar tribe, united the Chechens with fellow Dagestani Muslims in a desperate struggle against the might of the trans-continental Russian imperium. The Russians responded to this often fanatical defense with scorched earth tactics that burned scores of Chechen villages and displaced their populations. Policies such as cutting down forests where the Chechen fighters hid, collectively punishing villagers for ambushes of Russian armies by Chechen highlander guerrillas, and constructing fortresses such as Grozny, which translates to "Terrible" in Russian, enabled the Russians to subdue the out-numbered Chechen mountain clans by the 1860s.

While the Chechens were nominally subdued and brought into the Russian Empire after the defeat of Imam Shamil, they never truly accepted Russian rule. Revolts in Chechnia were suppressed with great bloodshed on several occasions during the tsarist period. The traditional Muslim, clan-based society of the Chechens came under further assault during the succeeding Soviet period.

During the Soviet period the Chechens experienced the horrors of anti-religious campaigns which included execution of community religious leaders, forced collectivization of property, and finally state-sponsored ethnic cleansing. One cannot understand the Chechens today without understanding how the collective memory of these traumas continue to shape their identity. Special mention must be made of the brutal ethnic cleansing to which this people was subjected by Josef Stalin during the general conflagration of World War II. Using false charges of mass treason as a pretext, Stalin ordered that the Chechens, Ingush, and other distrusted Muslim groups in the region, such as the Crimean Tatars, Karachai, and Balkars, be forcefully deported en masse from their mountain homelands to the depths of Soviet Central Asia in February 1944.

Newly declassified state security (KGB) documents brought the horrors of this tragedy to life. They describe the destruction of Chechen villages, mass executions, starvation, loss of life from illness, and the disruption of families and villages that were scattered across the harsh steppes of the Central Asian republic of Kazakhstan. Villagers in highland hamlets such as Khaibek were doused with gasoline and burnt alive by Soviet troops while thousands of pitiful survivors died in their places of exile. Approximately one in three died in the process of deportation. While many Chechens later adapted to life in the Soviet system, some Chechen deportees never forgave the Soviet system, which they often equated with Russia, for this genocidal attack. Trans-generational stories describing the horrors of the deportation continue to shape generations of Chechens who grew up long after the event and instilled in the Chechens a deep distrust of any outside authority, especially one based in Moscow.

Following the death of Stalin the Chechen survivors were allowed to return to their reconstituted homeland-republic in 1956 by the new Soviet leader Nikita Khrushchev. For the remaining years of the USSR the Chechens proved to be a relatively docile if distrusted nation in the Soviet Union. For example, Chechens were not allowed into the highest administrative positions of their home territory known as the Chechen-Ingush Autonomous Soviet Socialist Republic, which was headed by Russians. The Chechens also underwent anti-religious campaigns designed to eradicate what the atheistic state saw as sufi Islamic superstitions, and the Chechens ranked among the poorest peoples in the Soviet state. While the Chechen capital of Grozny grew during the Soviet period to be the largest city on the north Caucasus flank, with a population of 400,000, Chechens were often excluded, and it remained a predominately Russian town. Although Chechnia had one of the largest oil refineries in the former USSR, the average Chechen did not benefit from the oil industry and the Chechen highlands remained one of the most backward regions in the entire USSR. Consequently many Chechens became seasonal migrant workers and scattered throughout the USSR as guest workers. This formed the basis of the highly publicized Chechen mafia which, along with the Azeri and Russian mafias, became one of the most powerful ethno-mafias in the USSR.

Upon the collapse of the USSR in 1991 the Chechen leadership took advantage of Russian president Boris Yeltsin's offer to the various regions of the Soviet Union to seize as much autonomy as they could and unilaterally declared Chechnia independent of the Russian Federation. The neighboring Ingush, who were traditionally less anti-Russian, peacefully separated themselves from the secessionist Chechen republic in order to receive financial benefits from a grateful Moscow. Under the confrontational leadership of Djohar Dudaev, an ex-Soviet air force general and the highest ranking Chechen military officer in the USSR, a secessionist segment of the Chechen leadership led the Chechen people in creating a de facto independent Chechen statelet known as Ichkeria in the early 1990s.

This situation was seen as intolerable by the Russian General Staff which feared a domino effect in other non-Russian ethnic republics in the multi-ethnic Russian Federation, and the Russian military made several attempts to overthrow the break-away republic on Russia's strategic Caucasian border. Finally, in the fall of 1994 Russian leader Boris Yeltsin ordered the invasion of the Connecticut-sized republic of Ichkeria, to reign in lawlessness in the Chechen statelet which was described in the Russian press as a mafiaocracy. Moscow's hopes of a small, victorious war in Chechnia similar to the US intervention in Haiti were soon dashed when Chechen street fighters and guerrillas destroyed Russian invading divisions and launched a full-scale partisan war from Chechnia's southern mountains. After losing approximately 7,500 soldiers and killing 35,000 civilians in Chechnia, the humiliated Russian Federation Army signed a peace treaty delaying the final decision on Chechnia's status and retreated from a devastated land in summer of 1996. Despite their numeric inferiority, the highly motivated Chechen fighters, led by popular field commanders such as Shamil Basaev, Arab jihadi warlord Emir Khattab, and moderate commander Aslan Maskhadov, outfought the Russian conscript army in the first Russo-Chechen War of 1994-1996.

From 1996 to 1999 a lawless situation prevailed in Chechnia as the secular-moderate president of the Chechens, Aslan Maskhadov, vied with radical Chechen field commanders such as Shamil Basaev, who was stridently anti-Russian, for control of Chechnia. Russia subsequently used the provocative invasion by a small band of Khattab and Basaev's men into the neighboring Russian republic of Dagestan in the autumn of 1999, and a series of unexplained bombings in Russia, which were nonetheless blamed on Chechens, as a pretext for launching a massive second invasion of Chechnia in the fall of 1999. Although the vast majority of Chechens, including the pragmatist president Maskhadov who disavowed Basaev's invasion, were moderates who disliked the extremist Wahhabi warlords such as Khattab, Russia accused the Chechen nation of terrorism. In response to a growing problem of Chechen kidnappings and jihadi incursions into Russian territory from Chechnia, the Kremlin invaded the independent state in October 1999 with the stated aim of destroying international terrorism in Chechnia.

With the fall of the Chechen capital of Grozny in February 2000 after a stubborn defense against a Russian Federation force of approximately 100,000, the Chechen leadership retreated to the Caucasus Mountains which make up the southern third of the Chechen republic. There the Chechens and a small band of Arab jihadi supporters continued to wage a deadly guerrilla war against Russian Federation forces. Russia's utilization of prison camps, known as filtration points, indiscriminate bombing of civilian targets, extrajudicial killings of suspected rebel sympathizers, search and destroy cleansing (zachistka) missions, and brutal reprisals against villages for attacks by guerrillas, drove many apolitical Chechens into the arms of extremist field commanders such as Shamil Basaev. Basaev and his Arab supporters are also suspected of carrying out terrorism against Russian targets including the October 2002 Nord Ost Theater hostage-taking in Moscow and a rash of suicide bombings in 2003.

Russo-Chechen wars of 1994-1996 and 1999-present have obliterated the Chechens' economic infrastructure, destroyed their traditional patriarchal society, and led to the radicalization of Islam amongst certain segments of the Chechen population. One must not make the mistake of seeing the Chechens, who have a moderate form of Sufi Islam, as Osama bin Laden-financed Islamic fundamentalists as Russia would have the West believe. Since the terrorist attacks on the US World Trade Centers on 11 September 2001 the Russian government has aimed to portray its Chechen opponents as Al Qaeda-sponsored terrorists in an effort to discredit their struggle for independence. While there is evidence that sympathetic Arabs, such as a recently slain Arab warlord named Emir Khattab and his successor Abu Walid, both jihadi commanders who lead a group of approximately 200 well-financed Arab Wahhabi fighters in the so-called International Islamic Brigade, have joined the fight against the Russian infidels, the majority of anti-Russian Chechen fighters are secular nationalists and have no interest in Bin Laden's global jihad against Zionists and American crusaders.

As of 2003 the Chechen conflict shows no signs of ending and the Russian Army has been incapable of capturing elusive Chechen field commanders such as Shamil Basaev, Russia's most wanted man, or the head of the Chechen resistance, Aslan Maskhadov. Over 5,000 Russian Federation troops have been killed in this new round of conflict, yet the Russian government appears to be committed to destroying both bona fide terrorist groups operating from Chechen territory and those powerful secular elements in Chechnia who seek independence from Russia.

Bibliography: Lesley Blanch, *Sabres of Paradise* (New York, 1960); Khassan Baiev. *The Oath. A Surgeon Under Fire.* (New York 2003). James Critchlow, *The Punished Peoples of the Soviet Union* (New York, 1991); John Dunlop, *Russia Confronts Chechnya* (Cambridge, 1998); Anatol Lieven, *Chechnya, Tombstone of Russian Power* (New Haven, Conn., 1999); Anne Nisvat, *Chienne de Guerre. A Woman Reporter Behind the Lines of War in Chechnya* (New York, 2001); Brian Glyn Williams, "Commemorating 'The Deportation' in Post-Soviet Chechnya. The Role of Memorialization and Collective Memory in the 1994-1996 and 1999-2000 Russo-Chechen Wars," *History and Memory,* Vol. 12, No. 1, (2000), "Jihad and Ethnicity in Post Communist Eurasia. On the Trail of Trans-national Islamic Holy Warriors in Kashmir, Afghanistan, Central Asia, Chechnya and Kosovo," *The Global Review of Ethnopolitics,* Vol. 2, No. 3 (2003), "The Russo-Chechen War. A Threat to Stability in the Middle East and Eurasia?" *Middle East Policy,* Vol. 8, No.1 (2001), "Unravelling the Links Between the Middle East and Islamic Militants in Chechnya," *Central Asia Caucasus Analyst,* 12 February, 2003; Robert Seely, *Russo-Chechen Conflict. A Deadly Embrace* (London, 2001); Sebastian Smith, *Allah's Mountains. The Battle for Chechnya* (London, 1998); Anna Zelkina, *In Quest for God and Freedom. Sufi Responses to the Russian Advance in the North Caucasus* (London, 2000).

Brian Glyn Williams

CHEKANOVSKY, ALEKSANDR LAVRENTIEVICH (1833-1876). Geologist, explorer of central Siberia.

Chekanovsky was born on 12 February 1833 in Kremenets in Volynia province to a Polish gentry family. He studied medicine at Kiev University from 1850 to 1855 and at Derpt, now Tartu, University from 1855 to 1856. He left his medical studies incomplete to devote himself to the study of geology and mineralogy, transferring to the mineralogy department of Derpt University. From 1857 to 1863 he worked for the Siemens & Galske company in Kiev, which was running a telegraph line to India. Chekanovsky participated in the Polish uprising of 1863, for which he was sentenced to exile in Siberia for six years.

In exile in the village of Padun in Bratsk district of Irkutsk province he conducted regular meteorological observations and studied the geology of the Angara River. He was first to sketch a cross section of the Silurian deposits of the region and first to discover and describe outcroppings of trap rock, a word he coined. In 1868 he moved to Irkutsk, where he worked in the Siberian branch of the Imperial Russian Geographical Society. From 1869 to 1872 Chekanovsky carried out geological explorations of Irkutsk province. He studied deposits of lazurite near Lake Baikal, discovered a rich complex of flora and fauna of the Jurassic period at the village of Ust-Balei, and established that the yellow sandstone of the Irkutsk region dates from the Jurassic, which allowed him to date mountain ridges of the Baikal region. Chekanovsky also evaluated the coal-bearing capacity of the Jurassic sandstone. In 1874 he published a monograph about his geological exploration of Irkutsk province. This appeared as a separate volume in the Notes of the Siberian Branch of the Imperial Russian Geographical Society

From 1873 to 1875 Chekanovsky conducted three trans-Siberian expeditions, to the Lower Tunguska, Olenek, and Lena rivers. As a result of these expeditions he discovered a huge trap rock deposit in Eastern Siberia. He divided trap rock for the first time into three facies, intrusive trap rock, lavas, and tuffs. He also distinguished dikes as a special sort of intrusive trap rock. Chekanovsky further established that the coal-bearing sandstone of the Lower Tunguska River Valley belonged to the Carboniferous period, discovered Mezozoic deposits in the Lower Tunguska River basin and chalk deposits in the lower reaches of the Lena River, and amassed large collections of fossil and living flora and fauna.

A.L. Chekanovsky provided a basic geographic and geological description of a large part of Eastern Siberia and compiled the first geographic and geological maps of that region. His geological map of Irkutsk province was awarded the highest prize, a gold medal first class, at the International Geographical Congress in Paris in 1875. In 1876 Chekanovsky moved to St. Petersburg and worked in the Mineralogical Museum of the Imperial Academy of Sciences. On 18 October 1876 during a period of depression he committed suicide. Thirteen fossil animals, ten fossil plants, four living plants, a mountain ridge in Yakutia, a mountain in the Khamar-Daban range, and a village near Bratsk in Irkutsk province are all named for A.L. Chekanovsky. A number of scholars have described his botanical and zoological collections.

Bibliography: I.L. Kleopov, *Aleksandr Lavrent'evich Chekanovskii* (L., 1972); "Dnevnik ekspeditsii Aleksandra Lavrent'evicha Chekanovskogo po rekam Nizhnei Tunguske, Oleneku i Lene v 1873-1875 godakh" in *Zapiski Imperatorskogo Russkogo geograficheskogo obshchestva po obshchei geografii*, Vol. XX, Nos. 1-3 (SPb., 1896); A.L. Chekanovskii, "Geologicheskoe issledovanie v Irkutskoi gubernii" in *Zapiski Sibirskogo otdela Imperatorskogo Russkogo geograficheskogo obshchestva*, Vol. XI (Irkutsk, 1873); J. Chudzikovska and J. Jaster, *Na bezbrozach Dalekiej Polnosy. Opowiesc of Aleksadrze Chekanowskim* (Warsaw, 1958).

Nikolay Komedchikov

CHEKHONIN, SERGEI VASILIEVICH (1878-1936). French: Tchekhonine. Artist, illustrator, ceramicist.

Sergei Vasilievich Chekhonin was born in the village of Lykoshino near Tver in 1878. He was a draughtsman of enormous technical skill and came to be regarded by some as the most outstanding book illustrator in pre-revolutionary Russia. He was also a major figure in the history of Russian enamels and ceramics, most notable for his famous revolutionary porcelains.

Chekhonin studied at the school of the Society for the Encouragement of the Arts in Saint Petersburg (Obshchestvo pooshchreniia khudozhestv) in 1896-97 and under Ilia Repin at Princess Tenisheva's Studio from 1897 to 1900. Between 1904 and 1907 he worked at Abramtsevo with Petr Vaulin, the director of the Ceramics Studio, and with Mikhail Vrubel. He later worked at Princess Tenisheva's Talashkino school and in Vaulin's Kikerin factory near St. Petersburg. Chekhonin's radicalism was stimulated by the Revolution of 1905. He worked at the journal Satirikon and on other critically-minded periodicals. He visited Paris in 1906-1907.

Chekhonin's interest in ceramics developed early and lasted until the end of his life. Among his early achievements were the majolica panels on the façade of the Metropole Hotel in Moscow on which he worked with Vrubel. He subsequently did the majolicas for the church erected in honor of the Romanov tercentenary, suggesting that ideology did not always trump the opportunity to advance his career.

Chekhonin was one of the best known members of the second generation of the World of Art (Mir iskusstva) and exhibited with them off and on between 1911 and 1924. He participated in the exhibitions sponsored by the Golden Fleece (Zolotoe runo) in Moscow in 1909-1910. Although he was interested in Russian folk art, he was quite cosmopolitan and knowledge of much of the art of the Russian Empire enriched his later work, as did his connection with Abramtsevo and the World of Art movement in general. Between 1913 and 1918 he was director of a school specializing in decorative enamel work in Yaroslavl province. He also produced a series of murals for the Yussupov palace on the Moika Canal in St. Petersburg.

With his radical sympathies, Chekhonin made an easy transition to the post-1917 world. He helped Lunacharsky reorganize the People's Commissariat of Enlightenment, while producing a number of agitational posters and turning his attention to radical ceramics. In 1918 he was appointed to direct the art section of the State Porcelain Factory, formerly the Imperial Porcelain Factory. His designs for agitational ceramics with revolutionary mottoes were the first produced for the new Soviet state. He remained at the State Porcelain Factory for almost ten years, with the exception of 1923-1924 when he served as director of the Volkhov Factory near Novgorod. In the final World of Art exhibition in 1924 he produced portraits of Lenin and Zinoviev.

Chekhonin emigrated to Paris in 1928, where he expanded and varied his range. He turned his talents to advertising and other commercial activities. He drew for Vogue magazine. He also continued his activities in theater design and worked for the Ballets Russes, producing a new set for The Snow Maiden in 1930. He died at Lörrach near Basel in 1932.

Bibliography: Galina Dmitrievna Agarkova, et. al., *Russkii farfor* (M., 1993); John Bowlt, *Khudozhniki russkago teatra. Sobranie Nikity i Niny Lobanovykh-Rostovskykh* (M., 1991); V.I. Dudakov and David Elliott, *100 Years of Russian Art.*

From Private Collections in the USSR (London, 1989); Alexander Efros and N. Punin, *S. Chekhonin* (M., 1923); John Milner, *A Dictionary of Russian and Soviet Artists* (Woodbridge, Eng., 1993), pp. 106-108; Nina Lobanov-Rostovsky, *Revolutionary Ceramics* (New York, 1990); O.S. Ostroi and I.S. Saksonova, *Izobrazitel'noe i prikladnoe iskusstvo* (SPb., 2002); Evgeniia Petrova, et al., *Mir iskusstva* (SPb., 1998); Deborah Sampson Shinn, *Soviet Porcelains, 1918-1985* (New York, 1992); A.S. Vinogradova and G.E. Klimov, *Grafika russkikh khudozhnikov ot A do Ia* (M., 2002).

Abbott Gleason

CHEKHOV, ANTON PAVLOVICH (1860-1904). Renowned short-story writer and dramatist.

Chekhov was born in Taganrog on the Black Sea, the grandson of a serf who purchased his freedom before emancipation and the son of a small-scale shopkeeper. He attended the school of the Greek church and from 1868 the Taganrog Gymnasium. In 1876 Chekhov's father went bankrupt and the family moved to Moscow while Chekhov remained in Taganrog to finish the gymnasium. In 1879 Chekhov joined his family in Moscow and entered the medical faculty of Moscow University. While in medical school Chekhov began to write short pieces for the satirical journals, weekly periodicals that featured comic stories and drawings, the most prominent of which was Fragments (Oskolki), edited by N.A. Leikin (1841-1906). Chekhov completed his medical courses in 1884 but by this time he had developed a reputation as a writer for the satirical journals, using a variety of synonyms such as Antosha Chekhonte. In 1886 he began to write under his own name for New Times, the most widely read newspaper in Russia, which was owned and edited by the newspaper baron A.S. Suvorin (1834-1912). In 1888 Chekhov began to contribute to so-called thick journals, first to Northern Herald (Severnyi vestnik) and later to Russian Thought (Russkaia mysl), which were read primarily by members of the intelligentsia. From then until the end of his career he was recognized as the most important writer of his generation, although critics often castigated his works for supposed indifference and lack of direction. Although his literary activity became the main focus of his career and the principal means of support for himself and his family, Chekhov maintained his interest in medicine throughout his life, at times actively, as when he served as a district medical officer during a cholera outbreak.

In his early works Chekhov often conformed to requirements imposed by the satirical journals, such as brevity, comic dialogue and word play, and a surprise ending. Many of these stories are variants of the so-called little scene (stsenka), comic situations featuring familiar social types, such as officials, actors, and clerics, engaged in activities or in settings appropriate to the time of year, the beginning of the theater or dacha season, Christmas or New Year, Easter. Some of Chekhov's best-known early stories, such as Death of a Civil Servant (Smert chinovnika, 1883), Fat and Thin (Tolsti i tonky, 1883), The Chameleon (Khameleon, 1884), and A Horsy Name (Loshadinnaia familiia, 1885), are of this type, whereas other early stories, such as Oysters (Ustritsy, 1884), The Huntsman (Eger, 1885), and Grief

(Toska, 1886), give clearer evidence of a more profound interest in psychological experience and social dislocation.

As he was able to publish in more serious newspapers and then in thick journals, Chekhov addressed increasingly complex issues and employed more sophisticated literary strategies, as evident in such works as Sleepy (Spat khochetsia), The Steppe (Step), The Name-Day Party (Imeniny), all 1888, A Boring Story (Skuchnaia istoriia, 1889), The Duel (Duel, 1891), The Student (Student, 1894), My Life (Moia zhizn, 1896), and The Lady with a Lapdog (Dama s sobachkoi, 1899), which are recognized as among the greatest achievements of the modern short story. In many of these works Chekhov explored the situation of members of the Russian intelligentsia, who were disillusioned with received ideas and tentatively seeking new principles (The Duel, My Life), and of women in a society still ambivalent about their status (The Name-Day Party, The Lady with a Lapdog).

Chekhov's interest in drama began at an early age, even prior to his participation in the satirical journals, although his earliest surviving play, usually called Platonov in English after the central character's surname, and Fatherlessness (Bezottsov-shchina) in Russian, remained unknown until after the author's death. In the 1880s and early 1890s Chekhov gained popularity on the stage with such one-act farces as The Bear (also known as The Boor, Medved, 1888), and A Jubilee (Yubilei, 1892), but success as an author of full-length dramas eluded him. Both the early Ivanov (1888) and The Seagull (Chaika, 1895) in their first production in St. Petersburg were failures, the latter play spectacularly so. Only with a production of The Seagull by the newly-formed Moscow Art Theater in 1898, based on innovative principles of staging and acting developed by the theater's co-founder and director, Konstantin Sergeevich Stanislavsky (1863-1938), did the play receive recognition as a radically new and original sort of drama. Subsequent Moscow Art Theater productions of Uncle Vanya (Diadia Vania, staged 1899), Three Sisters (Tri sestry, 1901), and The Cherry Orchard (Vishnevy sad, 1904), the last two written specifically for the Moscow Art Theater, made Chekhov one of the most important modern dramatists and gained the Art Theater a world-wide reputation for theatrical innovation. Particularly in his final two plays Chekhov, though by no means an advocate of radical change, created a poetic vision of Russian society in transition, aware of traditional cultural values, yet anticipating a world in which social relations will be profoundly changed. Chekhov's association with the Moscow Art Theater also led to romance. He married one of the theater's actresses, Olga Leonardovna Knipper (1868-1959), in 1901.

Chekhov not only depicted a wide range of the social reality of his day in his works, he also took a direct interest in many of the issues of the period. He assisted schools and organized book donations to libraries in his hometown of Taganrog, in Melikhovo, the village near the estate he purchased in 1892, and in Yalta, where he moved in 1898. He also initiated practical programs for famine relief during a crop failure in 1891-1892. In 1890 he traveled across Siberia to Sakhalin, which served at the time as a Russian penal colony. There Chekhov conducted a detailed sociological survey of the population, publishing his observations as his only book and non-fictional work, *The Island of Sakhalin* (1895), which eventually led to improvements on the island and in general terms of penal servitude. Chekhov also broke with his long time friend, patron, and editor Suvorin over Suvorin's support of Alfred Dreyfus's conviction for espionage in France and opposed the anti-Semitic stance taken by Suvorin's paper New Times.

From the 1880s until his death Chekhov suffered from tuberculosis. In 1904 he went to Germany in search of treatment and died in Badenweiler in southern Germany in July of that year.

Bibliography: Ernest J. Simmons, *Chekhov. A Biography* (Boston, Mass., 1962); Michael Henry Heim and Simon Karlinsky, trans. and commentary, *Anton Chekhov's Life and Thought. Selected Letters and Commentary* (Berkeley, Cal., 1973); Toby W. Clyman, *A Chekhov Companion* (Westport, Conn., 1985); Robert Louis Jackson, ed., *Reading Chekhov's Text* (Evanston, Ill., 1993); Donald Rayfield, *Anton Chekhov. A Life* (New York, 1998); Vladimir Kataev, *If Only We Could Know! An Interpretation of Chekhov*, trans. by Harvey Pitcher (Chicago, Ill., 2002).

Andrew R. Durkin

CHEKHOV, MICHAEL (1891-1955). Actor, director, educator.

A nephew of Anton Chekhov and a disciple of Konstantin Stanislavsky, Michael Chekhov (Mikhail Aleksandrovich Chekhov) developed an acting technique that combined elements of the major acting theories of the twentieth century. In his acting Chekhov embodied the distorted consciousness of modernism and Viktor Shklovsky's notion of ostranenie, the splitting of an actor's consciousness into the I of the actor and the I of a character, which defines the product of an actor's activity, a stage mask, as an aesthetic object. Chekhov worked on his technique throughout his life, in different languages and artistic venues, including theater, film, and opera, as an actor, a director and an educator.

Chekhov began to study acting at age sixteen. In 1910 he completed Aleksandr Suvorin's theater school and was admitted to St. Petersburg's Suvorin Theater, where he spent his first professional season. In April 1912 Stanislavsky invited the young actor to start his career at the Moscow Art Theater and to join MAT's First Studio. The best parts of Chekhov's early repertoire at the studio included Fribe in Hauptman's Festival of Peace (1913), Caleb in Dickens' The Cricket on the Hearth (1914), Frazer in Berger's The Deluge (1916), Malvolio in The Twelfth Night (1917), and Erik XIV in Strindberg's Erik XIV (1921). In 1921 at MAT he performed what Vsevolod Meyerhold called the best Khlestakov of the Russian stage in Gogol's Inspector General, which was directed by Stanislavsky.

After 1918 Chekhov's life developed in several directions including his pedagogical career. In 1922 he became the leader of the First Studio, and in 1924 he was one of the first Soviet actors to receive the title of Honored Artist of the Russian Federation. On the stage of MAT II Chekhov directed and performed among other roles Hamlet (1924), Ableukhov in Bely's Peterburg (1925), and Muromsky in Sukhovo-Kobylin's Delo (1927). At the same time Chekhov led the life of a spiritual searcher, as a member of Russian Anthroposophic Society, and modified his acting technique in accordance with the spiritual and aesthetic ideas of Rudolf Steiner. The troupe of MAT II did not welcome Chekhov's tutelage and a series of conflicts ensued. By 1928 Chekhov considered it too dangerous to stay in the country and emigrated to Germany.

Chekhov was always interested in how an actor could call upon creativity and inspiration. *O tekhnike aktera* (1946) is his major theoretical work, the result of a life-long study of acting. He published his first article on the subject (O systeme Stanislavskogo) as early as 1919. Unlike Stanislavsky, Chekhov did not want to probe an actor's subconscious. Instead, he advised actors to use their imagination, which would bring them to the realms of the subconscious and inspiration without damaging their individuality. Chekhov stressed the importance of improvisation, rhythm and movement. Interested in the processes of inner and outer characterization, he advocated the actor's technique of imitating an ideal character originating in the imagination. Chekhov argued that an actor's only aim on stage is the creation of a stage mask by means of transformation and characterization through imaginary center, imaginary body, psychological gesture and atmosphere.

After he fled Russia, Chekhov worked in Germany, France, Latvia, Lithuania, England, and the United States. He was constantly improving his technique, seeing acting as a messianic activity that embodies both an actor's professional training and his personal purification. Chekhov's experience in exile, his encounter with different languages and cultures, gave him the idea of creating an international theater, comprehensible to spectators of any national or linguistic origin.

Chekhov's acting career in the west was subject to language limitations. Although he started his emigre life as an actor in Max Reinhardt's theater and performed three roles in German, later even pursuing a career in film, he was not satisfied. He moved to Paris to open a theater company for Russian audiences, but the attempt was not successful, and Chekhov went to Riga to spend several years acting in Russian and teaching Latvian and Lithuanian actors. There Chekhov performed the best roles in his emigre repertoire: Ivan the Terrible in Alexei Tolstoy's Death of Ivan the Terrible (1932) and Foma Opiskin in Dostoevsky's The Village of Stepanchikovo (1932).

Chekhov gradually shifted his focus to directing and teaching. In 1930 he directed The Twelfth Night at the Gabima Theater in Berlin. In 1932 he taught an acting course at the Kaunas National Theater and prepared the first version of his book in German.

The happiest period of Chekhov's life in the west was between 1935 and 1939, when Dorothy and Leonard Elmhirst invited him to organize an acting school and theater at their Dartington Hall estate in England. There Chekhov continued his pedagogic practice and worked on the English version of his acting manual. In 1938, together with his studio, Chekhov moved to the United States. The American Michael Chekhov Studio functioned until 1942 and put on several productions, among which Dostoevsky's The Possessed (1939) was the most successful. This studio closed due to war mobilization.

Chekhov spent the last fifteen years of his career in Hollywood, where he made approximately ten movies. He was nominated for an Oscar in the category of Best Supporting Actor for his role of Brulov in Hitchcock's Spellbound (1945), directed several productions, and tutored Hollywood celebrities, including Marilyn Monroe and Gregory Peck. He published *O teknike aktera* in Russian in 1946 and the English translation, *To the Actor*, in 1953, dedicating both of them to creating an ideal actor. Chekhov died in 1955 in Los Angeles.

Bibliography: M. Chekhov, *To the Actor. On the Technique of Acting* (New York, 1953); *Michael Chekhov's To the Director and Playwright* (New York, 1963); *Lessons for the Professional Actor* (New York, 1985); *Literaturnoe nasledie* (M.-L., 1995); L.C. Black, *Michael Chekhov as Actor, Director and Teacher* (Ann Arbor, Mich., 1987); G. Boner, *Tschechow M., Werkgeheimnisse der Schauspiel-kunst* (Zurich, 1979); L. Byckling. *Mikhail Chekhov v zapadnom teatre i kino* (SPb., 2000).

Yana Meerzon

CHELPANOV, GEORGY IVANOVICH (1862-1936). Psychologist, philosopher, logician, and educator.

Born in Odessa, Chelpanov studied in the History and Philology Department of that city's Novorossiisky University from 1882 to 1887. During this time he became interested in psychology, falling under the influence of the pioneering German psychologist and physiologist Wilhelm Wundt (1832-1920).

After graduation Chelpanov briefly taught psychology in a gymnasium before beginning his studies in philosophy at Moscow University in 1890. Two years later he moved to Kiev University's Philosophy Department. In 1897 he was appointed professor and head of the department. Over the next ten years he completed his doctoral dissertation and established a small laboratory for experimental psychology.

Foreshadowing his later role as educator and facilitator, Chelpanov turned his home in Kiev into one of Russia's great centers of intellectual life. Students and fellow intellectuals, including Nikolai Aleksandrovich Berdiaev (1874-1948), Lev Shestov (1866-1938), Vasily Vasilievich Vodovozov (1864-1933), and Sergei Nikolaevich Bulgakov (1871-1944), gathered there to discuss science, religion, and politics.

During this period Chelpanov's approach most closely matched that of the British structuralist Edward Titchener (1867-1927), the most faithful of Wundt's students. Like Titchener and Wundt, Chelpanov believed that psychologists should study conscious experience by manipulating physical stimuli applied to a subject, who would then report back the results. Chelpanov's methods, while introspective, were designed to minimize the subject's inferences, thus sidestepping the phenomenon of pure internal thought, so that the investigator could study perception and unadulterated sensation.

In adopting this stance Chelpanov distanced himself from the tradition associated with the father of Russian psychology, Ivan Mikhailovich Sechenov (1829-1905), and Chelpanov's own contemporaries, Ivan Petrovich Pavlov (1849-1936) and

Vladimir Mikhailovich Bekhterev (1857-1927). These scientists, who saw mental activity as the product of mechanical neural systems and conditioned reflexes, sought to study externally observable behaviors. Chelpanov derided behaviorism or reflexology, as it came to be called, as superficial, overly reductionistic, and even dilettantish. He believed that absent a priori philosophizing, behaviorism threatened to turn psychology into a mere mechanical trade. Chelpanov publicly sparred with the educational psychologist Alexandr Petrovich Nechaev (1870-1948), declaring psychology a young science whose purity and public standing were threatened by those quick to derive general theories of behavior or apply psychology's lessons to other fields, such as education.

In 1907 Chelpanov returned to Moscow University, taking over the chair of philosophy held by the late Sergei Nikolaevich Trubetskoi (1862-1905). After visiting Germany and the United States in 1910 and 1911 to study psychological facilities, Chelpanov informally established the Institute of Experimental Psychology at Moscow University in 1912. The institute, named after its patron, art dealer S.I. Shchukin, officially opened in 1914 with Chelpanov as its director. The second of its kind in Russia, after the St. Petersburg Psycho-Neurological Institute founded by Bekhterev in 1908, it was better equipped than any in Europe. The hallmark of the Institute was Chelpanov's insistence that his students gain a thorough grasp of the underlying philosophical questions before tackling the scientific problems of the field.

The Bolsheviks' accession to power in 1917 presented Chelpanov with a dilemma. Though he supported the new government's educational and social reforms, he rejected its efforts to assert ideological and political control of scientists and philosophers. As a result he steadfastly refused to support the Bolsheviks, even as some younger researchers began to introduce a brand of psychology based on Marxism. In an environment increasingly hostile to intellectuals who did not toe the line, Chelpanov's own intellectual development complicated his situation in the 1910s and early 1920s as he drew closer to the Würzburg school and its emphasis on introspection.

The showdown over the emerging lines of Soviet psychology sharpened in January 1923 at the First All-Russian Psychoneurological Congress, where Chelpanov engaged in a sharp debate with one of his students, Konstantin Nikolaevich Kornilov (1879-1957). Later Soviet scientists and historians maintained that Kornilov, who promoted an explicitly Marxist approach to psychology called reactology, won the debate by popular acclaim. In truth, he conceded most of Chelpanov's technical points, while loudly denouncing Chelpanov as a bourgeois reactionary. Soviet authorities concurred, and in November 1923 Chelpanov was replaced as director of the institute and chairman of philosophy at Moscow University by his erstwhile student.

Toward the end of his life Chelpanov retreated further into psychological idealism, adopting a position similar to Edmund Husserl's phenomenology. Psychologists, Chelpanov believed, should study pure consciousness, free from all physical and verbal stimuli. Relegated to the shadows because of his rejection of Bolshevik politics and Marxist science, his death in 1936 went largely unnoticed. Although Chelpanov's works on philosophy and psychology passed out of print in the 1930s, he was not forgotten entirely. When Soviet universities revived the teaching of logic in the late 1940s, publishers rushed a late edition of Chelpanov's textbook on the subject into print.

In terms of his own scientific contributions Chelpanov is rightfully overshadowed by his rivals Pavlov, Bekhterev, and Nechaev. His real significance, in which he rivals any Russian scientist of his day, was as a teacher. As director of the Shchukin Institute and professor of philosophy and psychology, he educated the first generation of Soviet psychologists, including Kornilov and the more sophisticated Pavel Petrovich Blonsky (1884-1942), Nikolai Aleksandrovich Rybnikov (1880-1961), and Anatoly Alexandrovich Smirnov (1894-1980). Although Chelpanov rejected materialism and refused to employ Marxist modes of thought, his emphasis on the philosophical roots of psychology ironically equipped many of his students to find their own philosophical and ideological accommodations in the 1920s. Under his tutelage a cohort of experimental psychologists emerged who had both the philosophical bent and methodological rigor to set about creating Marxist psychology in the 1920s and early 1930s.

Bibliography: Chelpanov's most influential and representative works are *Mozg i dusha* (SPb., 1900), *Vvedenie v filosofiiu* (Kiev, 1905), *Lektsii po eksperimental'noi psikhologii* (M., 1908), *Psikhologiia i shkola* (M., 1912), and *Uchebnik logik,* 10th ed. (M., 1918). In English, see David Joravsky, *Russian Psychology* (Oxford, 1989).

Randall D. Law

CHEMISTRY IN RUSSIA AND THE SOVIET UNION. A physical science as it developed in Russia and the USSR.

At the beginning of the eighteenth century it was quite difficult to define chemistry as a field of natural philosophy anywhere in Europe, and Russia was no exception. The study of the properties and reactions of various substances is an area of intense investigation since antiquity, but the separation of what was to become a rigorous experimental branch of the natural sciences apart from the separate trends of learned alchemy, popular alchemy, Paracelsian medicine, apothecaries' practices, mining, and practical trades such as gunpowder production was not yet accomplished. At the accession of Tsar Peter the Great (r. 1682-1725), while there existed a disorganized collection of apothecaries, metallurgists, paper and gunpowder manufacturers, and other tradesmen later classified under the general rubric of chemistry, the science proper had not taken root in Russia yet. It only recently did so in the late seventeenth century in western and central Europe.

The introduction of chemistry to Russia was largely the product of Peter's founding of the Imperial Academy of Sciences in St. Petersburg in 1725 and the importation of European savants to serve as academicians and professors at the accompanying, but short-lived university. Chemistry was one of the original ten fields specified by Peter's project for the Academy of Sciences, and the science has maintained a presence at the institution through all of its turbulent incarnations. Perhaps partly because of the strong associations of chemistry with pharmacy and medicine, academicians in this field produced works of far less import than their counterparts in sciences such as mathematics or astronomy. It was only in the late nineteenth century, when chemistry became the dominant science in all strata of the Russian intellectual hierarchy, that academicians in chemistry were as distinguished as their peers.

Because recruitment of a competent chemist who was willing to relocate to the infant city of St. Petersburg was so difficult, the academy settled for Michael Burger, a Baltic German, as its first chemist in September 1725. He died in late July 1726 after falling off a carriage, allegedly while drunk. His replacement was Johann Georg Gmelin (1709-1755), a young medical doctor with credentials from Tübingen and a member of a distinguished scientific family that left its imprint on chemistry for the next hundred years. Gmelin was first appointed as a curator at the academy, but two significant publications, now believed to be based on his father's earlier experimental work in Stockholm, led to his election to the post of academician in 1731. Gmelin spent 1733-1743 on the Great Northern Expedition to Siberia, where he mostly engaged in botanical and ethnographic researches. He resigned upon his return, once again vacating the chemistry post which seemed perpetually difficult to fill.

Essentially all later Russian and Soviet histories of chemistry date the dawn of a truly Russian tradition in the science to the work of Mikhail Vasilievich Lomonosov (1711-1765). Lomonosov is widely known as the first native Russian academician, the founder of Moscow University, and the composer of a canonical body of Russian lyric poetry. His claim as a distinguished chemist rests on much shakier ground, to say nothing of his failure to establish a tradition of chemistry through disciples. Lomonosov did expend a great deal of his seemingly boundless energy on chemistry, metallurgy, and allied sciences, including the construction of a fully-equipped chemical laboratory at the Academy of Sciences on Vasilievsky Island in St. Petersburg. Still his claims to original discoveries are in fact quite limited despite his own protestations and those of later historians.

Like many other native Russian academicians throughout the next hundred years, yet unlike the professors of chemistry at the universities, who were largely from noble stock until the advent of Mendeleev's generation, Lomonosov was not a member of the nobility (dvorianstvo). He attended the gymnasium and university of the Petersburg Academy of Sciences and was an adjunct of chemistry there from 1742 until his promotion to full academician upon Gmelin's resignation in 1745. Before this promotion Lomonosov went abroad to study with Christian Wolff (1679-1754) in Marburg. His study in Germany was part of a longstanding tradition that remained central to Russian chemical education until the late nineteenth century. Wolff, a disciple of Gottfried Wilhelm Leibniz (1646-1716), taught Lomonosov widely in natural philosophy but studiously avoided inculcating the young Russian with aspects of Newtonian thought, which left a detrimental impact on the latter's research. Lomonosov's early publications in chemistry in Latin received severe criticism in western Europe. He eventually refrained from publishing and, several years before his death, even from research. Lomonosov is often cited as the formulator of the concept of conservation of mass, that matter is neither created nor destroyed in chemical or physical reactions and therefore the amount of products must exactly balance the amount of reactants, a doctrine almost universally attributed outside Soviet historiography to Antoine-Laurent Lavoisier (1743-1794). While he did engage in some valuable chemical experimentation, Lomonosov's work was largely ignored, and his energy was often dissipated in his myriad other activities. His largest contribution was his effort to construct a chemistry laboratory at the academy, but even this did not survive him for very long, as it quickly fell into disuse and disrepair and was dismantled in the 1780s.

The story of chemistry in imperial Russia from the age of Lomonosov to the birth of the Soviet Union is one of the gradual decline of the academy as the central location of chemical activity and the corresponding rise of alternative sites, mostly universities, and the rise in the importance of laboratories of the chemical industry in the latter half of the nineteenth century. The first university to herald this transition was Kazan University, founded in 1804, which was unquestionably the center of chemical knowledge in the Russian Empire until the 1860s when it was eclipsed by St. Petersburg University. Although not the first chemist at Kazan, the founder of its chemical tradition was Nikolai Nikolaevich Zinin (1812-1880). Zinin had no particular interest or training in chemistry in 1835, when the holder of the chair in chemistry was let go pursuant to that year's new University Statute and Zinin was pushed by the physico-mathematical faculty to take on the task of educating himself in chemistry despite his formal training in mathematics. He was sent abroad in this process of re-education, spending significant research time in Berlin, Giessen, and Paris, and visiting several other countries. Upon his return he began a series of experiments in organic chemistry that later led to remarkable discoveries that gained him a prominent European reputation. He also trained Aleksandr Butlerov in Kazan and after 1847 moved to the Military-Medical Academy, later the Military-Surgical Academy, in St. Petersburg, eventually rising in the 1860s to a chair (kafedra) at the Academy of Sciences. In Petersburg his legacy of training continued as did his substantial original researches.

While there was a continuous, though faint chemical tradition since the formation of the Academy of Sciences, there was an undoubted explosion in the number and diversity, both geographical and topical, of chemists and chemical works beginning in the 1860s and continuing at this elevated level until the collapse of the Soviet Union. Until the Soviets reversed it, the trend in chemistry was towards the rise of university-based science with a heavy emphasis on teaching and research combined, as opposed to the academy's separation of these two functions. The expansion of the number of chemists was largely driven by the tsarist state's interest in technical modernization after its defeat in the Crimean War in 1855, which influential individuals in the Ministry of Finance and the Ministry of Education, among others, blamed on inadequate domestic technical expertise.

The plan for expansion was written into the liberal University Statute of 1863. Instead of importing new institutions and scholars as Peter the Great had done, talented postdoctoral and graduate students were sent abroad, most of them on government stipends, to study at the major educational centers of Germany and France. The majority of Russian chemists sent abroad in the 1860s selected Heidelberg as their destination. Paris was the second most popular destination. At Heidelberg they worked more with the younger chemist Emil Erlenmeyer (1825-1909) than with luminaries such as Robert Wilhelm Bunsen (1811-1899), Gustav Kirchhoff (1824-1887), and Hermann von Helmholtz (1821-1894), who were also responsible for the attractiveness of Baden as an educational center. While abroad, several of these chemists, especially Dmitry Ivanovich Mendeleev (1834-1907), Aleksandr Porfirievich Borodin (1833-1887), who is better known from his later vocation as a composer, and physiologist Ivan Mikhailovich Sechenov (1829-1905) began to appreciate the value of organized chemical meetings and mutual interactions. In the later 1860s these Heidelbergers, along with chemists who had remained in the capital, interacted to establish the new institutions of Russian chemistry.

There were two main transformations beginning in the 1860s, both of which left distinctive characteristics which permanently shaped the development of chemistry in Russia. The first of these changes was institutional. The interest in expanding postdoctoral education by sending young chemists to Germany was conceived as temporary. Upon their return these scientists filled posts at the major education institutions of Russian cities, following the expansion of science faculties at universities according to the University Statute of 1863 and the proliferation of agricultural and technological institutions. As an increasing number of students began to study chemistry, graduate education expanded, and chemists recognized a need to replicate many of the professional structures available in the west. For example, since the only previous attempt at publishing a chemical journal in Russian, N. Sokolov's and A. Engel'gardt's Chemical Journal (Khimichesky zhurnal N. Sokolova i A. Engelgardta) foundered after just two years in the late 1850s, Russian chemists had to turn to either the Bulletin of the St. Petersburg Academy of Sciences or to foreign chemical journals in order to publicize their researches. All these journals published in German or French. Russians disproportionately patronized Emil Erlenmeyer's Zeitschrift für Chemie und Pharmacie, continuing to publish there even after Erlenmeyer relinquished control of the journal in 1864. As a domestic market for both the production and consumption of chemical research grew, however, the Zeitschrift lost its appeal.

In October 1868 the Ministry of Popular Enlightenment approved the proposal made by the chemistry section of the First Congress of Russian Natural Scientists and Doctors to establish a Russian Chemical Society, thus making official the various informal chemical circles that developed in St. Petersburg over the course of the decade. Along with the right to convene formally and organize chemical discussion, the society was granted the imprimatur to publish the Journal of the Russian Chemical Society (Zhurnal russkogo khimicheskogo obshchestva). The journal, edited for over thirty years by St. Petersburg University chemist Nikolai Aleksandrovich Menshutkin (1842-1907), became the template for Russian scientific organization. An increasing number of Russian chemists published their research here before sending articles abroad, and many chose to publish only in Russian, as foreign chemical societies increasingly began to abstract the Russian articles in response to the rising stature of the Russian community. The Russian Physical Society, formed in 1874, also used the chemists as their model, and the two societies fused in 1878 to form the Russian Physico-Chemical Society, publishing a joint journal until after the 1917 Revolution. This society soon expanded its membership across the empire, diluting the dominance of Petersburgers, but not eliminating it entirely until the Soviet period.

The second major transformation of the late nineteenth century was conceptual. Beginning in the early 1860s a series of discoveries emerged from Russian chemists' research in chemical theory in both organic and inorganic chemistry, forming the bedrock of chemical knowledge to the present day. The best known of these is the 1869 formulation of the periodic table of chemical elements by D.I. Mendeleev. Mendeleev in 1867, six years after his return from Heidelberg, obtained the leading post as professor of general chemistry at St. Petersburg University. Given the recent reform of atomic weights at the Karlsruhe congress of chemists in September 1860, Mendeleev found no adequate textbook in Russian and considered that any Russian translation of a western European book was bound to be out of date by the time it appeared. He began to compose his own textbook of general chemistry directed to first-year students at the physical-mathematical faculty of his university. While composing this text, *The Principles of Chemistry* (first edition, 1868-1871, eight editions in Mendeleev's lifetime), he confronted the problem of how to organize all of the knowledge of chemical elements in a pedagogically accessible format. After several halting attempts Mendeleev arranged them by order of increasing atomic weight and in natural families. By 1871 he developed a complete version of the periodic system which allowed for the prediction of three new elements. Upon the discovery of these predicted elements, gallium in 1876, scandium in 1880, and germanium in 1886, Mendeleev's system received wide recognition and still forms the basis of almost all chemistry education across the globe.

The contribution of Russian chemists in organic chemistry was also substantial. During the course of his lectures in this subject at Kazan University in the late 1850s and early 1860s Aleksandr Mikhailovich Butlerov (1828-1886) developed a theoretical framework for organic chemistry which argued that one could best explain the properties of compounds by analyzing the topological distribution and connectivity of atoms within a molecule, rejecting earlier treatments of organic chemistry which argued that such intramolecular knowledge was beyond the scope of the science. Using this theory, Butlerov was able to explain the phenomenon of organic isomerism, where compounds contained the same elements in the same proportions but with vastly different properties, by arguing that they differed in terms of connectivity. He went on to predict several novel compounds which were later discovered. Similar theories were being developed simultaneously in western Europe, most notably by August Kekulé (1829-1896), and these two chemists engaged in a vigorous dispute about priority which has not yet disappeared from the historiography. Butlerov also founded a strong school of organic chemists, including Vladimir Vasilievich Markovnikov (1838-1904), known in the western literature as Markownikoff, and Aleksandr Mikhailovich Zaitsev (1841-1910), known in the west as Saytzeff, both of whom made fundamental contributions to organic theory. Markovnikov also initiated a broad research endeavor to analyze the composition of Baku petroleum, the start of a distinguished Russian tradition of oil chemistry.

Since Russian chemistry was both the most professionalized of the sciences at the dawn of the twentieth century and the one with the clearest links to industry, it was quick to become involved in the political, social, and economic transformations of war, revolution, and Bolshevism. Before the approach of the World War I chemistry in particular received its fair share of the ballooning enrollment of students, and the strain this imposed on all disciplines was acutely felt, given the importance of material supplies in chemical pedagogy. The coming shocks to the educational establishment of the Russian Empire, therefore, were easy for chemists to interpret as a set of opportunities to develop the science's position in society.

When war broke out in 1914, Russia experienced numerous economic shocks as crucial industrial chemicals and products imported primarily from Germany were cut off by hostilities. Russia now had to develop its own sources of various chemicals, as well as specialty items such as optical glass. This need was exacerbated by the flight of foreign capital during the war. Chemists responded by offering their services to the state. Chemists were important participants in the Commission for the Study of Natural Resources, formed in 1915 to advise the government on military needs through the Academy of Sciences and continued to function past the October Revolution. The Chemistry Section of the Russian Physico-Chemical Society was tremendously influential in coordinating the activities of its members for the war effort, and when fighting ceased, chemists were not about to let the previous dependence on foreign supplies resume. This led to heavy investment by the state into the development of an almost fully self-sufficient chemical and pharmaceutical industry, especially during the Stalin years. More than other scientists, chemists threw their lot in with the communists as the best hope for their discipline.

This early enthusiasm for the Soviet government, which was only discernable as enthusiasm because the other sciences were so cold to the new government's overtures of patronage, meant that chemists benefitted directly from the industrial expansion of the coming decades and suffered less in the principal academic reorganization of the Stalin years, the resurgence of the Academy of Sciences. In the late imperial period the Academy of Sciences lost ground to the universities, which fast became the central sites of original scientific research. Throughout the 1920s the Bolshevik regime began to sideline the universities, separating research from teaching in an effort to keep tsarist-era bourgeois experts from access to impressionable young Soviet minds. This culminated during the years of the cultural revolution (1928-1931) in the reform of the Academy of Sciences into a Soviet-friendly institution. In the process teaching was almost totally severed from research in an institutional sense. It was not until after the Second World War that world-class chemists emerged from universities in the Soviet Union since the best chemists flocked to the Academy of Sciences and its labyrinth of subsidiary institutes. In November 1930 all chemical societies and subdivisions were abolished except the Russian Chemical Society, which was granted existence for one more year, when it was finally taken over and transformed into the D.I. Mendeleev All-Union Chemical Society in 1933. This society survived the collapse of the Soviet Union with a slight emendation in name.

The history of chemistry during the Soviet period has been very sparsely studied. The only exception to this general neglect was the debate over resonance theory, in many ways a consequence of the coziness of chemists with the regime and the top-heavy dominance of the academy. Resonance theory was developed by American chemist Linus Pauling (1901-1994) in 1930 to account for the fact that many organic molecules could be written as having several distinct molecular structures, even though there was only one molecule present. Pauling argued that each of the structures counted as part of the molecule's true structure, which was in the end a weighted average of all the various possible formulations. In 1949 Gennady V. Chelintsev, an ambitious but not particularly remarkable chemist, argued for an alternative way of writing organic formulas, which would account for the findings of quantum mechanics but not require multiple representations for each molecule, and claimed that this was more in accordance with dialectical materialism. The debate over the theory of resonance occupied the higher levels of the Academy of Sciences and was later interpreted as an attempt to establish an orthodox Lysenkoism in chemistry akin to that in genetics. This interpretation fails on several accounts. First, this debate was initiated from below, by chemists, and not from above, as the analogy with Lysenko would suggest. Second, claims made against resonance actually had philosophical coherence and were received somewhat sympathetically even outside the Soviet Union. Third, this effort failed to become orthodoxy, eventually fading away as a critique, much as resonance itself faded away with the more-comprehensive quantum chemistry of molecular orbital theory.

It is difficult to disentangle the end of Soviet chemistry from the fate of the other sciences, as excessive centralization in the Academy of Sciences, fragmentation into various specialized and classified institutes, and inadequate material supplies and funding hurt all the sciences. Chemistry, unlike ecology or physics, did not play an especially significant role in the collapse of the Soviet order, although a new phase may have opened with the end of the Cold War because chemists' expertise is necessary to help destroy the stocks of chemical agents they helped build for a state whose patronage no longer sustained the science.

Bibliography: In general, see Iurii Ivanovich Solov'ev, *Istoriia khimii v Rossii. Nauchnye tsentry i osnovnye napravleniia issledovanii* (M., 1985), and V.V. Kozlov, *Vsesoiuznoe khimicheskoe obshchestvo imeni D.I. Mendeleeva, 1868-1968* (M., 1971). On the genesis of a chemical community in imperial Russia, see especially Nathan Marc Brooks, "The Formation of a Community of Chemists in Russia, 1700-1870" (Ph.D. diss., Columbia University, 1989), and Alexander Vucinich, *Science in Russian Culture*, 2 vols. (Stanford, Cal., 1963-1970). On the transition from imperial to Soviet chemistry, see Nathan M. Brooks, "Chemistry in War, Revolution, and Upheaval. Russia and the Soviet Union, 1900-1929," *Centaurus*, Vol. 39 (1997), 349-367. On the particulars of Soviet chemistry, see Alexander Vucinich, *Empire of Knowledge. The Academy of Sciences of the USSR, 1917-1970* (Berkeley, Cal., 1984), and Loren R. Graham, *Science, Philosophy, and Human Behavior in the Soviet Union* (New York, 1987), especially Chapter 9 on the resonance controversy.

Michael D. Gordin

CHEPTSOV, EFIM MIKHAILOVICH (1874-1950). Socialist realist painter.

Cheptsov ranks among the leading Soviet genre painters of the revolutionary era. He was born in the village of Medvenka, near Kursk, in 1874. His initial training came at the icon painting school at the Monastery of the Caves in Kiev, after which he worked as an icon painter and illustrator. He also studied at the Tenisheva School and between 1905 and 1911 at the St. Petersburg Academy of the Arts. Between 1911 and 1913 he traveled and studied in Germany, Austria-Hungary, France, and Italy. His work from as late as 1918 has been described as bearing the obvious stamp of late academicism.

After the Bolshevik Revolution he adapted the quasi-documentary style associated with Vasily Perov and other Russian painters of the 1860s to Soviet subjects in the 1920s and 1930s. Among his most famous works are A Meeting of the Village Communist Cell (1924) and the Retraining of Teachers (1925). He was an influential teacher at the Soviet Academy of Art in Leningrad from 1937 and at the Potemkin Pedagogical Institute in Moscow. His later work is completely typical of socialist realism. Representative works are included in the collections of the Tretiakov Gallery and the Kursk Art Museum. He died in Moscow in 1950.

Bibliography: Hirshhorn Museum and Sculpture Garden, *Russian and Soviet Paintings, 1900-1930* (Washington, 1988); John Milner, *A Dictionary of Russian and Soviet Artists* (Woodbridge, Eng., 1993); A.M. Muratov, V. Manin, et al., *Zhivopis' 20-30kh godov* (SPb., 1991); O.S. Ostroi and I.S. Saksonova, *Izobrazitel'noe i prikladnoe iskusstvo* (SPb., 2002); *Russkoe iskusstvo. Illiustrirovannia entsiklopediia* (M., 2001).

Abbott Gleason

CHERDYN. Capital of Cherdyn territory (raion) of Perm district (oblast).

Cherdyn is located 185 miles (300 km) north of Perm on the right bank of the Kolva River, a tributary of the Vishera, which flows into the Kama. The Russian town arose on the site of a settlement that was continuously occupied from the eighth to the fifteenth century by the Komi- Permiak, an aboriginal people of the Urals. It is first mentioned in the Vychegda-Vymsky chronicle in 1451 in connection with the appointment of viceroy (namestnik) Mikhail Ermolich by the Moscow prince

Vasily II. In the official list of fifteenth- to seventeenth-century chronicles the town is called Great Perm Cherdyn. In 1462 the population of the town and region accepted Orthodoxy. In that same year the Ioann Bogoslovsky Monastery, the first to be established in the Urals, was founded at Cherdyn. Great Perm Cherdyn was incorporated into the Russian state in 1472. In 1535 a fortress was erected at the town to protect the eastern borders of Muscovy from raids by Siberian Tatars and Voguls (Mansi).

In the middle of the sixteenth century Cherdyn became the center of Cherdyn district, the largest in the Urals. Moscow's viceroys were replaced by commanders (voevody) in 1572. In 1579 there were 290 households in Cherdyn, including 326 men. Sixty-five merchants and five forges did business there. In the sixteenth and seventeenth centuries the town and district supplied servicemen and supplies to the newly founded cities and settlements beyond the Urals. In the sixteenth and seventeenth centuries Cherdyn district was increasingly populated and dominated by Russian peasants, who had come from the Northern Dvina River basin and Lake Onega area. In the mid-seventeenth century Russians became the dominant ethnic group not only in Cherdyn district but throughout the northern Urals.

Cherdyn ceased to be important as an administrative and defensive center in the eastern borderlands in the seventeenth and eighteenth centuries. It ceded that role to Solikamsk, Kungur, Stroganovsky Novy Usol, and then to Perm. Despite that, Cherdyn remained the center of a district containing extensive lands of the northern Kama and the upper Pechora rivers. The borders of Cherdyn district remained unchanged from the seventeenth century until 1923.

As a district center Cherdyn remained relatively important. Cherdyn merchants controlled most of the transit trade among the Kama, Pechora, and Vychegda river basins. The district zemstvo, which was established in 1870, contributed greatly to the economic development of the area.

Stone churches and cathedrals soon replaced wooden structures in Cherdyn. The Ioanno-Bogoslovsky Cathedral was erected in 1718. The Voskresensky (1750-1785, reconstructed 1908-1911), Preobrazhensky (1756, 1853), Bogoiavlensky (1751-1778), Uspensky (1754-1784, 1884), Troitsky (1817-1838), and Vsesviatsky (1815-1817) cathedrals followed during the next century. In 1857 a stone shopping arcade with an open gallery was constructed on market square. Other public buildings and the estates of the wealthier merchant families helped shape the appearance of Cherdyn. The merchant house of cooperatives built in 1891, the town's administrative center in the second half of the nineteenth-early twentieth century, the women's high school and the parish school in the late nineteenth-early twentieth centuries, the trade school in 1900, district hospital in 1913, and the complex of buildings of the G.M. Lunegov almshouse and shelter of the late nineteenth century were among the most significant. The Aliny, Gusev, Cherny, Protopopov, Michurin, and Merkuriev family estates in the second half of the nineteenth and early twentieth centuries were among the most architecturally impressive.

The oldest parts of the city reflect early planning assumptions. They are dominated by the market square and cathedrals, which are oriented to the direction of light rather than to the grid of streets. Most of the rest of the town follows the rectangular grid of streets and avenues laid out in the first half of the nineteenth century. The view of the town from the river is dominated by hills with picturesquely arranged complexes of church buildings and residential properties. The highest point in the town as in earlier days remains the Grado-Cherdynsky Voskresensky Cathedral. Some residents consider the burial ground of eighty-five defenders of Great Perm, who died in battle with Siberian Tatars in 1547, a sacred place. It is located within the town at the gates of Kondratiev Settlement on the Vishera River. A chapel containing an icon representing the martyrs and an iron plate inscribed with their names once stood at the gravesite. The Orthodox Church raised the town's defenders to the rank of local saints, and they were worshiped as patrons and intercessors. At the present time a wooden cross stands at the spot.

In 1911 the women's monastery, which was abolished in the 1760s, was reopened. In 1915 it became a shelter for orphans whose parents died at the front in World War I. The monastery was closed again in 1919, but Abbess Rufinia managed to reorganize it in Shanghai. In the 1940s, in accordance with the testament of Rufinia, the nuns led by Abbess Ariadna moved to San Francisco where they founded the Bogoroditsa-Vladimir cloister, the successor to the Cherdyn monastery.

Many explorers, travelers and other notable personages visited Cherdyn. They include N.P. Rychkov (1770), A.I. Shergen (1828), E.K. Gofman (1847-1850), M.E. Saltykov-Shchedrin (1854-1855), D.N. Mamin-Sibiriak (1888), Charles Rabot (1890), Yu.M. Shokalsky (1890), and O.E. Mandelshtam (1934). Their writings are excellent sources for the study of the history and culture of the region.

A Society of Lovers of History, Archaeology, and Ethnography of Cherdyn Region functioned in Cherdyn between 1898 and 1918. It established a Museum of Antiquity. In 1899 the Cherdyn district zemstvo administration opened the A.S. Pushkin Museum for General Education. The collections of those two museums became the foundation of Cherdyn's A.S. Pushkin Regional Studies Museum that operates today. The museum has unique archeological finds, documents, and other materials on the merchant dynasties, the town, and peasant life, and local icons. In 2000 a museum of the history of Orthodoxy was opened in Cherdyn, the second in Russia after the museum of the history of religion in St. Petersburg.

The population of Cherdyn in 2002 was 6,500. Offices of local and regional businesses are located in the town, which has several libraries, a regional artistic center (formerly dom kultury), and model middle and other specialized schools.

Bibliography: G.N. Chagrin, *Goroda Permi Velikoi Cherdyn' i Solikamsk* (Perm, 2004); G.N. Chagrin, ed., *Cherdyn'. Kratkii istoricheskii ocherk* (Perm, 1972), *Na drevnei Permskoi zemle* (M., 1988), *Iz proshlogo Cherdynskogo kraia* (Perm, 1974); V.V. Kostochkin, *Cherdyn'. Solikamsk. Usol'e* (M., 1988); *Perm Velikaia Cherdyn'* (Perm, 1999); *Cherdyn' i Ural v istoricheskom i kul'turnom nasledii Rossii* (Perm, 1999); *Pravoslavie v russkoi kul'ture* (Cherdyn', 2001); William C. Brumfield, "Photographic Documentation of Architectural Monuments in the Northern Districts of Perm Province, Russia," *Visual Resources,* Vol. 18 (2002), 17-48.

Georgii N. Chagin

CHERENKOV, PAVEL ALEKSEEVICH (1904-1990). Physicist, Nobel Prize winner.

Cherenkov's career in science can be seen as a strikingly successful result of Soviet policies that made advanced education more open to representatives of the lower classes, thereby accelerating their promotion into established professional and academic elites. Particularly strong until the mid-1930s, those policies included reversed class privileges in education and relaxation of formal barriers between successive stages, allowing one, for example, to start university without completing secondary education, or to be hired as professor without a Ph.D. Such opportunities enabled Cherenkov to receive higher education, opening up what became an illustrious life in science.

Cherenkov was born into a peasant family on 28 July 1904 in the village of Novaia Chigla in Voronezh province. When he was two, his mother died and his father remarried. The boy started working as a manual laborer at the age of thirteen with only two years of elementary schooling. In 1920, when a Soviet secondary school opened in his village, Cherenkov resumed his education while supporting himself by occasional work at a grocery. In 1924 he enrolled in the Pedagogical Department of Voronezh State University and after graduation in 1928 became a teacher of physics and mathematics at an evening school for workers in Kozlov, now Michurinsk, in Tambov province. Several major changes occurred in Cherenkov's life in 1930. He married the daughter of a philology professor from Voronezh and was admitted to the newly established graduate program at the Physico-Mathematical Institute of the USSR Academy of Sciences and moved to Leningrad. In the same year his father-in-law was arrested as a bourgeois professor and sent to work in a prison camp, and his own father was persecuted and exiled as a kulak.

In Leningrad the course of Cherenkov's study took a new turn in 1932 when the academy appointed S.I. Vavilov to head the institute's physics division and develop it into a full-fledged Physical Institute of the Academy (FIAN). A specialist in luminescence, the emission of light by some substances in the absence of high temperatures, Vavilov wanted to encourage the development of novel fields despite the lack of senior experts. He directed several graduate students to start a nuclear physics laboratory on their own and asked Cherenkov to study whether luminescence in some solutions, ordinarily induced by incoming light, can also be caused by gamma rays from a radioactive source. A clever experimental method developed by Vavilov in the 1920s, when equipment was scarce, allowed observations of faint luminescence, almost at the threshold of single quanta, by the naked eye after two hours of adaptation in complete darkness. Following this technique Cherenkov noticed, in addition to expected luminescence, that passing gamma rays produced a faint background glow that remained present in pure liquids like water, not only in luminescent solutions. Vavilov's expertise helped recognize this phenomenon as a novel, heretofore unknown kind of radiation. They published the discovery of blue light in 1934 as two related papers, the experimental by Cherenkov and the theoretical by Vavilov.

In 1935 Cherenkov defended his thesis (kandidat nauk) and remained at FIAN as a research associate when the institute moved to Moscow. In the preceding decades physics saw several cases of widely publicized discoveries of spurious rays. Some Soviet colleagues and foreign visitors believed FIAN's search for an almost invisible radiation in the dark more spiritism and ghost-hunting. In the face of widespread skepticism Cherenkov stubbornly persisted, and in a series of subsequent studies that became the basis of his second thesis (doktor nauk, defended in 1940), discovered unexpected properties of the new radiation, including its distinctive directedness. This feature helped FIAN theoreticians I.E. Tamm and I.M. Frank explain the phenomenon in 1937.

The Cherenkov or Vavilov-Cherenkov radiation is produced when electrons travel through a substance faster than light does, but slower than light travels in a vacuum so that no contradiction with Einstein's theory of relativity arises. It is the optical analog of shock waves in acoustics, the sound produced in the air by an ultrasonic projectile or jet aircraft. The phenomenon of Vavilov-Cherenkov radiation can thus be used for registering fast-traveling subatomic particles. Such new detectors, called Cherenkov counters, were designed and became widely used in high-energy accelerators after World War II when they helped physicists discover new elementary particles, for example the antiproton. The 1958 Nobel Prize in physics was awarded to Cherenkov, Tamm, and Frank for the discovery and the interpretation of the Cherenkov effect. Vavilov was no longer alive and thus could not be nominated. In the Soviet Union the discovery received the Stalin Prize in 1946.

Cherenkov worked at FIAN for the rest of his life. He contributed to the establishment of the first Soviet high-altitude cosmic ray stations and improved detectors for them. During World War II FIAN was evacuated to Kazan where Cherenkov worked on acoustical systems for air defense. In 1944 he joined the Communist Party. Between 1946 and 1958 Cherenkov assisted V.I. Veksler in the design of new generations of particle accelerators, the betatron and the synchrotron, for which he, among other contributors, received the 1951 Stalin Prize. Most of the work he did in those years was classified at the time, although not necessarily for good reasons. Starting in 1959 he directed the FIAN laboratory that studied how photons interact with mesons and nucleons, a series of studies that was awarded the USSR State Prize of 1977, and he was instrumental in the establishment of a new synchrotron laboratory in Troitsk, near Moscow. Between 1951 and 1977 he also taught as a professor at the Moscow Institute of Physical Engineers (MIFI).

After the war, as the use of Cherenkov's 1934 discovery and his fame grew in the West, his reputation and standing at home remained modest, overshadowed by more illustrious colleagues. Cherenkov was elected to the USSR Academy of Sciences only after he received the Nobel Prize. In 1965 he became a corresponding member and in 1970 an ordinary member of the academy. In 1985 he was elected to the US National Academy of Sciences as a foreign member. He was reluctant to allow the use of his famous name in order to promote projects and for public relation purposes. In speech and writing he also tried to avoid using the phrases "the Cherenkov effect" and "Cherenkov counters," which had become standard terminology in physics.

Besides the research in physics that occupied him until his death, Cherenkov was also active in the Soviet Peace Committee, the Soviet Committee of the Organization for Security and Co-operation in Europe Committee, and in the Pugwash Conferences on Science and World Affairs. He was fond of tennis and photography. His family lived in a communal apartment until 1962, when they finally moved into a separate flat. His two children, a son and a daughter, became scientists. The death of his wife in 1978 was a very severe blow to him. Cherenkov died in Moscow on 6 January 1990.

Bibliography: Pavel Alekseevich Cherenkov, 1904-1990. Materialy k biobibliografii uchenykh (M., 1997); A.N. Gorbunov and E.P.Cherenkova, eds., *Pavel Alekseevich Cherenkov. Chelovek i otkrytie* (M., 1999); I.M. Frank, "A Conceptual History of the Vavilov-Cherenkov Radiation," *Soviet Physics Uspekhi*, Vol. 27 (1984), 385-95; *Nobel lectures, including presentation speeches and laureates' biographies. Physics* (Amsterdam, 1967).

Alexei B. Kojevnikov

CHEREPNIN, ALEKSANDR NIKOLAEVICH (1899-1977). French: Tcherepnin. Polystylist composer.

Cherepnin was born on 8 January 1899 in St. Petersburg, the son of composer Nikolai Cherepnin and Marie Benois. While his early musical education was somewhat spotty, the prominence of his father in Russian musical circles brought him into contact with such important musical personalities of the day as Anatol Liadov (1855-1914), César Cui (1835-1918), Nikolai Rimsky-Korsakov (1844-1908), Igor Stravinsky (1882-1971), and Sergei Prokofiev (1891-1953). He began his composition early and by age fourteen had produced numerous small piano pieces which he later published. In 1918 the elder Cherepnin moved his family to Tiflis (Tbilisi), Georgia, where his son absorbed much of the local musical color. After three years the family moved to Paris where Alexander studied piano with Isidore Philippe, who encouraged and championed the young composer's music. In Paris Cherepnin composed his first large-scale works, such as his Symphony No. 1 (1927)

In 1938 Cherepnin married Lee Hsien Ming, a pianist he met in China. The couple returned to Paris, where Cherepnin prepared a compilation entitled *Anthology of Russian Music* (1938). He also composed a series of works for unusual solo instruments, including the elegant Sonatine sportive (1939) for alto saxophone and piano. During World War II the Cherepnin family was trapped in Paris during the German occupation, but Nikolai managed to make a living by preparing musical arrangements.

In 1948 DePaul University in Chicago invited him to teach composition, analysis, and music history, and in 1949 he moved his family to Chicago, where they remained for fifteen years. In 1958 the Cherepnins became citizens of the United States. During his stay in Chicago Cherepnin was an active teacher and promoter of new American music. He numbered among his students Robert Muczynski

(1929-), Gloria Coates (1938-), John Downey (1927-), and Phillip Ramey (1939-). At the same time he composed and premiered his Divertimento (1955), Fourth Symphony (1956), and Symphonic Prayer (1959).

After retiring from DePaul University in 1964 he moved to New York and began an active career as a pianist, conductor and composer. In 1967 Cherepnin gave a concert tour of Russia at the invitation of the Soviet government, an event that was personally important in that it allowed him to visit places associated with his youth. He died in Paris of a heart attack on 29 September 1977. At the time of his death he was working on two symphonies, one for percussion alone.

In terms of musical language Cherepnin could be described as a polystylist. He created artificial scales from which he derived his harmonies. For example, he employs a nine-step scale in his early Sonatine romantique for solo piano (1918), which through transposition and permutation yields thirty-six variants. In his much later Piano Sonata No. 2 (1961) he employed an eight-step scale derived from a Greek tetrachord. Together with traditional major-minor tonality and modality derived from Georgian and Asian folk music and Russian liturgical chant, these combine to create an extended tonal musical language. His music also distinguishes itself for its clear structural logic, rhythmic and contrapuntal textures, and use of neglected instruments.

Works: Operas: Die Hochzeit der Sobeide, op. 45 (after Hofmannsthal), 1930 (Vienna, 1933); Die Heirat, op. 53, 1933 (Essen, 1937); The Farmer and the Nymph, op.72 (Aspen, Colo., 1952). Ballets: Ajanta's Frescoes, op. 32 (London, 1923); La Femme et Son Ombre, op. 79 (after Claudel) (Paris, 1948); Le Gouffre (after Andreev), 1953 (Nuremberg, 1969). Orchestral Works: Piano Concerto No. 1, op. 12, 1919; Rhapsodie Georgienne, op. 25, for violoncello and orchestra, 1922; Symphony No. 2, op. 77, 1947; Piano Concerto No. 4, op. 78, 1947; Symphony No. 3, op. 83, 1952; Harmonica Concerto, op. 86, 1953. Vocal: Les Douze, op. 73, for speaker and chamber orchestra, 1945; Seven Chinese Folksongs, op. 95, voice, piano, 1962; Six Liturgical Songs, op. 103, for chorus, 1967. Chamber: String Quartet No. 1, op. 36, 1922; String Quartet No. 2, op. 40, 1926; Piano Quintet, op. 44, 1927; Sonatine Sportive, op. 63, alto saxophone, piano, 1939; Sonata da Chiesa, op. 101, viola da gamba, organ (flute, strings, harpsichord), 1966. Keyboard, etc.: Bagatelles, op. 5, piano, 1913; Sonatine Romantique, piano, 1918; Piano Sonata No. 1, op. 22, 1918; Piano Sonata No. 2, op. 94, 1961; Processional and Recessional, organ, 1962; Tzigane, accordion, 1966; Caprices Diatoniques, Celtic harp, 1973.

References: A. Tcherepnin, "A Short Autobiography," *Tempo,* no. 130 (1979), 12; E. Arias, "Alexander Tcherepnin's Thoughts on Music," *PNM,* Vol. 21 (1982), 138, "The Symphonies of Alexander Tcherepnin," *Tempo,* no. 158 (1986), 23, *Alexander Tcherepnin. A Bio-Bibliography* (Westport, Conn., 1989).

Gregory Myers

CHEREPNIN, NIKOLAI NIKOLAEVICH (1873-1945). French: Tcherepnin. Ballet composer, conductor, teacher.

Cherepnin was born in St. Petersburg on 3 May 1873, the son of a prominent physician. The Cherepnin household was a musical one. His father held regular musical soirees every Tuesday evening. In accordance with his father's wishes Cherepnin pursued a law degree but composed on the side. In 1897 he married Marie Benois, niece of the celebrated painter and set designer, and in 1898 he received an advanced diploma in composition from the St. Petersburg Conservatory where he was a student of Nikolai Rimsky-Korsakov (1844-1908). Over the years Cherepnin developed a close friendship with the older composer.

After his graduation from the conservatory Cherepnin joined the Mariinsky Theater as a choral conductor, eventually becoming one of the house's leading opera and ballet conductors. From this point on Cherepnin made steady progress on both fronts of his dual composing and conducting career. He began one of his important ballet scores, Le Pavillon d'Armide, Op. 29, followed by another successful programmatic piece, Le Royaume Enchanté, in 1904. At the same time his skill as an operatic conductor was such that Rimsky-Korsakov often requested that Cherepnin lead every important performance of his works. For example, when the Paris Opéra Comique decided to mount Rimsky's The Snow Maiden (Snegurochka) in 1908, they wrote to the composer and asked him to recommend a Russian conductor for the performance. Without hesitation Rimsky sent Cherepnin to Paris.

His success as a conductor and composer served to raise his prestige and profile in the musical world, and he soon caught the attention of Sergei Diaghilev, who chose Cherepnin to conduct for the 1909 spring season of his ballet in Paris. Diaghilev was impressed by the suite Cherepnin had made from his 1907 ballet Pavillon d'Armide and programmed a performance of the entire ballet as one of three works for the spring season.

In addition to his work with Diaghilev's Ballet Russe, Cherepnin continued his employment with the Mariinsky Theater. He joined the faculty of the St. Petersburg Conservatory in 1908 where he taught composition and conducting. These duties brought him into contact with his star pupil, the precocious Sergei Prokofiev. In contrast to the rather negative response to his modernistic tendencies that the young Prokofiev received from the conservatory's director, Alexander Glazunov, Cherepnin encouraged him in his experiments. Their relationship was such that Prokofiev dedicated his Piano Concerto No. 1 to Cherepnin. In 1911 Cherepnin scored another success with his ballet Narcisse, which was premiered by the Ballet Russe in Monte Carlo. It was at this time that another rising star appeared on the horizon, one whose presence nearly eclipsed Cherepnin, the young Igor Stravinsky.

In spite of the hardships brought about by World War I and the growing political and social unrest that climaxed with the Russian Revolution, Cherepnin managed to successfully mount another stage work, The Masque of the Red Death, based on Edgar Allen Poe's story. Because of the World War and the Civil War that immediately ensued, life became increasingly difficult because of the growing food shortage in Petrograd. In 1918 Nikolai Cherepnin received an offer to become director of the National Conservatory in Tiflis (Tblisi), Georgia, which escaped much of the impact of the World War and was not experiencing yet the effects of the Revolution of 1917. He and his family disposed of their possessions and left Petrograd to undertake an arduous summer journey to the Caucasus.

The Cherepnins remained in Georgia for three years, and while there he absorbed much of that musical landscape in the form of folk music. The Revolution then caught up with the family and they fled to Batumi. The increasing Bolshevik presence finally prompted the family to apply for emigration, and on 16 June 1921 they sailed to Constantinople, where they waited for a French visa. On 4 August they left Turkey and reached France nine days later.

Cherepnin only achieved a modicum of success in Paris. For a time he was director of the Russian Conservatory, and Diaghilev mounted his ballets Dionysus (1922) and Russian Fairy Tale (1923). Diaghilev, however, was losing interest in Cherepnin. Cherepnin completed Mussorgsky's comic opera Sorochinsky Fair (Sorochinskaia Yarmarka), which was accepted by the Monte Carlo opera. It was mounted under his direction in 1924. Six years later it was staged by the Metropolitan Opera in New York. Meanwhile, Cherepnin found only occasional work in Paris as a conductor, performing the operas of Rimsky-Korsakov.

Cherepnin once again tasted success when in 1932 he was invited by Serge Koussevitsky to guest conduct the Boston Symphony. Koussevitsky commissioned Cherepnin's Three Pieces for Orchestra after a Tale of Edgar Allan Poe, Op. 59, and the celebrated piano virtuoso Benno Moiseivitch championed Cherepnin's Piano Concerto in C-sharp Minor, Op. 30. About this time Cherepnin expanded his compositional output and made his first forays into composing opera, although his most famous and ambitious work was his 1937 oratorio, The Descent of the Virgin into Hell (Khozhdenie Bogoroditsy po mukam), which premiered in Paris that year. In 1941 the Cherepnin family attempted to flee Paris ahead of the Nazi invasion. They did not succeed and remained trapped in the city. Cherepnin died there on 26 June 1945. Cherepnin never again achieved the success he had known in the years before World War I, living in the musical shadow of his more famous contemporaries, Prokofiev and Stravinsky, yet his music contains much that is fresh and original.

Works: Operas: Svat (after N. Ostrovsky, *Bednost' ne porok*), 1930 (Paris, 1930); Van'ka-kliuchnik (after F. Sologub), 1932 (Belgrade, 1933). Ballets: Le pavillon d'Armide (A. Benois, after T. Gautier), 1907 (St. Petersburg, Mariinsky, 1907); Nartsiss (Narcisse et Echo) (L. Bakst, after Ovid, Metamorphoses), 1911 (Monte Carlo, Casino, 1911); Maska krasnoi smerti (choreodrama, after E.A. Poe), 1915 (Brussels, La Monnaie, 1956); Vakkh, 1922 (London, Covent Garden, 1922); Russkaia volshebnaia skazka, 1923 (London, 1923); Roman mumii (after Gautier), 1924 (London, Covent Garden, 1924). Choral: 2 khora, chorus, orchestra, 1899; Pesn' Safo (cantata on texts by Ye. Zarin), soprano, female chorus, orchestra, 1899. Oratorio: Khozhdenie Bogoroditsy po mukam (Russian oratorio on apocryphal texts), 1934. Orchestral: La princesse lointaine, 1896; Iz kraia v krai, 1903; Zacharovannoe tsarstvo, 1910; Tale about the Fisherman and the Fish, 1917; Sud'ba, 1938. Chamber and Solo Instrumental: String Quartet, 1898; Liricheskaia poema,

1900; Azbuka v kartinkakh; Cadence fantastique, violin and piano, 1915. Orchestrations: Musorgsky, Sorochinskaia iarmaka, 1923.

References: Yu. Shaporin, "Moi uchitelia," *Sovetskaia muzyka*, No. 9 (1962), 96; O. Tompakova, "N.N. Cherepnin," *Muzykal'naia zhizn'*, No. 1 (1974), 15; M. Bikhter, "Listki iz knigi vospominanii. N.N. Cherepnin," *Sovetskaia muzyka*, No. 9 (1959), 130; N. Cherepnin, *Vospominaniia muzykanta* (L., 1976); D. Street, "A Forgotten Firebird," *Musical Times*, Vol. 119 (1978), 674.

Gregory Myers

CHERKASHENIN, MIKHAIL (?-1581). Ataman of the Don Cossack Host.

Mikhail Cherkashenin is mentioned only a few times in historical documents of the sixteenth century, but he figures prominently in Cossack folklore. He is first mentioned in 1548 in connection with the establishment of Cossack forts at the Great Portage (perevoz) between the Volga and Don rivers, where the Volga-Don Canal is now located. These were settlements surrounded by sharpened poles from which the Cossacks ventured to do battle with Tatars led by Elbuzuk.

In extant literary sources Cherkashenin is written with small letters, cherkahsenin, indicating that he belonged to the Cherkas, or Ukrainian, people. A description of the naval battle at Kerch in 1556 mentions that Mishka cherkashenin dispatched two pagans, or prisoners. In 1559 Mikhail Cherkashenin defeated the Crimeans on the northern Donets River and sent four pagans to the tsar in Moscow. It was in this time, during the military campaigns of 1556-1559, that the Don Cossacks demonstrated their mastery of naval warfare in battles with the Crimean Tatars. The Cossacks led by Cherkashenin dared ever more frequently to venture into the Sea of Azov and approached the Kerch Strait ever more closely, preparing for expeditions into the Black Sea.

Cherkashenin shows up next at the beginning of 1570 in a charter from Tsar Ivan the Terrible, conveying his envoy Ivan Novosiltstsev to the Turkish sultan Selim. "The tsar and grand prince sent him to the Turkish sultan and ordered Misha Cherkashenin and the atamans and Cossacks to accompany him from Rylsk to the Azov Sea...." As this is one of the first extant tsarist charters concerning the Don, historians usually date the official beginning of the Don Cossack Host from it and from other charters of that period. Mikhail Cherkashenin is one of the first Don Cossack atamans known from historical sources.

Ataman M. Cherkashenin is next mentioned during the destruction of the army of the Crimean khan Devlet-Girei near Moscow in 1572. Cherkashenin's son Danil was captured by the Tatars during this battle and executed in 1574. The Cossacks avenged his execution with the seizure of Taprokalov, also known as Earthen (Zemliany) Town for the ditches and earthen walls that surrounded it. Taprokalov was the first line of defense for the fortress of Azov. According to historian N.M. Karamzin, the bravery of the Don Cossacks led by Cherkashenin amazed Constantinople. Sultan Selim II angrily censured Khan Devlet-Girei that his execution of Danil aroused the anger of the Cossacks, who consequently seized Azov and "took the best people from Azov." As a consequence Ataman Cherkashenin was given the cognomen Wrath of Azov. The Cossacks could not hold Azov for long, partly because Moscow did not want war with Turkey and the Crimea while they were involved in the exhausting Livonian War and partly because Turkish and Crimean forces were still superior.

Cherkashenin also led Cossacks to the western front and participated in the Livonian War. He fought and died at the defense of Pskov, which was besieged by 100,000 troops of Stefan Batory, king of the Rech Pospolita, or Polish-Lithuanian Commonwealth. Approximately 20,000 troops, including 500 Don Cossacks, defended the city during the twenty-week siege. When the main attack took place on 8 September 1581, Pskov's commander (voevoda) I.P. Shuisky ordered the Svinuzsky tower be blown up together with the attacking enemy. The Cossacks blew up the tower, burying hundreds of besiegers under its walls, but Cherkashenin also died in the explosion. His death proved to be not in vain. Soon thereafter Stefan Batory concluded the Yam-Zampolsky Treaty with Moscow (1582). Cherkashenin's heroic death formed the basis of many Cossack legends until they were supplanted by the folklore of Ermak Timofeevich (d. 1584) and Stepan Razin (1630?-1671).

Bibliography: Akty, otnosiashchiesia k istorii Voiska Donskogo, sobrannye General-Maiurom A.A. Lishinym, Vol. 1 (Novocherkassk, 1891); Mikhail Astapenko, *Donskie kazach'i atamany. Istoricheskie ocherki-biografii, 1550-1920 g.g.* (Rostov on Don, 1996); I.F. Bykadorov, *Donskoe voisko v bor'be za vykhod k moriu, 1546-1646* (Paris, 1937); *Istoricheskie pesni XIII-XVI vekov* (M.-L., 1960); N.M. Karamzin, *Istoriia gosudarstva rossiiskogo,* Vol. 3 (Rostov on Don, 1990); S.M. Markedonov, "Kazachii ataman Mikhail Cherkashenin," *Donskoi vremennik* (Rostov on Don, 2000), 75-78; N.A. Mininkov, *Donskoe kazachestvo na zare svoei istorii* (Rostov on Don, 1992); O.P. Nikolaev, "Gibel' atamana Mikhaila Cherkashenina vo vremia oborony Pskova v 1581 godu. Opyt rekonstruktsii lokal'noi legendy" in *Kazachii Peterburg* (SPb., 1995); *Razriadnaia kniga 1475-1598 g.g.* (M., 1966). In English: Linda Gordon, *Cossack Rebellion. Social Turmoil in Sixteenth-Century Ukraine* (Albany, 1983); George G. Grabowicz, *The History of the Myth of Cossack Ukraine in Polish and Russian Romantic Literature* (Ph.D. diss., Harvard University, 1975); Albert Seaton, *The Horseman of the Steppes. The Story of the Cossacks* (London, 1985).

Evgenii I. Kirsanov

CHERKESS. A Caucasian people related to the Abkhazians. Also called Adyge, Kabardin.

Before the Russian revolutions in 1917 the people called the Cherkess, Adygey, and Kabardin were known as Circassians. Today they represent remnants of a once large and powerful group which fought against the Russians during much of the first half of the nineteenth century. Ninety percent of them were killed or forced to flee to the neighboring Ottoman Empire by 1864. Because of this diaspora they are difficult to enumerate. In 1989 the people formerly called Circassians numbered 560,000 in the USSR, although they were much more numerous abroad, including nearly two million persons of Circassian heritage in Southwest Asia alone.

Against the wishes of the Circassian people, the Bolsheviks initially divided the group into two nations, an eastern group known as Kabardin and a western one designated Cherkess. In the 1930s the western branch was subdivided into the Adygey (western Circassians) and the Cherkess (central Circassians). The self-designation of all three peoples has always been Adyge. In 1989 there were 386,000 Kabardins, 123,000 Adygeys, and 51,000 Cherkess in the Soviet Union. The term "Cherkess" is a derivative of the ancient Greek term kerket, which became the common designation of the Russians and Turks for all Circassians.

The majority of Russian Cherkess live in seventeen scattered villages in the northern steppes of the Republic of Karachaevo-Cherkessia on the first of three south-to-north-dipping cuestas (cotes in French) of the Greater Caucasus Mountains. To the west is the vast Kuban River plain and to the east is the Stavropol Upland. Outside Russia most Cherkess live in parts of Southwest Asia and North Africa. All Cherkess are descended from the once united Adyge tribes who, before the Russian advance, occupied the steppes between the Don and Kuban rivers. Modern Cherkess speak the same language as the Kabardins, which is similar to and mutually intelligible with that of the Adygeys. Each language descends from the Abkhaz-Adyge group of Caucasian languages. In the early nineteenth century a Circassian literary language arose on the basis of the Baksan dialect. The original Arabic script was superseded by the Latin in 1923 and by the Cyrillic in 1936. Most Cherkess are Sunni Muslims of the Hanafi school.

Despite protection from and alliance with the Crimean Tatars and other Turkic tribes, including the Karachais, with whom they are now paired in their republic, the Cherkess came under Russian control during the reign of Ivan the Terrible (r. 1533-1584). Relations with the Russians soured as Russian settlers encroached on the Cherkess homelands. After the Treaty of Adrianople (1829), by which the Ottomans ceded the Caucasus region to Russia, the Caucasian tribes, including the Cherkess, rose up in periodic rebellions only to meet with harsh Russian reprisals. After three decades of continual bloodshed the Russians finally conquered the Caucasus region.

In 1928 Stalinist authorities created a Cherkess Autonomous District (oblast, AO), which they later merged with the nearby Karachai AO to become the Karachaevo-Cherkess AO. The Caucasian Cherkess and Turkic Karachais were never happy with the arrangement. During the Second World War the Karachais were banished to Central Asia, but the Cherkess were allowed to stay. Between 1943 and 1957, when the Karachais returned, the district was named simply the Cherkess AO. In 1992 Karachaevo-Cherkessia was recognized as a republic within the Russian Federation.

A turning point in the relations between the Cherkess and Karachais came during the republic's first presidential elections on 12 May 1999. An ethnic Cherkess won 40 percent of the votes in the first round but only 12 percent in the runoff. Simultaneously an ethnic Karachai secured only 18 percent of the first-round votes and 85 percent in the second. The apparent irregularities provoked violence and ethnic unrest. The republic's Supreme Court validated the vote in favor of the Karachais. The Cherkess have continued to stew and have demanded the reconstitution of the Cherkess AO inside the contiguous Stavropol Territory (Krai). The events have also aroused the disapproval of other Circassian groups.

The republic's labor force is roughly divided between industry (23.0 percent) and agriculture (19.3 percent). Agriculture leads in value of output. The Kuban River plain is the most fertile region in the Russian Federation, yielding bumper harvests of winter wheat, spring barley, rice, sunflower seeds, sugar beets, and vegetables, raised primarily by Cherkess. Substantial herds of cattle, sheep, and goats are raised on both steppe and mountain pastures. In non-Muslim areas pigs may be found wandering the village streets. The republic's primary industries are petrochemicals, mechanical engineering, metal work, building materials, wood processing, and coal mining. Since the collapse of the USSR more than 2,000 small businesses have sprung up.

Bibliography: On the precise location and homeland of the Cherkess, see *Atlas SSSR* (M., 1983). On their language and ethnic relations, see two books by Ronald Wixman, *Language Aspects of Ethnic Patterns and Processes in the North Caucasus* (Chicago, Ill., 1980) and *The Peoples of the USSR. An Ethnographic Handbook* (Armonk, N.Y., 1984). On their history, economy, and other characteristics, see V.A. Tishkov, ed., *Narody Rossii. Entsiklopediia* (M., 1994) and Philip Hanson and Michael J. Bradshaw, *The Territories of the Russian Federation, 2001* (London, 2001).

Victor L. Mote

CHERNOBYL. Ukrainian city. To the end of the nineteenth century also spelled Chernobol. Since the independence of Ukraine in the 1990s written Chornobyl. In Belorussian Czarnobyl.

The city is situated in north-central Ukraine, seventy miles (113 km) from the Ukrainian capital Kiev (Kyiv), on the Pripiat River at its confluence with the Uzh. Its name derives from the Eastern Slavic name for wormwood (Latin, Artemisia vulgaris; Russian chernobylnik), an aromatic spice and leaf mainly used by the liqueur industry. Chernobyl became widely known after a nuclear accident occurred at an atomic power plant ten miles (16 km) from the city on 26 April 1986.

Chernobyl is first mentioned in medieval chronicles at the end of the twelfth century (Hypatian Chronicle, 1193). It became part of the Grand Duchy of Lithuania in 1362 and received the status of a town (mestechko) in 1566. After the Union of Lublin (1569) Chernobyl came under the power of the shliachta (nobility) of Poland. Between 1648 and 1654 residents of Chernobyl took part in the Ukrainian war of liberation. As a consequence of the second partition of Poland in 1793 under Catherine II (r. 1762-1796) Chernobyl became Russian territory. During Catherine's reign dissident sectarians (raskolniki) from the Starodubsky district were resettled to Chernobyl (1775). This was part of Catherine's policy to settle people of different faiths in the newly conquered borderlands in addition to Orthodox Cossacks. In the 1897 census Chernobyl was located in the Radomyslsky district of Kiev province.

It then had 9,351 residents. In 1926, following the World War and the Russian Civil War, Chernobyl's population fell to 9,000. It achieved the status of a city in 1941. When construction of the Chernobyl atomic power plant began in 1971, the city had 10,000 inhabitants. In independent Ukraine Chornobyl is part of the Yvakivsky region in the province of Kiev.

Burial mounds or tumuli (kurgany) of a semi-nomadic pastoralist culture that spread from the Russian steppes to Danubian Europe around 3500 B.C. have been excavated in the vicinity of Chernobyl. Iron weapons and pieces of gold and silver have been found in them. A hoard of silver Roman coins from approximately 139 B.C. to A.D. 40 also was unearthed in the area.

Chernobyl has two Orthodox churches dating back to the thirteenth century and one Catholic church, constructed in the sixteenth century. Until 1832 Chernobyl had a Dominican monastery, and in the nineteenth century two Orthodox chapels, two parish schools, and a Jewish poorhouse operated in the city. Jews first came to Chernobyl at the end of the seventeenth century. By 1765, 700 Jews lived in the Chernobyl community. A century later the Chernobyl Jewish community numbered 3,482. It sponsored a talmud torah school, and in 1910 it opened a high school for Jewish women. By the time of the 1897 census more than 50 percent of Chernobyl's population were Jewish (5,536). Since the first Jewish settlers arrived in the seventeenth century the city has been residence of the Chernobyl Hasidic masters (tsaddikim).

In the nineteenth century Chernobyl had three market places in which the trade of local products, such as resin, birch tar, tobacco, and fish, predominated. Following the nuclear accident in 1986 all of Chernobyl's residents were evacuated and have not been permitted to return.

See also Chernobyl Nuclear Accident, SMERSH, Vol. 5.

Bibliography: "Chernobyl (Czarnobyl)," *Evreiskaia entsiklopediia,* Vol. 15 (SPb., 1908- 1913), 859; "Chernobylskaia familiia tsadikov," ibid., 859-860; Petr T. Tutkovskii, "Chernobyl," *Entsiklopedicheskii slovar',* Vol. 78 (SPb., 1903), 607; *Bolshaia sovetskaia entsiklopediia,* Vol. 29 (M., 1978), 88; *Entsiklopediia Ukrainoznasvtva,* Vol. 10 (Kiev, 1984), 376; *Ukraïnska radianska entsiklopediia,* Vol. 12 (1985), 336; O.M. Marinich and E.I. Stetsenko, "Chernobyl," *Geografichna entsiklopediia Ukraïny,* Vol. 3 (Kyiv, 1993), 428.

Markus Wolf

CHERNOBYL NUCLEAR ACCIDENT (1986). To date, the world's worst nuclear reactor accident.

A sage once said that nuclear power is a Faustian bargain. Before 26 April 1986 the Chernobyl (Ukrainian: Chornobyl) nuclear power plant ranked among the ten largest electric power producers in the Soviet Union. Located ten miles (16 km) south of the Belarus border on the outskirts of the Ukrainian town of Pripiat, approximately eleven miles (18 km) northwest of the town of Chernobyl (51°16' N 30°14' E) and seventy miles (113 km) north of Kiev (Kyiv), the capital and largest Ukrainian city, the power plant included four recently-built reactors with rated capacities of 1,000 megawatts (mw) each. Plant construction began in the 1970s. Reactor No. 1 was commissioned in 1977, followed by No. 2 in 1978, No. 3 in 1981, and No. 4 in 1983. The planned addition of two more 1,000 mw reactors later in the 1980s would have made Chernobyl the largest nuclear power station and the second most powerful producer of electricity in the USSR. In the spring of 1986 it produced 10 percent of Ukraine's total electric output. A year before the disaster the Chernobyl plant was featured in the journal Soviet Life, which touted it as a model of cleanliness and efficiency, the very quintessence of Soviet technological supe-riority. Because of this superiority the Chernobyl reactors, like all Soviet nuclear reactors at the time, were free of allegedly needless, expensive containment domes. Moreover, the Chernobyl reactors used graphite-moderated technology, a type rejected in a highly classified report as unsafe by the US Atomic Energy Commission as early as 1956. This information unfortunately never was shared with Soviet sci-entists. Such was strategy during the Cold War.

At 12:23:58 a.m. on 26 April 1986 two to possibly five explosions destroyed the reactor and reactor building of Chernobyl No. 4, sending flames and chunks of red-hot nuclear fuel and graphite high into the night sky. A radioactive plume of fifty tons (45.5 metric tons) of evaporated nuclear fuel soared to altitudes between 3,300 (approx. 1,000 m) and 36,000 feet (approx. 11,000 m), carrying with it uranium dioxide particles and highly radioactive radio nuclides of iodine-131, plutonium-239, neptunium-139, cesium-137, strontium-90, and dozens of other radioactive isotopes of varying half-lives. The torrent of ejected fuel eventually reached 15,000 to 20,000 roentgens per hour borne by southeasterly winds that blew across Belorussia (Belarus), the Baltic republics, and deep into Scandinavia. Because of shifting winds much of eastern and some of western Europe experienced some fallout. The explosion and its subsequent impact was the equivalent of ten Hiroshima atomic bombs, in addition to seventy tons (63.6 metric tons) of fuel and 700 tons (636 metric tons) of radioactive graphite, which landed in and around the damaged reactor unit. Everyone and everything in the town of Pripiat glowed for several days during and after the tragedy at somewhere between 0.5 and 1 roentgen per hour.

Grigori Medvedev, author of *The Truth about Chernobyl*, dispassionately noted that "timely and truthful [reporting] would have saved tens of thousands of people from high doses of radiation" (p. 80). Instead, information about the explosion did not reach authorities in Moscow for hours. In fact Polish and Swedish scientists announced a mysterious spike of radiation to a worried world public before Mikhail Gorbachev, the general secretary of the Communist Party, admitted on 28 April that there had "been an incredible misfortune." The sad part was that Gorbachev prob-ably was not deliberately hiding the truth, as had so many general secretaries before him. He simply had not received accurate information. Certainly Gorbachev would have known earlier had the winds been blowing in their normal southwesterly path, which would have carried the radioactivity directly to Moscow. Indeed, the anomalous southeasterly vector on the lee of an east-moving high-pressure cell spared the Soviet Union a far higher casualty rate. Despite the delay in reporting the event to the Soviet public, some scholars believe that it was the Chernobyl catastrophe that convinced Gorbachev to establish his now-famous glasnost policy.

The true heroes at Chernobyl were the firefighters, some of whom exposed themselves to 20,000 to 30,000 roentgens per hour in order to smother the crater with 5,500 tons (5,000 metric tons) of lead, boron, sand, and clay. Underneath the reactor they laid a second concrete foundation to preclude groundwater contamination. Finally, together with other workers they erected a huge concrete-and-steel sarcophagus to prevent the emission of further radioactivity. By 2003 the hastily built twenty-four-story high sarcophagus was leaky and so unsound structurally that it conceivably could topple and disperse radioactive particles again. Two workers at the No. 4 reactor died instantly as a consequence of the explosion. By mid-August 1986 the figure was raised to thirty-one, including firefighters and other workers who were exposed to the highest doses of radiation during the cleanup. It was already apparent by then that they would not be the only casualties of the disaster.

As many as 200,000 persons were evacuated in stages from areas in and outside a nineteen-mile (30 km) radius around Pripiat, half of these coming during the first weeks after the explosions. This came to be called the permanent control zone or the thirty-kilometer zone. The 35,000 residents of Pripiat were compelled to leave within the first thirty-six hours. On 3 May Soviet authorities began to evacuate up to 75,000 more from the permanent control zone, 50,000 evacuees going to other parts of Ukraine and 25,000 to other parts of Belorussia. In 1986 and 1987 another 50,000 Belarus inhabitants were evacuated from areas outside the thirty-kilometer zone, followed by 30,000 more in 1991 and 1993. Between 1991 and 1996, 50,000 more Ukrainians were moved to other parts of Ukraine.

Since 1986 tens of thousands of Ukrainians and Belarus have been disabled by Chernobyl-related illnesses. Although the aftereffects of the disaster on human health have been elusive, thyroid cancer has been directly linked to Chernobyl. In perhaps the worst-impacted area, the Homyel region (oblast) in Belorussia, thyroid cancer among children soared twenty-two-fold from 1986 through 1990 compared to the period from 1981 through 1985. Before the collapse of the USSR as many as 3.3 million people, including 1.5 million children, who were exposed to the harmful effects of the radiation, received generous Soviet social benefits. As a result of the depressed post-Soviet economies the victims now suffer from inadequate health care. In the spring of 2003 thousands of Chernobyl survivors marched in the streets of Kyiv, demanding restitution.

The worst physical effects have been on arable land and groundwater. People near Chernobyl used, and continue to use, conventional wells. In the immediate aftermath of the catastrophe one-fifth of Belorussia's farmland had to be abandoned, stripped, and buried, almost 10,000 square miles (30,000 sq. km) of it seriously contaminated with more than five curies of radioactive cesium. The worst affected provinces remain Homyel, Mahilyow, and Brest in Belarus. Similar contamination has been recorded in the Ukrainian areas of Kyiv, Zhytomyr, and Chernihiv, and in the Russian area of Briansk. Wells have been sealed, and runoff from the contaminated area has been redirected so as not to pollute the Dnipro (Dnieper) River, which provides the bulk of Kyiv's water supply.

In December 2000 the Chernobyl nuclear power plant finally shut down, five years after it was slated to do so. In 1990 the Ukrainian parliament voted to close the facility permanently by 1995, but economic exigencies would not permit it. In 1996 the Ukrainian government and the G-7 countries concluded an agreement to decommission the plant by the end of the millennium. In addition the G-7 pledged $300 million to bolster the sarcophagus at reactor No. 4. Almost three decades had passed. The once technological marvel proved itself to be a nightmare. Funds worth billions of dollars were wasted, thousands of human lives destroyed, and the damage promises to linger for centuries. This part of the Faustian bargain was fleeting and devastating.

Bibliography: On the precise location and homeland of the Chernobyl nuclear power plant, see Victor L. Mote, *An Industrial Atlas of the Soviet Successor States* (Houston, Tex., 1994). On the events that took place during the Chernobyl catastrophe, see Gregori Medvedev, *The Truth about Chernobyl* (New York, 1991). For the aftermath of Chernobyl see Mike Edwards, "Chornobyl. Living with the Monster" in *World Geography. A Study Guide*, ed. by Michael A. Modica and Dennis L. Morrison (Waterbury, Conn., 2002).

Victor L. Mote

CHERNYSHEV, NIKOLAI MIKHAILOVICH (1885-1973). Painter, monumental artist, teacher.

Chernyshev was born 21 March 1885 in the village of Nikolskoe in Borisoglebsk district of Tambov province. A great grandson of serfs, he was the fourth son in a middle-class family of ten children. His father died in 1890, and the family moved to Moscow in 1892. In 1901 he entered the Moscow School of Art, Sculpture, and Architecture, from which he graduated in 1911. There he studied with Abram Efimovich Arkhipov (1862-1930), Konstantin Alekseevich Kovrovin (1861-1939), and Valentin Aleksandrovich Serov (1865-1911). In 1910 he visited Paris where he painted at the Académie Julien. In the Paris museums and galleries Leonardo, Puvis de Chavannes, and Cézanne made particularly strong impressions on him. From 1911 until 1915 he studied at the Imperial Academy of Arts in St. Petersburg. From 1912 to 1916 he exhibited at the Moscow Salon. In 1916 and 1917 he served in the Russian Army.

Chernyshev's artistic outlook was shaped in part by late symbolism, as propounded in the journal Milky Way (Mlechny put, 1914-1916), which was edited by his brother, the poet Aleksei Chernyshev (1880-?). Using the pseudonyms Omutov and O-v, Chernyshev published short stories and drawings from his series Mythological Alphabet in Milky Way. In the same years he began to paint monumental works with religious themes, organized by the principles of Gesamtkunstwerk.

In 1918-1920 Chernyshev served as director of the depository of works of contemporary art within Commissariat of People's Education (Narkompros). In 1918-1919 he took part in decorating Moscow for Soviet holidays. He worked on decorating the bridges in May 1918, painted the mural, Science and Art Bring their Gifts to Labor, on the city Duma building, and in May 1919 he was in charge of decorating Red Square. In spring 1919 he became artistic director of the Artistic Industrial Workshops at the I.D. Sytin printing house. In August 1919, when he was a cadet at the Higher School of Military Camouflage, he was sent on temporary duty to the Higher Artistic and Technical Workshops (Vkhutemas) as a professor in the department of monumental painting. He remained there until 1930.

In the summer of 1921 Chernyshev joined the World of Art group but left it in December 1921 when the Society of Artists and Poets, better known as Makovets, was established. Aleksei Chernysev was editor in chief of the Makovets' journal, Art is Life. The program of artistic unification espoused by Makovets appealed to Chernyshev's desire for a synthesis of art and inspired realism.

In the late teens and early 1920s several artists and movements prominent in that period influenced Chernyshev's art, Picasso, Cezanne (Still Life With Red Bucket and Bottle, 1919), cubism, and rayism (Lithographs of the Four from the Mansard collection, 1920) among them. In the first half of the 1920s he painted homeless children, beggars, blind people, adolescents in children's homes, schools, and summer camps, and completed a series of drawings and paintings at Isadora Duncan's dance school. Most of his work from this time on featured adolescent girls in the transition from childhood to young womanhood, thin, fragile, with skinny legs, and sharp knees and elbows. In Chernyshev's opinion their grace was comparable to the beauty of Greek statues. The elongated proportions characteristic of their age at the same time brought to mind Russian medieval art and in that way served as a metaphor for inspiration and purity.

Chernyshev's pictures can be read as scenes from contemporary daily life and on a metaphorical level about human life in general. An example of a painting that could be interpreted variously is Pussy Willow in Bloom (1926). Pussy willow is a symbol of the arrival of spring and images of skinny adolescent girls are associated with its slim, fuzzy branches. At the same time, the conjunction of the standing girl selling pussy willow, an attribute of Russian Easter, and of the two approaching schoolgirls with books allows one to interpret the picture as a depiction of the meeting of the old, religious and passive, and the new, constantly in motion.

Easel painting represents the greater part of Chernyshev's oeuvre. Over the course of decades the artist's attention became more focused on monumental art, particularly fresco, which he considered his ideal. At Vkhutemas Chernyshev taught mural painting to monumental artists. Chernyshev also paid particular attention to the revival of mosaic art and forgotten techniques of wall painting, such as sgraffito.

In 1935 Chernyshev helped organize the workshop of monumental art of the Academy of Architecture of the USSR. He remained there until 1948. In 1938-1941 he worked as director for wall art during the planning of the Palace of Soviets. During the 1930s and 1940s he completed only a small number of independent paintings, doing some of them in the provinces. Those included the theater hall in the House of Pioneers and Octobrists (Moscow, 1935), living quarters for MKhAT (Moscow, 1937-1938), the Palace of Culture (Zlatoust, 1946-1947), and the Opera and Ballet Theater in Ulan-Ude (1948-1952).

In his effort to establish the importance of fresco for socialist art, Chernyshev hoped by turning to ancient traditions to return to contemporary art the significance that images and spirituality had in medieval art. In Soviet conditions this effort unavoidably led to a number of compromises, which are reflected in his published works where, for example, he accentuated the supposedly realistic traditions of early Russian masters.

In 1949 Chernyshev, along with other teachers accused of formalism, was removed from the Moscow Art Institute, where he had taught since 1936. Despite his advanced age, to his last days he retained his creative energy and worked on paintings and mosaics. In the 1960s and 1970s he created a series of imagined portraits of Russian medieval painters, called Masters of the Moscow School. In 1970 he was awarded the order of the Red Banner of Labor and the title People's Artist of the RSFSR.

Bibliography: N.M. Chernyshev, *Tekhnika stennykh rospisei* (M., 1930), *Iskusstvo freski v Drevnei Rusi* (M., 1954); L. Bubnova, *Nikolai Mikhailovich Chernyshev* (M., 1960); *N.M. Chernyshev. Zhivopis', grafika, monumental'noe iskusstvo* (L., 1983); *N.M. Chernyshev. Sbornik materialov i katalog vystavki proisvedenii iskusstva, k 90-letiiu so dnia rozhdeniia khudozhnika,* comp. by V.L. Lapshin (M., 1978); *N.M. Chernyshev, 1885-1973. Katalog vystavki proizvedenii,* comp. by L.I. Gromova, P.N. Chernysheva (M., 1990); "Chernyshev, Nikolai Mikhailovich" in John Milner, *A Dictionary of Russian and Soviet Artists* (Woodbridge, Eng., 1993), 111-112.

Ilia Dorontchenkov

CHERSONESUS. City established as a Greek city-state on the southern shore of the Crimea.

Chersonesus was founded at the southern tip of the Crimean peninsula as a colony of Heraclea Pontica, a Greek city-state on the southern shore of the Black Sea. Archaeological evidence dates the foundation of the colony to c. 525 B.C. The city was located at the shortest direct point across the Black Sea and possessed excellent protected bays and harbors favorable for trade. The economy was based on rich fisheries, fertile land, salt extraction, and maritime and overland trade. The city, which was built on a grid plan, was one of a number of Greek city-states in Crimea and possessed its own mint and government. It maintained close economic and political ties with the Greek city-states of the southern Black Sea. It also possessed an extensive agricultural hinterland. The foundations of many farm buildings and much of the grid of country lanes that divided the Heraklean Peninsula are still evident.

Uneasy relations with nomadic neighbors to the north, Scythians and later Sarmatians, resulted in gradual loss of arable countryside. At the end of the second century B.C. under the leadership of Diophantes the inhabitants of Chersonesus defeated the Scythians, enabling the city to regain its agricultural lands temporarily. The city lost its political autonomy to Mithridates VI Eupator (120-63 B.C.) the king of Pontus. Following the defeat of Mithridates by the Romans in 63 B.C., Chersonesus became a Roman satellite. From the second half of the first century the city served as the main military base of the Roman, and later Byzantine, forces in the Crimea.

The Roman presence is strongly reflected in the archaeology of the city. Three bath complexes have been discovered, a network of ceramic pipes brought water from distant springs into the city, cement became a construction material, and epigraphic monuments feature Latin inscriptions. During the Roman period Chersonesus produced garum, the famous Roman fish sauce, on an industrial scale and traded it widely within the empire.

The Roman citadel was reinforced in A.D. 245 in anticipation of a Gothic invasion, but Roman troops left the city in the 270s and were replaced by a local force. Archaeological remains of Hunnic settlements in the Crimean hinterland testify to the end of intensive agricultural production. After that time the city relied on grain supplies from other parts of the Roman Empire.

It is not certain when Christianity was established in Chersonesus. The rich hagiographic sources ascribe the conversion of the population to the apostle Andrew and the pope Clement during the first century. Chersonesus definitely had a bishop by 382, as attested in the list of bishops present at the Second Ecumenical Council in Ephesos. A number of burial chambers decorated with Christian frescoes date from the early fifth century. A limestone plaque with representation of a menorah and Hebrew graffiti on plaster indicate that a synagogue also existed in the city during late antiquity.

In the Byzantine period Chersonesus became an important center of transcontinental commerce. In the fifth and sixth centuries the city was a bustling center along the Silk Route and participated in trade with the northern steppe peoples. Furs, slaves, and leather were exchanged for textiles, wine, jewelry, etc. Chersonesus also had a large fish-salting industry. In the seventh and eighth centuries the city experienced an economic decline as a result of general trends of urban and economic shifts in the Mediterranean. The great industrial-size cisterns for fish-salting were replaced by smaller household units, suggesting a decline in trade and diminished production.

The geopolitical situation in Crimea changed in the seventh century with the rise of the Khazar khaganate, which extended its political influence to Crimea. In Byzantine sources the city gained notoriety as place of exile for dangerous political opponents of the emperor. Pope Martin I and the emperor Justinian II were banished in the seventh century. In the eighth century Leo IV banished plotters and as late as the eleventh century Alexios I Komnenos exiled a pretender. In the ninth century the Byzantine emperor Theophilos reestablished Byzantine control over Chersonesus and created the theme (military division and territorial unit) of Klimata in the early 830s.

Between the ninth and twelfth centuries Chersonesus became an important trading center and outpost of the Byzantine Empire. Chersonesus served as a commercial intermediary with the steppe to the north. Residents depended heavily on the trade of hides and wax, which they bought from the nomads and traded within the empire. Port facilities were expanded and improved and defensive lines along land and sea were reinforced. A long wall of 1.5 miles (2.5 km) enclosed 75 acres (30 hectares), which could accommodate a population of 6,000-7,000.

The political importance of Chersonesus during this period also cannot be underestimated. It served as an intelligence-gathering point and diplomatic post for relations with Byzantium's neighbors to the north, including the Khazars, Pechenegs, Rus, and Polovtsians. The Byzantines maintained alliances with certain groups in order to employ them against others. One result of this diplomacy was the baptism of the Rus prince Vladimir in 988-989. Emperor Basil II enlisted Vladimir's military support in a civil war in exchange for the hand of his sister in marriage. After the capture of Chersonesus by the Rus, Basil II promptly sent his sister Anna to Vladimir. According to the Russian Primary Chronicle Vladimir was also baptized there. In the nineteenth century a St. Vladimir cathedral was built on the site where the baptism was thought to have occurred, and it became a center of active pilgrimage.

After the tenth century very little is known about the history of the city due to paucity of literary and epigraphic sources. The city suffered from an extensive fire some time in the late tenth or early eleventh century. The entire western part was not repopulated and became a rubbish dump. The city was still an important center in the mid eleventh century, as attested in an inscription of 1059 relating that city and port defenses were restored and improved.

In the twelfth century the importance of Chersonesus declined again as Byzantine influence in the north waned. International trade shifted to the towns in eastern Crimea where Sudak, which was controlled by the Polovtsians, emerged in the twelfth century as the most important Black Sea port. Ceramics and metalwork finds suggest that Chersonesus retained its role as an important commercial center for southwest Crimea.

After the Genoese secured a trade monopoly in the Black Sea from the Byzantine government in 1261, their presence in Crimea rapidly increased. Although the ports in eastern Crimea continued to be the main commercial centers on the peninsula, Chersonesus was used by the Genoese for the grain and salted fish trade. In 1299 Chersonesus and other Crimean cities were destroyed by Tatar khan Nogai in retaliation for the murder of Nogai's grandson in Kaffa. A considerable part of the city was rebuilt, and the Catholic Church established a number of institutions in the city. By 1320 a Franciscan monastery existed in Chersonesus, and in 1333 a Catholic bishopric and cathedral of St. Clement were established.

The bubonic plague reached Crimea in 1348. Chersonesus apparently never recovered. Patriarchal documents from Constantionple stress the poverty of the bishopric, and in 1390 the bishop left the town because of a lack of funds. The last bishop of Chersonesus, a Uniate, was appointed in 1440, but he did not reside there. Archaeological evidence points to the devastation of the city at the end of the fourteenth century. Many buildings were burned, church treasures were discovered in molten accumulations, and unburied corpses displayed skull wounds. This destruction perhaps was connected with the invasion of Crimea by Tamerlane in 1396.

In the fifteenth century Chersonesus ceased to exist. In a Geneoese document dated to 1472, three years prior to the Ottoman conquest of Crimea, Chersonesus and a neighboring town are called uninhabited places (loci non habitati). A seventeenth-century Ottoman traveler in Crimea recorded that the ruins of Chersonesus' defensive walls served as giant sheep corral. After the Russian conquest of Crimea the ruins of Chersonesus served as a stone quarry for the construction of Sevastopol. Regular excavations have been conducted in Chersonesus since 1876, and intensive excavations have been conducted since the 1930s. Chersonesus played an important role in the development of classical archaeology in the Russian Empire and Soviet Union. Excavations of medieval strata, pioneered by A.L. Yakobson in the 1950s and continued by others, have greatly enriched the scholarly understanding of daily life and material culture in the Byzantine period. In 1993 Chersonesus was declared an archeological preserve by the government of Ukraine, but coastal erosion and urban encroachment continued to threaten the future of the site.

Bibliography: A.L. Iakobson, *Srednevekovyi Khersones, XII-XIV vv.* (M., 1950); V.I. Kadeev, *Khersones Tavricheskii. Byt i kul'tura, I-III vv. n.e.* (Kharkov, 1996); Omeljan Pritsak and Anthony Cutler, "Chersones" in *The Oxford Dictionary of Byzantium,* Vol. 1 (Oxford, 1997), 418-19; S.B. Sorochan and L.V. Marchenko, *Zhizn' i gibel' Khersonesa* (Kharkov, 2000); V.M. Zubar', *Khersones Tavricheskii. Osnovnye etapy istoricheskogo razvitiia v antichnuiu epokhu* (Kiev, 1997).

Elena N. Boeck and **Brian J. Boeck**

CHESS IN RUSSIA. A popular board game, component of national culture, tool for social engineering, and Cold War weapon.

When and how chess came into Russian lands has been extensively investigated by Soviet scholars. Linguistic and archaeological evidence indicates an Arabic origin. The game apparently accompanied goods along trade routes from the Baghdad caliphate into Kievan Russia no later than the ninth century. Once it was introduced, chess spread rapidly. Evidence of its popularity is seen in the heroic epics (byliny) of Kievan times, which portray chess prowess as an important attribute for warriors and princes. Merchants and upper-class women also were depicted as skilled players. The wide dissemination of chess suggested by the byliny is supported by archaeology. Chess pieces dating to the Kievan period have been found in dozens of sites.

Popular though it was, Russian chess had a powerful enemy, the Orthodox clergy. In Constantinople chess was associated with infidel Persia, where Byzantine chess originated. The Russian church inherited the Byzantine animus for chess and added its condemnation of chess as a pagan survival. Clerical hostility peaked in the sixteenth century when Ivan the Terrible (r. 1533-1584) banned chess from his realm. There is no evidence of any sustained effort to enforce the tsar's edict, not even at his court where chess grew in popularity.

In addition to enthusiasm for chess among Russian elites, there is also evidence for the game's popularity at other levels of sixteenth- and seventeenth-century Russian society, especially among merchants. The great annual fairs were hotbeds of chess competition. Foreign travelers commented on the popularity of chess and praised the skill of Russian players.

The game played in pre-Petrine Russia was not the modern form of chess. Modern chess took shape in western Europe after 1450, when new rules radically changed the nature of the game, speeding it up, making it more exciting and less forgiving. Pawns, bishops, and especially the queen received enhanced powers. Prior to the reign of Peter I (r. 1682-1725) Russian chess was untouched by these innovations.

A passionate chess player, Peter encouraged chess in his family and court, but his most important contribution to Russian chess was its westernization. Not surprisingly, he favored the western game and facilitated its adoption at his court. Western chess was not adopted outside of elite circles, however. Soviet writers have indicated that a sort of schism occurred over chess which paralleled the gulf raised between a westernized aristocracy and the rest of society.

Elite adoption of the new chess allowed Russia to participate in Europe's progressive chess culture, including a rapidly developing chess literature. The first chess book printed in Russia was a translation of *The Morals of Chess* by Benjamin Franklin (1706-1790). Published in St. Petersburg in 1791, Franklin's treatise anticipated Bolshevik ideas about the character-shaping virtues of chess. In 1824 Alexander Dmitrievich Petrov (Petroff, 1794-1867) published the first important chess book written in Russia. Considered Russia's first master player, today Petrov's name is associated with an aggressive opening system that he popularized.

The preeminent pre-revolutionary Russian chess master was Mikhail Ivanovich Chigorin (Tchigorin, 1850-1908). Russia's first truly great player, he competed successfully in international tournaments and matches. Although primarily remembered in the west for his unsuccessful matches against world champion Wilhelm Steinitz (1836-1900), Chigorin later was apotheosized as the inspiration for the creative instinct in Soviet chess. He also worked hard to popularize chess in Russia. By the end of his life Russian masters were a common sight in international tournaments.

Russia's top players were competing in an international tournament in Mannheim, Germany when World War I broke out. They were interned there for the duration, but internment conditions were not particularly onerous, allowing players leisure to both hone their tactical skills and ponder the strategic depths of their game. Two young Russian internees in particular, Aleksander Aleksandrovich Alekhin (Alekhine, 1892-1946) and Efim Dmitrievich Bogoliubov (1889-1952), developed into world-class players during these years. When they returned home their social origins made them politically suspect in the revolutionary state.

Although Vladimir Ilich Lenin (1870-1924) and other Bolsheviks were avid chess players, the early Soviet government saw no special significance for chess in the new society. Chess acquired greater importance later on due to its perceived utility, initially as a training tool for military and party cadre, secondly as a cultural tool for refashioning Russian society, and finally as a propaganda tool for touting the superiority of Soviet culture.

Soviet recognition of chess's utility began in 1920 when Aleksander Fedorovich Ilin-Zhenevsky (1894-1941), a veteran Bolshevik and a chess master, was appointed commissar of the Red Army's universal military training organization, Vsevobuch. He introduced chess into the curriculum, citing parallels between qualities desired in soldiers and attributes developed by chess. At the end of the Civil War and the onset of the New Economic Policy a less martial version of this theme developed, drawing parallels between qualities instilled by chess and characteristics of the ideal communist.

The year 1920 also saw the first Soviet championship, played under the harsh conditions of War Communism. Russia's top players were in effect requisitioned for the tournament. Once it was underway dissatisfaction over conditions developed, and the players threatened to walk out. Ilin-Zhenevsky was narrowly able to avert an embarrassing strike by increasing food and cigarette rations. Another Soviet championship was not attempted until 1923.

The year 1924 was pivotal for Soviet chess. Groups representing apolitical and political views of the game's role in Soviet society vied for control of the fledgling Soviet chess establishment. The apolitical position was championed by the recently revived, tsarist-era All-Russian Chess Federation. The chess section of the Trade Union Council, a creation of Ilin-Zhenevsky, espoused the political view. The triumph of Ilin-Zhenevsky's political position was signaled by the creation of an official government office, the All-Union Chess Section of the Supreme Council for Physical Culture. The significance of the elevation of chess to governmental status was underscored by the selection of Nikolai Vasilievich Krylenko (1885–1938), a veteran Bolshevik of considerable standing, to head the Chess Section.

The position of chess was further enhanced in 1925 when a state-sponsored psychological study supported the utility of chess. The study reached two key conclusions. First, it confirmed the dialectical nature of chess, giving it the critical stamp of ideological approval. Second, it concluded that skills developed in chess generalized to other activities, thereby raising the overall cultural and intellectual level of the player, a finding in harmony with Marxist beliefs about human malleability. This study marks an important shift in official thinking about the role of chess in building socialism. Originally a tool for training soldiers and party cadre, chess was now also seen as a means for general cultural, intellectual, and political elevation of the masses.

In the spirit of this study Krylenko expanded the mission of Soviet chess to include the cultural enlightenment of the people. The rationale and target of his campaign are illustrated by slogans adopted by Krylenko's chess section: "Chess is a powerful weapon of intellectual culture!" and "Take chess to the workers!"

Krylenko had another goal. He wanted to create a vanguard of Soviet masters capable of competing successfully on the world stage. The two objectives merged in the Moscow International Chess Tournament of 1925, the first international chess tournament in Soviet Russia. Organized, financed, and conducted according to a special decree of the Council of Peoples' Commissars, the Moscow tournament has the distinction of being the first government-sponsored international chess tournament. There were twenty-one participants, ten Soviet players and eleven leading foreign masters. The latter included Cuban world champion, Jose Raul Capablanca (1888-1942). Conspicuously absent was future world champion, Alekhine, now in emigration.

The winner of the tournament, Bogoliubov, was another player of the prerevolutionary generation. He soon joined Alekhine in voluntary emigration. Many of the new Soviet players performed quite respectably despite facing their first test against world-class competition. Even so, it was ten years before Krylenko was ready to repeat the experiment. If Moscow was only partially successful in testing Soviet masters, it had great success in popularizing chess. The tournament was a sensation in Moscow, and crowds filled the playing hall, spilling out into the street. Chess Fever, a short comedy film shot during the tournament by Soviet producer Vsevold Ilarionovich Pudovkin (1893-1953), captured Moscow's enthusiasm.

At the end of the 1920s, as the state extended its reach into all aspects of society, state control of the chess bureaucracy was tightened. In the spirit of the industrial five year plans, results were demanded in all areas of the chess program. In the climate of the purges, persons suspected of holding the discredited apolitical view of chess became class enemies. The chess establishment was hit hard by the purges of 1937 and 1938, when Krylenko was executed.

In spite of dislocation and fear, Soviet chess made great strides in the 1930s. In 1929 there were twenty-five Soviet masters, and by 1934 forty-three. In 1935 the Soviet system produced its first grandmaster, Mikhail Moiseevich Botvinnik (1911-1995). By 1940 there were five, some of whom had lived in newly annexed territories.

As Soviet Russia sought a united front against fascism in the mid-1930s, appearances by Soviet grandmasters in western tournaments signaled a renewed interest in friendly cultural exchanges. Additional evidence of the shift was seen in 1935 with Moscow's resumption, after a ten-year hiatus, of hosting international chess tournaments.

In 1935 Botvinnik traveled to Europe for his debut in international competition. In 1935 and 1936 he had fine results in Moscow's international tournaments. When Botvinnik returned to Europe in 1936, he tied for first at Nottingham, one of the strongest tournaments ever held. Botvinnik's triumph was heralded in Pravda, the Communist Party newspaper, which featured a long article reiterating the purpose and goal of Soviet chess and reaffirming the commitment to chess in the Soviet Union, which Pravda termed the classical land of chess.

The successes of the 1930s led Soviet theorists to postulate the existence of a Soviet school of chess. Although derided in the west, this view is consistent with fundamental tenets of Marxism. Since chess, like other cultural components of a society's superstructure, is dependent upon the economic underpinnings, a different style of chess play under socialism would be expected. The Soviet school was characterized as dialectical, that is creative, flexible, opposed to dogma, and above all, committed to the idea of struggle. Botvinnik, the chief theorist and strongest representative of the Soviet school, wanted to challenge the world champion in 1936, but Alekhine's status as a renegade made official contacts difficult. Negotiations for a match were still in progress when the war intervened.

Like every aspect of Soviet society, chess was called upon to contribute to the Soviet victory in the Great Patriotic War, as World War II was termed in the USSR. The top players served in a variety of areas, and Soviet masters toured the hospitals and field units, giving lectures and exhibitions. Meanwhile the Soviet chess establishment, poised in 1941 to deliver the first Soviet world champion, did not relax. There were tournaments and top-level matches during the war years, and the Soviet Union emerged from the war in a position of unprecedented superiority, an accomplishment of great significance on the cultural front in the ensuing Cold War.

The first postwar Soviet chess triumph came in 1945. In the spirit of goodwill which still prevailed, the Soviets played a radio match with the United States chess team. In team matches, players contest games individually against the corresponding member of the opposing team, with each team counting its points collectively. Wins equal one point and draws equal one-half point. Many expected a close match, but the result was a stunning, 15-1/2 to 4-1/2, Soviet victory. The next year the American team was invited to Moscow for another drubbing. The British team was equally outclassed in a 1946 match. Soviet players also dominated postwar international tournaments.

After the war Soviet chess affiliated with the international chess body, Fédération Internationale des Echecs (FIDE), formerly disdained as a bourgeois organization. FIDE wanted to regularize the selection of challengers for the world title, the Soviets wanted Botvinnik to take the crown. The situation was complicated by the controversy surrounding the reigning champion. Already considered a renegade by Soviet authorities, Alekhine was now under a cloud in the rest of the world for pro-Nazi activities. But Alekhine died suddenly in 1946, and FIDE stepped into the vacuum. A complicated match-tournament was conducted in 1948 under FIDE auspices, and Botvinnik emerged as the clear victor.

Although a certain amount of self-congratulation was natural and justified as Soviet superiority manifested itself, initial official Soviet pronouncements were careful to emphasize the role of chess in advancing international friendship. As relations cooled, the tone changed. Soon Soviet chess was opening an aggressive cultural front in the developing Cold War. When Botvinnik captured the world championship in 1948, the event was heavily politicized and hailed as proof of Soviet cultural superiority. Soviet claims were well-supported by events. From

1948 until 1972 Soviet possession of the world title was never threatened. FIDE control allowed for an orderly system of tournaments and matches, culminating every three years in the selection of a new challenger. The entire process was dominated by Soviet players.

Botvinnik retained the title until 1963, with two brief interruptions. All four of his challengers were Soviet players. In 1951 and 1954 Botvinnik played even matches with David Ionovich Bronstein (1924-) and Vasily Vasilievich Smyslov (1921-), respectively. Botvinnik retained the title in the event of a tied match. Then in 1957 Smyslov defeated the champion but lost the title a year later when Botvinnik exercised his rematch right. In 1960 Mikhail Nekhemevich Tal (1936-1992), a young Soviet player renowned for his sharp tactical ability, decisively defeated Botvinnik, but the seemingly indefatigable Botvinnik again reclaimed the title in a rematch. Finally in 1963 Soviet grandmaster Tigran Vartanovich Petrosian (1929-1984) defeated Botvinnik. Stripped of his automatic rematch right, Botvinnik declined to undertake the arduous process required to challenge the sitting champion. The Botvinnik era ended, but the Soviet monopoly of the title continued.

While Petrosian was deposing Botvinnik, a player poised to challenge the Soviet chess monopoly also won a great victory. In 1963-1964 Robert James Fischer (1953-) swept the United States Championship, without conceding even a draw. Fischer's total domination of American chess stood in stark contrast to Botvinnik's status as first among equals. Many expected Fischer to take the world championship in 1966 or 1969, yet factors having little or nothing to do with ability hampered his quest. Fischer wrestled with a variety of demons, some seemingly personal, some certainly Soviet.

Fischer charged the Soviets with a variety of offenses, especially collusion at the candidates' tournaments, the first step in FIDE's multi-stage process for selecting the challenger to the world champion. Fischer alleged that the Soviets, who were heavily represented in these events, played as a team, conceding early draws or even prearranged losses to their top players, but playing all-out against him. The accusation was not new. Capablanca made similar complaints directly to Stalin in the 1930s. Fischer went public with his complaints about Soviet conduct in 1962, when Sports Illustrated published his article, "The Russians Have Fixed World Chess."

FIDE made some reforms, but these were too modest to lure Fischer back, and the title remained in Soviet hands. In 1966 Petrosian beat back the challenge of Boris Vasilievich Spassky (1937-), but in 1969 Spassky was able to wrest the crown from Petrosian.

The United States Chess Federation (USCF) began to maneuver on behalf of Fischer, who was still boycotting the preliminary stages of the qualifying process. Another American grandmaster generously gave up his position, placing Fischer directly into the second stage, a series of individual matches where Soviet collusion was impossible. In an unprecedented demonstration of world dominance Fischer disposed of his first two opponents without losing or drawing a game. His third opponent, Petrosian, managed to slow Fischer down with a couple of draws, even winning a game, but Fischer rallied and convincingly vanquished the former world champion. Now only Spassky stood between Fischer and the world title.

The 1972 match between the solitary Fischer and Spassky, the tip of the Soviet chess iceberg, was staged in Reykjavik, Iceland. Billed as the match of the century, and framed as a Cold War clash par excellence, the match proceeded in a veritable circus atmosphere. Fischer, portrayed as arrogant and rapacious, seemed to represent everything unattractive about the United States. Spassky, who maintained a calm and courteous facade throughout, appeared to represent the best of Soviet society. But Fischer was clearly the better player, and after an inauspicious start, he soundly defeated his Soviet rival.

Fischer's reign was short. In 1975 he declined to defend his title. Vying for the vacated throne were two Soviet grandmasters, Anatoly Yevgenievich Karpov (1951-) and Viktor Lvovich Korchnoi (1931-). Karpov, groomed to regain the title for the Soviets, inherited the crown. Korchnoi, who felt poorly used by the Soviet chess establishment, soon defected. In 1978, when the two clashed again, the Cold War once again provided the backdrop. The match, and the incredible spectacle surrounding it, went on for months, with Karpov the eventual winner.

Karpov, now the darling of the Soviet chess establishment, went on to defend his title successfully twice more, against Korchnoi in 1981, and then against a new Soviet challenger, Garry Kimovich Kasparov (1963-) in 1984-1985. The latter match, played under a new, open-ended format, in which draws no longer counted, refused to end. It was terminated under murky circumstances after forty-eight games, ostensibly to protect the health of the players. A new match was begun later in 1985 under the old, best of twenty-four games, format. This time Kasparov prevailed and became the youngest world champion.

The rivals met twice more in matches for the championship, in 1986-1987 and 1990. Each time Kasparov retained his title. The long and bitter rivalry between the two Soviet grandmasters, under the relative relaxation of glasnost, split Soviet chess into competing camps. Upon the breakup of the Soviet Union in 1992 the remnant of the Soviet Chess Federation broke into corresponding factions. Then FIDE, long supported by the Soviet Federation, fragmented under the strain. Kasparov's organization left FIDE in 1993 to form the Professional Chess Association (PCA), and the rump FIDE returned the world title to Karpov. Like rival medieval popes, each champion claimed exclusive right to the title.

With new leadership at the helm, FIDE was radically revamped. Under very controversial rules, Aleksandr Valerievich Khalifman (1966-), a Soviet-era emigré who returned to Russia, won the FIDE world championship in 1999. The next FIDE Champion was an Indian player, Viswanathan Anand (1969-). Although few now took the FIDE title seriously, its departure from post-Soviet hands was significant. In 2000 Kasparov lost his crown to the young Russian Vladimir Kramnik (1975-) in a surprising upset. Kasparov's fifteen-year reign, the last seven years unofficial, but generally recognized, ended.

At this writing, a plan is in place to reintegrate FIDE. The world's top four players are slated to compete in an ad hoc competition to heal the rift. Three of the players are from the former Soviet Union, the other is Hungarian. Although many now represent new independent nations, the players of the old Soviet school still dominate world chess. Young players who came of age after the Soviet collapse are poised to continue in the same tradition of excellence. Although chess no longer enjoys state sponsorship, post-Soviet players in the early twenty-first century still benefit from their Soviet inheritance.

Bibliography: Nicolai Grekov, *Soviet Chess* (New York, 1949); Anatoly Karpov, I.Iu. Averbakh, "Shakhmaty," *Entsiklopedicheskii slovar'* (M., 1990); Isaak Maksovich Linder, *Shakhmaty na Rusi* (M., 1975); David John Richards, *Soviet Chess. Chess And Communism in the USSR* (Oxford, 1965); Andy Soltis, *Soviet Chess, 1917-1991* (Jefferson, N.C., 2000).

Michael A. Hudson

CONTENTS